D0421546

ve

100580527

Beyond Cognitive
Metaphor Theory

Routledge Studies in Rhetoric and Stylistics

MICHAEL BURKE, *Series Editor*

Beyond Cognitive Metaphor Theory

Perspectives on Literary Metaphor

**Edited by
Monika Fludernik**

Routledge
Taylor & Francis Group
New York   London

100580527

808
BEY

First published 2011
by Routledge
711 Third Avenue, New York, NY 10017

Simultaneously published in the UK
by Routledge
2 Park Square, Milton Park, Abingdon, Oxon OX14 4RN

Routledge is an imprint of the Taylor & Francis Group, an informa business

© 2011 Taylor & Francis

The right of the Monika Fludernik to be identified as the author of the editorial
material, and of the authors for their individual chapters, has been asserted in
accordance with sections 77 and 78 of the Copyright, Designs and Patents Act 1988.

Typeset in Sabon by IBT Global.

All rights reserved. No part of this book may be reprinted or reproduced or utilised
in any form or by any electronic, mechanical, or other means, now known or hereaf-
ter invented, including photocopying and recording, or in any information storage or
retrieval system, without permission in writing from the publishers.

Trademark Notice: Product or corporate names may be trademarks or registered trademarks, and are used only for identification and explanation without intent to infringe.

Library of Congress Cataloging-in-Publication Data

Beyond cognitive metaphor theory : perspectives on literary metaphor / edited by
    Monika Fludernik.
        p. cm. — (Routledge studies in rhetoric and stylistics ; 3)
    Includes bibliographical references and index.
    1. Metaphor in literature.   2. Metaphor.   3. Figures of speech in literature
4. Cognition in literature.   5. Discourse analysis, Literary.   I. Fludernik, Monika.
    P302.5.B49 2011
    809'.915—dc22
    2010048810

ISBN13: 978-0-415-88828-8 (hbk)
ISBN13: 978-0-203-81580-9 (ebk)

Contents

Figures

Tables

Acknowledgments

This collection has profited immensely from the constructive collaboration of its participants, for which I would like to express my thankfulness. My special gratitude extends to Beatrix Busse and Margaret Freeman, who gave me invaluable feedback on specific points of cognitive metaphor theory.

Thanks also go to Erica Wetter at Routledge (New York), who shut both eyes to the length of the manuscript, and to Michael Burke, who agreed to adopt the book for his series and was extremely efficient and helpful in seeing it into print.

The editor and authors are also grateful for permission to reprint the following texts. Thanks go to Faber and Faber Limited (Essex) for permission to cite from T. S. Eliot's *Four Quartets: Burnt Norton, East Coker, The Dry Salvages, Little Gidding* [1944], London: Faber & Faber, 1983 (see Ina Habermann's chapter); to Henry Holt and Company (New York) for permission to print excerpts from *The Brooklyn Follies* (2006) by Paul Auster (see Beatrix Busse's chapter); to Rowohlt (Reinbek) for permission to cite from Robert Musil's *Gesammelte Werke. Prosa und Stücke, Kleine Prosa, Aphorismen, Autobiographisches, Essays und Reden, Kritik*, edited by Adolf Frisé, Reinbek: Rowohlt, 1978; and to Verba Mundi Books and David R. Gobine, Publisher, for permission to cite extracts from *Five Women* by Robert Musil, translated from the German by Eithne Wilkins and Ernst Kaiser, © 1966 by Dell Publishing Company (see Ralph Müller's contribution); as well as to Kwok-bun Chan for permission to quote an extract from "The Importance of Sympathy", *South China Morning Post*, December 20, 2003 (see Andrew Goatly's chapter).

Last but certainly not least, I would like to thank my staff at Freiburg for their time and dedication to this project. I am particularly grateful to Ramona Früh, Theresa Hamilton, Luise Lohmann and Rebecca Reichl as well as to Caroline Pirlet, who did the final reformatting of the manuscript.

Introduction

Monika Fludernik

RECENT DEVELOPMENTS IN METAPHOR THEORY

CLAUDIO:	Is there no remedy?
ISABELLA:	None, but such remedy as, to save a head,
	To cleave a heart in twain.
CLAUDIO:	But is there any?
ISABELLA:	Yes, brother, you may live;
	There is a devilish mercy in the judge,
	If you'll implore it, that will free your life,
	But fetter you till death.
CLAUDIO:	Perpetual durance?
ISABELLA:	Ay, just, perpetual durance; a restraint,
	Though all the world's vastidity you had,
	To a determin'd scope.
CLAUDIO:	But in what nature?
ISABELLA:	In such a one as, you consenting to't,
	Would bark your honour from that trunk you bear,
	And leave you naked.
CLAUDIO:	Let me know the point.
ISABELLA:	O, I do fear thee, Claudio, and I quake
	Lest thou a feverous life shouldst entertain,
	And six or seven winters more respect
	Than a perpetual honour.
	(*Measure for Measure* III, i, 60–76; Shakespeare 1994:
	70–71)

In Act III, Scene i of *Measure for Measure*, Isabella fulfils the thankless task of telling her brother Claudio the result of her mission to the Duke's deputy Angelo: if she sleeps with him, Angelo is willing to pardon her brother. Recognizing that Claudio is liable to grasp at straws and desire life over honour, she avoids telling him the whole story straight until she has moved him to the pitch of manly courage ("If I must die, / I will encounter darkness as a bride / And hug it in mine arms", lines 82–84). Before this point she applies circumlocution, indirection and metaphor in hinting at the truth and in order to prepare Claudio for his role as victim.

Claudio does not know what she is talking about—unlike the audience, who have just witnessed Angelo delivering his dishonourable conditions to the noviciate Isabella. While the prospective nun talks about a future in which her brother will be "fetter[ed] [. . .] till death" (line 65), referring to Claudio's virtual bondage by remorse should he allow his sister to be robbed of her honour, Claudio takes this metaphor literally to mean life imprisonment, "[p]erpetual durance". In response she elaborates the metaphor by again contrasting freedom ("free your life"—"all the world's vastidity"—lines 65, 68) not with a "fetter" (lines 69, 66), but with "restraint" (line 67), this time "to a determined scope".

Claudio's repeated questions, his requests for clarification, subsequently no longer focus on bondage but on the loss of honour, which is figured as nakedness. In contrast to the later opposition between virtue and vice in the imagery of being and seeming (the "devil" Angelo is an "outward-sainted deputy", whose "filth" exposes him to be "a pond as deep as hell"—lines 91, 88, 92–93), Isabella here images honour as a skin-like garment that is part of the body and yet can be torn off, resulting in the death of the subject. A tree shorn of its bark cannot survive, nor would Isabella be able to survive after she has been disrobed (i.e. violated) by Angelo. The term *trunk* refers to the literal tree trunk in the virtual scene projected by the source domain of the metaphor, but it also resonates with an allusion to Claudio's trunk or body, from which his head will have been lopped off in the impending execution. A tree, Isabella implies, can survive without its head (crown), but not without its bark. Like the honourless Angelo and the barkless tree, Isabella, who will be despoiled of her virginity, will be left naked and unable to fend for herself after Angelo's cruel conquest of her. By extending the tree-bark image to Isabella, one notices that it seems as if Angelo is actually planning to peel off her skin, flaying her alive, an action that would not merely leave her naked but dead; he would kill her by exposing her flesh (the body covered up chastely by her monastic habit and virtuous mind). At the same time, this shameful bereavement of honour and virginity (after all, rape would ingressively tear her hymen) applies in equal measure to Claudio, who will be flayed metaphorically if he allows Angelo to dishonour his sister. Angelo's arboral despoliation—a gardener or forester destroying the plants which are under his protection—will therefore cause a double deprivation in the siblings. He will rape both Isabella and Claudio; whereas this violation is literal as well as figurative in the sister's case, it is only metaphorical in Claudio's.

In reverting to Claudio's initial question about a "remedy" (line 60), Isabella uses the medical metaphor to express her fear of Claudio's weakness, suggesting that he may prefer a brief life to a quick death resulting in "perpetual honour": "I quake / Lest thou a feverous life shouldst entertain, / And six or seven winters more respect / Than a perpetual honour" (lines 73–76).

Here the "perpetual durance" of remorse (line 66) has been transformed into an imprisonment in disease, an unenviable lingering out of life on a sickbed. Compared to this option, a clean swift departure to heaven (cf. lines 56–59 earlier) which promises an indestructible gift of honour, a spiritual life that will outlive death, emerges as more attractive, and Claudio's mettle is finally aroused to the point of "resolution" (line 81) where he appears prepared to "encounter darkness as a bride / And hug it in [his] arms" (lines 83–84).

The traditional terminology of the New Critics and their successors (I. A. Richards 1936; Abrams 1953) referred to the metaphorical grounding of a passage such as this one by the *tenor*, *vehicle* and *ground* concepts. In order to talk about Angelo's threatened rape, Isabella displaces the effects of this action from herself onto Claudio. She figures his preserved life (the tenor) as a life imprisonment (vehicle) in guilt or remorse (ground); as a violent loss of honour (vehicle: tree losing its bark) and a resultant nakedness (ground); and as a miserable existence in sickness (vehicle), where the fever presumably also implies a guilty conscience or a maimed honour (ground). Death, by contrast, is figured positively as a journey to heaven (lines 56–60):

> CLAUDIO: Now, sister, what's the comfort?
> ISABELLA: Why,
>   As all comforts are; most good, most good, indeed.
>   Lord Angelo, having affairs to heaven,
>   Intends you for his swift ambassador,
>   Where you shall be an everlasting leiger.
>   Therefore, your best appointment make with speed;
>   To-morrow you set on. (III, i, 54–60)

Death in this metaphor does not seem an end but a beginning, a voyage with a destination that will then afford a lasting resting place in paradise ("everlasting leiger"—line 58), where Claudio will receive "perpetual honour" (line 76). It is noticeable that in Isabella's rhetorical manipulation the loss of Claudio's head and his loss of sensation are entirely displaced by her focus on that which she fears for herself rather than on what Claudio might fear (he will articulate his dread of dying later in lines 117–31 when her persuasive strategy has failed).

Cognitive metaphor theory in its classic mode replaces the terms *vehicle* and *tenor* by those of *source domain* and *target domain* respectively. It also paraphrases the metaphors in the mould of idealized cognitive models (ICMs). In the example passage above, we would therefore move from DEATH IS A JOURNEY TO HEAVEN to a series of LOSS OF HONOUR IS IMPRISONMENT, LOSS OF HONOUR IS NAKEDNESS and LOSS OF HONOUR IS SICKNESS. All of these would be grouped under a more general cognitive metaphor or image schema, in which POSSESSION IS POSITIVE and, inversely, LOSS/DEPRIVATION IS NEGATIVE. This helps us see that, for Isabella, Claudio's impending death correlates with the opposites or antonyms of loss and is hence positively associated with the poles of FREEDOM, CLOTHING AND HEALTH. In fact, it is the last of these source domains that Claudio sees as relevant to his rescue from execution when he asks Isabella to provide a "remedy" for his predicament (sickness).

The development from classic cognitive metaphor theory (Lakoff & Johnson 1980; Johnson 1987; Lakoff 1987; Turner 1987, among others) towards blending theory (Fauconnier 1984, 1997; Turner 1996; Fauconnier & Turner 2002) adds another basic insight to the study of metaphors. Rather than looking for the essential common denominator of a "ground" between vehicle and tenor, or trying to describe the semantic effects of a metaphor in terms of the projection of features from source domain to target domain, this approach allows for a functional transfer of the generic pattern which can be traced in both source and target domains and results in a blending of these, in which the aspects of both domains begin to coalesce into a new whole. Thus, in the well-known metaphor "My surgeon is a butcher", the generic space consists of a subject wielding a knife-like implement and an object lying passively on a table. In the blend, the surgeon's scalpel from the target domain (input space 1) becomes a kind of cleaver (taken from the source domain or input space 2). The transfer implies that the patient operated on by that surgeon is treated violently and insensitively as if he or she were a piece of meat. In fact, the patient is threatened with becoming just that by being turned into a corpse through the butchery of the surgeon (with additional associations of the operation turning into an autopsy).

In the passage from *Measure for Measure*, the usefulness of the blending model comes out most forcefully in the image of the tree bereft of its bark. As I noted earlier, this image manages to blend the tree of the source domain, including a possible crown of the tree and its bark, on the one hand, with, on the other, the two people threatened with fatal deprivation: Claudio with the loss of his head and Isabella with that of her virginity. At the same time, the image parallels Isabella's violation as deprivation and her resulting shame with the consequences of these events for Claudio, who will lose his honour. In this example of single-scope blending, then, the basic pattern of ripping off a vital cover to expose and kill the body beneath it constitutes the generic space which reappears in input space 1 (the tree having its bark torn off) and in the parallel input spaces 2 and 3 (Isabella's rape and Claudio's loss of honour and resultant remorse). In the blend, Isabella's loss of (sexual and moral) honour and Claudio's nakedness stand out as the effect of Angelo's sexually motivated 'ripping'.

Still more recent developments of blending theory and conceptual integration theory in Turner's and Fauconnier's double-scope blending[1] and their alignment of metaphor, fictionality and, possibly, narrative open yet wider ranges of application of these theoretical models for literature (Fauconnier & Turner 2008; Turner 2008). Blending is characterized by its emergent structure and its spontaneous and easy merging of input spaces to produce ad hoc solutions or scenarios (cf. Dancygier 2006: 5–6, 9).

Even more importantly, conceptual integration theory in its newest format (Turner 2006) claims to solve the main problem that had seemed to stand in the way of literary scholars' appreciation of the cognitive model—its seeming inability to account for literary creativity.

The above necessarily very one-sided summary of what I have called the 'cognitive revolution' in metaphor studies tries to explain some major aspects of cognitive metaphor theory for readers as yet unfamiliar with this approach. It therefore neglects to provide a history of "metaphorology" (Forceville & Urios-Aparisi 2009: 4) and fails to mention such important contributions as Max Black's interaction theory (Black 1979), Paul Ricoeur's *The Rule of Metaphor* (1975), Harold Weinrich's "kühne Metapher" ('bold metaphor') essay (1963), or Hans Blumenberg's *Metaphorologie* (1989). Readers interested in a history of metaphor studies are referred to Jäkel (1999), Rolf (2005) and Kohl (2007). The title of this volume is meant to focus on the two major aspects thematized in this collection of essays: the impact of cognitive metaphor theory and its (sometimes fraught) relationship to literary studies. In particular, this collection will document both the objections to the cognitive metaphor model in literary criticism and the gradual absorption and creative appropriation of this model in literary circles. Conversely, we will see how cognitive metaphor theoreticians handle metaphors in literary texts and how they react to literary scholars' criticisms.

LITERARY CRITICISM AND COGNITIVE METAPHOR THEORY (CMT)

This volume arose from the perceived need to address the status of literary metaphor within metaphor theory. In the Anglophone world (and therefore in English studies world-wide), cognitive metaphor theory has had a tremendous impact, displacing almost all other theoretical approaches to metaphor, and has resulted in what could well be described as a paradigm shift in the Kuhnian sense. However, that paradigm shift preponderantly affected linguistics rather than literary studies. In continental European literature departments, especially in French or Romance studies, a number of different approaches have continued to evolve and only recently, and often somewhat reluctantly, have scholars begun to confront the ruling CMT methodology and mode of argument. Two issues have been particularly important for the (lack of) communication between literary and linguistic scholars. CMT, which emerged from (cognitive) linguistics, has tended to focus on the metaphoric nature of our thinking, moving away from surface structure textual analysis to universal, or at least language-specific, cognitive base metaphors, captured in formulas like LIFE IS A JOURNEY. CMT attempts to describe "the way we think" (Fauconnier & Turner 2002). Although some critics like Reuven Tsur (1992), Mark Turner (1987, 1991, 1996), Margaret H. Freeman (2007, 2009) and Elena Semino (2008) have clearly focused on individual texts and their local meanings in a framework of interpretation, much CMT work has concentrated on tracing specific cognitive metaphors in individual texts or on elaborating a system of cognitive metaphors and their relation to one another (see esp. Andrew Goatly and his associates' METALUDE database). However, more recently cognitive metaphor theoreticians have started to research cultural differences in metaphor use (Gibbs 1999; Musolff 2004; Goatly 2007; Kövecses 2005, 2010). They have also begun to confront the second problematic area between literature and linguistics, the issue of metaphoric creativity (see Holyoak & Thagard 1995; Fauconnier & Turner 1999; Moreno 2007; Glucksberg 2008). Lakoff and Turner (1989: 67–72) have outlined four mechanisms of creativity, by means of which metaphors that are familiar to us from everyday language are modified and contextualized in literary texts and thereby acquire a semblance of originality: (1) elaboration, (2) extension, (3) questioning and (4) combining (see Kövecses 2002: 43–53, 2010; Semino 2008: 44–66). To this list one must add contextualization, which plays a key role in shaping our interpretation of metaphors as semantically significant and aesthetically innovative (see Douthwaite in this volume). Moreover, although not included in this collection, work on metaphor recognition (Steen 2002; Steen et al. 2010; Goodblatt 2001; Goodblatt & Glicksohn 2002) also helps to refocus and revise classic CMT's emphasis on cognitive metaphor as a basic cognitive tool that determines our linguistic expressions, since metaphor recognition allows one to analyse which metaphors are more creative and therefore more noticeable than others.

For literary critics, then, cognitive metaphor theory has been problematic on two accounts: one, universality or reductivism in opposition to textual specificity; and, two, its theoretical position regarding the creativity or originality of metaphors. Traditional literary critics insist on seeing metaphors as singular achievements in poetic creativity which open a particularly direct access to a poet's genius. Hence, metaphors appear as the incarnation of creativity and aesthetic achievement. They moreover allow the critic a window into the author's intellectual or creative workshop, almost into the poet's subconscious. (One can here point to Wolfgang Clemen's [1951] and Caroline Spurgeon's [1952] classic studies of Shakespeare's metaphors.) Besides being unduly steeped in romantic ideology, such an approach downplays the prevalence of metaphors in prose texts, where they often cannot be linked to an author's genius; it also privileges poetic language over everyday speech in an inversion of the cognitive linguists' preference for natural over poetic language. The traditional literary treatment of metaphor, though affording extensive micro-level analyses of poetic passages, additionally fails to explain the quality of metaphoric creativity from a more systematic perspective, or to offer a theory of *literary* metaphor (in contrast to the non-literary use of metaphors). It can elucidate a particular metaphor in a poem or the network of metaphors in a specific poem with great brilliance, but it cannot say much on the position of metaphor in literary language and how (if at all) it differs from that of non-literary speech and writing. Literary metaphor studies therefore often focus on interpretative specificity to the detriment of theoretical generality; they highlight individuality and microcontext rather than systematic explanations on a language-wide level of analysis.

Both literary and linguistic approaches to metaphor have traditionally concentrated on verbal metaphor, neglecting other media, especially pictures, audiovisual media and gestures. Only recently has this lacuna been explored by Charles Forceville (1996, 2006, 2008) and in the essays in Forceville and Urios-Aparisi (2009). Given the current great popularity of multimediality and multimodality studies (Page 2010), this certainly promises to be an area that should prove to be of common interest to linguists and literary scholars.

The chapters in the second part of this collection trace the adoption of cognitive metaphor theory in literary studies (Douthwaite, Müller, Sinding) and the active engagement of CMT theoreticians with literary texts (Freeman, Busse, Kimmel). Part II moreover shows how the cognitive metaphor approach has resulted in creative applications of the theory to genre studies (Sinding), ideology (Goatly) and film (Forceville).

Part I of the volume, *à contretemps*, introduces the English-language reader to a panoply of approaches to metaphor which have their origin outside cognitive metaphor theory. Some of these position themselves in contrast to CMT (Coenen, Pettersson, Chrzanowska-Kluczewska); others either attempt a cautious merging of traditional literary analysis with CMT (Habermann) or situate CMT in relation to their own theoretical frameworks (Biebuyck & Martens, Yacobi). What these studies make apparent is that the NOUN ONE IS NOUN TWO formula of CMT oversimplifies what is going on in most literary texts (cf. Forceville & Urios-Aparisi 2009: 11); they moreover point up extensive affinities between the traditional approaches and CMT that seem to have disappeared from view in the CMT paradigm shift. In fact, as some of the chapters in Part II demonstrate, more recent developments in conceptual integration or blending theory significantly complement literary approaches to imagery and overcome some of the drawbacks of CMT from a literary perspective.

FROM ANALOGY TO NARRATOLOGY: APPROACHES TO LITERARY METAPHOR OUTSIDE THE COGNITIVE PARADIGM

Part I, Indigenous Non-Cognitive Approaches to Metaphor, opens with a chapter by the German Romance scholar Hans Georg Coenen, who in "Systematizing Verbal Imagery: On a Sonnet by Du Bellay" provides a summary of his theory of analogy to metaphor (Coenen 2002). Coenen's chapter taps a long tradition of rhetorical analyses of metaphor in which the affinity between source and target domains (anticipated by Weinrich in the terms *Bildspender* and *Bildempfänger*) lies less in the projection of a (set of) specific feature(s) of the source onto the target than in the analogies subsisting or created between the two domains. This has been acknowledged implicitly by blending theory in its creation of a generic space, which extrapolates precisely such relations of analogy. Coenen moreover concentrates on examples that set three or more items in relation to one another, thus extending metaphor studies beyond the syntactic *of*-constructions analysed by Mark Turner in *Death Is the Mother of Beauty* (1987), in which two concepts are set in relation to one another and generate an analogical set:

> X is the mother of Y
> Death is the mother of Beauty
> Cowardice is the mother of Fear
> Necessity is the mother of Invention
> Fear is the mother of Morality
> Ignorance is the mother of Devotion
> Invention is the mother of Creativity

Coenen's contribution moreover lies in a formalisation of such analogies into tables of sets that allow one to perceive empty slots in the analogies textualized in his example poem, and to thereby provide evidence for implicit analogies. These, one could argue, to some extent emerge within blending theory as part of the 'added meaning' of the blend, although analogy by itself does not exhaust such additional meaning. (Thus, the idea of incompetence generated in "My surgeon is a butcher" cannot be totally explained by analogy.) Coenen's contribution, moreover, historically opens a window into a subgenre of poetry in which extended similes and metaphors are constitutive of the poetic argument.

A completely different rhetorical tradition is brought to bear on the issue of metaphor by Elżbieta Chrzanowska-Kluczewska, who utilizes the concept of catachresis to discuss three denotations of that term, Catachresis One, Catachresis Two and Catachresis Three. These three different types of catachresis end up deconstructing the concept, and they also open up a scale of perceptible metaphoricity. At one end of the scale, one has metaphors that are almost non-metaphorical since they have become lexicalized (*table leg*, *bottle neck*, etc.); at the other end, there are the 'bold' foregrounded metaphors that Weinrich (1963) characterized as *kühne Metaphern*. The third type corresponds to Foucault's atopic notion of catachrestic discourse, a figure of discontinuity. Chrzanowska-Kluczewska, besides integrating into her analysis the classical rhetorical tradition enshrined in Lausberg's *Handbook of Rhetoric* (1960), also taps a school of Polish rhetorical study represented by the scholars Dobrzyńska (1984), Kulawik (1994) and Nycz (2000). Her contribution "Catachresis—A Metaphor or a Figure in Its Own Right?" suggests that rhetorical analysis, far from being outdated, can in fact provide a systematic access to the questions of metaphoric creativity and metaphor recognition.

The next chapter, by Benjamin Biebuyck and Gunther Martens, represents the school of metaphor studies located at Ghent University in Belgium. Biebuyck and Martens have for some time been engaging in the metaphor analysis of narratives, creating a model of how metaphor in some authors supplies an entire semiotic level of signification. Metaphors are analysed in great textual detail, paying particular attention also to verbs (Biebuyck 1998, 2009). Biebuyck and Martens's chapter "Literary Metaphor between Cognition and Narration: *The Sandman* Revisited" demonstrates with particular incisiveness how narrativity is enhanced on the level of metaphors and how these metaphors affect the reading process and generate and enhance metaphoric narrativity through the accumulation and eventual amalgamation of textual metaphors on the narrative discourse level.

Ina Habermann and Bo Pettersson, by contrast, are not representative of a specific school of metaphor thought, but of a broad literary outlook that has usually been defined in opposition to linguistic approaches. While Habermann resorts to cognitive metaphor theory as an additional prop to support her poetic analysis, Pettersson is more critical of CMT, wanting linguistics to take account of contextual and particularly generic frames. Habermann in her "Reaching Beyond Silence: Metaphors of Ineffability in English Poetry—Donne, Wordsworth, Keats, Eliot" concentrates on the fact that metaphor refuses denotation, operating indirectly by means of non-literality. She chooses silence and the unspeakable as particularly apt topics of metaphoric speech—metaphor enables the poet to say the unsayable. Her examples range from metaphysical poetry to Romanticism and Modernism, thus positioning her analysis within a historical and developmental framework.

This semiotic and incipiently deconstructive approach is complemented in Pettersson's chapter by a more traditional textual and historical analysis. Pettersson's reservations regarding cognitive metaphor theory do not so much concern details like the invariance principle (the fact that only some features of the source are projected onto the target, namely those that are compatible with the intrinsic structure of the target—thus the red, red rose of the source may have thorns and need daily watering, but these aspects are not thematized in application to the beloved)[2]; instead, Pettersson focuses his critique on the abstract and general level of CMT research and argues for the specificity of literary metaphor and for the complex generic and historical framing of literary texts that need to be taken into consideration when discussing an individual metaphor. Pettersson's "Literary Criticism Writes Back to Metaphor Theory: Exploring the Relation between Extended Metaphor and Narrative in Literature" thus represents the unease engendered by CMT among literary scholars, whose major concern is the individual poem and the specific metaphor that is especially striking or resonates with other texts in a particularly apt manner. By discussing Blake's poetry and Magnus Mills's fiction, Pettersson attempts to demonstrate the affinity between extended metaphors and narratives and their use in the service of allegory. Metaphors, in such a framework, are not interesting as *linguistic* or *cognitive* patterns, or for their semantic generation of meaning through set formulae, but as salient markers of poetic achievement that constitute part of a network of echoes across the centuries of the poetic tradition.

Tamar Yacobi's "Metaphors in Context: The Communicative Structure of Figurative Language" approaches metaphor through its operation within the communicative act as a whole. Like her earlier work on unreliability (e.g. Yacobi 2000), this approach is based on Tel Aviv functional poetics and narratology, which examines discourse in terms of the effect(s) that an addressor seeks to create in the addressee. More specifically, the argument here is related to quotation theory (Sternberg 1982), which argues that all quoting involves the montage of perspectives between quoter and quotee. In discourse as communication, the workings of metaphor depend both on its object and on the addressor's goal(s) concerning the effect on the addressee(s). Since in fiction metaphor is always quoted, Yacobi thus goes beyond the question of voice to account for the possibility of reading a metaphor as directed to two different audiences. The examples, from poetry and prose (especially Henry James), illustrate a variety of effects which vary according to their reference to fictive inset as against authorial framing of the figurative discourse. Like Pettersson, Yacobi thus instantiates a contextualist and highly literary approach to metaphor study.

EXTENDING COGNITIVE METAPHOR AND BLENDING THEORY

Part II, Cognitive Metaphor Theory and Literary Analysis, opens with the contribution of John Douthwaite, and with a plea for the consideration of Gricean conversational implicature in metaphor study. Douthwaite is critical of cognitive metaphor theory and, like Pettersson and Yacobi, misses a more contextual situating of metaphors. In "Conceptual Metaphor and Communication: An Austinian and Gricean Analysis of Brian Clark's *Whose Life Is It Anyway?*", Douthwaite takes conversational implicature, flanked by speech act theory[3], as the theoretical angle from whose vantage point he wants to reform CMT. Douthwaite concentrates in particular on the individual speech act and its metaphoric instantiations, thus linking with Habermann's emphasis on the indirection of speaking about the unsayable through metaphoric language. His chapter proposes a fruitful marriage between conversational implicature and a CMT approach. Douthwaite's chapter is the only one in this collection to deal with drama.

After this somewhat critical opening, the chapters by Margaret H. Freeman and Beatrix Busse illustrate cognitive metaphor theory research in its application to literary texts, poetry in the case of Freeman and novels in the case of Busse. Freeman in her "The Role of Metaphor in Poetic Iconicity" compares Shelley's and Horace Smith's poems "Ozymandias". Following Hiraga's (2005) work on metaphor and iconicity, she explores how Charles Sanders Pearce's semiotic theory might explain how metaphor creates iconicity by fusing diagram with image (Freeman 2007, 2009). Freeman's most original contribution concerns the stipulation that iconicity can serve as a criterion of poetic quality.

Busse analyses Paul Auster's novelistic oeuvre from the perspective of the medical metaphors WRITING IS MEDICINE and WRITING IS DISEASE. Her "'One should never underestimate the power of books': Writing and Reading as Therapy in Paul Auster's Novels" is a linguistic chapter that engages with the level of metanarrative argument in Auster's fiction, thus linking with metaphors such as WRITING IS FOOD FOR THE READER in Fielding (cf. Fludernik 2010). Busse anticipates some paradoxes and ambivalences in the conceptualization of medicine that we will also encounter in Goatly's more openly ideological analysis.

Michael Kimmel's contribution is the first of a series of chapters to move off into new applications of cognitive metaphor theory. In "Metaphor Sets in *The Turn of the Screw*: What Conceptual Metaphors Reveal about Narrative Functions" he uses CMT as a theoretical basis, but with the help of the computer programme *Atlas.ti* establishes a systematic textual metaphor analysis that is able to provide a much more comprehensive and statistically comparable analysis of narrative texts. He provides an in-depth illustration of his approach on the example of Henry James's short story.

Ralph Müller's chapter "Hyperliteralist Metaphor: The Cognitive Poetics of Robert Musil in His Novella 'Die Portugiesin'" employs cognitive metaphor theory to focus on a phenomenon that resembles Biebuyck and Martens's chains of metaphoric expressions but constitutes a separate category. He calls this strategy "hyperliteralism" and outlines its theoretical and practical manifestations. Müller is particularly interested in elucidating the cognitive principles at work in the chosen story and in the technique of hyperliteralism.

Michael Sinding's chapter "Storyworld Metaphors in Swift's Satire" takes cognitive metaphor theory into genre theory in an attempt to discuss allegory and satire on the example of Swift's *A Tale of a Tub*. Sinding concentrates on the interplay of metaphor and story and its larger narratological significance. He moreover outlines the important role of metaphor in macrotextual meaning effects. Given the continuous allegorical shape of *A Tale of a Tub*, Sinding is placed advantageously to analyse metaphor coherence and literary structure. His chapter interfaces not only with work on literary satire but also with narratology, especially with research into storyworlds.

Andrew Goatly's contribution ("Conventional Metaphor and the Latent Ideology of Racism") does not per se deal with literature but with ideology and its textual manifestations, whether in literature or non-literary texts. Goatly uses newspaper articles available online in order to illustrate discourses of racism and their typical metaphoric textualizations. He also addresses the issue of metaphoric creativity by introducing an ideological latency scale. In this respect, his chapter echoes Chrzanowska-Kluczewska's metaphoricity scale. Like Kimmel, Goatly in his analysis foregrounds the function of image schemas; he also discusses various disease metaphors (IDEAS ARE DISEASES), thus establishing a link with the imagery analysed by Busse in Auster's fiction. Goatly's chapter develops Lakoff's work on the ideological thrust of cognitive metaphor (e.g. Lakoff 2006) and reaches out into cultural studies (see also Fludernik 2005a).

The final chapter in the volume, Charles Forceville's "The JOURNEY Metaphor and the Source-Path-Goal Schema in Agnès Varda's Auto-biographical *Gleaning* Documentaries", broadens the predominantly verbal and textual emphasis in metaphor studies (and in this collection) to confront visual and multimodal metaphor, a topic of intensive earlier research by Forceville (1996, 2006, 2008). Taking a film by Agnès Varda as his example, Forceville here uncovers aspects of metaphor that are specific to the pictorial and sonic mode without necessarily surfacing in language. Visual, verbal and aural aspects of metaphor include the possibility of simultaneous rather than sequential cuing, the enhanced potential for blending in the visual medium and the greater ambiguity or openness of metaphoric interpretation.

OUTLOOK

As this volume documents, linguistic cognitive metaphor theory and blending theory and literary analysis of imagery have begun to communicate in a fruitful and mutually beneficial manner. Increasingly, CMT theoreticians are interested in specific uses of metaphor rather than merely the systematic and cognitive aspects of individual textual manifestations. At the same time, literary scholars are more frequently willing to spend time on CMT and to familiarize themselves with blending theory. Despite some remaining qualms on either side, the chapters in this collection are evidence of a fair-minded intellectual exchange.

The contributors to this volume moreover suggest a need to integrate more clearly approaches to metaphor that have developed outside the framework of cognitive metaphor theory. They also show the benefits of extending CMT and blending theory into areas that are particularly relevant for literary critics: issues of genre, ideology, the media, narrative, reception, iconicity and aesthetics. Metonymy and its link to realism have also recently come in for extensive study (Panther & Radden 1999; Barcelona 2000; Fludernik 2005b; Panther & Thornburg 2007). A particularly important concern is the relationship between metaphor and narrative, an issue raised by blending both theorists (Fauconnier & Turner 2002; Turner

2008) and literary scholars (Pettersson 2001; Fludernik 2010). Alongside CMT's recent interest in cultural grounding and variation, all of these aspects of literary framing can be regarded as pragmatic modifications of the original universalist principles of CMT. In a sense, CMT and blending theory—like Saussurian linguistics—started out as analyses of a *langue*, and this *langue* is increasingly being complemented and displaced by a focus on the *parole* of metaphor: actual instances of metaphor use and their verbal and visual manifestations. I hope this volume will have made its own little contribution to the emergence of such a change.

NOTES

1. Briefly, double-scope blending allows projection from input space 2 to input space 1, thus shelving the invariance hypothesis (see below). An easy introduction to blending theory is provided in Fludernik, Freeman and Freeman (1999).
2. The invariance hypothesis was first introduced by Lakoff and Turner (1989) and modified in Lakoff (1990). For a critique of the unidirectionality and target structure preservation claimed in the invariance principle which focuses on literary metaphor see also Stockwell (1999).
3. On speech act theory see Austin (1962), Searle (1969) and Grice (1975); relevance theory is linked to Sperber and Wilson (1995).

WORKS CITED

Abrams, Meyer H. (1953) *The Mirror and the Lamp: Romantic Theory and the Critical Tradition.* New York and Oxford: Oxford University Press.
Austin, John L. (1962) *How to Do Things with Words.* Cambridge, MA: Harvard University Press.
Barcelona, Antonio (2000) Ed. *Metaphor and Metonymy at the Crossroads: A Cognitive Perspective.* Topics in English Linguistics, 30. Berlin: de Gruyter.
Biebuyck, Benjamin (1998) *Die poietische Metapher: Ein Beitrag zur Theorie der Figürlichkeit.* Würzburg: Königshausen & Neumann.
———. (2009) "Acting Figuratively, Telling Tropically: Figures of Insanity in Günter Grass's *Die Blechtrommel*". *Style* 43.3 (Fall): 322–40.
Black, Max (1979) "More about Metaphor". *Metaphor and Thought.* Ed. Andrew Ortony. Cambridge: Cambridge University Press. 19–43.
Blumenberg, Hans (1989) *Paradigmen zu einer Metaphorologie* [1960]. Frankfurt: Suhrkamp.
Clemen, Wolfgang (1977) *The Development of Shakespeare's Imagery* [1951]. Second Edition. London: Methuen.
Coenen, Hans Georg (2002) *Analogie und Metapher: Grundlegung einer Theorie der bildlichen Rede.* Berlin: de Gruyter.
Dancygier, Barbara (2006) "What Can Blending Do for You?". *Language and Literature* 15: 5–16.
Dobrzyńska, Teresa (1984) *Metafora.* Wrocław: Zakład Narodowy im. Ossolińskich, Wydawnictwo PAN.
Fauconnier, Gilles (1998) *Mental Spaces: Aspects of Meaning Construction in Natural Language* [*Espace mentaux*, 1984]. Cambridge: Cambridge University Press.

———. (1999) *Mappings in Thought and Language* [1997]. Cambridge: Cambridge University Press.

Fauconnier, Gilles, and Mark Turner (1999) "A Mechanism of Creativity". *Poetics Today* 20.3: 397–418.

———. (2002) *The Way We Think: Conceptual Blending and the Mind's Hidden Complexities*. New York: Basic Books.

———. (2008) "Rethinking Metaphor". *The Cambridge Handbook of Metaphor and Thought*. Ed. Ray Gibbs. Cambridge: Cambridge University Press. 53–66.

Fludernik, Monika (2005a) "Metaphoric (Im)Prison(ment) and the Constitution of a Carceral Imaginary". *Anglia* 123: 1–25.

———. (2005b) "The Metaphorics and Metonymics of Carcerality: Reflections on Imprisonment as Source and Target Domain in Literary Texts". *English Studies* 86.3: 226–44.

———. (2010) "Narrative and Metaphor". *Language and Style: In Honour of Mick Short*. Eds. Dan McIntyre and Beatrix Busse. Basingstoke: Palgrave. 347–63.

Fludernik, Monika, Donald C. Freeman and Margaret H. Freeman (1999) "Metaphor and Beyond: An Introduction". *Poetics Today* 20.3: 383–96.

Forceville, Charles (1996) *Pictorial Metaphor in Advertising*. London and New York: Routledge.

———. (2006) "Non-verbal and Multimodal Metaphor in a Cognitivist Framework: Agendas for Research". *Cognitive Linguistics: Current Applications and Future Perspectives*. Eds. Gitte Kristiansen et al. Berlin and New York: de Gruyter. 379–402.

———. (2008) "Metaphor in Pictures and Multimodal Representations". *The Cambridge Handbook of Metaphor and Thought*. Ed. Raymond W. Gibbs, Jr. Cambridge: Cambridge University Press. 462–82.

Forceville, Charles, and Eduardo Urios-Aparisi (2009) Eds. *Multimodal Metaphor*. Berlin and New York: de Gruyter.

Freeman, Margaret H. (2007) "Poetic Iconicity". *Cognition in Language: Volume in Honour of Professor Elżbieta Tabakowska*. Eds. Władislaw Chłopicki, Andrzej Pawelec and Agnieszka Pokojska. Kraków: Tertium. 472–501.

———. (2009) "Minding: Feeling, Form, and Meaning in the Creation of Poetic Iconicity". *Cognitive Poetics: Goals, Gains, and Gaps*. Eds. Geert Brône and Jeroen Vandaele. Berlin: de Gruyter. 169–96.

Gibbs, Raymond W., Jr. (1999) "Taking Metaphor Out of Our Heads and Putting It into the Cultural World". *Metaphor in Cognitive Linguistics: Selected Papers from the Fifth International Cognitive Linguistics Conference, Amsterdam, July 1997*. Eds. Raymond W. Gibbs, Jr., and Gerard J. Steen. Amsterdam: John Benjamins. 145–66.

Glucksberg, Sam (2008) "How Metaphors Create Categories—Quickly". *The Cambridge Handbook of Metaphor and Thought*. Ed. Raymond W. Gibbs, Jr. Cambridge: Cambridge University Press. 67–83.

Goatly, Andrew (2007) *Washing the Brain: Metaphor and Hidden Ideology*. Amsterdam: John Benjamins.

Goodblatt, Chanita (2001) "Adding an Empirical Dimension to the Study of Poetic Metaphor". *Journal of Literary Semantics* 30: 167–80.

Goodblatt, Chanita, and Joseph Glicksohn (2002) "Metaphor Comprehension as Problem Solving: An Online Study of the Reading Process". *Style*. Special Issue on Cognitive Approaches to Figurative Language. 36: 428–45.

Grice, Paul (1975) "Logic and Conversation". *Syntax and Semantics*, Vol. 3. Eds. Peter Cole and Jerry L. Morgan. New York: Academic Press. 41–58.

Hiraga, Masako K. (2005) *Metaphor and Iconicity: A Cognitive Approach to Analysing Texts*. Houndsmill, Basingstoke and New York: Palgrave Macmillan.

Holyoak, Keith J., and Paul Thagard (1995) *Mental Leaps: Analogy in Creative Thought*. Cambridge, MA: MIT Press.

Jäkel, Olaf (1999) "Kant, Blumenberg, Weinrich: Some Forgotten Contributions to the Cognitive Theory of Metaphor". *Metaphor in Cognitive Linguistics: Selected Papers from the Fifth International Cognitive Linguistics Conference, Amsterdam, July 1997*. Eds. Raymond W. Gibbs and Gerard J. Steen. Amsterdam and Philadelphia: John Benjamins. 9–27.

Johnson, Mark (1987) *The Body in the Mind: The Bodily Basis of Meaning, Imagination, and Reading*. Chicago: University of Chicago Press.

Kohl, Katrin (2007) *Metapher*. Stuttgart: Metzler.

Kövecses, Zoltán (2002) *Metaphor: A Practical Introduction*. Oxford: Oxford University Press.

———. (2005) *Metaphor in Culture: Universality and Variation*. Cambridge: Cambridge University Press.

———. (2010) "A new look at metaphorical creativity in cognitive linguistics". Unpublished ms.

Kulawik, Adam (1994) *Poetyka: Wstęp do teorii dzieła literackiego*. Cracow: Antykwa.

Lakoff, George (1987) *Women, Fire, and Dangerous Things: What Categories Reveal about the Mind*. Chicago: University of Chicago Press.

———. (1990) "The Invariance Hypothesis: Is Abstract Reason Based on Image Schemas?" *Cognitive Linguistics* 1.1: 39–74.

———. (2006) *Whose Freedom? The Battle Over America's Most Important Idea*. New York: Picador.

Lakoff, George, and Mark Johnson (1980) *Metaphors We Live By*. Chicago: University of Chicago Press.

Lakoff, George, and Mark Turner (1989) *More than Cool Reason: A Field Guide to Poetic Metaphor*. Chicago: University of Chicago Press.

Lausberg, Heinrich (1960) *Handbuch der literarischen Rhetorik: Eine Grundlegung der Literaturwissenschaft*. München: M. Hueber.

Moreno, Rosa E. Vega (2007) *Creativity and Convention: The Pragmatics of Everyday Figurative Speech*. Amsterdam: John Benjamins.

Musolff, Andreas (2004) *Metaphor and Political Discourse: Analogical Reasoning in Debates about Europe*. London: Palgrave Macmillan.

Nycz, Ryszard (2000) *Tekstowy świat: Poststrukturalizm a wiedza o literaturze*. Cracow: Universitas.

Page, Ruth (2010) *New Perspectives on Narrative and Multimodality*. London and New York: Routledge.

Panther, Klaus-Uwe, and Günter Radden (1999) Eds. *Metonymy in Language and Thought*. Amsterdam: John Benjamins.

Panther, Klaus-Uwe, and Linda L. Thornburg (2007) "Metonymy". *The Oxford Handbook of Cognitive Linguistics*. Eds. Dirk Geeraerts and Hubert Cuyckens. Oxford and New York: Oxford University Press. 236–63.

Pettersson, Bo (2001) "On LIFE IS A JOURNEY as Link between Analogy and Narrative". *Language, Learning, Literature: Studies Presented to Håkan Ringborn*. Eds. Martin Gill, Anthony W. Johnson, Lena M. Koski, Roger D. Sell and Brita Wårvik. Turku: Åbo Akademi University. 199–214.

Richards, Ivor A. (1967) *The Philosophy of Rhetoric* [1936]. New York and Oxford: Oxford University Press.

Ricoeur, Paul (2003) *The Rule of Metaphor* [*La métaphore vive*, 1975]. Transl. Robert Czerny, with Kathleen McLaughlin and John Costello, SJ. Routledge Classics. London: Routledge.

Rolf, Eckard (2005) *Metaphertheorien: Typologie, Darstellung, Bibliographie*. Berlin: de Gruyter.

Searle, John (1969) *Speech Acts: An Essay in the Philosophy of Language.* Cambridge: Cambridge University Press.

Semino, Elena (2008) *Metaphor in Discourse.* Cambridge: Cambridge University Press.

Shakespeare, William (1994) *Measure for Measure* [1623]. Ed. J. W. Lever. The Arden Shakespeare, Third Series. London: Routledge.

Sperber, Dan, and Deirdre Wilson (1995) *Relevance: Communication and Cognition.* Second Edition. Oxford: Blackwell.

Spurgeon, Caroline (1952) *Shakespeare's Imagery and What It Tells Us.* Cambridge: Cambridge University Press.

Steen, Gerard (2002) "Identifying Metaphor in Language: A Cognitive Approach". *Style* 36.3: 386–407.

Steen, Gerard, Aletta G. Dorst, J. Berenike Herrmann, Anna A. Kaal, Tina Krennmayr and Trijntje Pasma (2010) *A Method for Linguistic Metaphor Identification: From MIP to MIPVU.* Amsterdam: John Benjamins.

Sternberg, Meir (1982) "Proteus in Quotation-Land: Mimesis and the Forms of Reported Discourse". *Poetics Today* 3: 107–56.

Stockwell, Peter (1999) "The Inflexibility of Invariance". *Language and Literature* 8.2: 125–42.

Tsur, Reuven (2008) *Toward a Theory of Cognitive Poetics* [1992]. Second Edition. Brighton: Sussex Academic Press.

Turner, Mark (1987) *Death Is the Mother of Beauty: Mind, Metaphor, Criticism.* Chicago: University of Chicago Press.

———. (1991) *Reading Minds: The Study of English in the Age of Cognitive Science.* Princeton: Princeton University Press.

———. (1996) *The Literary Mind.* New York and Oxford: Oxford University Press.

———. (2006) Ed. *The Artful Mind: Cognitive Science and the Riddle of Human Creativity.* New York: Oxford University Press.

———. (2008) "The Mind Is an Autocatalytic Vortex". *The Literary Mind: REAL Yearbook of Research in English and American Literature*, 24. Eds. Jürgen Schlaeger and Gesa Stedman. Tübingen: Gunter Narr. 13–43.

Weinrich, Harald (1963) "Semantik der kühnen Metapher". *Deutsche Vierteljahrsschrift für Literaturwissenschaft und Geistesgeschichte* 37: 324–44.

Yacobi, Tamar (2000) "Interart Narrative: (Un)Reliability and Ekphrasis". *Poetics Today* 21.4: 711–50.

Part I

Indigenous Non-Cognitive Approaches to Metaphor

1 Systematizing Verbal Imagery
On a Sonnet by Du Bellay

Hans Georg Coenen

This chapter falls into two sections. In the second, more important section, the interrelations of images in a sonnet by Du Bellay will be analysed. In the first section, the relevant terminology and the theoretical foundations on which this analysis rests will be outlined. This investigation is based on elements of a theory developed from Aristotelian ideas and enriched by some insights from modern logic. This theory is expounded in detail in Coenen (2002). The first section of this chapter summarizes the theory only insofar as will be required for the present analysis.

1 TERMINOLOGY

One of the premises of the present analysis of images, admittedly a controversial premise but not to be defended further at this point, is the axiom that verbal imagery, including metaphors, is based on analogy. Analogy, in turn, requires description. It will therefore first be established what in the present context is meant by description.

1.1 Description

We understand description as the attribution of a **descriptive content** (*Beschreibungsinhalt*) to an **object of description** (*Beschreibungsgegenstand*). The latter is regarded as carrying the properties constituting the descriptive content. The act of description is a speech act that is performed through the production of texts, just as are ordering, threatening, admonishing, complaining, flattering, swearing an oath and many others. Objects of description neither have to be real nor need they be assumed to be real; the motto *esse est describi* applies to them. The object of a description, therefore, need not be a concrete item such as Charlemagne's crown or a concrete person such as Charlemagne himself. Groups, classes and collectives can also be objects of description, as can facts, cases, processes, states, situations, institutions, locations, periods of time or indeed any abstract concepts. Anything which is described is *ipso facto* an object of description.

In order to apply the term *description* for the explication of analogy, a slight complication of the concept must first be introduced: one can distinguish between descriptions that are polyadic or polyvalent (*mehrstellig*) and those that are monadic or monovalent (*einstellig*). The sentence *Charlemagne was a Frank* may serve as an example of a monovalent description: in this sentence Charlemagne is the object of description (*Beschreibungsgegenstand*) and "... was a Frank" is the descriptive content (*Beschreibungsinhalt*). The sentence *Charlemagne was the eldest son of Pepin the Short* can be viewed as a bivalent (*zweistellig*) description, with the descriptive content "... was the eldest son of ..." providing the relation of two objects. Charlemagne is described through his relation to Pepin the Short, and *vice versa*. A triadic or trivalent (*dreistellig*) description could be exemplified by the sentence *Charlemagne bequeathed to Louis the Pious a multiethnic state*. Here, three objects are described through their interrelations, namely Charlemagne, Louis the Pious and a multiethnic state. A description may, of course, be more than trivalent. Any attempt to set a maximum number of possible valences would prove arbitrary, particularly since the linguistic medium of a description need not consist of a single sentence but may comprise a complete text.

In order to account for differences in valency, the definition of the term *description* is here extended to the attribution of a descriptive content to an ordered set of described objects. At the limit would be a set which holds only one object to be described. The descriptive content may best be imagined as a text with numbered vacancies such as in the following formula:

[1] bequeathed [2] [3].

This abstraction is, however, ambiguous in that the information that [3] is to be replaced with the receiver of the legacy and [2] with the legacy itself is missing. The descriptive content correlates with the objects of description occupying its vacancies in the same manner as the functor in logic does with its arguments. The account of a description comprises the set of objects ([Charlemagne], [Louis the Pious], [a multiethnic state]) and the descriptive content (*Beschreibungsinhalt*): ([1] bequeathed [2] [3]). The number of the valencies reflects the positions of the objects within their ordered set. In the case of polyvalent descriptions, the term *descriptive content* is perhaps confusing: the objects are not described by the descriptive content alone, but rather by the descriptive content *and all other objects within the set*. In the example above, Charlemagne is not described merely through the formula "[1] bequeathed [2] [3]" but also through the filling of the vacancies [2] and [3].

The suggested way of handling descriptions, which rests upon predicate logic, can be viewed as the result of a meaning-preserving transformation applied to linguistic expressions. There is, however, no strict system of processing rules whose application would automatically lead from the actual form of linguistic expression to our kind of notation. The dissecting of a linguistic description into a **set of items** and a **descriptive content** is not a regulated process, like a logical derivation within the language of calculus, but a more or less plausible act of interpretation. One and the same linguistic expression can be dissected into different sets of items and different descriptive contents. The following sentence may serve as an example: *Rhetoric is an invention of the Greeks*. An initial analysis might interpret "Rhetoric" as the only element of the set and "[1] is an invention of the Greeks" as the descriptive content. However, an alternative analysis might interpret "Rhetoric" and "the Greeks" as the two elements of the set and "[1] is an invention of [2]" as the descriptive content. The first analysis would be useful if one wanted to highlight the analogy of rhetoric to grammar, for instance. The sentence *Grammar is an invention of the Greeks* could be viewed as a monovalent description, just like the sentence on rhetoric. Rhetoric and grammar would thus serve as two alternative occupants of a vacancy (*Leerstellenfüller*) in relation to the same descriptive content. They are, then, *analogous*, as will become more apparent in the next section. Rhetoric is a sibling of grammar. The second analysis, for instance, would be useful in application to the sentence *The pyramids are an invention of the Egyptians*, if, that is, the analogies of the respective item pairs rhetoric/Greeks and pyramids/Egyptians were to be highlighted. The pyramids do for the glory of the Egyptians what rhetoric does for the glory of the Greeks. The pyramids are the rhetoric of the Egyptians and rhetoric corresponds to the pyramids of the Greeks. It is therefore the case that a linguistic description can be parsed into a set of items and a descriptive content in different ways, but this process is by no means arbitrary. The purpose of the parsing is to reveal specific analogies and their interrelations.

1.2 Analogy

We understand analogy as a symmetrical relationship between two items or item sets in a universe of discourse (*Diskursuniversum*). This relationship is actualized when a description with the same descriptive content applies to both items or item sets. Rhetoric and grammar are analogous insofar as they result in valid descriptions as alternative occupants of the vacancy of the descriptive content "[1] is an invention of the Greeks". The item pairs "evening"/"day" and "age"/"life" are analogous insofar as they result in valid descriptions as alternative occupants of the vacancies of the descriptive content "[1] is the final phase of [2]". Based on this analogy, age can be described figuratively as the evening of life or the evening as the old age of the day. Aristotle has used these figurative expressions as examples of analogy-based metaphors in his *Poetics* (1456b). Our concept of analogy is a generalisation of the Aristotelian one. It additionally allows us to explain metaphors which Aristotle would not have regarded as analogy-based.

Two analogous items or item sets constitute an **analogy set** (*Analogie-menge*), for example the items "rhetoric" and "grammar" or the item sets "evening"/"day" and "age"/"life". An analogy set contains at least two elements. There are also larger analogy sets. We will, therefore, define *analogy set* as a set of items in which each item is a set that contains two or more elements and in which each element in one set is analogous to each element of the other set due to their shared descriptive content. For illustration, let us propose an analogy set of three item sets, in which each in turn contains three elements. The three item sets shall be the following:

A   [breeds of dogs, wolf, poodle]
B   [Romance languages, Latin, French]
C   [Western tragedies, classical Greek tragedy, French Classicist tragedy]

The shared descriptive content providing the analogy between the item sets might be

All [1] descend from [2]. Of the descendants of [2], [3] constitutes a particularly highly refined variety.

This descriptive content results in three valid descriptions with the item sets as alternative occupants of the vacancies, establishing four three-element analogy sets: the first one contains the three item sets themselves while the other three contain the items occupying the same position within the respective sets, namely [breeds of dogs, Romance languages, Western tragedies], [wolf, Latin, classical Greek tragedy], and [poodle, French, French Classicist tragedy]:

Taking the latter analogy set as an example, there is an analogous relationship between poodles and French, between poodles and French Classicist tragedy and between French and French Classicist tragedy. The first

| position sets | global analogy | 1.
[A, B, C]
A [breeds of dogs, wolf, poodle]
B [Romance languages, Latin, French]
C [Western tragedies, classical Greek tragedy, French Classicist tragedy] | | |
| | local analogy | 2.
breeds of dogs
Romance languages

Western tragedies | 3.
Wolf
Latin

classical Greek tragedy | 4.
Poodle
French

French Classicist tragedy |

Figure 1.1   Analogy sets—global and local analogy illustrated.

one of these analogies might be the basis for the metaphorical statement *French is the poodle among the Romance languages.*

The *analogous relationship* between those item sets that result in valid descriptions as alternative occupants of the vacancies of the same descriptive content shall be called *global analogy.* The item sets [breeds of dogs, wolf, poodle] and [Romance languages, Latin, French] are hence linked by such **global analogy.** The analogous relationship between the individual elements of different globally analogous item sets, on the other hand, shall be called **local analogy** (*Detailanalogie*). Assuming the validity of the three descriptions above, we can then specify a local analogy between breeds of dogs and Romance languages, between wolves and Latin and between poodles and French, respectively. The items sharing a local analogy constitute a **position set** (*Positionsmenge*) because they occupy the same position in different item sets. The sets [breeds of dogs, Romance languages, Western tragedies], [wolf, Latin, classical Greek tragedy] and [poodle, French, French Classicist tragedy] are, therefore, position sets. If an analogy is based on a monovalent description, in which the item sets contain only one element each, global analogy and local analogy get conflated. Rhetoric and grammar as alternative occupants of the vacancies of the descriptive content "[1] is an invention of the Greeks" share a global as well as a local analogy.

Two items are analogous if they share a descriptive content. The existence of shared descriptive content does not preclude the existence of other descriptive contents applicable to only one of the items. Thus, Greek tragedy, besides being described as the origin of Western drama, could equally well be described as the secularized equivalent of Dionysian religious rites. Two items sharing all possible descriptive contents, however, would have to be identical.

An analogy based on a monovalent descriptive content may be trivial or non-trivial. It is trivial if the shared descriptive content of the analogous items results from a conventional shared denotation (*Bezeichnung*) or from a familiar conceptual classification. The analogy between Peter and Paul is trivial if based on the descriptive content "[1] is an apostle", for 'apostle' is a conventional denotation shared by both. It is also trivial if based on the shared descriptive content "[1] is human" because 'human' is a conventional hypernym for both apostles. The analogy between a hammer and pliers is trivial if based on the descriptive content "[1] is a tool", for 'tool' is a conventional hypernym for both. Equally trivial is the analogy between Monday and Friday if based on the descriptive content "[1] is a weekday". It is non-trivial if the shared descriptive content is "[1] is the last working day of the week". An employee whose vacation starts on a Tuesday could be told by a colleague "Monday is your Friday". The triviality of an analogy therefore depends on the descriptive content it is based on. Between the members of one and the same item pair several valid analogies may exist, both trivial and non-trivial. Analogies based on polyvalent descriptions are usually non-trivial.

1.3   Root Identity

Linguistic imagery (*sprachliche Bilder*) is based on non-trivial analogies. One could not use the word *hammer* metaphorically in order to describe pliers, arguing that both are tools. The fact that both are tools affords only a trivial analogy. By contrast, the word *coin* may be used to describe a word, since both owe their value to convention. The analogy between, say, sun and death is trivial if it is based on the descriptive content "[1] is a phenomenon of our world". It is non-trivial, however, if the descriptive content "[1] cannot be looked at without winking" is assumed, as in La Rochefoucauld's maxim 26 (1967 [1664]: 13): "Le soleil ni la mort ne se peuvent regarder fixement". ('Neither the sun nor death can be looked at without winking.'[1])

Every analogy set—that is, every set of items analogous due to the same common features—has an **analogy root** (*Analogiewurzel*). An analogy root shall be defined as *the description on which the analogy between the members of an analogy set rests.* Baudelaire's sonnet "Correspondances" begins with the words "La Nature est un temple [. . .]" (1982: 193). The statement puts "Nature" and "temple" into a relationship of analogy. This two-element analogy set can be assigned the following pair of descriptions as its root:

> In Nature a murmuring ulterior world becomes manifest.
> In a temple a murmuring ulterior world becomes manifest.

The analogy root could also be described by the item set and the shared descriptive content:

> [Nature, temple]
> In [1] a murmuring ulterior world becomes manifest.

Analogy roots are composed of as many descriptions as there are items contained in the analogy set. Naturally, these descriptions may be polyvalent. The analogy set then consists of item sets rather than individual items.

Language offers different options for the expression of an analogy. One can place a literal (Nature) and a metaphorical reference (temple) of the same item in corresponding syntactic positions, as in the above sonnet by Baudelaire. Or one can present the analogy in the form of its own root, i.e. as a description set (cf. Coenen 2008: 107–9):

> La fortune fait paraître nos vertus et nos vices, comme la lumière fait paraître les objets. (Maxime 380; La Rochefoucauld 1967 [1664]: 90)

> Fortune makes visible our virtues or our vices, as light does objects.[2]

The maxim connects two descriptions which illustrate the same bivalent descriptive content by means of the conjunction *comme* (as): "[1] makes visible [2]". The item sets serving as alternative occupants of the vacancies in this case are [Fortune, virtues/vices] and [light, objects]. The same analogy root could be the basis of a metaphorical statement such as "Fortune is the light which makes visible our virtues or our vices".

One and the same root can be the basis of several local analogies. For instance, the analogy between Fortune and light—to return to La Rochefoucauld's maxim—is based on the same root as the analogy between virtues and vices on the one hand and material objects on the other hand. Root identity engenders a **systematic affinity** (*systematische Verwandtschaft*) between different analogies. It is grounded in the identity of the descriptive content utilized by analogy-generating descriptions. The two analogies between Fortune and light, and between virtues/vices and material objects, are based on the descriptive content "[1] makes visible [2]" used in both cases to describe the respective analogy partners. The term **root identity** (*Wurzelgleichheit*) renders more precise the classical term *metaphora continuata*, i.e. "continued" or "spun out" metaphor. Quintilian uses this term in his description of allegory in the *Institutio oratoria* (bk. VIII, ch. 6, par. 44):[3]

> Ἀλληγορία [...] presents one thing in words and another in sense, or sometimes a sense quite contrary to the words. Of the first sort, the following is an example [...]:
>
>> O ship, shall new waves bear thee back into the sea?
>> O what art thou doing? Make resolutely for the harbour
>
> and all that ode of Horace, in which he puts the ship for the commonwealth, the tempests of the waves for civil wars, and the harbour for peace and concord. (2001: 450)

The connection between the metaphors which Quintilian describes as *metaphorae continuatae* rests on root identity. The common root of the cited metaphors consists of two four-element item sets and a common descriptive content, for whose four vacancies the two item sets offer alternative occupants. The item sets in question are respectively [ship, waves, sea, harbour] and [commonwealth, civil wars, danger of ruin, peace/concord]. The shared descriptive content linking the four analogies could be proposed as follows: "[1] is pushed by [2] towards the threatening [3]; turning towards [4], however, saves [1] from [3]".

1.4   Matrix and Figurative Field

In order to illustrate a more complex analogy root, a two-dimensional matrix will be employed in the second section of this chapter. Its structure shall be explained at this point. As expounded above, an analogy root consists of descriptions using the same descriptive content with vacancies which are filled by analogous items. Any descriptive content present in an analogy root is an element of two sets: on the one hand, a set which is related to at least one other set on the basis of a global analogy, and, on the other hand, a position set (*Positionsmenge*) whose elements are related by means of local analogy. The schematic representation of analogy roots yields a two-dimensional positioning of items in rows and columns. The elements of a set related to other sets by means of global analogy share the same rows. Consequently, the globally analogous item sets are placed in subsequent rows. The vertical columns, by contrast, contain elements in the same positions within the different globally analogous sets. The different columns, therefore, contain different position sets. The globally analogous sets shall be referred to as **domains** (*Bereiche*) and are marked by capital letters labelling the rows. The position sets shall be distinguished by Arabic numbers marking the positions within the globally analogous sets and labelling the respective columns. For an analogy root with three globally analogous item sets containing three elements each and offering alternative realizations of the same descriptive content in the vacancy slots, the objects of description could be placed in the matrix in Table 1.1.

The nine items fitting into the nine cells are distributed between the three domains A, B and C, as well as between the position sets 1, 2 and 3. Each item is marked by its domain and by its position set. This abstract matrix becomes more comprehensible if the boxes are filled with actual items, as in Table 1.2.

If the matrix of items is complemented by the always implicit common descriptive content, a **figurative field** (*Bildfeld*) emerges. For the matrix below (Table 1.2), for instance, the following descriptive content could be elaborated: "[2] is the desirable middle between extreme [1], which corresponds to a radical lack, and extreme [3], which refers to an excess of the quality of [2]".

Table 1.1   Matrix of Root Analogies

	1	2	3
A			
B			
C			

Table 1.2   Matrix Domains and Position Sets

	1	2	3
A	anorexia	healthy eating	bulimia
B	cowardice	courage	foolhardiness
C	Arctic cold	temperate climate	tropical heat

I employ the expression *figurative field* here despite the fact that Harald Weinrich has already introduced this term into literary studies, though with a different meaning (Weinrich 1958). Weinrich's figurative field refers to the structure of the lexicon of one language or even of several languages. Our figurative field, on the other hand, is a semantic paradigm underlying the use of images in an individual text or passage.

From the matrix of items, several kinds of analogies, as well as their relationships, can be extracted. The three domains A, B and C are globally analogous by pairs. Likewise, the elements of a position set display pairwise local analogy. The matrix thus elucidates nine (three times three) local analogies. Three kinds of relationships between analogies can be discerned. First, there is the close relationship through membership in the same analogy set between the elements of two analogies. In this way, the global analogy between the domains A and B (eating habits and morale), for example, is related to the global analogy between the domains B and C (morale and climate). In the same way, the local analogy between the items A1 and B1 (anorexia and cowardice) is related to the local analogy between the items B1 and C1 (cowardice and Arctic cold).

A second relationship obtains between the local analogies connecting the same domains in different position sets, such as A1 with B1 or A2 with B2. These items are related less closely but in a more interesting way. The analogy between anorexia and cowardice is related to that between healthy eating and courage. So is the analogy between courage and a temperate climate (B2 and C2) to that between foolhardiness and tropical heat (B3 and C3).

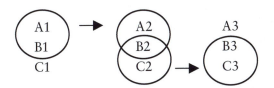

The third type of relationship can be observed to subsist between local analogies connecting different domains in different position sets, for instance anorexia and cowardice (A1 and B1) with healthy eating and a temperate climate (A2 and C2):

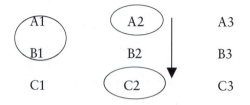

The figurative field is a kind of paradigm underlying the analogies drawn within a text or passage. The above figurative field could, for instance, underlie the following statements:

> Healthy eating is the desirable middle between anorexia and bulimia, as a temperate climate is the desirable middle between Arctic cold and tropical heat.

> Bulimia is foolhardiness in eating.

> Courage is the temperate climate of morale.

The process of reconstructing an underlying figurative field can be treated as a special approach to text interpretation, which helps to reveal the motivation for employing the given analogies as well as the potential affinities arising from these analogies. In some cases, one encounters a text which is determined by one simple figurative field that can be demonstrated to underlie the entire text. We will now turn to such an example as our case study.

2   TEXT ANALYSIS

> Ces cheveux d'or sont les liens, Madame,
> Dont fut premier ma liberté surprise,
> Amour la flamme autour du cœur éprise,
> Ces yeux le trait qui me transperce l'âme.   4
>
> Forts sont les nœuds, âpre et vive la flamme,
> Le coup de main à tirer bien apprise,
> Et toutefois j'aime, j'adore et prise
> Ce qui m'étreint, qui me brûle et entame.   8
>
> Pour briser donc, pour éteindre et guérir
> Ce dur lien, cette ardeur, cette plaie,
> Je ne quiers fer, liqueur, ni médecine: 11

L'heur et plaisir que ce m'est de périr
De telle main ne permet que j'essaie
Glaive tranchant, ni froideur, ni racine. (Du Bellay 1974: 64)   14

Those snary locks are those same nets, my Dear!
Wherewith my liberty, thou didst surprise!
Love was the flame that fired me so near:
The dart transpiercing were those crystal eyes.   4

Strong is the net, and fervent is the flame;
Deep is the wound, my sighs do well report.
Yet I do love, adore, and praise the same
That holds, that burns, that wounds in this sort;   8

And list not seek to break, to quench,
The bond, the flame, the wound that festereth so,
By knife, by liquor, or by salve to deal:
So much I please to perish in my woe.   12

Yet lest long travails be above my strength
Good Delia! Loose, quench, heal me, now at length!   14
                     (transl. Kastner 1908: 271–72)

This love poem, reproduced here in modernised orthography, is taken from the sonnet cycle *L'Olive* by the French Renaissance poet Joachim Du Bellay (1522–60). The cycle was first published in 1549 and republished in 1550 in a substantially expanded edition. It is composed in the Petrarchan tradition. The sonnet, the tenth poem in a series of fifty in the first edition, additionally draws on a work by Ariosto. The relationship of the sonnet to its sources is, however, not the subject of this article. While Du Bellay's text with its masochistic commitment to the throes of love may perhaps nowadays no longer be appreciated greatly as one of the masterpieces of Western poetry, this poem is certainly representative of the historical Mannerist treatment of analogy and metaphor which at times even had a Europe-wide following.

The text consists of fourteen lines of ten syllables each, with a regular caesura after the fourth syllable. The rhyming pattern is abba abba cde cde. The rhymes are female with the exception of rhyme c; the regular alternation of male and female endings, which subsequently became obligatory, is not yet in force. Typographically, the fourteen lines are grouped into two quartets and two tercets, as is conventionally the case in French sonnets. The transition from the quartets to the tercets, marked by a volta or turning point in the content, is also highlighted by a change in the rhyming pattern.

The sonnet describes the narrator's love for a lady named Olive—Du Bellay's counterpart of Petrarch's Laura, and it does so by means of the threefold conventional imagery of (B) bondage, (C) a burning castle and (D) the soul pierced by an arrow. The lover suffers the pain of one subdued in battle, a prisoner of war (B). Appropriate remedies (*remedia amoris*) to ease these sufferings are named. In accordance with the poem's imagery, these remedies are given as (B) a sword cutting the fetters, (C) water quenching the fire and (D) medicine for the wounded soul. The startling twist at the turn from the octave to the sestet, the volta of the sonnet, consists in the narrator's declaration that he will renounce the *remedia amoris*. The second tercet, the obligatory *chute* (closure) of the sonnet, establishes the reason for this renunciation: for the lover, the suffered pain, paradoxically, is at the same time his joy and delight (line 12: "l'heur et plaisir"). In face of the menacing imagery describing the state of the lover's suffering this masochistic punch line is as unexpected as is the renunciation itself.

The text is based on a four-domain figurative field. The thematic domain A is the speaker's love for Olive. The remaining three domains (B to D) furnish images for this love's description: the bondage of a prisoner (B), the burning of a castle (C) and the wounding by an arrow (D).[4] For each of these domains, five positions can be distinguished: (1) a painful state, (2) the means by which this state has been effectuated, (3) its specific effect, (4) the remedy that could end the pain and (5) liberation from the pain. Position 1 in domain A refers to the tortured state of the speaker in his immoderate infatuation with Olive, which is, however, only illustrated in the image domains B to D: in domain B bondage, in C the abode in a burning castle and in D the wounding by an arrow (see Table 1.3 below). The filling of position 2, referring to the cause of the state of suffering, requires some elaboration for domain A. The sonnet names three factors triggering the speaker's love for Olive: the golden hair of the beloved, her eyes and another attribute termed *Amour*. If the figurative field is to remain internally consistent, *Amour* has to be interpreted in such a way that the strict formal equivalence to *Ces cheveux d'or* and *Ces yeux* is justified. This equivalence derives from the line-initial position of *Amour* as the subject of one of three coordinated phrases and is additionally based on the metaphorical equation of *Amour* with a cause of suffering. The beloved's hair is figured as the fetters arresting the prisoner; her eyes are the arrow piercing the victim; and *Amour* is the fire incendiarizing the castle of the heart. This demand for equivalence is not met by the interpretation of *Amour* as 'the speaker's love for Olive,' nor by 'Olive's love for the speaker.' (The latter would imply that the speaker has fallen in love with Olive because she has been in love with him first.) The slot is best filled if one interprets *Amour* as the beauty and grace which emanate from Olive's appearance and nature, and which are a gift of the god Amor. In modern French usage, too, *Amour* can denote that which makes a person or object loveable:[5]

C'est un Amour, se dit d'une personne, d'un enfant très joli, et aussi de quelque objet très joli. (*Petit Littré*, 1959)

While the filling of slot A2 required some explication, B2 to D2 are straight-forward. In domain B, the cause of the speaker's suffering are the ropes binding the prisoner; in C, it is the fire burning down the castle, and in D the arrow inflicting a life-threatening wound.

Continuing to go over the positions, let us now turn to the remaining slots. The effect, or one could say the quality of suffering (position 3), is again not described in A. In B it is "to constrict" (line 8: *étreindre*), in C it is "to burn" (line 8: *brûler*) and in D it is "to wound" (line 8: *entamer*). Positions 4 and 5 operate analogously. In domain A there is no explicit filling of the slot, whereas domains B to D are provided with items for the position set. As regards position 4 (the remedy), the following means of ending the speaker's suffering are named: in B it is the sword cutting the fetters; in C it is water and the cold; in D it is a medical balm. When one uses the remedy, suffering will cease. In domain A, this would compound to the termination of the love relationship, but the text does not name this possibility. In domain B, position 5 is filled by the ripping apart of the fetters, in C by the extinction of the fire and in D by the healing of the wound that has been inflicted by the arrow.

The matrix given in Table 1.3 below constitutes a figurative field. It sorts the items explicitly mentioned in the text as well as those implic-itly present into the four domains and into the five position sets. The cells of the matrix are filled with the expressions used in the text which denote the respective items. If the text does not offer an expression, the cell remains empty. It then indicates an item which is significant but remains unnamed.

Table 1.3   The Imagery Field of Du Bellay's "Ces cheveux d'or"

	1	2	3	4	5
A		cheveux d'or, yeux, amour *golden hair, eyes, charm*			
B	liberté surprise *caught liberty*	liens, nœuds *bonds, knots*	étreindre *constrict*	fer, glaive *iron, sword*	briser *cut*
C	cœur enflammé *enflamed heart*	Flamme *flame*	brûler *burn*	liqueur, froideur *water, cold*	éteindre *put out*
D	âme transpercé *pierced soul*	trait *arrow*	entamer *wound*	médecine, racine *medicine, root*	guérir *heal*

This illustration is, however, incomplete without the identification of the descriptive content whose vacancies are occupied by the items of the four alternative domains. The descriptive content in this case can be outlined as follows

> The speaker has fallen into the painful state [1]. This state has been brought about by the means [2] yielding the effect [3]. It would be possible for the speaker to use the remedy [4] against state [1], effecting his liberation [5]. However, he renounces [5] because he "loves, adores and praises" state [1] in spite of his suffering.

Finally, the three image domains (B to D) are not merely analogous as alternative realizations for the vacancies in a shared descriptive content. They can also be subsumed under an obvious generic term: warfare. The beloved Olive is a victorious foe binding the prisoner in fetters, burning down his castle and slaying him with an arrow. The vanquished antagonist accepts his defeat with relish. He forswears righting himself. Within the world of the imagery (the source domain in the cognitive model), this stance would be absurd. One goes to war in order to win, not in order to enjoy one's defeat. The absurdity of the speaker's resolution is meant to reflect on his love and, generally, on domain A. The speaker's excessive devotion to the beloved appears as a plausible absurdity, so to speak. Du Bellay's depiction of love is a witty play with a paradox. It cultivates the rhetoric virtue of the *genus acutum*.[6]

In the thematic domain A, four out of five positions remain vacant. The topic of painful yet delightful love is elaborated as a "mixed" analogy of three images ("permixtae apertis allegoriae", cf. Lausberg 1990, §897). The presentation of the images juxtaposes expressions from each image domain with expressions from the thematic domain A. Only the means of erotic conquest (position 2) is named both in the thematic domain A and in the respective image domains (B to D). In each case, the analogous expressions stand in corresponding syntactic positions. Each of the three expressions occupying position 2 in domain A is adopted into a different mixed analogy: the beloved's hair into that of bondage, grace into that of burning and the eyes into that of wounding. In the first case, the connection is metonymically motivated by the fact that hair could actually serve to make ropes. The other two allegories rely on familiar metaphors: the grace endowed by Amor scorches the heart of the beholder, just as the beloved's eyes shoot arrows at the lover, which pierce his soul. In domain C, the heart is represented by the burned castle. The term *cœur* (line 3: 'heart'), it may be assumed, is not meant by Du Bellay to be metaphorical but is the literal expression for the anatomical organ of love. It therefore belongs to domain A, as does the term *âme* (line 4: 'soul'). When Du Bellay speaks of the arrow piercing the soul rather than the body, he temporarily shifts from the image domain to the thematic domain (the target domain). The soul is the invisible location of love. It cannot be pierced by arrows.

In this poem, the figurative field is somewhat complex, with its four domains containing five positions each. Nonetheless it is not exceedingly difficult to reconstruct. The author does not mix the domains at random. In the first quartet he highlights the analogous relationship between the thematic domain and each of the three image domains by correlating corresponding items. In each of the three sentences of the first quartet, a subject denoting an item from the thematic domain is assigned a corresponding item from one of the image domains as a predicate noun; hence: A2 = B2, A2 = C2, A2 = D2. In the second quartet and the tercets, Du Bellay closely coordinates corresponding items from the three image domains. The allegories are mixed not merely insofar as each image domain employs vocabulary from the thematic domain, but to the extent that the image domains themselves are mixed.

It is only as an exception that the close co-ordinations contain expressions from the same domain (line 7: *j'aime, j'adore, prise*; 'love, adore, praise'). Generally, items from the same position set but from different domains appear in conjunction, as in "Ce dur lien, cette ardeur, cette plaie" (line 10: 'The bond, the flame, the wound that festereth so'). All co-ordinations of items from the same position set constitute a rapport frame (*Rapportschema*; cf. Curtius 1961: 290–91) because within them the order of items from the three domains remains constant: B—C—D.

> Pour briser [B] donc, pour éteindre [C] et guérir [D]
> Ce dur lien [B], cette ardeur [C], cette plaie [D] [. . .] (lines 9–10)

This triple coordination (*Dreierkoordination*) is a principle of composition in the sonnet. The text contains eight of these triplets of varying syntactic complexity. Of the 140 metric syllables in the sonnet, 120 are involved in a triple co-ordination. Only lines 12 and 13 do not follow this principle. They provide a general pause before the poem closes powerfully with yet one more triple co-ordination. The first triad occupies the first quartet and consists of three analogies presenting a first layout of the figurative field. The second triad occupies lines 5 and 6, the third one line 7 and the fourth one line 8. The fifth triad occupies line 9, the sixth line 10, the seventh line 11 and the eighth line 14. In spite of two lines without co-ordinations, the sestet thus contains as many triple co-ordinations as the longer octave—an example of the structural compression in the sestets which one frequently finds in sonnets. Out of the eight triads, six juxtapose item denominations from the corresponding positions in three different image domains in the order B—C—D.

*   *   *

For the cognitivist George Lakoff (Lakoff & Johnson 1989, 1980) this sonnet would probably exemplify a poetic elaboration of the basic metaphor LOVE IS WAR. For Harald Weinrich (1958) it would be a recurrence to the figurative field of the topos "war of love" (*Liebeskrieg*). Lakoff's basic metaphor and Weinrich's figurative field both refer to a state transcending the structure of an individual text; it describes a common habit of thought, i.e. the propensity observable within languages or language families to proceed selectively rather than arbitrarily when coupling semantic fields with analogies. Weinrich views every figurative use of language as the conjunction of two "zones of meaning". The phrase "The offended paid the offender in his own coin", for example, couples the zone of verbal with that of monetary transactions. The lexicon of a language can be divided into countless such meaning zones. Even greater is the number of conceivable conjunctions between any two of them. According to Weinrich, however, the total number of linguistic uses of imagery can be reduced to a manageable number of recurrent conjunctions of meaning zones, which he has dubbed figurative fields (1976: 284). One of these he calls "verbal coin" (*Wortmünze*). As could be observed in the above example, the verbal coin metaphor couples the meaning zones of language and of finance. Neither Weinrich's concept of the figurative field nor Lakoff's concept of basic metaphor in any way relies on an analogy root. Neither is defined by a descriptive content shared by the combined meaning zones. Analogies belonging to the same figurative field (as defined by Weinrich) therefore need not be related in the manner discussed in this article. Assigning a metaphor to one of Weinrich's figurative fields does not serve to explain an analogy but rather highlights a field of higher probability for an explanation. The actual explanation both of the cognitive motivation of a particular analogy and of the systematic connection between related analogies is provided only by the analogy root: a set of two or more descriptions sharing the same descriptive content. The analogy root, one could argue, is the grammar of imagery, so to speak, and can be reconstructed from a particular text employing it. The form that this reconstruction has taken in the analysis conducted above constitutes a figurative field. This figurative field, however, as opposed to the figurative field as defined by Weinrich, refers to concrete texts and is explicative. In contrast to Lakoff, who views basic metaphor as neurally conditioned, the figurative field, as proposed here, offers an abstractive, and therefore rationally grounded, motivation for the use of imagery.

(Translated from the German by Lars Franßen and Monika Fludernik)

NOTES

1. Transl. J. W. Willis Bund and J. Hain Friswell. Gutenberg Library: http://www.gutenberg.org/files/9105/9105-h/9105-h.htm.
2. Transl. J. W. Willis Bund and J. Hain Friswell.
3. The original reads as follows: *Allegoria, quam inversionem interpretantur, aut aliud verbis, aliud sensu ostendit, aut etiam interim contrarium. Prius fit genus plerumque continuatis tralationibus, ut "O navis, referent in mare*

te novi fluctus: o quid agis? Fortiter occupa portum", *totusque ille Horati locus, quo navem pro re publica, fluctus et tempestates pro bellis civilibus, portum pro pace atque concordia dicit* (Quintilianus 2001: 51).
4. Compare Table 1.3 below for the domains A to D and the positions (1) to (5).
5. Compare the German expression *Du bist ein Schatz* ('you are a treasure').
6. See Lausberg 1990, §540, 3,5.

WORKS CITED

Aristotle (1989) *Poetik*. Ed. and transl. Manfred Fuhrmann. Stuttgart: Reclam.
—— (1960) *The Poetics*. Transl. W. Hamilton Fyfe. London: Heinemann and Cambridge.
Baudelaire, Charles (1982) "Correspondances" [1857]. *Les fleurs du mal*. With a translation by Richard Howard. Brighton: The Harvester Press. 15 (English translation); 193 (French original).
Coenen, Hans Georg (2002) *Analogie und Metapher: Grundlegung einer Theorie der bildlichen Rede*. Berlin: de Gruyter.
—— (2008) *Die vierte Kränkung: Das Maximenwerk La Rochefoucaulds*. Baden-Baden: Deutscher Wissenschafts-Verlag.
Curtius, Ernst Robert (1961) *Europäische Literatur und lateinisches Mittelalter* [1948]. Third Edition. Tübingen: Francke.
Du Bellay, Joachim (1974) *L'Olive*. Ed. E. Caldarini. Geneva: Droz.
Kastner, L. E. (1908) "The Elizabethan Sonneteers and the French Poets". *The Modern Language Review* 3.3: 268–77.
Lakoff, George, and Mark Johnson (1980) *Metaphors We Live By*. Chicago: University of Chicago Press.
—— (1989) *More than Cool Reason: A Field Guide to Poetic Metaphor*. Chicago: University of Chicago Press.
—— (1871) *Reflections: Or Sentences and Moral Maxims*. Transl. J. W. Willis Bund and J. Hain Friswell. London: Simpson, Low, Son and Marston. [Gutenberg Library: http://www.gutenberg.org/files/9105/9105-h/9105-h.htm]
Lausberg, Heinrich (1990) *Handbuch der literarischen Rhetorik: Eine Grundlegung der Literaturwissenschaft*. Third Edition. 2 vols. Stuttgart: Steiner.
Littré, Emile, and Amédée Beaujean (1959) Eds. *Dictionnaire de la langue française*. Paris: Gallimard.
Quintilianus, Marcus Fabius (2001) *The Orator's Education. Vol. III: Books 6–8*. 5 vols. Ed. Donald Russel. Loeb Classical Editions. Cambridge, MA: Harvard University Press.
Weinrich, Harald (1958) "Münze und Wort: Untersuchungen an einem Bildfeld". *Romanica: Festschrift für Gerhard Rohlfs*. Ed. Heinrich Lausberg. Halle: Niemeyer. 508–21. (Extended version in Weinrich 1976: 276–90.)
Weinrich, Harald (1976) *Sprache in Texten*. Stuttgart: Klett.

2 Catachresis—A Metaphor or a Figure in Its Own Right?

Elżbieta Chrzanowska-Kluczewska

> *Humans are the symbol-making, symbol-using, symbol-misusing animal.*
>
> —*Kenneth Burke*

INTRODUCTION

Catachresis has been a figure of dubious status ever since it was described in classical rhetoric as an instance of *semantic abuse*. It has also been a neglected trope, with few works entirely devoted to it alone. Rather, the term *catachresis* has appeared *en passant*, scattered across the vast literature on poetics and rhetoric. And yet, catachresis definitely deserves a more thorough reflection, for it discloses the fuzziness of traditional stylistic taxonomies and, even more conspicuously, showcases the need to consider stylistic figures according to their functional scope within the text. For this reason I reject the unclear traditional taxonomy of figures into *figurae elocutionis* (figures of language, figures of expression) and *figurae sententiae* (figures of thought) (cf. Lausberg 2002: 345–46, §602–4; 417, §755–57); I do so not only in consideration of a frequently disputed borderline between the two but for more serious methodological reasons. Contrary to the so-called rhetorical theory of tropes with its roots in antiquity, I believe that nothing exists in language that would not have existed previously in the mind. Consequently, I assume all figures to be primarily conceptual constructs and indispensable instruments of our cognition, for which verbalization is only a secondary realization. In this I follow the line of thinking best represented by George Lakoff, Mark Johnson and Mark Turner; however, I treat metaphor not as the key pattern of our conceptualizations but as one of several figures that are responsible for what I would like to call the 'figurative and rhetorical bent' of the human mind.

For the purpose of a more objective description of stylistic and rhetorical devices, I find it more useful to subdivide figures in two ways. The **first subdivision** is in accordance with the level of linguistic description. This yields (a) **phonetic,** (b) **morphological,** (c) **syntactic,** (d) **semantic, and** (e) **graphic figures,** and allows also for possible combinations of these classes, especially at the syntactic-semantic interface. In this group I reserve the term *trope* for *semantic figures* alone. Among these, metaphor represents a prototypical figure, whose importance, however, should be neither under-nor overestimated. This family of semantic figures or tropes, which in classical rhetoric consisted of thirteen or fourteen major items (cf. Lausberg 2002: 315, §557), includes metaphor, metonymy and synecdoche (traditionally treated as relatives of metaphor), irony, hyperbole, euphemism, oxymoron and allegory, to mention only the best known and most frequently described members of this set.

The **second subdivision**, which I outlined in some detail in Chrzanowska-Kluczewska (2004b), seems of greater importance to me. In brief, in this group I propose to distinguish stylistic devices, but tropes in particular, according to their *scope*, viz. the range of the text which constitutes their functional domain. **Microtropes**, the semantic figures of traditional poetics and rhetoric, operate within syntagms that cover phrases and, maximally, sentences. **Macrotropes**, in turn, organise sequences of sentences, i.e. fragments of texts or even whole texts (to wit, short lyric poems). They are best illustrated by extended similes and extended metaphors, with roots traceable to Homeric figuration. The third level of description, which I will call **metatropes**, consists of 'large figures' that construe entire discourses at a higher level of organisation, and that act as an external commentary on them. In contrast to micro-and macrotropes, which are always overt (that is explicitly present in the text), metatropes are figures of the second order, tacitly structuring the text and requiring a certain interpretative effort in order to be recognized. In brief, they have to be processed by a sort of inferring mechanism that belongs to what might be called *stylistic competence*. As such, metafigures address a more mature readership.[1] In accordance with its etymology, a metatrope should be understood as a 'self-aware' and 'auto-reflexive' figure capable of 'referring to itself' and possibly to figures subordinate to it. Thus a metatrope, which is part of a rhetorical metacode at our disposal, can refer to the language of which it is part and can transcend and comment upon it from a 'bird's-eye' perspective. However, I will use the term **metatrope** in a broader sense, meaning by it a 'large figure', indeed a **megatrope**,[2] which may, but does not necessarily have to, be exclusively self-referential. Historically speaking, the concept of metatropes originates in Jakobson's 1956 essay introducing the well-known distinction between the metaphoric and metonymic modes, which operates across various semiotic systems, including the fine arts and cinematography. (See below in the section on Catachresis Three.)

For the sake of a more practical explanation of the terms proposed, let us consider the following short poem by Christina Rossetti:

(1) Never on this side of the grave again,
    On this side of the river,
  On this side of the garner of the grain,
    Never—

Ever while time flows on and on and on,   5
    That narrow noiseless river,
Ever while corn bows heavy-headed, wan,
    Ever—

Never despairing, often fainting, rueing,
    But looking back, ah never!   10
Faint yet pursuing, faint yet still pursuing
    Ever. ("A Life's Parallels"; Rossetti 2001: 218)

Not much happens within this poem at the level of microtropes. There are two metaphors: time as "that narrow noiseless river" (line 6), and the anthropomorphization (possibly personification) of "corn" that "bows heavy-headed" and looks "wan" (line 7). At the level of macrofiguration, that is of big figures operating across a larger stretch of the text, we notice the pervading antithetical construction of "never" vs. "ever" in the description of time and human life. This figure of antithesis is supported, additionally, by consistently parallel syntactic constructions; the poem is a nice example of how semantic and structural layers of language work in tandem. The last stanza of the poem is interesting syntactically and phonetically in that its core is a stylistic device called *homoioteleuton*, the grammatical rhyme based on the repetition of participial endings -*ing*. Yet, the stanza lacks a subject, which—when supplied—makes of it a macro-metaphor of human existence always torn between despair and hope. Once we reach the meta- (or mega-) level of figuration, we have to ask ourselves the question: what is this melancholic lyric really about? If the title is suppressed, the interpretation of the metafigure may be harder, but if the title is provided ("A Life's Parallels"), we can see that we are here dealing with an antithetical representation of a peculiar parallelism of human existence: things never repeat themselves, but life continues forever. A meta-metaphor and meta-antithesis are here neatly at work.

An even more interesting instance of how figuration is distributed among different levels of stylistic analysis is Langston Hughes's poem "The Negro Speaks of Rivers" (1921). The poem is written in a straightforward and, apparently, rather literal language, with micro-metaphors occurring only in the refrain-like simile (lines 4, 13) that likens the soul's growth to the depth of rivers (where metaphor is strengthened additionally by means of a simile) and in the anthropomorphic description of a river's "muddy/ bosom" (lines 9–10). It is also strongly narrative-oriented. The macrofigurative patterning consists in the all-pervasive synecdoche, the figure of generalisation, marked by the repetition of the pronouns "I" and "my" at the beginning of successive lines. This special type of synecdochical *pars pro toto* goes by the name of *singular for plural*. "I" and "me" do not refer to one particular individual but have an obvious generic referent in a group of people and should be interpreted as 'we, the black people'. Interestingly, the macro-synecdoche that organises the entire text can be seen as consisting of a chain of micro-synecdoches at the lower functional level. At the meta-level of description, however, the poem will be taken as a large metaphor merging into allegory that summarizes the history of mankind, originating from Africa and gradually spread over other continents. It also points to the fact that major centres of human civilization were always connected with large rivers and closes with an allusion to the fate of Afro-American slavery. The poem demonstrates that human language can be colloquial and rather plain at the low level of stylistic description but rich in tropological connotations at the higher conceptual, supra-textual level of metatropes. It also shows a smooth transition from the micro- to the macro- and ultimately to the meta-level of figuration.

This triple model will be applied below and in the context of our considerations of catachresis in its various guises.

CATACHRESIS ONE

If you open a dictionary on stylistics or rhetoric, you are bound to find two distinct definitions under the entry *catachresis* (derived from the Greek *katáchresis*, translated into Latin as *abusio*). I will refer to them henceforward as Catachresis One and Catachresis Two. Further below, I will argue for the need to introduce a category of Catachresis Three as a—what seems to me—necessary extension of the traditional rhetorical analysis.

Catachresis One is a figure of venerable ancestry, with a genealogy in ancient rhetoric. Quintilian, in his *Institutio oratoria* (after Lausberg 2002: 320–22, §562; see also Preminger 1974: 104), refers to it as a 'necessary misuse', a *translatio cum virtute*. In this capacity it stands for the application of an already existing word to something not yet lexicalized. Cicero (*De oratore* 3, after Lausberg 2002: 203, §562) calls this application of catachresis *inopiae causa*, i.e. 'caused by lack of a proper expression' (lexical gap, in modern terminology). For this reason Catachresis One has sometimes been referred to as *inopian* (such is its official 'nickname' in the Polish school of stylistics, represented by Dobrzyńska 1984).[3] To illustrate it, Quintilian refers to the famous example taken from Virgil's *Aeneid*: "They build a horse", referring to the Trojan horse. Horses have never been built before so the word *build* has acquired a new meaning in this legendary context. Though inopian catachresis abounds in every language, due to its clichéd, highly lexicalized character, it is rarely perceived as a truly poetic device. *The foot of a mountain, the mouth of a river, a bottle neck, the lip of a jug, a shuttle bus, a computer mouse* are all instances of Catachresis One. They all possess a clearly referential (denotational) function in that they have become names for hitherto unnamed entities. In this respect Catachresis One is, undoubtedly, a very useful figure. It saves us the trouble of importing foreign lexemes or phrases to patch up the gappy semantic fields of our mother tongue; it also saves us the effort to coin more ambitious neologisms. As such, Catachresis One has been traditionally praised as a practical device and an instance of the economy displayed by natural language in enlarging its vocabulary (Quintilian; Dobrzyńska 1984).

Though the merits of Catachresis One are quite undisputed, its figurative status has always been rather low-key. Although Quintilian (and Dobrzyńska 1984) treat Catachresis One as a phenomenon of its own, that is a figure distinct from metaphor, the long tradition of poetics and rhetoric has wavered on this point. Even Lausberg (2002: 320, §562), while commenting on Quintilian, refers to it as a "necessary metaphor", though Quintilian clearly clarifies the distinction between catachresis and metaphor. While inopian catachresis refers to the use of an old term for something that does not as yet have its own name, metaphor consists in the application of a new term to something that has a name in its own right. Hence, according to Quintilian, in this respect metaphor should not be equated with Catachresis One. Dobrzyńska points to a second *differentium specificum* between inopian catachresis and 'genuine metaphor'. Catachresis is language-specific, highly idiomatized and often untranslatable. By contrast, metaphor should always be translatable (which does not mean 'always interpretable')[4]: we translate a genuine metaphor 'as it goes' (word by word), and what emerges should also be a metaphor.

The trouble is that the majority of catachrestic expressions, including the rather trivial examples I have enumerated above, possesses a clear metaphorical or metonymical flavour. Hence, stylisticians use terms such as *metaphorical/metonymical/synecdochical catachresis*, thus pointing directly to its figurative source (cf. Lausberg 2002: 320, §562; 330–31, §577, referring to the Greek stylistician Tryphon, as well as to Quintilian and Cicero). Thus, metaphorical catachresis, based on likeness, is visible in expressions such as *shuttle plane* (*shuttle* is, originally, a weaving instrument), *the apple of somebody's eye*, or *to surf the net*. Metonymical catachresis appears in such phrases as *trousers torn at the knee* (adjacency to the knee as part of the body). Ancient rhetoric fails to distinguish between metonymy and synecdoche within catachresis, but we could claim that all catachrestic expressions that contain names of conspicuous (salient) body parts are synecdochic in nature (cf. *the eye of a hurricane, to nose into documents*) for in this way they point to one outstanding property of an individual or an object. Metaphoric, metonymic and synecdochic qualities are often difficult to distinguish, which only corroborates the fact that the borderlines between these related figures are often blurred.

Cognitive poetics is well prepared to neatly accommodate inopian catachresis under the metaphorical or metonymical extension of the central meaning of a lexeme, which ultimately positions this figure within the huge semantic relation of polysemy (cf. Taylor 1995). Assuming that we agree to recognize the metaphorical nature of the larger part of the territory covered by Catachresis One, we have to classify it as a boundary case of conventionalized metaphor; it is tropologically not very exciting and hence often overlooked as a stylistic device: indispensable but not very sophisticated, we could say. The huge amount of literature on poetics and stylistics abounds in descriptions of inopian catachresis, several of which are in themselves metaphorical. Let me quote only the best known attributes of this figure: *genetic, linguistic, habitual, conventional, yellowed ('faded'), frozen, petrified, fossilized* or *stereotyped.*[5]

It has often been claimed that Catachresis One becomes, with time, the case of "zero figuration" or "applied figure" (Cohen 1979), inclining ultimately towards "zero deviation" and "zero tension" (Dobrzyńska 1984). On this extreme interpretation, Catachresis One illustrates a paradoxical situation in which a dead metaphor is at the same time very much alive (cf. Lakoff & Johnson 1980 on conventional metaphors): alive in the sense of being frequently and quite automatically applied, dead in the sense of being almost completely demetaphorized.

Yet, it occasionally happens that inopian catachresis may suddenly become revitalized and its metaphoricity restored and refreshed. It has been observed that not yet fully competent users of a language such as foreigners in the process of Second Language Acquisition or children beginning to master their native tongue unintentionally revert to inopian catachreses, which can be marked by a high degree of inventiveness.

Functionally speaking, inopian catachresis is a small figure, with its semantic scope limited to nominal or verbal phrases, as in *black holes* and *to head the Department.*[6] As such it is of little interest for literary semantics or discourse analysis, whose main concerns are larger stretches of texts or entire discourses. Inopian catachresis is also the most colloquial and the least poetic out of the three subtypes of this figure discussed in the present chapter.

CATACHRESIS TWO

In contrast to Catachresis One, Catachresis Two is a full-blown metaphor which tends to occupy the other end of the metaphorical cline. It is a metaphor marked by the feature of illogicality, often close to absurdity, and generates far-fetched, strained associations. Already George Puttenham in *The Arte of English Poesie* (1589) presented Catachresis Two as a figure of "plain abuse" (cf. Cuddon 1998: 114). In this role Catachresis Two shows a strong clash or incongruity, conflict or discordance between its two constitutive elements, the vehicle and tenor[7] or the source and target domains.[8] Catachrestic metaphor often relies on synaesthetic effects, the use of nonce words, malapropisms, and glaring juxtapositions (violations of selectional restrictions), etc. The most often cited examples in English literature come from celebrated classics such as Shakespeare (a real master of catachrestic constructions in drama) or Milton:

(2a) [. . .] for supple knees / *Feed* arrogance [. . .]

(Troilus and Cressida, III, iii, 48–49)

(2b) [. . .] my face I'll grime with filth,
[. . .] *elf* all my hair in knots [. . .]

(King Lear, II, ii, 180–81)[9]

(3) [T]o take arms against a *sea* of troubles [. . .]

(Hamlet, III, i, 59)

(4) *Blind* mouthes! that scarce themselves know how to hold / A sheep hook, [. . .]

("Lycidas"; Milton 1980: 44, lines 119–20)[10]

For a more modern example see the following line from Stephen Spender's first version of the poem "Seascape":[11]

(5) Afternoon *burns* upon *the wires* of the sea.

Here we encounter two catachreses combined in a chain, forming a double metaphor with a sentential scope.

Two observations emerge at this point. Examples (2) to (4) cited above can all be classified as microfigures (microtropes). The *microcatachrestic* reading refers to semantic dissonance within verb phrases (2a, 2b) or in (2a) even more conspicuously between subject and predicate; in (3), it operates within a single noun phrase, whose head may be thought to be unusual; while in (4), the discordance is built between the adjectival modifier and head noun in the nominal phrase; (4) is also synaesthetic in nature.

The second point that I would like to make is the existence of a continuum between Catachresis Two and 'ordinary' metaphor: it is difficult to find an exact point at which non-catachrestic metaphoric quality ends and Catachresis Two begins. After all, figures and tropes by definition are all constituted by what Cohen (1979) dubs *écart*, that is by a shift, a 'turn' or departure from the literal (precisely what the Greek word *trópos* denotes).[12] All metaphors are unusual combinations of terms, puzzles or enigmas in the Aristotelian terminology (cf. Lausberg 2002: 315, §556). It is barely possible to pinpoint the exact moment at which a metaphor becomes 'abusive' enough to be classified as 'genuine catachresis'. The reader's response has obviously to be taken into consideration, for the ease or difficulty in interpreting metaphors is a highly subjective issue, dependent on a wide variety of factors, such as an individual predilection for strangeness, a general level of literary education, and even on what I choose to call *tropological competence*.[13]

In one of the best studies devoted entirely to Catachresis Two, the article "The Semantics of Bold Metaphor", Harald Weinrich (1963/1971),[14] discusses the poetic currents and schools that made Catachresis Two their artistic motto, treating this device as the pivot of their poetic design. This trend was already strong in the European Baroque literature, including the *conceit* in English metaphysical poetry (cf. next section), and it then reappeared in nineteenth-century French poetry, an exemplary case being Jean-Arthur Rimbaud's poetic works. In 1918 Pierre Reverdy formulated the "metaphoric rule": the more distant (but at the same time more pertinent) the relationship between the two metaphorical terms (tenor and vehicle), the stronger the created image. In his first manifesto of the surrealist movement André Breton adopted Reverdy's rule as a slogan.[15]

Indeed, modernist poetry tends to be heavily catachrestic, thus becoming a *crux interpretum*, the interpreter's cross, a real challenge to the reader, critic and translator alike. It is worth noting that Catachresis Two need not be limited to phrasal or sentential contexts. It can freely permeate a longer textual stretch (often in lyric poetry), thus acquiring the functional status of a *big* figure, a *macrotrope*. Dylan Thomas is an excellent example of a 'catachrestic poet'. Let us note the catachrestic chain of semantic enigmas which are heightened by unusual syntax and their *macrocatachrestic* stanzaic scope in his "Poem in October" (1971). Among the many catachreses of this poem are "the *neighbour* wood", the "mussel *pooled*" and the "*heron priested* shore", "water *praying*", or the "*net webbed* wall". The remaining six stanzas follow the same pattern of catachrestic design (though, for instance, the second stanza is definitely less catachrestic and easier to process). As a result, the entire poem can be seen as a continuous macrocatachrestic structure. The above-mentioned rule for the apparent translatability of Catachresis Two (as a genuine metaphor) is well exemplified by the Polish version of the poem, authored by Jerzy Pietrkiewicz (1997). His translation faithfully recreates the macrocatachrestic chain, in which the interpretative defiance shown by the text is visible in the translator's struggle with the poem, which the reader is invited to share.

As in the case of Catachresis One, one encounters a whole spectrum of defining expressions that characterize Catachresis Two, namely: *tensive, immediate, occasional, one-shot/fleeting* (Lakoff & Turner 1989), *nonbanal, poetic, fanciful* (Cohen), *live, distant* (Bally 1909), and, in extreme cases, *unintelligible, destructive* or *non-tropical metaphor*. In fact, the evaluation of Catachresis Two as an instance of a radical semantico-logical transgression has never been consistent or unanimous. Although Quintilian recognized the existence of Catachresis Two (cf. Lausberg 2002: 316, §558; 321, §562), he never used the name *catachresis* for its designation and never praised its utility; on the contrary, he perceived in it a vice, a *vitium* directed against good taste and the perfection of style. He called it *translatio dura*, that is "hard" or "difficult metaphor". The followers of traditional rhetorical thinking (e.g. Dobrzyńska 1984: 200ff) treat passages containing Catachresis Two as erroneous and nonsensical and as requiring excessive processing and exerting a disruptive effect on the coherence mechanism of the text. By contrast, *The Princeton Encyclopedia* tries to depict Catachresis Two more positively, claiming that "[i]t need not be a ridiculous misapplication as in bad poetry, but may be a deliberate wresting of a term from its normal and proper significance. Sometimes it is deliberately humorous" (Preminger 1974: 104). More critical analyses have also claimed that, *pace* the laudatory opinions of the French symbolists, dadaists and surrealists, catachrestic constructions may not only be unintelligible, but can even prove to be unimaginable.

The issue of image-creation is a vast and interesting topic far exceeding my immediate frame of reference and worthy of in-depth elaboration. Suffice it to say that the requirement of being image-productive need not be seen as a *sine qua non* of metaphors and other tropes. Human cognitive capacity goes well beyond pictorial representation. Although we heavily depend on visual imagery in our cognition, we have other non-visual representational schemas at our disposal. The charge levied against Catachresis Two of being potentially non-visual can thus be easily repudiated.[16]

THE METAPHORICAL CONTINUUM

Our previous considerations, backed up by contemporary research on metaphor (Lakoff & Johnson 1980), led us to postulate a scalar approach to metaphoricity, with Catachresis One marking one end of the continuum (verging on dead metaphor) and Catachresis Two occupying the opposite end of the cline (one-shot, innovative metaphor). In between extends a vast area covered by non-catachrestic metaphors, which among themselves will also display various degrees of conventionalization.

The heterogeneous nature of Catachresis Two, on one side approaching 'normal' metaphor, on the other inclining towards nonsense, shows very conspicuously in the subgenre of English metaphysical poetry.[17] Its most outstanding device, called the *conceit*, is a complex phenomenon, in fact a whole bundle of different figurative devices, whose aim was to surprise and sometimes to shock and delight the reader. The metaphysical conceit frequently reverted to oxymoron, paradox and hyperbole as its main instruments. All in all, the metaphysical conceit played with unusual configurations of linguistic elements and, in Cuddon's words, produced "abstruse" and "recondite" effects (1998: 165–71). Catachresis Two, in its 'metaphysical shape,' had two contrasting aspects. One, positive, showed a high degree of poetic ingenuity combined with exquisite technical skill. It appears, for instance, in John Donne's catachrestic macro-metaphor that structures the poem "A Valediction: Forbidding Mourning", playing on the far-fetched comparison of two lovers (or rather their souls) to the legs of the compasses. This famous catachresis is striking due to a particularly apt juxtaposition of two dissimilar domains. Such a meta-phor, which in traditional poetics is referred to as *reification* (depersoni-fying a human being and treating it like an object), can produce various effects, often depreciatory, but in the case of Donne's poem it has a highly emotional and moving effect.

The other face of the seventeenth-century English conceit is much less attractive. Consider the following excerpt from John Cleveland's "To the State of Love, or, the Senses' Festival":

(6) My sight *took pay*, but (thank my charm)
I now *impale* her in my arms,
(*Love's Compasses*) confining you
Good Angels, to a circle too.
(quoted in Cuddon 1998: 169, my emphasis)

In spite of the fact that the macro-metaphor that organises the entire poem is very similar to the imagery invoked by Donne (the compasses, the cir-cle, the enclosure), the excessive stacking of catachrestic constructions one upon another (coupled with a simplistic aa, bb rhyme) has a deleterious effect on the aesthetic quality of the text. The poem, though interpretable, is a failure, both aesthetically and emotively.

The issue of the relative (un)interpretability of Catachresis Two is closely linked to the problem of whether it is possible to combine "everything with everything" within a catachrestic construction (which, after all, has every right to become a 'semantic scandal').

Two opposing answers have been given to this question. A Polish poet, Tadeusz Peiper, often called the Pope of Polish modernism and considered the founding father of the Cracovian Avant-Garde in the 1920s, once said to Karol Irzykowski, an outstanding literary critic of the time, that any two words can be put together into a unit of meaning. As an illustration he pro-duced a catachrestic expression *typhoidal silence* to prove that the seman-tic system of human language, an open system *par excellence*, is based on *illimitable ways* of joining words together (quoted in Kulawik 1994: 103). A similar opinion was voiced by Robert S. Hartman (1967: 113), who claimed that "[a] metaphor is a set of predicates used as a variable. Hence it can, in principle, replace every other word of the language—and even itself as an ordinary word rather than that of a metaphor, as in 'a peach of a peach'".

Such free combinations of "everything with everything" are very pro-ductive in catachrestic expressions, which then appear to be unbound metaphorical games. Yet the ease of their production raises the question of the linguistic borders of metaphor and, consequently, of the boundary region between sense and nonsense. For illustration, let us consider below a specimen of the Victorian 'nonsense poetry', "Cold Are the Crabs" by Edward Lear:[18]

(7) Cold are the crabs that crawl on yonder hills
    Colder the cucumbers that grow beneath,
    And colder still the brazen chops that wreathe
    The tedious gloom of philosophic pills!
    For when the tardy gloom of nectar fills
    The simple bowls of demons and of men,
    There lurks the feeble mouse, the homely hen,
    And there the porcupine with all her quills.
    Yet much remains—to weave a solemn strain
    That lingering sadly—slowly dies away,
    Daily departing with departing day.
    A pea-green gamut on a distant plain
    When wily walrusses in congresses meet—
    Such such is life—

The poem is catachrestic at both the micro- and macro-level and the Catachreses Two that abound in it are definitely bizarre. Despite its limited interpretability, we can detect a distant intertextual allusion working between Lear's poem and Lewis Carroll's (1871/1981) "The Walrus and the Carpenter" and "A boat, beneath a sunny sky", the poem closing *Through the Looking Glass*.

At the end of the metaphorical scale the excessive freedom of linguistic juxtapositions has been reflected in experimental poetry or *écriture automatique*, where words are put together at random. Such haphazard combinations may result in catachrestic metaphors, but very often this *licentia poetica* is not regulated by any exigencies of semantic compositionality but, for instance, by considerations of its phonetic character.

Such extreme play with linguistic material can also be found in Raymond Roussel's prose, which fascinates readers by its auto-referential, mostly nonsensical nature and its experiments with syntactic figuration. Michel Foucault (1963), in fact, perceived in Roussel's writings a eulogy on the catachrestic potential of natural language. I will return to Foucault's preoccupation with catachresis below.

The second answer to the question about the combinatorial possibilities within catachresis has been quite different. Stylisticians working within the poststructural but non-cognitive paradigm for metaphor, based mostly on the tensive theory of Ivor A. Richards and Max Black, have always posited the existence of limits to catachrestic metaphor: catachresis should be unusual but not utterly nonsensical. Some limitations have been postulated regarding the distance between tenor and vehicle, which ought to share certain common semantic elements (features, sememes, etc.). In their opinion (such has also been the standpoint of the Polish school of poststructural stylistics; see also Nowottny 1962: 242), a metaphor has three functions: (1) cognitive (=epistemic), (2) emotive and (3) ornamental. If the first function is missing, the expression must not be treated as a metaphor at all.

In turn, within the cognitive school, Lakoff and Turner (1989) and Lakoff (1990a, 1990b) set certain restrictions on mappings between metaphoric domains. According to Lakoff, the target domain ought to preserve its inherent structure in the process of mapping. The so-called *Invariance Principle* moreover imposes a condition on the maintenance of the image-schematic structure of the source domain.[19]

All these requirements appear too stringent, however. Catachresis Two, an exceptional case of metaphor, does not quite conform to them since its concept-generating function, especially in the case of near-to-nonsense or totally absurd formations, may be suppressed.

CATACHRESIS THREE

It is to Jakobson (1956) that we owe the idea that figuration can extend far beyond a phrase, a sentence, a sequence of sentences or even a short text, though such a proposal has distant roots in the *tropi sermonis* of ancient rhetoric. A 'large figure' of traditional and structural stylistics and criticism, in Jakobson's understanding of this term, becomes a device for the construal of entire discourses and especially of narrative (contrary to micro- and macrofiguration typically associated with poetry). Jakobson designated only metaphor and metonymy as apt candidates for this level of semiotic description, and his ideas were later practically implemented by David Lodge (1977) in his study of modernist prose. Both of them succeeded in demonstrating that large figures constitute an autonomous level of description in that, for instance, a metonymically constructed novel does not need to make use of metonymy at the micro- or even macro-level and may utilize metaphor instead. Thus, metafigures are not only covert but also largely dissociated from overt figuration.

Quite independently, Kenneth Burke in his Appendix to *A Grammar of Motives* (1962), which is titled "Four Master Tropes", discussed a progression from metaphor through metonymy and synecdoche to irony. This idea of four main figures reaches back to the neo-classical Renaissance rhetoricians active in the sixteenth century (Ramus and others). However, in referring to these figures as "styles of thinking", which can co-occur or dominate in certain genres (types of discourses), Burke is an obvious precursor of the cognitive approach to metaphor. Hayden White (1973, 1978, 2000) in his influential account of historiographic discourse based himself on Giambattista Vico's tropology and Kenneth Burke's writings. Not surprisingly, he selected the same *master tropes* as candidates for the meta-level he proposes: *Metaphor, Metonymy, Synecdoche* and *Irony*. Late structuralists (Barthes) and some poststructuralist critical theorists (Paul de Man, Geoffrey Hartman, James Hillis Miller) then drew attention to the fact that other rhetorical and stylistic devices may also be at work on this tacit plane of discourse analysis. Drawing all these scattered postulates together, I was able to compile a list of fourteen possible metatropes. These large textual models are handy in describing narration and in particular fictional prose (Chrzanowska-Kluczewska 2004b). To White's initial tetrad I added *antithesis, inversion, chiasmus, catachresis, paronomasia, euphemism, suppression, exaggeration, anomaly* and *allegory*.

What I would like to call Catachresis Three has found its place in this inventory as a generalised large figure of semantic abuse or misuse, a mother to all figures that depend on strongly marked DEVIATION. Elaborating the idea of White (1973/1987: 37) that catachresis, the figure of the absurd and aporia, works at the metatextual level, I regard it as a superordinate term for all figures based on various kinds of logical deviance such as: *paradox, oxymoron, hysteron-proteron* and *prolepsis* (the latter two creating a disturbance of temporal sequence), *metalepsis* (confusion of cause or circumstances for a particular effect), unjustified *hyperbole*, etc. In this guise Catachresis Three is basically a metafigure of broadly conceived ABUSE, inclusive of many figures that are illogical or paradoxical in nature. Importantly, Catachresis Three may, but does not need to be, metaphorical in nature.[20]

The real father of the conception of Catachresis Three in contemporary philosophical and rhetorical thinking is, however, Foucault (1963, 1966). His ideas articulated various postmodern and deconstructionist currents. Katie Wales refers to Foucault as the main propagator of the *pancatachrestic* nature of figurative language: "Indeed, he would go so far as to maintain that all language is catachrestic: literal meanings are not inherent in the signifier-signified relationship but have simply come to be conventionalized" (1989: 57).[21] And though Wales points to Foucault's major study *The Order of Things* (1966/2009) as the place where the theory of catachresis takes shape, it is already present in his earlier work devoted to Raymond Roussel's experiments with language.

In his summary overview of the great patterns underlying modern European rationalization and its various discourses as expounded in *The Order of Things*, Foucault claims that this project started with a slightly naïve search for the meanings of similitude (*ressemblance*) in the Renaissance. Such an analysis actually corresponds to a regular meta-metaphorical thinking (in my own terms). Seventeenth-century rationalism already had to cope with all kinds of errors, illusions, madnesses and logically ungrounded patterns of thinking. We can observe that these features mark the beginning of *catachrestic discourse*, which has been evolving ever since, to find a fuller expression in pre- and post-Second World War philosophical thought and literary experiments. Foucault invokes catachresis as a figure whose defining properties are *incongruity, juxtaposition of incompatible entities,* and *distortion of categorization*; in a word, catachresis is defined by what Foucault calls *atopia* (or *heterotopia*): a displacement that provokes the most remote things to approach one another, "a worse kind of disorder than that of the *incongruous*, the linking together of things that are inappropriate" (Foucault 1966/2009: xix, xx).

In *Archéologie du savoir* (1969), Foucault's earlier highly emotional and heavily figurative way of talking about great figures of human thought and language gives way to the concepts of *discontinuity, cleavage, split* or *break* as they affect human discourses and mark thresholds and boundaries of discourse formations. Nowhere in this essay does Foucault apply the term *catachresis*. Yet despite this, one can assume that the concept of a cleavage in discourse (marked by areas of incongruity, clashes of ideas, etc.) reveals the essence of catachresis to be that of a *fundamental incoherence*. It is in the light of these considerations that we can also conceive of Catachresis Three as a figure whose tropological range is basically that of a space of conflict.

Unlike Catachresis One and Catachresis Two, which will most often be related, respectively, to colloquial language or to linguistic innovations in poetry, Catachresis Three seems to be a structure-forming strategy for the narrative, whose distinguishing features are all transgressive on the lines identified by Foucault. No wonder, then, that Catachresis Three has been associated with certain experiments in twentieth-century modernist, but especially postmodernist, prose. Whether we talk about the *nouveau roman*, about experimental, autoreflexive and autothematic literature or about metafictional prose, all of these types of discourses arguably feature catachrestic qualities. Among these can be enumerated inconclusiveness, the dispersion or even the utter disintegration of sense, and the lack of definite reference and interpretation. Moreover, one can list sharp contrasts and the unexpected combination of themes: constellations that bring together extreme elements and lead to *aporias*, rifts in the textual structure, sudden shifts in narrative time (confusing flash-forwards or flashbacks), the superposition or overlap of various spaces, and many more. All these features share in catachrestic transgression or excess. It is on the basis of such characteristics of postmodern discourses that Jean-François Lyotard has christened them "decomposed", incoherent and disrupted narratives, in a word the *récit perdu* ('lost narrative', cf. Lyotard 1979: 31, 68). It is figured as the demise of master narrations,[22] in which the "narrative function [. . .] is dispersed into clouds of linguistic elements—narrative ones, but also denotative, prescriptive, descriptive, etc." (Lyotard 1979: 8, my translation; cf. also p. 105). And yet, notwithstanding Lyotard's pessimistic claims about *le récit perdu* as an unstructured discourse, we should recognize an obvious catachrestic backbone in postmodern narration. Postmodern narrative is not "lost" but constitutively metacatachrestic.

CONCLUSION: FUNCTIONS AND STATUS OF CATACHRESIS

Theories of metaphor usually mention three pivotal functions of this figure: (a) **cognitive** (epistemic, explanatory, exploratory), (b) **ludic** and (c) **expressive**. This division is an old idea, originating in classical rhetoric, best summarized in Cicero's description of the three *officia oratoris*, that is the three functions of rhetorical discourse achieved through figuration:

(1) *docere*—to teach, (2) *delectare*—to please and (3) *movere*—to move.[23] Looking back at our previous discussion, we can conclude that all three elements are present, in all the three kinds of catachresis, but to a varying degree. Since catachresis itself is a scalar phenomenon, having its point of departure in its contiguity to conventional metaphor and ending in sheer nonsense, we have to take into account with which kind of catachresis we are dealing. Contextual considerations and the reaction of interpreters can provide us with invaluable hints in this matter.

The epistemic value of metaphor has been emphasized not only in the ample literature of the cognitive analysis of metaphor, where one of the basic claims is that we use metaphor to understand the world (Lakoff, Johnson, Turner),[24] but also in philosophical writings. Susan Haack, in what can be called a pragmatic approach to figuration, stresses the exploratory role of metaphors, especially in the formulation of new scientific theories, calling them "the training wheels of inquiry" (Haack 1994: 15).

The motivation behind the use of Catachresis One is obviously **epistemic**: we describe a new phenomenon through reference to those elements of reality that are well-known to us and already have their name. This is especially visible in contemporary catachrestic formations like *space walk* or *mouse pad*. Catachresis One is a very useful designating device. In turn, Catachresis Two is even more prominently exploratory, since—by unusual juxtapositions of disparate elements of reality—it points to similarities present in the world which we may not have realized existed. The exploratory function is no less prominent in the basically non-metaphorical metafigure called Catachresis Three. In the understanding of several literary critics (Nycz 2000: 14; McHale 2005: 456–59; cf. also Cuddon 1998: 557), the overpowering features of inconsistency and strangeness that pervade postmodern narrative and its figurations reflect the keynote of poststructuralism: a pessimistic feeling that human knowledge is conditioned and determined by the reality which is radically 'inhuman', thus escaping human logic and cognition. This strange world, full of unsolved mysteries (and often referred to by such metaphors as the Other, *différance*, monstrosity, the Sublime, the unpresentable, etc.), can no longer be comprehended through well-known categories but only negatively, through "special analytic strategies".[25] In the preceding sections I have tried to show that Catachresis Three is a primary device allowing us to try to grasp the nature of the uncanny. It is in this capacity that catachresis holds a peculiar cognitive value—it helps us, albeit in a shocking manner, to deal with what escapes easy comprehension.

In what concerns the second, pleasure-producing or **ludic** function of metaphor, Catachresis Two displays a strong ludic character, especially in its more extravagant instances when linguistic experiments compensate for the loss of epistemic value. In such cases (cf. Lear's poem quoted as example (7) above), Catachresis Two becomes playfulness *par excellence*, offering a very special game of the author and the text with the reader. More often than not catachresis is *play* rather than *game* proper, since it refuses to adhere to any particular rules.[26]

The gamesome aspect of Catachresis Three in its text-structuring capacity is no less interesting. The need for what Viktor Shklovsky dubbed *ostranenie*,[27] that is "deformation by art", usually translated as *defamiliarization*, has been a leitmotif of modernism and, even more conspicuously, of postmodernism.

Barthes (1973) proposes that a text produces its own gamesome space. Barthes contrasts the *texte de plaisir* with the *texte de jouissance* (25), that is the text that gives us mere pleasure with the text that offers us delight and brings elation. He refers to the latter as the *texte paradisiaque*: it is impossible, full of ruptures and clashing contradictions (14–17). Barthes provides a very good reason to explain our craving for the "blissful texts" of pleasure and delight. It is to combat *ennui*, lurking boredom: "Le Nouveau, c'est la jouissance" (66). Novelty disrupts boredom and brings us joy. In his entry in the *Philosophical Dictionary* devoted to *boredom*, Robert Nisbet (1982: 22–28) describes boredom as the acute *malaise* of Western civilization: "[T]he pains and the results of boredom are everywhere to be seen, and nowhere more epidemically that in Western society at the present time". Even more emphatically, Harold Bloom (1975: 93) claims that tropes are linguistic mechanisms that work similarly to psychological mechanisms of defense. The tropes can thus be seen as a defense against "death". By "death" in this context he means a non-figurative, literal meaning. The reader will not fail to notice an analogy between literalness and boredom.

It should by now be obvious that both Catachresis Two and Three are instruments that help us in the construal of such blissful and delectable structures. A catachrestic text, though frequently failing to be meaningful or lacking images, can still please us. In its extreme version it can even be what Barthes (1973: 65) describes as "*hors-critique*".

A good summary of this postmodern drive to draw pleasure from the infinite layers of the ludic potential of human language comes from Jean Baudrillard's article with the tell-tale title "The Ecstasy of Communication":

> There is in effect a state of fascination and vertigo linked to this obscene delirium of communication. A singular form of pleasure perhaps, but aleatory and dizzying. [. . .] the whole tendency of our contemporary "culture" would lead us from a relative disappearance of forms of expression and competition [. . .] to the advantages of forms of risk and vertigo. (1990: 132)[28]

I hope to have shown that in Catachresis Two and Three the cognitive and the ludic functions are often closely combined. Both ways of figuration can open to us totally unexpected ways of conceptualization and imagery. Or else, if this type of figuration is strange enough and no immediate image schemas, meanings, connotations or pictorial imagery accompany it, it is

University of Ulster LIBRARY

still able to perform the function of *delectare*. Both types of catachrestic thinking, metaphorical and non-metaphorical alike, offer new trails for our cognitive wrestling with the world, during which we will at times have to move by leaps and bounds. I am alluding here to Seana Coulson's (2001) interesting suggestion to enrich the idea of conceptual blending with the notion of the *semantic leap*—a sudden shift in the creation and interpretation of new mental spaces. Catachresis Two is a good instance of such an unusual juxtaposition, leading to 'jumps' in the conceptual operations concerned with the production and reception of 'bold' linguistic expressions. Catachresis Three requires a similar processing strategy at the metatextual level. Catachresis Two and Three also give us an opportunity to revel in the 'symbol-misusing' capacity of human language.

Let us turn to the third power of metaphor, the power to express the emotions of the author and to affect the reader. Catachresis One loses with time its ability to 'move' the recipient but Catachresis Two fares much better in this respect. Nowottny (1962) stresses the emotive aspect of metaphor, which can sometimes override its conceptual import. And indeed, several catachreses through their incongruity play upon our emotions more than on our "cool reason" (cf. Lakoff & Turner 1989). Black (1962: 227) also stresses the dynamic side of the reader's response to non-banal metaphors (though he never uses the term *catachresis* explicitly). In his interactive (tensive) model of metaphor, Catachresis Two would count not only as the most tensive but also as the most emotionally-loaded and the most stimulating.

Whether Catachresis Three can exert a similar effect upon the reader has not yet been analysed in any detail and still remains a matter for future investigation.

The time has come to summarize briefly our considerations on the status of Catachresis and to venture an answer to the question contained in the title of this chapter. Catachresis One seems to have largely lost its metaphorical/metonymical/synecdochical status, though—diachronically speaking—it originated as a metaphor in the vast majority of cases. If so, it can be perceived as a figure functioning on its own but placed very close to dead, stereotyped metaphor. The fact that only a very thin line (if at all) separates clichéd metaphors from catachreses is reflected in the fact that such figures are described differently in various stylistic dictionaries that do not agree on their assumed metaphoricity. As to these figures' scope of operation, they function only at a micro-level of description, hence as 'small' figures.

Catachresis Two has to be classified as full-blown metaphor, running from very inventive and interpretable to nonsensical, barely interpretable or non-interpretable examples. Goodrich (2008: 47) succinctly grasps this aspect: "It is for this reason that Renaissance rhetorical handbooks term catachresis the most free and powerful of the tropes [...] Catachresis is in this sense the exemplary source of linguistic novelty because it is the most extreme form of metaphor [...]". Catachresis Two usually operates at the micro-level of description (single 'small' metaphor) but very often combines into chains that develop into a macro-figure, spanning larger portions of the text (as in the Dylan Thomas and Lear poems mentioned above).

Finally, Catachresis Three is a figure in its own right, a very general meta-figure of DEVIANCE and ABUSE, basically non-metaphorical in nature. As a text-forming (or rather, text-disrupting) strategy, it appears to work only at the metatextual level of description.

It must be striking to discover that the uniform term *catachresis* covers three quite distinct cases of figuration.[29] Despite all the differences, however, there exists a common denominator underlying the three phenomena: this is the element of novelty and strangeness perceived in the world and then coded in language. Thus the triadic figure of Catachresis makes a triple appeal to fundamental cognitive needs shared by human beings: of acquiring knowledge, experiencing pleasure and sharing in emotions. It shares this capacity with other tropes and figures but performs its duty in its own, peculiar way.

NOTES

1. It is in this sense that H. White (1973/1987) referred to irony as a sophisticated metafigure. See also B. McHale's short discussion of 'double-coding' in postmodern fiction (2005: 457).
2. *Megatrope* might, actually, be a better term but since my proposal to refer to a large textual figure as *metatrope* has already caught on, especially in Polish stylistics, I will abide by it. I should also clarify that P. Werth's (1994) 'extended metaphors'/'megametaphors', qua discursive phenomena, will belong to my metatropical level.
3. Interestingly, J. A. Cuddon (1998) and K. Wales (1989) ignore this facet of catachresis entirely.
4. This controversial claim made by T. Dobrzyńska touches on the much discussed issue of *translatability*. Different theories of translation, running from the extreme of treating every translator as a traitor (*traduttore traditore*), through theories of dynamic, culturally oriented equivalence of translated texts, end in another extreme: the belief that everything in human language is ultimately translatable. Translatability and interpretability are overlapping, not isomorphic phenomena. This leaves a margin for a translation which is not fully interpretable and which covers such difficult cases as Catachresis Two.
5. Compare also the French terms: *la métaphore endormie, oubliée, méconnue.*
6. Small figures, by my definition (cf. Introduction), have their scope limited to a single sentence. Catachresis One is genuinely small, since it resides in noun and verb phrases only. Non-catachrestic micro-metaphors can be nominal, verbal, but also—very typically—sentential, as in T. S. Eliot's April, which is metaphorically defined as "the cruellest month", or W. Wordsworth's "A slumber did my spirit seal" (a combination of a nominal and verbal metaphor with a sentential scope).
7. This is the terminology of the interactive theory (Richards 1936; Black 1962; Nowottny 1962; also Semino 1997).
8. This, in turn, is the terminology of the cognitive approach (Lakoff & Johnson 1980; Lakoff & Turner 1989).
9. See Wales (1989: 57, original emphasis).

10. Examples (4) and (5) are quoted in A. Preminger (1974: 104, original emphasis).
11. Quoted in W. Nowottny (1971: 229, original emphasis).
12. We should be cautious about falling into the trap of *pancatachresis*, smelling a semantic or logical abuse everywhere in language (a tendency ascribed to M. Foucault by Wales 1989), as we should eschew a related temptation of *panmetaphoricity* to the neglect of other conceptual schemas of cognition.
13. In 1843 F. Fénelon wrote that difficult and bold metaphors should be left to more temperamental nations. This squares with the nineteenth-century inclination (best exemplified by W. von Humboldt's writings) to search for signs of the national spirit, which shows also through a particular language (including its figurative devices).
14. In no place in his article does Weinrich use the term *catachresis*, preferring to call *kühne Metapher* what in the classical French tradition (Fénelon, Voltaire) was described as *la métaphore dure, hardie, agissante*.
15. "Plus les rapports des deux réalités rapprochées seront lointains et justes, plus l'image sera forte—plus elle aura de puissance emotive et de réalité poétique . . ." (Breton 1924/1929: 38): 'The more distant and precise the two different domains of the image are, the stronger that image is going to come across, the more emotive force and poetic impact it is going to have' (transl. Fludernik).
16. Although Lakoff and Turner (1989), while discussing one-shot, fleeting poetic metaphors, maintain that they rely on the mapping of images rather than conceptual schemas, we can perceive catachrestic metaphor as exempt from a strict dependence on visual imagery.
17. I am indebted to M. Fludernik for calling my attention to the metaphysical *conceit* as pertinent to the theme of Catachresis Two (and Catachresis Three at the meta-level of textual organisation).
18. The poem has been accessed at http://ingeb.org/songs/coldaret.html.
19. The issue of the at least partial preservation of the structure of source and target domains during the metaphorical transfer is one of the most interesting aspects of the cognitive approach to metaphor. A discussion of this question unfortunately exceeds the limits of the present chapter.
20. What is particularly striking in White's treatment of Catachresis Three is that he subsumes it under a very broadly understood mode of IRONY, an opinion I do not share (cf. also White 2000: 105).
21. It seems that Wales speaks here of Catachresis One as a pervasive feature of natural language (I am indebted to M. Fludernik for calling my attention to this interpretation). Foucault himself uses the term *catachresis* only in a few places in his writings, referring to Catachresis One and Two. Yet, the recurring theme of his entire ouevre is Catachresis at the metadiscursive level. White (1978/1985: 281) points to the fact that catachresis is also Jacques Derrida's favoured trope. The scope of this chapter does not allow me to develop this train of thought, however.
22. Also in a broader sense of discourse formations à la Foucault.
23. The discussion on this subject is contained in Cicero's *De oratore*. A good commentary on this triple role of rhetoric can be found in Burke's *A Rhetoric of Motives* (1962: 597 ff.).
24. The extreme version of the theory of 'embodied mind' sees our language as a huge metaphoric projection from body-related concepts, which for the human beings are the best understood reality. This opinion is only partly shared by the author of this chapter, who does not believe in the *panmetaphoricity* of natural language and defends the value of the other figures in cognition and language (cf. Introduction and fn. 12).

25. Such is the opinion of Nycz (2000) in one of the major studies devoted to poststructuralism in Polish literary criticism. McHale (2005: 457–59) also stresses this 'ontological dominant' in postmodern poetics.
26. See Chrzanowska-Kluczewska (2004a), where I discuss this issue in greater detail. Actually, the language-games theory is a promising model in this respect, capable of encompassing (under the label of *deviant games*) the methodological considerations on the border zone of metaphoricity, to which Catachresis Two in its extreme version obviously belongs.
27. The term introduced in 1917 in his book *Art as Device* (cf. Shukman 1977: 6, 40–42).
28. Both Baudrillard (1990) and F. Jameson (1990) refer also to some "schizophrenic" features of postmodern discourse. This is no longer a ludic function of language but the conceptualization and language of the psychotic.
29. The reasons why such disparate cases of figuration, of which only Catachresis Two is a full-fledged metaphor, have been given the same name is partly explained by Goodrich (2008: 47), who suggests that catachresis stands for "the extension [. . .] to a novel or improper meaning."

WORKS CITED

Bally, Charles (1909) *Traité de stylistique française*. Heidelberg: C. Winter.
Barthes, Roland (1973) *Le plaisir du texte*. Paris: Éditions du Seuil.
Baudrillard, Jean (1990) "The Ecstasy of Communication". *Postmodern Culture*. Ed. H. Foster. Tenth Edition. London, Concord, MA: Pluto Press. 126–34.
Black, Max (1962) *Models and Metaphors: Studies in Language and Philosophy*. Ithaca: Cornell University Press.
Bloom, Harold (1975) *A Map of Misreading: Studies in Language and Philosophy*. New York: Oxford University Press.
Breton, André (1929) *Manifeste du surrealism* [1924]. Paris: Éditions Kra.
Burke, Kenneth (1962) *A Grammar of Motives* and *A Rhetoric of Motives*. Cleveland and New York: The World Publishing Company (Meridian Books).
Carroll, Lewis (1981) *Alice's Adventures in Wonderland & Through the Looking-Glass* [1865, 1871]. New York: Bantam Books.
Chrzanowska-Kluczewska, Elżbieta (2004a) *Language-Games: Pro and Against*. Kraków: Universitas.
———. (2004b) "Microtropes, Macrotropes, Metatropes". *AAA—Arbeiten aus Anglistik und Amerikanistik* 29: 65–80.
Cohen, Jean (1979) "Théorie de la figure". *Sémantique de la poésie*. Eds. Tzvetan Todorov et al. Paris: Seuil. 84–127.
Coulson, Seana (2001) *Semantic Leaps: Frame-Shifting and Conceptual Blending in Meaning Construction*. Cambridge: Cambridge University Press.
Cuddon, J. A. (1998) *The Penguin Dictionary of Literary Terms and Literary Theory*. Revised C. E. Preston. Fourth Edition. London: Penguin Books.
Dobrzyńska, Teresa (1984) *Metafora*. Wrocław: Zakład Narodowy im. Ossolińskich & Wydawnictwo PAN.
Fénelon, François (1843) *Oeuvres*, Vol. 3 (Nouvelle édition). Paris: Charpentier.
Foucault, Michel (1963) *Raymond Roussel*. Paris: Gallimard.
———. (1969) *Archéologie du savoir*. Paris: Gallimard.
———. (2009) *The Order of Things: An Archaeology of Human Sciences* [1966]. London and New York: Routledge.
Goodrich, Peter (2008) "Catachresis". *Routledge Encyclopedia of Narrative Theory* [2005]. Eds. D. Herman, M. Jahn and M.-L. Ryan. London and New York: Routledge. 47.

Haack, Susan (1994) "Dry Truth and Real Knowledge: Epistemologies of Metaphor and Metaphors of Epistemology". *Aspects of Metaphor*. Ed. J. Hintikka. Dordrecht, Boston, London: Kluwer. 1–22.

Hartman, Robert S. (1967) *The Structure of Value: Foundations of Scientific Axiology*. Carbondale and Edwardsville: Southern Illinois University Press.

Hughes, Langston (1994) "The Negro Speaks of Rivers" [1921]. *The Collected Poems of Langston Hughes*. Eds. A. Rampersad and D. Roessel. New York: Vintage Books. 23.

Jakobson, Roman (1956) "Two Aspects of Language and Two Types of Aphasic Disturbances". *Fundamentals of Language* (*Janua Linguarum 1*). Eds. R. Jakobson and M. Halle. 'S-Gravenhage: Mouton & Co. 53–82.

Jameson, Fredric (1990) "Postmodernism and Consumer Society". *Postmodern Culture*. Ed. H. Foster. London, Concord, MA: Pluto Press. 111–25.

Kulawik, Adam (1994) *Poetyka: Wstęp do teorii dzieła literackiego*. Kraków: Antykwa.

Lakoff, George (1990a) "The Contemporary Theory of Metaphor". *Metaphor and Thought*. Ed. A. Ortony. Second Edition. Cambridge: Cambridge University Press. 201–51.

———. (1990b) "The Invariance Hypothesis: Is Abstract Reason Based on Image-Schemas?" *Cognitive Linguistics* 1.1: 39–74.

Lakoff, George, and Mark Johnson (1980) *Metaphors We Live By*. Chicago: Chicago University Press.

Lakoff, George, and Mark Turner (1989) *More than Cool Reason: A Field Guide to Poetic Metaphor*. Chicago and London: Chicago University Press.

Lausberg, Heinrich (1960) *Handbuch der literarischen Rhetorik: Eine Grundlegung der Literaturwissenschaft*. München: M. Hueber (Polish version: [2002] *Retoryka literacka. Podstawy wiedzy o literaturze*. Bydgoszcz: Wydawnictwo Homini).

Lear, Edward (2008) "Cold Are the Crabs". http://ingeb.org/songs/coldaret.html (accessed November 30, 2008).

Lodge, David (1977) *The Modes of Modern Writing. Metaphor, Metonymy, and the Typology of Modern Literature*. London: Edward Arnold.

Lyotard, Jean-François (1979) *La condition postmoderne*. Paris: Minuit.

McHale, Brian (2005) "Postmodern Narrative". *Routledge Encyclopedia of Narrative Theory*. Eds. D. Herman, M. Jahn and M-L. Ryan. London and New York: Routledge. 456–60.

Milton, John (1980) "Lycidas" [1637]. *The Complete Poems*. Ed. Bernard A. Wright. London: Dent. 44.

Nisbet, Robert (1982) "Boredom". *Prejudices: A Philosophical Dictionary*. Cambridge, MA, London: Harvard University Press. 22–28.

Nowottny, Winifred (1962) *The Language Poets Use*. London and New York: Oxford University Press (Polish translation of the chapter "Metaphor": (1971) *Pamiętnik Literacki* LXII, z. 4: 221–42).

Nycz, Ryszard (2000) *Tekstowy świat: Poststrukturalizm a wiedza o literaturze*. Kraków: Universitas.

Pietrkiewicz, Jerzy (1997) *Antologia liryki angielskiej 1300–1950*. Warszawa: Pax. 320–25.

Preminger, Alex (1974) Ed. *Princeton Encyclopedia of Poetry and Poetics*. Enlarged Edition. Princeton: Princeton University Press.

Richards, Ivor A. (1936) *The Philosophy of Rhetoric*. Oxford: Oxford University Press.

Rossetti, Christina (2001) "A Life's Parallels". *Selected Poems of Christina Rossetti*. Introduction and notes by K. McGowran. Ware, Hertfordshire: Wordsworth Editions. 218.

Semino, Elena (1997) *Language and World Creation in Poems and Other Texts.* London and New York: Longman.

Shakespeare, William (1982) *Hamlet.* Ed. Harold Jenkins. Arden Edition. London: Methuen.

———. (1997) *King Lear.* Ed. Reginald A. Foakes. Arden Edition. Walton-on-Thames: Nelson.

———. (1998) *Troilus and Cressida.* Ed. David Bevington. Arden Edition. Walton-on-Thames: Nelson.

Shukman, Ann (1977) *Literature and Semiotics: A Study of the Writings of Yu. M. Lotman.* Amsterdam, New York, Oxford: North-Holland Publishing Company.

Taylor, John R. (1995) *Linguistic Categorization: Prototypes in Linguistic Theory.* Second Edition. Oxford: Oxford University Press.

Thomas, Dylan (1971) "Poem in October". *Collected Poems, 1934–1952.* New York: New Directions. 113.

Wales, Katie (1989) *A Dictionary of Stylistics.* London, New York: Longman.

Weinrich, Harald (1963) "Semantik der kühnen Metapher". *Deutsche Vierteljahrsschrift für Literaturwissenschaft und Geistesgeschichte* 3: 325–44 (Polish translation: [1971] "Semantyka śmiałej metafory". *Pamiętnik Literacki* LXII, z. 4: 243–64).

Werth, Paul (1994) "Extended Metaphor—A Text-World Account". *Language and Literature* 3(2): 79–103.

White, Hayden (1978) *Tropics of Discourse: Essays in Cultural Criticism.* Baltimore: Johns Hopkins University Press.

———. (1987). *Metahistory: The Historical Imagination in Nineteenth-Century Europe* [1973]. Sixth Edition. Baltimore and London: Johns Hopkins University Press.

———. (2000) *Figural Realism: Studies in the Mimesis Effect.* Baltimore and London: Johns Hopkins University Press.

3 Literary Metaphor between Cognition and Narration

The Sandman Revisited

Benjamin Biebuyck and Gunther Martens[*]

INTRODUCTION

The introduction of a cognitive perspective to the study of literary metaphors is certainly one of the most striking revolutions in the history of literary studies. Even a superficial comparison of Paul Ricoeur's detailed and well-documented monograph *La métaphore vive* (1975), which is now considered the hallmark of traditional metaphor research, and Lakoff and Johnson's cognitive manifesto (*Metaphors We Live By*, 1980) will clearly reveal the deep chasm between the quarrelling *anciens* and *modernes*. Whereas Ricoeur's elaborate stock-taking covers all major theoretical approaches, from Aristotle to the contemporary philosophy of language, the pioneers of the cognitive turn seem to have found little inspiration in the rhetorical tradition and, as if *ex nihilo*, developed their own apparatus in the spirit of a generative model of language and cognition.[1] Lakoff and Johnson's conviction that metaphor was much more than a device for producing aesthetic pleasure opened up the perspective that placed metaphor research at the heart of contemporary attempts to understand human cognition in general, yet at the same time leaving many of those scholars who analysed metaphor as a distinguishing feature of artistic communication disgruntled. First and foremost, the cognitive paradigm explained literary metaphor as a special case, an extension of concepts and models inherent in language as such—the obvious example of this approach being Lakoff and Turner's *More than Cool Reason: A Field Guide to Poetic Metaphor* (1989). The next step was the development of an empirical-cognitive paradigm, which released literary metaphor from the insider ethos current in traditional literary circles. Inspired by reader-response-criticism and developments in linguistic pragmatism and (literary) sociology, these empirical proponents turned to actual readers and asked them what they thought or felt when confronted with poetic figurativeness (cf. Steen 1994). Both tendencies—the cognitive and the empirical—have expanded their own line of reasoning and established themselves as versatile models and catalysts for further developments.

Neither of these approaches, however, have convinced literary scholars that they have actually solved the problems related to the role of metaphor in literary texts. Today cognitive researchers admit that even in relatively simple ordinary speech (in real utterances, instead of prefabricated text dummies) we "need to face squarely the far greater complexity of integrations that lie behind observable metaphorical systems" (Fauconnier & Turner 2008: 65), a far greater complexity, that is, than current mapping and blending theories have so far assumed to exist. Such an acknowledgment may be regarded as an ominous indication of the degree of complexity that might emerge when analysing literary communication, in which, as Steen (1994: 231) suggests, a certain degree of ambiguity or lack of clarity serves to attract increased reader attention.[2] More importantly, Fauconnier and Turner acknowledge that in the case of recognizable metaphorical conceptual systems we have to "take into account their cultural history" as well as "the emergent structures they produce" (Fauconnier & Turner 2008: 65); this desideratum is undoubtedly even more relevant with respect to literary metaphors that explicitly appeal to cultural traditions (e.g. through intertextual allusions). Literary metaphors also facilitate creative ad-hoc-emergence and call for "polyvalent processing" (Steen 1994: 207).

In what follows, we will try to discuss some of the major problems of the cognitive approach to literary metaphor (Section 1). We will do so not in order to reject or discard the cognitive approach, but to complement it with an alternative model that preserves the benefits of the cognitive revolution, without ignoring the singularity of literary communication. We propose the idea that the interconnectedness of complex figurative networks is fundamentally narrative in nature (Section 2). Only by viewing the interplay of metaphors in literary texts as an additional dimension of narrativity, can literary scholars valorise cognitive findings without feeling alienated from what they conceive as the core of literary interaction.[3] To clarify our point, in Section 3 we will take a closer look at a novella that is often considered to contain a repertory of the most diverse forms of figurativeness: E. T. A. Hoffmann's 'night piece' (*Nachtstück*) *Der Sandmann* (1816; *The Sandman*). The novella tells the story of a sensitive student, Nathanael, who (without realizing it) falls in love with an automaton called Olimpia. One day, he witnesses a rude quarrel between Spalanzani, the professor who has manufactured Olimpia, and his supplier of optical instruments, Coppola, who tries to disassemble Olimpia. Since Coppola reminds Nathanael of the man he holds responsible for his father's violent death (Coppelius), the scene causes a first outburst of insanity in Nathanael, from which he recovers with the help of his loyal fiancée Clara. When the evil antagonist Coppola/Coppelius appears for the third time, Nathanael descends into ultimate madness. He mistakes Clara for Olimpia and attempts to murder her. In the end, he commits suicide by jumping from a tower. In the wake of Freud's interpretation of the novella in *Das Unheimliche* (1919), it became the object of wide-ranging critical interest.

1   A CRITICISM OF COGNITIVE METAPHOR THEORY

Already in one of the earliest critical essays discussing the plausibility of the cognitive model presented in Lakoff and Turner's "field guide", Jackendoff and Aaron ask the most relevant question *überhaupt* in this debate: on what do Lakoff and Turner base their argument that there is no fundamental distinction between 'conventional' and 'poetic' or 'literary' metaphors (Jackendoff & Aaron 1991: 320)? Many critics agree with Jackendoff and Aaron that the concept of metaphoricity used by Lakoff and his co-authors is fuzzy and indeterminate. This is not only problematic for the analysis of metaphor, but also on a cognitive level, since the indeterminacy of their concept of metaphoricity forces them to adopt a "correspondingly narrow view of the cognitive basis for concept formation" (Jackendoff & Aaron 1991: 331).[4] Lakoff et al.'s integrative notion of metaphor is further fostered by what McGlone has called their idiosyncratic combination of 'hyperliteralness' and 'hyperfigurativeness' (see Eder 2007: 186–87). On the one hand, these authors display an over-inclination to classify all forms of semantic mobility as metaphorical.[5] On the other hand, they deploy a sparsely motivated literal notion of the cognitive processing of sensorimotor impulses (automatic and immediate understanding) and of their transference onto abstract concepts (Jackendoff & Aaron 1991: 332). By contrast, Jackendoff and Aaron claim there is a difference between 'conventional' and 'literary' metaphors, and it is not a matter of degree or appearance. Literary metaphors are characterized by their "overt incongruence" (325) because they operate by means of a "split reference" (334)—a referential anomaly which in traditional metaphor research goes under the name of "stereoscopic vision".[6] Jackendoff and Aaron's point of criticism echoes Glucksberg and McGlone's findings that there is "no support for the hypothesis that people automatically retrieve specific source-target domain mappings in order to understand a novel metaphor" (quoted in Eder 2007: 176–77). This means *either* that 'literary' metaphors are not processed cognitively in the same manner as conventional metaphorical concepts *or* that generally Lakoff's description of metaphorical information structuring does not hold water.[7] The latter conclusion obviously raises questions that go well beyond the scope of our contribution. We will therefore here concentrate on the first conjecture.

Lakoff's cognitive model has indeed convincingly shown that metaphor is a matter of conceptual information and not of semantic meaning as such—one has to understand the meaning of an utterance in order to perceive its metaphoricity. But there are no (empirical) indications that conjoining two incongruous concepts in a literary metaphor instigates a process of mapping or blending or that the incongruity that lies at the heart of the metaphor is in any way annulled. On the contrary: there are two major arguments supporting the contention that the initial tension between the two concepts irrevocably remains in force throughout the metaphorical processing and that no mapping occurs at all. This would explain, firstly, why metaphors can be re-enacted; they do not lose their metaphoricity because we have encountered them before; nor do they lose their effectiveness, when they are repeated; in fact, this may even enhance their rhetorical force. Secondly, our assumption accounts for the fact that the direction in which conceptual information is processed does not go from the source domain to the target domain alone, but also in the opposite direction.[8] It is correct that this insight generated the replacement of original mapping processes (Lakoff & Johnson 1980) by blending theory (e.g. in Fauconnier 1998; Fauconnier & Turner 2002, 2008). Yet the supposed coalescence of concepts in blending theory, as Jackendoff and Aaron already noticed (1991: 334–35), turns out to be incompatible with the irresolvable tension that lies at the basis of metaphor perception. This tension can be traced back to the express acknowledgment of the originary negation inherent in the metaphorical process, illustrated by Jackendoff and Aaron's "Of course, X is not Y. But if it were"-test (1991: 328–30; cf. Punter 2007: 42). Hence, it is plausible to conclude that literary metaphor operates through the juxtaposition of conceptual information—a process in which chunks of conceptual information that can be neither reduced to one another nor integrated into one another—rather than by mapping or blending, cognitive operations implying conceptual integration or assimilation ("completion" and "elaboration", Fauconnier & Turner 2002: 43–44). The fact that literary metaphors themselves negate the identification of the juxtaposed concepts explains why these concepts remain unaffected through the metaphorical process. Even if mapping and blending of conceptual frames play a crucial role in all kinds of cognitive procedures, we can conclude that they are not part of the processing of literary metaphor and hence cannot apply as reading principles guiding metaphor interpretation.[9]

The reason why 'overt incongruity' is more fundamental to literary metaphor than the cognitive processes of mapping or blending is that metaphor mobilises two complex sets of knowledge simultaneously (cf. Kittay 1987: 15). The ad-hoc-manner in which this occurs is clearly in conflict with the Platonic strand of the cognitive view that only conceptual pairs are foregrounded that were already (conceptually) pre-existent. In his empirical approach, Steen shows that literary metaphors entail both "tenor" and "vehicle construction" (1994: 103, 41). The point is, however, that the information that needs to be mobilized for both processes of construction is not in the first place retrieved from our habitually available information about the world. Obviously, Jackendoff and Aaron are right when they state that any (conventional) notion of literalness is both linguistically and culturally determined and amenable to historical change (327). But how does this interact with the impact of "poetic composition" (333), which they also deem significant for literary metaphor? One therefore needs to discriminate metaphorical incongruity from other forms of innovative or experimental language use. It is crucial to recognize that metaphorical incongruity is established vis-à-vis an *intratextually* validated (and possibly varying) norm, whereas other experimental uses of language tend to transgress an *extratextual* norm of expectation. Literary metaphor thus relies on the incongruity between two distinct (i.e. irreducible) segments of knowledge *of the text*. As we will see when discussing *The Sandman*, only textual indices can show whether calling spectacles "eyes" is a metaphor or rather an instance of derangement or surreal vision. As a corollary, reading a literary metaphor may effect the activation of corresponding or complementary knowledge of the world, but this is secondary, insofar as it is not counteracted by the information provided by the text, or it is simply irrelevant.[10] This is consistent with Steen's observation that literary discourse, as a communicative form which focuses reader attention on itself, drastically enhances reader sensibility for literary metaphor (1994: 153, 243).

The idea that the incongruity characteristic of literary metaphor is generated in the first place on the basis of intratextual information matches with other empirically validated findings. Literary scholars generally agree that context is very important for metaphor comprehension (e.g. Punter 2007: 144), but the dynamics of relevant information retrieval indicate that it is indispensable for the perception of literary metaphor. Literary text types or genres not only facilitate metaphor reading, they also foster the intensity with which readers are willing to interpret literary metaphors. Obviously, this requires some degree of literary socialization (and of linguistic competence). Literary socialization enables readers not only to valorise the hermeneutic potential of literary discourse as it is, but also to devote specific attention to unconventional or innovative speech acts (Steen 1994: 47, 56–57; Jackendoff & Aaron 1991: 332–33). Thus, a double form of competence comes into play. On the one hand, *literary competence* stems from the audience's prior history of reading, in some cases reinforced by training, which mobilises reading strategies optimising the responsiveness to figural speech; on the other hand, the reading of a literary text itself generates a *textual competence*. This textual competence is in principle independent of the reader's background and can explain the facility with which non-native or non-contemporary readers, who do not (necessarily) dispose of the reservoir of pre-existing conceptual information that cognitive researchers posit to exist,[11] recognize the incidence of metaphor.

The question of what a literary metaphor means thus still remains unanswered. In his attempt to adjust Lakoff and Turner's approach, Pinker advocates the idea that metaphors do not particularly activate properties linked to concepts, but rather relationships between concepts (2007: 254, 264).[12] We agree that literary metaphor foregrounds the relational 'nesting' of concepts. But because of the way in which contextual information is retrieved, this 'nesting' also entails a reinforcement of the embeddedness of the metaphor in the context in which it is operative. Literary metaphor does not actually *mean* this network of relations; following Davidson (1979),[13] we prefer to say that it does not mean anything at all, because its meaning is entirely *potential*. In spite of this absence of meaning (or rather, because of it), metaphor initiates an interpretive activity which is not confined to the actual locus of figurativeness (or the standard conceptual information at hand), but implicates large chunks of context. As Steen shows, the appearance of other figures of speech in the context, both in sheer number and in the measure of their extendedness, increases the rhetorical weight of a literary metaphor (1999: 509–18). Because of its connectedness with literal and non-literal parts of the context alike, a literary metaphor disrupts the primary chronology at work in the literary text and transforms the reader—much more explicitly so than is usually believed—into a collaborator in the communicative transaction. This may partially explain why metaphors occur with such density in literary texts that are based on a poetics of reader activation and why they enable literary texts to functionalise what Pinker has called a "rhetorical payoff" (2007: 265): a feeling of accomplishment and reward that is experienced when readers can themselves contribute to the success of the communicative exchange. What the reader makes of the metaphor is not its resolution, however—on the contrary, the interpretation is as much ad hoc as is the incidence of metaphors themselves. The interpretation of metaphors remains open for revocation, adaptation and negotiation.

2   METAPHOR AND NARRATIVE

The cognitive approach alone is not enough to explain how metaphors operate in literary discourse. Let us now have a look at an example. In a recent German novel the nose of one of the characters is described as follows: "Sommersprossen umtanzten Meyers knollige Nase" (Kluger 2008: 17, 'Freckles danced around Meyer's bulbous nose'; our translation). We might argue that the author puts to work the concepts BODY FEATURES ARE PERSONS, FRECKLES ARE CHEERFULNESS, A CHEERFUL PERSON IS A DANCING PERSON, A PERSON'S FACE IS A SURFACE and A NOSE IS A TREE, but this would be a considerable diagnostic detour that offers little surplus explanation of the metaphor "umtanzten" ('danced around') itself. We believe that much more can be expected from an approach that takes the intrinsic relational disposition of literary metaphor not as an entrance to a static structure of complex blending, as Fauconnier and Turner assume ("a notion that emerges from the full network", 2008: 55), but as a key to unlock the narrative potential of the metaphor.

Both in literary criticism and in cognitive studies valuable impulses have been provided that explore the narrativity of literary metaphors. The traditional approach focuses on the manner in which a metaphor either is unfolded in the literary text or induces unfolding on behalf of the (interpreting) reader. In her recent monograph on poetological metaphors, Kathrin Kohl stresses the potential of verbal and nominal metaphors to expand into 'full scenarios' (2007: 47). But when looked at more closely, this view turns out to rely on what might be called a *genetic* epistemology: metaphors are supposed to carry in them the germs of a vast number of narrative extensions that are actualised within the text or implicitly transmitted to the reader to be actualised. Such scenarios undoubtedly exist and take the form of miniature embedded stories with internal agency and temporality (see the "micronarratives" discussed in Biebuyck & Martens 2009: 123). But the narrative potential of metaphor is not confined to this rather specific type of figurative imagination. Due to its genetic character the 'unfolding hypothesis' goes against some obvious counter-evidence. The most prominent objection concerns the 'genetic thesis' premise that narratively unfolding metaphors occupy a stable key position in the rhetorical repertoire of a text. This is clearly not the case. The salience with which figures of speech appear often fluctuates in the course of the narrative, and in some texts the characters explicitly argue about which figure of speech is the most appropriate in that specific narrative situation. This does not imply that there is no hierarchy within the rhetorical network. On the contrary, there usually exists a *master trope* that organises the entire figurative structure, but only does so at a specific time and place within the narrative (cf. Biebuyck & Martens 2009: 125). In most literary texts, the figurative complex is not dominated by one single master trope, but rather displays a kind of *rhetorical negotiation* between different tropes claiming, with varying success, the central position.[14] Hence, this crystallization point cannot form the stable start of a process of progressive unfolding, since the dynamics of negotiation makes it amenable to constant revaluation.

The second counter-indication to the genetic thesis is the fact that different tropes occurring in a literary text do not always support the figurative cohesion of the unfolding of the metaphors. They often imply a change of course in the unfolding or even its utter negation. One might object that in literary texts different concurrent processes can come about in which separate metaphors are unfolded apart from one another, but this argument altogether downplays the credibility of a more or less encompassing unfolding.

The third consideration is related to the observation that under the influence of changing contextual circumstances a figurative re-orientation of tropes may take place. What at first seemed to be a metaphor (e.g. "eyes" for spectacles) may well turn out to be a metonymy (spectacles as an aid for eyesight) or synecdoche ("eyes" as part of autonomously acting creatures) later on, only to regain some of its metaphorical quality in the end. This is again an instance of ongoing rhetorical negotiation in the figurative network that excludes the notion that a trope carries in it the germ of its unfolding. The figurative transformations at stake here do not mean that the first textual manifestation (in our example: the metaphorical one) was incorrect and needed replacement by a later and more correct one. All manifestations (metaphor, metonymy and synecdoche) are equally valid, if only measured in terms of the place and time in which they occur. This also holds for tropes that become rhetorically ambivalent in the course of the literary text.

The second way to approach the narrative potential of metaphor finds its origins in the cognitive paradigm itself. It claims that, from the cognitive repertoire readers have at their disposal, metaphors may retrieve conceptual scripts or scenarios, consisting of a source, a path and a goal (cf. Lakoff 1987: 285). Such scripts can be defined as the articulation of fairly general action frames, comprising all-round inferential patterns such as causality, sequentiality and temporality. There is not much doubt that such retrieval frequently takes place while reading literary metaphors. But it can only induce very general and simple chains of actions, which require ample additional specificity and orientation to become really productive at a narrative level. To obtain this type of specificity and orientation, the reader will once again fall back on the range of metaphors occurring in the literary text and the dispersed chunks of information they rely on. The emergence of the narrative dimension of the figurative network is thus compatible with the development of the (primary) narrative itself.

As we have already indicated, readers of literary texts are recorded as displaying an increased sensibility for figurative processes. This sparks off an interesting dynamic of recursiveness, which might be labelled a 'tropological circle' (Biebuyck 1998: 242–47; cf. Pimentel 1990: 34–67). Reading a powerful literary metaphor opens the door to reinterpreting non-figurative utterances in the literary text that refer to identical or related semantic fields, thereby allocating to them a surplus metaphorical dimension. In this manner, literary metaphors recuperate parts of the text that were reproduced as plain narrative sequences. A second consideration concerns the rhetorical interplay between different figures of speech which is the result of the de-automatization of text processing.[15] In some cases, this interplay is a matter of figurative syncretism; synecdoche and personification, for instance, often go hand in hand. In other cases, different figures of speech engage in negotiation or competition in order to obtain the stature of master trope (cf. Biebuyck 2009). This dynamic processual notion of network not only complicates the narrative situation; it reinforces what Iser has coined "the wandering viewpoint" (1976: 193–94)—the active engagement of the reader in processing the narrative.

Hence, it might be much more rewarding to approach the network of metaphors and other figures of speech in a literary text as an *additional layer of narrativity*, instead of tracing the unfolding of a guiding metaphor or merely falling back on already available cognitive scripts. This additional layer, which we have named *paranarrative* (Biebuyck & Martens 2009: 120), obviously requires the reading of the primary narrative of the text (which, for clarity's sake, might be called *epinarrative*), because it relates to the same story world and the same characters, but it expands its actional, temporal, spatial and aspectual scopes in ways that are not necessarily congruent or equivalent to those in the epinarrative. Hence, the paranarrative is neither instrumental nor superior to the epinarrative. It allows the reader to gain access to alternative segments of the storyworld and opens up a complementary spectrum of perspectives. In doing so, it displays new narrative agency: just like the epinarrative, the paranarrative relies on the ongoing reordering of (textual) information about the storyworld. The narrative setting within which this process occurs reinforces what has been termed a "rhetorical" (Fowler) or "point-driven reading" (Vipond and Hunt; for both see Steen 1994: 84). It encourages the reader to interpret the relations within the figurative network in a narrative sense (instead of a logical sense for example). We can see a similar narrative impulse at work when reading disparate textual phenomena such as landscape depictions in literary works: here, too, descriptive matter can be transformed into non-linear and non-continual, yet progressively developing narrative potential.

Such an additional layer of narrativity is not effectuated generically. In texts with a poor or monolithic metaphorical repertoire, or with extreme figurative heterogeneity, it may prove problematic to build up any narrative potential at all. But insofar as it is possible to build up such potential, any concept of a consistent narrator is thereby undermined. To claim that the paranarrative represents 'subconscious' aspects of a narrator would push the anthropomorphic chimera of a narrator-persona *ad absurdum*. Given that the paranarrative is stimulated by the figurative network in a literary text, but generated by the interpreting reader, in other words that it requires intensified reader activity and reader participation, it seems plausible not to attribute the figurative narrative to any narrator-gestalt, but to circumscribe it as an auto-poetic and self-organising practice with a strong feedback infrastructure. Evidently for this process to take place, reader sensibility and responsibility are of the utmost importance.

In our view, the most vulnerable spot in empirical metaphor research appears here. Empirical cognitive scholars tend to focus on readers' immediate and solitary responses to reading metaphors (cf. Steen 1994: 53, 107). Thus, they neglect the fundamentally reflexive and cooperative nature of metaphor comprehension. This weakening of the narrator's authority caused by literary metaphor and its narrative networking does not lead to the absolute hegemony of the individual (and solipsistic) interpreting reader. It brings the readers themselves into a position in which they dialogically exchange approaches to understanding literary metaphor. Thus, they are urged to continually revisit their own interpretive impulses. The exchange shows that metaphor comprehension is not the result of a solitary undertaking, but rather of a series of acts of interpretation and concurrent negotiations between different readers. As Steen argues (1994: 100), time is the "crucial factor in this discussion": within "leisurely metaphor processing" (101), the elaboration of the narrative potential of the trope will be much more probable than in a "time-limited" approach. Acknowledging the importance of negotiation and exchange may ultimately open the door to a more differentiated approach towards metaphor and figures of speech in general. Not only will it be possible to discriminate diachronically between divergent forms of incongruity and between different ways in which figurative networks emerge, but also between historically determined practices of metaphorical negotiation. But let us first cast a glance at a famous example of metaphor and narrative: *Der Sandmann*.

3   CIRCULATION OF ENERGY—AN ANALYSIS OF *THE SANDMAN*[16]

At the heart of the novella lies the fundamental uncertainty about what is real or imagination. Is the protagonist, Nathanael, reliable or mad? Are Coppelius and Coppola identical or not? And how do they relate to Spalanzani, who, very much like them, is characterized by his small, piercing eyes (E 96) and his "ghostly appearance" (E 110)?—a question to which only scant attention has been paid so far. In particular, the role of Clara remains unresolved. Although she is repeatedly represented as Nathanael's considerate guardian angel (E 116), she also induces (*entzünden* [G 31], 'inflame') some of his outbursts: she belittles his image of Coppelius as a "phantom of his own inner self" (E 23) and invites him to throw his "mad fairy tale", which clearly has a stabilizing effect on Nathanael's mental balance, "into the fire" (E 103). She lures her only just recovered fiancé to the tower ("let's climb up there one last time", E 117) and ignites his murderous and suicidal rage, during which he mistakes her for Olimpia.

At some places in the text, the characters are clearly different, but at others their differences dissolve. This uncanny situation is obviously linked to Nathanael's paranoid perception, but as the narrative renders a voice that is extremely conscious of its own narrative position and has protagonists who are presented expressly as both writers and readers, it seems odd that the narrator would simply imitate the protagonist's viewpoint. This is where the text's repertoire of metaphors comes in.

One of the densest instances of metaphoric phrasing occurs when the strange Italian optician Coppola visits Nathanael to sell him some of his merchandise. Nathanael has just moved into a new room, after his old home was burned down (E 104). From the window of this new room he can see Olimpia as a "stiff and motionless" person, to whom he is initially completely indifferent. The narrator describes—from the perspective of Nathanael—how Coppola "contort[s] his wide mouth into a hideous grin" and how his eyes start sparkling in a piercing, protractive manner ("giving a piercing look from under his long grey lashes", E 105). He addresses the perplexed student in poor, but recognizable German: "No barometer, no barometer! I'ave beautiful eyes-a to sell you, beautiful eyes-a" (E 105). Nathanael is deluded by his perception of the optician's small eyes ("die kleinen Augen", G 35) and misunderstands Coppola's figure of speech. The expression wavers between a metaphor (spectacles are eyes), a metonymy (spectacles are extensions of the eyes) and a simple, albeit fantastic reference to the facts. While attributing linguistic incompetence to his interlocutor, Nathanael himself proves to be rhetorically short-sighted: "these are my eyes-a", Coppola persists, resuming the original phrasing in a plain identity metaphor (E 105). This speech act serves as a catalyst for a broader, intensified figurative setting: "Thousands of eyes were looking and blinking convulsively and staring up at Nathanael; but he could not look away from the table, and Coppola put more and more spectacles on it, and their flaming eyes sprang to and fro ever more wildly, darting their blood-red rays into Nathanael's breast" (105, translation modified). Clearly, the surrealistic description of the scene can be traced back to the childhood trauma Nathanael already tried to give expression to in his mystical poems ("like bloody sparks"). But it remains peculiar that the glasses do not reinforce Nathanael's eye-sight; they imitate and mirror his looks and, in doing so, appear metaphorically as autonomous, living creatures ("flickered and winked and goggled", E 105). The protagonist loses his grip on the narrated situation entirely: as the glasses replicate his gaze, they gain control over his behaviour. Turned into a passive victim, he witnesses the increasing vehemence of his *Gegenüber* and finally has to undergo their "blood-red" beams (E 105) aimed at his chest. Thus, the relation between subject and object is reversed completely. At the same time, the borderline between the real and the surreal dissolves. The narrator describes the situation without indicating whether his description is influenced by Nathanael's delusional perception or not—a narrative technique typical of Hoffmann's literary practice (see Segebrecht 1996: 129). The narrative thus blurs the (literal) frame of reference necessary for figurative communication. As such, the scene gradually evolves into a sylleptic scenario, juxtaposing the literal (i.e. real/surreal) and the figurative (i.e. metaphorical/metonymical) as two competing reading styles amenable to rhetorical negotiation. That this negotiation takes place at the level of the characters becomes already clear in Nathanael's first letter to his friend, Clara's brother Lothar (which he sent, inadvertently, to Clara herself), in which he contrasts his mother's rational explanation for the sandman with the old childminder's gruesome version. The locus of negotiation is further confirmed by Clara's rebuttal of Nathanael's Coppelius-tale (E 21). There is even a third moment of metaphorical negotiation, when Nathanael's fellow student Siegmund tries to talk his friend out of his amorous phantasm. Siegmund immediately realizes that his questions do not undermine, but reinforce the delusion. In order to circumvent a conflict with Nathanael, he discursively withdraws into the haven of what we might call *virtual proto-metaphor*: "as though her every movement were produced by some mechanism like clockwork" (E 111). Siegmund avoids calling Olimpia a machine (in a literal sense) by grounding the association with cogwheels in a metaphorical connection he is about to execute (OLIMPIA IS A MACHINE, in a figurative sense)—or at least: he pretends to do so.

The rhetorical outline of scenes such as the ones discussed above demonstrates that since the metaphorical reading is negotiable, it presents itself as a feasible alternative within the discursive logic of the story.

The encounter with Coppola is the turning point in the novella. Nathanael starts feeling irresistibly attracted to Olimpia. Indirectly, this leads to the double catastrophe at the end of the text: first the laceration (or disassembling) of Olimpia by Spalanzani and Coppola, then Nathanael's attempted murder of Clara and his eventual suicide. Yet, the scene is not the re-enactment of Nathanael's traumatic encounter with Coppelius as a child, since Coppola—Coppelius's double—does not want to steal the protagonist's eyes, but rather offers supplementary 'eyes' for sale. The initial configuration of characters is reversed (comparable to the subject/object-switch mentioned earlier), which is difficult to explain when we read the story as an account of a delusional projection. However, the reversal aligns well with the way in which the tropes in the text interact, with what we have termed the paranarrative. In drawing up an inventory of all figures of speech, we can easily see that most of them signal a primordial relation of *reciprocity* (instead of projection), which lies at the basis of an extensive dynamics of *exchange* or *transfer*. The optical instruments, which serve as a leitmotif in the novella, turn out to be conduits in the paranarrative, instead of projective devices.

Numerous figures support this claim. In the opening lines Nathanael writes about Clara as "my sweet angel, whose image is so deeply engraved upon my heart and mind" (E 85), and describes a horrible experience that has "entered [his] life" (E 85; "ist in mein Leben getreten", G 11). In many cases, the transfer concerns warmth and heat, occasionally light, but light is also often configured as a transportation of warmth. Clara responds to the message in Nathanael's letter as follows: "the idea [. . .] pierced my heart like a red-hot dagger" (E 93). The metaphors indicate that the protagonists in the novella do not interact with each other as autonomous agents, but function as temporary spatial containers in a large scale circulation of energy. As a consequence they become interchangeable instances (instead of polar opposites), who involuntarily hand on vitality to one another; on the one hand, they associate this experience with influx and efflux, on the other with gaining and losing control. It is no coincidence that already in the beginning Nathanael indicates that his story is about to "burst from my lips like mad laughter" (our translation, see E 85) and that his fascination for Olimpia concurs with the observation that "a narrow strip of the glass door was left unconcealed by the curtain which is normally drawn across it" (E 96). Accommodating transfer is metaphorically referred to as a current (e.g. "he felt an indescribable sense of bliss permeating ["durchströmte", 'streaming through'] his being with mild, heavenly warmth", E 116 and G 47), whereas both the narrator and the characters use metaphorical allusions to indicate that circulation can also be hampered, obstructed or enhanced, particularly by optical instruments. In the sense that the figures of speech betray that there is an energetic transfer between the characters, the latter lose part of their individuality. On hearing Olimpia's "shrill voice, like a glass bell" (E 108) at the ball, Nathanael feels "as though red-hot arms had suddenly seized him" (E 108), as he does not attribute the heated mood he experiences to his own excitement, but to a force outside himself. Conspicuously, the current flows equally in the opposite direction, as his touch fills Olimpia with his vitality. Immediately, Nathanael has to discern that her sense of measure and rhythm surpasses his capacities brilliantly—that she has become practically more human than he is.

After Spalanzani's deceit has been exposed, society begins to be suspicious of civilized behaviour and elegance: at tea parties the honourable ladies and gentlemen expressly sing out of tune and yawn, to prove that they are not machines. This might explain why Nathanael scolds Clara, who is knitting while listening to his mystical poetry, calling her an "accursed, lifeless automaton" (E 103), and why he eventually mistakes Clara for Olimpia, acting himself as an automatic puppet without consciousness or will. The current of energy between the characters may also clarify why there is such a strong resemblance between Coppelius, Coppola and Spalanzani, and why precisely Nathanael is ultimately provoked into imitating their destructiveness. It may even make understandable why Clara reveals in her letter to Nathanael that, despite her "cold temperament" (E 94; "kalte Gemüt", G 22), her response when reading his letter was anticipatively identical to his reaction to Coppola.

More importantly, the metaphorical notion of circulating energy may be a clue to understanding the instability of affective interactions in the novella. In contrast to what the reading of the text as the description of a delusion may suggest, romantic love is not merely a private experience of a solipsistic devotee: it flows quickly back and forth between communicating vessels. By means of the metaphorical denomination "love star" ("Liebesstern", G 37, 40), Nathanael twice indicates that Olimpia is the original source of his affection. He responds to the energy he receives from her by pouring out an incessant flow of poetry which he addresses to her (E 112). This poetological fancy, in which story-telling itself (just as much as letter writing) becomes part of the ambient circulation of energy, is typical of Hoffmann's self-reflexive prose. Literature itself describes a process of exteriorization and influx, in which nothing has a definite place or becomes one's definitive possession. Clara's and Nathanael's reciprocal declaration of love, in the style of the ancient love rhymes—"Now you're mine again!" and "My own—my own Clara!" (E 116)—therefore remains provisional and ironic.

From this perspective, it is no coincidence that Clara indirectly inherits a small house in the vicinity of the town from an old miserly uncle shortly before the final catastrophe—a material version of involuntary circulation. Nathanael's subsequent outburst not only goes hand in hand with his characteristic overflow of vitality ("rivers of fire were glowing and sparkling in ["durch"] his rolling eyes", E 117, see G 48), which Clara refuses to absorb, but it instigates a transfer at an unexpected level. The narrator first signals that the high tower throws its "gigantic shadow" (E 117; "Riesenschatten", G 48) over the market place. Only moments later, the two lovers are on top of this same tower contemplating the bluish landscape, which metaphorically arises "like a giant city" (E 117; "Riesenstadt", G 48), as if inflated by the accumulation of circulating energy. Whereas Clara acts here as a passive, petrified victim, it is her brother Lothar who attracts the circulating vitality and gains "prodigious strength" ("Riesenkraft") to save his sister and punch the madman in his face. But the ultimate trigger to Nathanael's suicide is the appearance of the "gigantic figure" ("riesengroß", G 49) Coppelius, on whose presence Clara had previously focused Nathanael's attention when referring to the "funny little grey bush" below (E 118). The narrator's oblique remark that the lawyer has already disappeared "into the throng" (E 118), as soon as Nathanael lies dead on the pavement, indicates that the circulation of energy simply goes on, without the protagonist. That Clara is said to have found not much later a friendly man, who managed to give her "the quiet domestic happiness which suited her cheerful, sunny disposition, which she could have never enjoyed with the tormented, self-divided Nathanael" (E 118), indicates that the circulation of energy has reached a final and conclusive state of stability and homeostasis.

This short analysis of the metaphorical paranarrative in E. T. A. Hoffmann's *Der Sandmann* is in our view not an alternative to existing readings, but rather a supplement to them. It shows that the ambivalence typical of all characters is not merely the result of delusional, unreliable perception, but also the effect of the transfer and circulation of energy, which makes any characterization of the protagonists inconclusive. Circulation in this novella does not mean uniform dispersion. It enacts unsteady processes of diffusion and osmosis, which give the story its typical speed with respect to the vicissitudes of the characters and to the emerging catastrophes. For Nathanael the circulation abruptly comes to a halt; he ceases to operate as a container—gloomily visualized in terms of his "shattered head" (E 118). It would require much more research to unfold this hypothesis entirely, but we believe it to be compatible with Hoffmann's poetics of the Serapiontic principle—the combination of the romantic dictum that literary imagination is unbounded with the Hoffmannesque restriction that it should always take its departure from ordinary, material reality—and his fascination for animal magnetism.[17] On the paranarrative level, the characters are not simply driven by their personal psychology; they much rather appear as carriers of a mobile will or of a circulating vitality. In the paranarrative they assume more and varying positions in the configuration than they do in the epinarrative. Moreover, the paranarrative focuses our attention on the intriguing reciprocity of consciousness that the characters display in their epistolary discourse—a strange phenomenon in a text type envisaging first and foremost the expression of internality. When Nathanael writes to Lothar, he already systematically anticipates the reactions he attributes to his addressees when they hear the words he has not even uttered.[18] This is a subtle example of a form of narrative complexity which can be explained much more conveniently when looking at the paranarrative: the speaker generates a (real) efflux on the basis of the (virtual) influx he receives from the addressee responding (hypothetically) to the (imminent, but not yet realized) efflux from the speaker himself. The idea of circulation thus underpins a process of *autopoesis*, of self-regeneration within a transpersonal circuit.[19]

4   CONCLUSIONS

For a cognitive approach to metaphor in its blending theory version, Hoffmann's novella seems to be an ideal object of analysis. Humans are mixed up with the inanimate and the mechanical and vice versa. But it is not simply a blend: the entire range of extended figurativeness provides the scaffolding for the novella's action. This makes a supplementary narrative dimension available that encompasses both isolated and syntagmatic instances of figurative speech and makes additional processes and phenomena in the storyworld visible and understandable, particularly with respect to the ensuing uncertainties as to what is real or unreal.[20] In reading a literary metaphor, we need to pay close attention to the interaction it sustains with other tropes and to the narrative potential that thus emerges. In Hoffmann's novella, we have observed the remarkable salience of identity metaphors and verbal metaphors and their continuing entanglement and syncretism with personification, metonymy, syllepsis, zeugma and synecdoche (most prominently in the motif of the loss of self-control and the autonomous body parts). Some of these figures signal threshold positions between the epinarrative and the paranarrative: here syllepsis and proto-metaphor turned out to be vital components.

This narrative dimension (and its emergence) has been the blind spot in the cognitive approach to literary metaphor so far. Natural narratology has induced a necessary shift in emphasis from structure to competence (cf. Fludernik 1996: *passim*) and has thus enabled us to distinguish effectively between marked and unmarked tropes and to avoid the pitfalls of hyperliteralism and hyperfigurativeness. Highlighting competence, however, does not reduce metaphor to the contingency of the reader's response. In our model, which integrates cognitive, rhetorical and narratological approaches, the reader's competence is drastically altered by his/her engagement with the text. This dynamic is more likely to occur in processing the rich texture provided by literary texts and the detailed attention they induce. Moreover, it displays the crucial importance of rhetorical negotiation as an integral part of the metaphoric process. This is why we describe literary metaphor as an auto-poetic and self-organising phenomenon with a strong feedback infrastructure and why we insist on the necessity of studying metaphor in interaction with narrators and focalisers, and why we believe one needs to explicate the polyvalence of the copula ("is") so central to the cognitive approach to figurativeness.

Thus extended figurative constellations, as they unfold in literary settings, create a type of meaning that at least partly falls outside the scope of contemporary cognitive research. As metaphors emerge as an event that "befalls" the narrative process (to use Reimer and Camp's graphic description [2007: 40]), they elicit a reader attitude that is more reflexive, more cooperative and less authoritative than the type of metaphor comprehension cognitive research describes, acting less locally and hinging more strongly on dynamic inference. Rather than turning the reader into a passive processor of pre-existing conceptual categorizations, figurative meaning is here argued to enfranchise the reader. Therefore, it can focus more attention on instances of a speaker's self-exposure so frequent in literary discourse, to the dynamics of figurative metamorphosis and even to the possibility of *negative metaphors*, i.e. implicit metaphors that present themselves as being erased, yet whose erasure appears exactly from its submerged contours within a larger metaphoric framework.

The current versions of cognitive poetics remain too one-sidedly focused on the dynamics of the mental apparatus of the language user. They thus tend to remain blind to the dynamics within the text due to be processed, as well as unattuned to instances of figurativeness that do not take place at the level of phrasing, but rather at that of metaphorical actions or events, objects, characters and eventually narration itself. The concept of blending is of little help in remedying this lack of dynamism. We hope to have demonstrated that approaching literary metaphor and figures of speech in general from their narrative angle offers more promising access to this problem.

NOTES

* We thank Monika Fludernik, Liesbeth Korthals-Altes and Peter Flynn for their valuable comments.
1. See Jackendoff and Aaron's (1991: 321–22) critical remarks on Lakoff and Turner's lack of dialogue with existing theories of literary metaphor.
2. See Steen's empirical observation that "relatively unclear metaphors received more attention from readers than relatively clear metaphors" (1999: 505).
3. Steen argues that "subjectivity, fictionality, polyvalence, and form orientation" are the main characteristics of literary reception, for which metaphors "may function as important crystallization points" (1994: 35–36).
4. See also Jackendoff and Aaron (1991: 331, 333). For further criticism, note Steen (1994: 25), Pinker's explorations on 'the metaphor metaphor' (2007: 235–78) and Eder's references to Tsur (2007: 190).
5. Jackendoff and Aaron (1991: 331) rebut for instance Lakoff and Turner's argument that calling a dog 'loyal' is metaphorical. For examples of 'metaphorical concepts' that can also be explained as instances of polysemy see Lakoff and Johnson (1980: 211).

6. See Biebuyck (1998: 183) and Punter (2007: 42). The term refers to "the ability to entertain two different points of view at the same time" (Berggren, quoted in Ricoeur 1979: 152).

7. Pinker (2007: 261) argues that Lakoff overestimates the manipulative effects of language: humans are no slaves to their metaphors; metaphors are rather symptoms of the ways in which humans cognitively manipulate their surroundings. A consequence of this point of view is, according to Pinker, that many conventional speech acts display creativeness through deviations and adaptations of metaphor-based conceptual systems.

8. See Shen (2008: 296–97) with respect to the 'directionality principle'. Shen's finding that in the case of "clashing structures" informants sometimes inverted the direction may indeed "suggest that the cognitive bias toward considering more accessible concepts as sources and less accessible ones as targets may override the relevant default convention when the two clash" (306); it may also imply that in communicative settings with heightened reader participation the cognitive hierarchy between more and less accessible concepts becomes less relevant—which would underpin the idea that literary metaphors operate bi-directionally.

9. Our view differs from what Lakoff has termed "the Invariance Hypothesis" (1990). He argues that in abstract thinking the source domain partially maintains its cognitive topology in the process of metaphorical mapping.

10. See also Eco's "adventurous inference": "for too long it has been thought that in order to understand metaphors it is necessary to know the code (or the encyclopedia). The truth is that the metaphor is the tool that permits us to understand the code (or the encyclopedia) better" (Eco 1984: 270).

11. Cf. Fauconnier and Turner's use of common sense phrasings like "typically" (2008: 56) or "naturally" (59).

12. Cf. Kittay's argument that metaphorical meaning is "a transference of relations of contrast and affinity across semantic fields" (1987: 138).

13. See his provocative statement: "We must give up the idea that a metaphor carries a message, that it has a content or meaning" (Davidson 1979: 43).

14. This *rhetorical negotiation*—an interplay between tropes as nodes of a figurative network in a literary text—is not to be mixed up with *interpretive negotiation*, carried out by readers interpreting the text. Both forms of negotiation underline, however, the interactional character of figurative speech.

15. We prefer to use the cognitive term 'de-automatization' to the well-known concept of 'defamiliarization' introduced by the Russian Formalist Victor Shklovsky in his famous article "Art as Technique" (2005: 16), because we do not allude to an encompassing aesthetic strategy characteristic of the literary work of art as such, but rather to a specific reader response, in which an already established reading fluency is disrupted.

16. References to the English translation (Hoffmann 2009) will be marked by the abbreviation "E", to the German original (Hoffmann 1985) by the abbreviation "G".

17. See Feldges and Stadler 1986: 27–32; Segebrecht 1996: 119–30.

18. For instance: "As I prepare to begin, I hear you laugh, while Clara says [. . .]" (E 86).

19. This is comparable to the automatic current we have attributed to the metaphoric paranarrative elsewhere (Biebuyck & Martens 2009: 122–23).

20. Crisp claims that blending—in his "narrow" definition: a conceptual or phenomenological identification or assimilation (2008: 301)—is the differential element between extended metaphor and allegory. Remarkably, he ignores the fact that allegory is essentially a narrative text type and sees interaction between tropes only in terms of an encompassing "integration network"

(304). In our view, no 'fusion' takes place, either in metaphor or in allegory, precisely because they both kindle narrative potential.

WORKS CITED

Biebuyck, Benjamin (1998) *Die poietische Metapher: Ein Beitrag zur Theorie der Figürlichkeit*. Würzburg: Königshausen & Neumann.

––––––. (2009) "Acting Figuratively, Telling Tropically: Figures of Insanity in Günter Grass's *Die Blechtrommel*". *Style* 43.3: 322–40.

Biebuyck, Benjamin, and Gunther Martens (2009) "Metaphor and Narrative: With References to Nietzsche's *Bildungsanstalten*". *In Search of (Non)Sense: Literary Semantics and the Related Fields and Disciplines*. Eds. E. Kluszewska and G. Spila. Newcastle: Cambridge Scholars. 115–27.

Crisp, Peter (2008) "Between Extended Metaphor and Allegory: Is Blending Enough?" *Language and Literature* 17.4: 291–308.

Davidson, Donald (1979) "What Metaphors Mean". *On Metaphor*. Ed. Sheldon Sacks. Chicago: University of Chicago Press. 29–45.

Eco, Umberto (1984) "Metaphor, Dictionary, and Encyclopedia". *New Literary History* 15.2: 255–71.

Eder, Thomas (2007) "Zur kognitiven Theorie der Metapher in der Literaturwissenschaft: Eine kritische Bestandaufnahme". *Zur Metapher: Die Metapher in Philosophie, Wissenschaft und Kultur*. Eds. F. J. Czernin and T. Eder. München: Fink. 167–95.

Fauconnier, Gilles (1998) *Mental Spaces: Aspects of Meaning Construction in Natural Language*. Cambridge: Cambridge University Press.

Fauconnier, Gilles, and Mark Turner (2002) *The Way We Think: Conceptual Blending and the Mind's Hidden Complexities*. New York: Basic Books.

––––––. (2008) "Rethinking Metaphor". *The Cambridge Handbook of Metaphor and Thought*. Ed. R. W. Gibbs. Cambridge: Cambridge University Press. 53–66.

Feldges, Brigitte, and Ulrich Stadler (1986) *E. T. A. Hoffmann: Epoche, Werk, Wirkung*. München: Beck.

Fludernik, Monika (1996) *Towards a 'Natural' Narratology*. London and New York: Routledge.

Hoffmann, E. T. A. (1985) "Der Sandmann" [1816]. *Nachtstücke; Kleine Zaches; Prinzessin Brambilla; Werke 1816–1820*. Ed. H. Steinecke. Frankfurt am Main: Deutscher Klassiker Verlag. 11–49.

––––––. (2009) "The Sandman" [1816]. *The Golden Pot and Other Tales*. Transl. R. Robertson. Oxford: Oxford University Press. 85–117.

Iser, Wolfgang (1976) *Der Akt des Lesens: Theorie ästhetischer Wirkung*. München: Fink.

Jackendoff, Ray, and David Aaron (1991) "Review Article on G. Lakoff and M. Turner, *More than Cool Reason A Field Guide to Poetic Metaphor*". *Language* 67.2: 320–38.

Kittay, Eva Feder (1987) *Metaphor: Its Cognitive Force and Linguistic Structure*. Oxford: Oxford University Press.

Kluger, Martin (2008) *Der Vogel, der spazieren ging*. Köln: DuMont.

Kohl, Kathrin (2007) *Metapher*. Stuttgart and Weimar: Metzler.

Lakoff, George (1987) *Women, Fire and Dangerous Things: What Categories Reveal about the Mind*. Chicago: University of Chicago Press.

––––––. (1990) "The Invariance Hypothesis: Is Abstract Reason Based on Image-Schemas?" *Cognitive Linguistics* 1: 39–74.

Lakoff, George, and Mark Johnson (1980) *Metaphors We Live By*. Chicago: University of Chicago Press.

Lakoff, George, and Mark Turner (1989) *More than Cool Reason: A Field Guide to Poetic Metaphor*. Chicago: University of Chicago Press.

Pimentel, Luz Aurora (1990) *Metaphoric Narration: Paranarrative Dimensions in A la recherche du temps perdu*. Toronto: University of Toronto Press.

Pinker, Steven (2007) *The Stuff of Thought: Language as a Window into Human Nature*. New York: Viking.

Punter, David (2007) *Metaphor*. London and New York: Routlegde.

Reimer, Marga, and Elisabeth Camp (2007) "Metapher". *Zur Metapher: Die Metapher in Philosophie, Wissenschaft und Literatur*. Eds. F. J. Czernin and T. Eder. München: Fink. 23–44.

Ricoeur, Paul (1975) *La métaphore vive*. Paris: Seuil.

———. (1979) "The Metaphorical Process as Cognition, Imagination, and Feeling". *On Metaphor*. Ed. S. Sacks. London and Chicago: University of Chicago Press. 141–57.

Segebrecht, Wulf (1996) *Heterogenität und Integration: Studien zu Leben, Werk und Wirkung E. T. A. Hoffmanns*. Bern: Lang.

Shen, Yeshayahu (2008) "Metaphor and Poetic Figures". *The Cambridge Handbook of Metaphor and Thought*. Ed. R. W. Gibbs. Cambridge: Cambridge University Press. 295–307.

Shklovsky, Victor (2005) "Art as Technique". *Literary Theory: An Anthology*. Second Edition. Eds. J. Rivkin and M. Ryan. Oxford: Blackwell. 15–21.

Steen, Gerard (1994) *Understanding Metaphor in Literature: An Empirical Approach*. London and New York: Longman.

———. (1999) "Analyzing Metaphor in Literature: With Examples from William Wordsworth's 'I Wandered Lonely as a Cloud'". *Poetics Today* 20.3: 499–522.

4 Reaching Beyond Silence

Metaphors of Ineffability in English Poetry—Donne, Wordsworth, Keats, Eliot

Ina Habermann

1 TROPES OF SILENCE[1]

It has traditionally been one of the functions of literature, and especially poetry, to stretch the limits of language in search of ways to express the ineffable—ideas and feelings that resist or defy expression, such as the emotional extremes of love or religious experience or the responses to beauty or violence. One important way of expanding language is through tropes—forms of 'translated' speech like metaphors and symbols or allegories.

Traditionally, in theories of rhetoric from classical antiquity to the early modern period, tropes had their place as embellishments and energizing elements within rhetorical *elocutio*. With the cognitive revolution, their heuristic value and their central role in all kinds of thought processes have been recognized and theorized in the fields of literary studies, linguistic semantics and pragmatics, philosophy and cognitive science (Blumenberg 1960/1989; Ricoeur 1975; Lakoff & Johnson 1980; Lakoff & Turner 1989; Turner 1991, 1996; Fauconnier & Turner 2002). Cognitive linguists and critics like Lakoff, Johnson and Turner insist that "[m]etaphorical understanding is not a matter of mere word play; it is endemically conceptual in nature. It is indispensable to comprehending and reasoning about concepts like life, death, and time" (Lakoff & Turner 1989: 50). Along these lines, they distinguish between conceptual metaphors, which express basic structures of language and thought, like LIFE IS A JOURNEY (Lakoff & Turner 1989: 9 and *passim*); image schemas like up/down, rising, container, source, path, etc. (Lakoff & Turner 1989: 97–100); and a more idiosyncratic production of image metaphors (Lakoff & Turner 1989: 89–96). For literary criticism, Turner's work has been particularly important. In *Reading Minds* (1991), he presents his project of cognitive rhetoric, which amounts to a revolution of literary criticism in the age of cognitive science, and in *The Literary Mind*, he identifies 'parable' as "the root of the human mind—of thinking, knowing, acting, creating, and plausibly even of speaking" (Turner 1996: v), introducing the concept of 'blending' as a more precise explanation of how images from various sources are cognitively mapped onto each other and interact or 'blend'.

Lakoff and Turner argue that in poetry, conceptual metaphors may simply be versified, or they may be combined in more sophisticated ways into strong images. A third possibility is

> to attempt to step outside the ordinary ways we think metaphorically and either to offer new modes of metaphorical thought or to make the use of our conventional basic metaphors less automatic by employing them in unusual ways, or otherwise to destabilize them and thus reveal their inadequacies for making sense of reality. The third stance is part of what characterizes the avant-garde in any age. (Lakoff & Turner 1989: 51–52)

Thus, it emerges that 'the metaphorical' can no longer be opposed to 'the literal'; instead metaphorical thinking on various levels of complexity and sophistication determines our interaction with the world, importantly even in development of abstract concepts. As Turner states with regard to indeterminate target structure,

> metaphor has exceptionally wide power to *impart* meaning to the target. [. . .] Much of the structure of an abstract concept may have been created by imparting to it through metaphor the image schematic structure of a source. Much of our abstract reasoning may be a metaphoric version of image schematic reasoning. (Turner 1991: 61; original emphasis)

Taking my cue from these insights, I will explore how tropes are used in literary discourse to express the ineffable. Speaking about the unsayable implies a transcendence of the dichotomy between speech and silence, and I suggest that tropes themselves can be seen as forms of deliberate, strategic silence: giving shape to something they cannot name. At one level, silence functions as a metaphor for the ineffable—silence as the source domain of the image and ineffability as the target domain. However, since silence, conceived as a type of negativity or absence, cannot be represented directly, it is in turn represented either metonymically or metaphorically, thus moving from the source to the target domain to create a double-layered system. Metonymically, silence is often framed, visually as in the famous concrete poem by Eugen Gomringer (1969),

> schweigen schweigen schweigen
> schweigen schweigen schweigen
> schweigen   schweigen
> schweigen schweigen schweigen
> schweigen schweigen schweigen

or acoustically, as in John Cage's piece *4'33''* (1952). Silence as event or experience becomes noticeable only within a frame. As an example of metaphorical representation, one might think of the silence which the ghost of Hamlet's father keeps about his experience in purgatory. His terrified son figures this as the "undiscovered country" (*Hamlet* III, i, 81; Shakespeare 1997: 1706), a spatial metaphor which expresses the inevitable silence which surrounds a state of non-being unknown to the living. Through readings of some English poems, whose canonicity ensures a certain cultural resonance, I will argue that silence figures ineffability, and that the metaphorical representations and explorations of silence in turn impart meaning, as Mark Turner suggests, to the abstract and indeterminate concept of ineffability. The journey of 'silence' from the source to the target domain is the space of the poem.

2 JOHN DONNE'S "THE EXTASIE": SOUL'S LANGUAGE

In the early seventeenth century, some of the poets who have subsequently been called 'metaphysical' looked for new ways to understand and express the ineffable. In John Donne's "The Extasie" (1633) for example, the unsayable is the experience of 'romantic' love—'romantic' in the sense of a heterosexual, individualized relationship which involves an emotional, spiritual and sexual union. In a spiritually eloquent but outwardly silent scene, where the speaker and his love lie on a bank surrounded by flowers, the poem describes this union as a *unio mystica* in analogy to the union of the soul with God. Sexual connotations are introduced as the "[p]regnant" (Donne 1912: line 2) bank is likened to a bed, but the speaker emphasizes that "as yet" (line 9), all bodily contact has been restricted to hands and eyes. Here, however, the lovers' hands are "firmely cimented" (line 5), "eyebeames twisted" (line 7), and their eyes placed like pearls "upon one double string" (line 8) in a silent moment of *ekstasis* in which the two souls have left their bodies behind and are united with one another.

> And whil'st our soules negotiate there,
> Wee like sepulchrall statues lay;
> All day, the same our postures were,
> And wee said nothing, all the day. (lines 17–20)

An uninitiated person who happened to pass by would hear and see nothing but two silent and immobile creatures, unless the observer was

> so by love refin'd
> That he soules language understood, [. . .]
> He (though he knew not which soule spake,
> Because both meant, both spake the same)

> Might thence a new concoction take,
> And part farre purer than he came. (lines 21–22, 25–28)

Silence thus figures the ineffable—love's mysteries. Still, through the idea that the mind, or the soul, is a BODY MOVING IN SPACE (Turner 1991: 79), the poem finds a way of reaching beyond silence. Two souls communicate in "soules language", which is not subject to the impurities of the sublunary sphere but akin to the *lingua adamica*, the powerful and perfect language spoken before the Fall. The muteness of the physical world points metonymically to a higher form of eloquence; absence is presence elsewhere. Therefore, the argument of the poem is not mystical or neoplatonic in the sense of the Catholic tradition, where sexual imagery is used as an allegorical expression of the union with God. Its trajectory is far more complex and ingenious than the familiar spiritual sublimation of an erotic attraction or the translation of holy rapture into physical terms. The departure from the traditional point of view is signalled in images like eyes threaded "upon one double string" (line 8) as well as the suspicious image of the ecstatic souls as "two equall Armies" at the mercy of a personified, rather pagan-sounding "Fate" (line 13).

The material quality of soul's language, initially cast in the image of the two negotiating armies, is then enhanced by the discourse of alchemy. According to the alchemical 'conceit', each individual soul is a mixture of things. In analogy to the alchemists' aspiration to create gold out of lesser metals, Love, the alchemist, combines them in a new mixture to produce an "abler soul" (line 43) purified of the "Defects of loneliness" (line 44). This is a clever move, because the logic of alchemy abolishes the somewhat unproductive dichotomy between physical and spiritual elements, which riddles neoplatonic discourses. Emphasis on the material throws into relief the pragmatic aspect of language, equating speech act with love act. Now it appears only logical to ask "But O alas, so long, so farre / Our bodies why doe wee forbeare?" (lines 49–50). And indeed, the purified soul needs to return to the individual bodies, which are not "drosse to us, but allay" (line 56), strengthening rather than contaminating the new 'golden' soul and giving it a seat in the world. The soul, conceived as a body moving in space, has taken a journey and must now return to its 'home' in the physical body: "Loves mysteries" (line 71) "in soules doe grow, / But yet the body is his booke." (lines 71–72). In order to overcome silence, souls must be (re) located in feeling bodies which communicate with the world through the senses: "Else a great Prince in prison lies" (line 68). The ultimate goal of Love the alchemist, or the magician, is a golden soul substance uniting two bodies. The speaker concludes:

> And if some lover, such as wee,
> Have heard this dialogue of one,
> Let him still marke us, he shall see
> Small change, when we'are to bodies gone. (lines 73–76)

Body and soul can separate and still be inseparable, just as the eloquence of the soul is a kind of silent speech, a "dialogue of one". Rather than relying on the traditional topos of ineffability that words are too weak to express the intensity of feelings adequately (see Benthien 2006: 300–08 and *passim*), the poem has given 'scientific' proof, as it were, that the prevailing silence figures a higher eloquence elsewhere, where language is illocutionary. Through the blending which has taken place, these realms are no longer separate. In a witty dialogue with mysticism, the *unio mystica* is blended with occult practices of alchemy and white—or possibly black?— magic on the basis of their joint defiance of ordinary logic. The poem manages to vindicate heterosexual love, presumably in the form of Protestant companionate marriage, and clear it from all charges of impurity. It does so on the strength of both religious and scientific authority, at the same time hiding love in a private emotional space.[2] The transcendent and transformative quality of the experience colours the ineffability of Love's mysteries, resignifying its silence as eloquence elsewhere.

3   WILLIAM WORDSWORTH'S "ODE ON IMMORTALITY": SIGNPOSTS INTO THE VOID

William Wordsworth's "Ode: Intimations of Immortality from Recollections of Early Childhood" (1807) offers a Romantic evocation of eternity. While Donne's poem is centred around an emotion ultimately impossible to describe but possible to experience, eternity is an abstract, sublime idea which tends to overwhelm the human mind. It is therefore more radically ineffable, so to speak, because the failure to grasp the concept does not proceed from the inadequacies of linguistic expression, but from cognition itself. Consequently, Wordsworth's speaker must be content with 'intimations' of immortality, explored as far as possible with figurative language. The speaker deplores the fact that a certain "celestial light" (Wordsworth 1883: line 4) which illuminated his early childhood has now disappeared, leaving behind a prosaic world lit by common daylight.

> Our birth is but a sleep and a forgetting:
> The Soul that rises with us, our life's Star,
> Hath had elsewhere its setting,
> And cometh from afar:
> Not in entire forgetfulness,
> And not in utter nakedness,
> But trailing clouds of glory do we come
> From God, who is our home:
> Heaven lies about us in our infancy! (lines 58–66)

Approaching his theme, the speaker draws on a number of appropriately fundamental basic conceptual metaphors for existence as described by

Lakoff and Turner, such as BIRTH IS ARRIVAL, LIFE IS BEING PRESENT HERE (Lakoff & Turner 1989: 1), LIFE IS A JOURNEY (Lakoff & Turner 1989: 3), A LIFETIME IS A DAY (Lakoff & Turner 1989: 5) or LIFE IS LIGHT (Lakoff & Turner 1989: 29). In order to convey a sense of his existential crisis, the speaker then proceeds to complicate or even deconstruct these assumptions. Birth may be a beginning, but it is also the end of something else, marking the loss of a divine presence. Rather than being connected to wakefulness and consciousness, as would be expected, birth is associated with oblivion. It is indeed seen as a sunrise and an arrival, but simultaneously as a sunset and a departure from another realm suffused with divine presence. Thus, life is not really a day, as the basic conceptual metaphor suggests, but more like the afterglow of a more glorious and illuminated day in another realm.[3] This realm is not located 'high up' in 'heaven', again, as might be expected in accordance with the customary image schema, but rather horizontally at a great distance. The soul has travelled far, "trailing clouds of glory", as the famous image has it. It follows that life must subsequently be lived in recognition of an initial loss, and rather than progressing towards a goal, as suggested in the permutations of the LIFE IS A JOURNEY metaphor, the traveller wanders ever further away from an initial state of grace.

The world that tries to engross the speaker is full of sounds—birdsong, the shepherd's tabor, cataracts which "blow their trumpets from the steep" (line 25), and of course the babble of everyday situations, where the growing child will "fit his tongue / To dialogues of business, love, or strife" (lines 97–98). Such speech is characterized as artificial—words that the "little Actor" (line 103) has rehearsed for his "'humorous stage'" (line 104). Here, the conceptual metaphors LIFE IS A PLAY and LIFE IS A BURDEN (Lakoff & Turner 1989: 20, 25) are employed to signal tedium and an element of inauthenticity. In contrast to this, true speech is silent and opaque:

> But there's a Tree, of many, one,
> A single Field which I have looked upon,
> Both of them speak of something that is gone. (lines 51–53)

Only the tree and the field, certain features of the natural world, still "speak" of this lost "something". As it seems, the really important things cannot be expressed, and the child, the "best Philosopher" (line 111), is "deaf and silent" as he reads the "eternal deep" (line 113). The more grown-up, worldly and eloquent we become, the less we know, or remember, about this "eternal deep".

As in Donne, speaking silence is central to the poem, but it could be understood as "soul's language" only if the communications of the natural world were taken to be imaginary–not true dialogue, but a kind of ventriloquism. Believing in a world beyond the self, the speaker gives thanks

for those first affections,
Those shadowy recollections,
Which, be they what they may,
Are yet the fountain light of all our day,
Are yet a master light of all our seeing;
Uphold us, cherish, and have power to make
Our noisy years seem moments in the being
Of the eternal Silence[.] [. . .]
Hence in a season of calm weather
Though inland far we be,
Our Souls have sight of that immortal sea
Which brought us hither,
Can in a moment travel thither,
And see the Children sport upon the shore,
And hear the mighty waters rolling evermore. (lines 149–56, 162–68)

Unlike Donne, who framed silence with spiritual eloquence, Wordsworth frames the "noisy years" of life with silence, which figures eternity as the ineffable. Silence belongs to the source domain here, but since the soul, conceived again as a body moving in space, is capable of swift movement, the soul can "see" that silence is an "immortal sea", thus imparting the qualities of the ocean to the abstract idea of eternity and making it sensually perceptible through the steady, rhythmic and perpetual rolling of the waves. It becomes clear at this point why the imagery of the elements is so archetypal: as the creation of basic conceptual metaphors, image schemas and mental spaces shows, the spatial situation of human beings within the natural world forms the very bedrock of any cognitive engagment and interaction with that world. Intriguingly, at the end of the poem, the speaker expresses thankfulness for the human heart, thanks to which tiny things can give rise to profound ideas: "the meanest flower that blows can give / Thoughts that do often lie too deep for tears" (lines 203–04) Here, the poet relies on an image schema which sees the self as a container where the things at the bottom or at a kind of core are most difficult to reach. "Too deep for tears" may mean 'too profound to be adequately expressed by crying' or 'too remote to be touched by expressions of emotion'; this the poem leaves open. In any case, the passage concerns thoughts rather than feelings, as if the speaker wishes to emphasize that rather than engaging in a sentimental discourse of nature, his reflection tends precisely towards the fundamentals of cognition itself.

Spatialization plays a crucial role in this context. When closing in on the ineffable, Wordsworth tends to use pointers without a clear referent, like "something", "elsewhere" or "afar"—not only in the "Ode" but also already in "Tintern Abbey", which addresses similar questions. "We see into the life of things" (Wordsworth 1936: 164; line 49), says the speaker about the meditative attitude which enables a spiritual experience:

> a sense sublime
> Of *something* far more deeply interfused,
> Whose dwelling is the light of setting suns,
> And the round ocean and the living air,
> And the blue sky, and in the mind of man:
> A motion and a spirit, that impels
> All thinking things, all objects of all thought,
> And rolls through all things. (164; lines 95–102; my emphasis)

Embedded in cosmic archetypal imagery—the air, the sea, the sun and stars—such empty, vaguely deictic words are like signposts into the void. They conjure up shapes and spaces which cannot be seen clearly with the 'eye of the mind'.

Translating this into philosophical discourse, these indeterminate shapes and spaces are reminiscent of the *khora* Plato described in his socratic dialogue *Timaeus*. The *khora* is an invisible and formless space which can be discerned only in a dreamlike state, metaphorically described as a 'vessel' or a 'nurse'—a kind of receptacle for impregnation.[4] Wordsworth's tropes achieve a spatialization of the ineffable, thus making a space, or "carving out a void" (Budick & Iser 1989: xi) for a type of knowledge and experience constitutive of our being and—therefore?—especially hard to communicate: intimations of immortality, eternity and divine presence. They must of necessity be couched in images *and* point beyond them, which begs the question about the metaphorical quality of such discourse. Read in the light of Derrida's thinking about negative theology, Wordsworth's approach could be seen as a radical (a)voiding strategy, a process of emptying and deferral. Derrida outlines the subject of negative theology:

> Suppose, by a provisional hypothesis, that negative theology consists of considering that every predicative language is inadequate to the essence, in truth to the hyperessentiality (the being beyond Being) of God; consequently, only a negative ("apophatic") attribution can claim to approach God, and to prepare us for a silent intuition of God. (Derrida 1989: 4)

Still, the silent intuition has to be framed somehow to be communicated, which entails the risk of premature affirmation. In his aptly entitled essay "How to Avoid Speaking", therefore, Derrida is concerned to defer speaking about the subject of negative theology, because to speak of it would be to take up the "ontological wager of hyperessentiality" (Derrida 1989: 8) inherent in such discourse. He prefers to think in terms of *differance*:

> What *differance*, the *trace*, and so on "mean"—which hence *does not mean anything*—is "before" the concept, the name, the word,

"something" that would be nothing, that no longer arises from Being, from presence or from the presence of the present, nor even from absence, and even less from some hyperessentiality. (Derrida 1989: 9; original emphasis)

In his poem, Wordsworth casts aspects of the natural world as traces coming from, or leading to, the ineffable "something". "Trailing clouds of glory do we come" is a striking image for the 'trace', which in turn is an image for a spatialized notion of "elsewhere", or the non-place of the *khora*:

The import of receptivity or of receptacle which, one may say, forms the elementary nonvariable of this word's determination, seems to me to transcend the opposition between figurative and proper meaning. The spacing of *khora* introduces a dissociation or a difference in the proper meaning that it renders possible, thereby compelling tropic detours which are no longer rhetorical figures. The typography and the tropics to which the *khora* gives place, *without giving anything*, are explicitly marked in the *Timaeus* (50bc). Hence Plato says this in his way: it is necessary to avoid speaking of *khora* as of "something" that is or is not, that could be present or absent, intelligible, sensible, or both at once, active or passive, the Good (*epekeina tes ousias*) or the Evil, God or man, the living or the nonliving. Every theomorphic or anthropomorphic schema would thus also have to be avoided. (Derrida 1989: 37; original emphasis)

Wordsworth's "tropic detours" suggest a material grounding and a spatialization of the transcendental, and (necessarily?) transient, experience of divine presence. 'Presence' is a figure of speech too, a metaphor for something ineffable of which there can be only intimations, or traces, which human beings interpret in accordance with the conceptual metaphors and image schemas that make the world intelligible to them. In blended images of this nature, it becomes impossible to identify or distinguish source and target domains, which would seem to be the precondition of figurative speech, because the hierarchy of 'proper' and 'translated' meanings has been revealed as illusionary.

4   JOHN KEATS'S "ODE ON A GRECIAN URN": INEFFABLE INEFFABILITY

John Keats's "Ode on a Grecian Urn" (1819/20) has been read as a celebration of visual art, as a supreme example of *ekphrasis* and an intervention into the time-honoured debate about the respective merits of the 'sister arts'. Readers have seen Keats come down in favour of painting and sculpture, or they have read the praise of visuals as ironic, cunningly reasserting the special merits of poetry (Kelley 2001). Behind such readings are assumptions about the meaning of classical art, both for the Romantics and for us today. In the early twentieth century, the art historian and cultural anthropologist Aby Warburg famously argued that while for nineteenth-century viewers, classical art mainly signified calm and serenity, interest in the classics was first revived in the Renaissance because of their depictions of motion and *energeia* (Michaud 2007). Indeed, Keats's ode dwells on the image of arrested motion in the scenes described and their effects on the viewer. While these debates provide a framework for my argument, I want to focus in my reading on the preoccupation with the silence of the inscrutable object at the centre of the ode's evocation of ineffability.

The urn is an inviolate "bride of quietness", the "foster-child of silence and slow time". It would have been easy, in unquiet times, to 'ravish' and shatter the fragile vessel; the undertone of sexualized violence is quite audible, but since this has not happened yet, the urn remains as a "historian" of the woods ("Sylvan"). This is a puzzling image, since a historian is someone who studies the past rather than belonging to the past, and the woods would be neither the most likely origin nor subject of the historian. These would rather be the legends, deities and people, myths and rituals evoked in the poem. In any case, the urn can "thus express / A flowery tale more sweetly than our rhyme" (lines 3–4): "thus" because is has been preserved against the odds or because it is "Sylvan"? "Express" because it cannot 'tell' the tale? Foregoing the alliteration, the speaker takes the urn to suggest that there *are* tales to tell about times gone by while withholding them, because tales are about narrative movement and progression, and 'parable', as Mark Turner might say. Taking the unfulfilled promise at face value, the speaker fires a volley of questions at the urn, which are of course greeted with silence. This tacit-urnity figures again at the end of stanza four, where the speaker addresses the empty little town depicted on the urn, finding it in his own heart to commiserate with it since "thy streets for evermore / Will silent be; and not a soul to tell / Why thou art desolate, can e'er return" (lines 38–40). A tension is created between the recurring "never" and "for ever" in the description of the scene of amorous pursuit on the urn—suggestions of a paradoxical eternity of tortured need, as in a Dantean hell, and perpetual ecstasy, which is profoundly inhuman. This insight darkens the tone and leads on to the scene of imminent sacrifice, the suggestion of ancient mysteries and the deserted town. The figures on the urn cannot live, and neither can they die. While Wordsworth's speaker is yearning for immortality and eternity, this speaker appears utterly appalled by the notion, and while the yearning in the former is created by tantalizing glimpses, the horror in the latter is produced by equally tantalizing over-exposure. Both, however, are engaged in a metaphorical exploration of the ineffability surrounding a mortal's intellectual and emotional grapple with a term that—going back via Derrida to Heidegger—we may do well to put under erasure: ~~eternity~~. In the fifth and last stanza, the speaker, rhyming on the "Attic shape", reflects on the urn's "fair attitude" (line 41). I read this as an ironic comment on a certain dishonesty perceived in the work of art as it is accosted once more by the speaker: "Thou, silent form, dost tease us out of thought / As doth eternity: Cold Pastoral!" (lines 44–45).[5] If we are teased "out of" thought by silence and eternity, where does that leave us? The beginning of the second stanza with its proverbial-sounding "Heard melodies are sweet, but those unheard / Are sweeter" (lines 11–12) almost feels like a false start; it quotes the neoplatonic dichotomy between "the sensual ear" (line 13) and "the spirit" (line 14), which John Donne had already moved beyond. The urn's silence or inscrutability is its most conspicuous characteristic. Silence does not figure eternity here, as it does in Wordsworth's "Ode", but the physical object, the urn itself, embodies both silence and eternity, drawing the mind of the viewer into a state of contemplation "out of thought" (line 44).

Again, we encounter the paradox of speaking silence with the urn as a mute ambassador from another world. When the urn does "speak" eventually, it offers a somewhat qualified consolation: "'Beauty is truth, truth beauty',—that is all / Ye know on earth, and all ye need to know" (lines 49–50). Through this statement, three concepts are aligned on the same level of abstraction—eternity, beauty and truth—and a linguistic evocation of a physical object, i.e. a symbol rather than a metaphor, is conjured up to impart its meanings to the targets. Blending occurs as in Wordsworth's poem, but the whole system appears more finite, closed and circular, like the shape of the urn itself, which is a cultural artefact rather than belonging to the natural world. In the spatial organisation of Wordsworth's "Ode", the ineffable is placed "beyond", whereas in Keats's "Ode", the images bounce around as in a mirror cabinet—beauty reflecting on truth reflecting on eternity reflecting on beauty and so on. This places the emphasis on the ultimately self-reflexive aspect of cognition and the extent to which consciousness is enclosed in a space where it is difficult to hear the "mighty waters rolling evermore". The urn's "all ye need to know" appears like an expression of Keats's notion of *negative capability* (Keats 1942: 72), the capacity to accept uncertainty and let ineffability be ineffable. Still, the exasperated tone of the poem suggests that such equanimity is hard won and that it entails an element of capitulation. Comparing the two Romantic poets with respect to *negative capability*, or the "via naturaliter negativa" (Hartman 1964: 31), Wordsworth may be said to practice as Keats preaches.

5   T. S. ELIOT, *FOUR QUARTETS*: TONGUES OF FIRE

If the classic work of art is trying to "tease us out of thought", the beginning of T. S. Eliot's *The Four Quartets* (1944) chases us out of thought at gun-point; insofar as it is possible to pinpoint the subject of the poem, Eliot appears to explore the secret of life—the ineffable which the poem struggles to express. In order to escape cliché, the speaker deconstructs the basic conceptual metaphors concerning time and space which uphold our sense of being in the world. Beginning with time, he confounds customary assumptions. Usually, TIME MOVES (Lakoff & Turner 1989: 44), the future is before us, the past behind us and LIFE IS A JOURNEY in time, which involves progress towards some goal. Not so, it appears, in "Burnt Norton":

> Time present and time past
> Are both perhaps present in time future,
> And time future contained in time past. [. . .]
> What might have been and what has been
> Point to one end, which is always present.
> Footfalls echo in the memory
> Down the passage which we did not take
> Towards the door we never opened
> Into the rose-garden. [. . .] (Eliot 1983: 13; lines 1–3, 9–15)

Notions of linearity, chronology and progression are overturned, and once the usual temporal framework is radically undermined, the image of the rose garden appears suspended in cosmic space. The subsequent epiphany in that rose garden, which "we" apparently entered although the door was never opened, gains a primal, prelapsarian quality—the surface of an empty pool glittering for a moment "out of heart of light" (14; line 37). There is a tension between the apodictic quality of the statements about time and their paradoxical content, which appears calculated to alert readers to the metaphorical nature of the usual assumptions about time, urging them to think beyond the usual scaffolding.

Having dismantled the temporal framework, the speaker in "Burnt Norton" proceeds with space:

> At the still point of the turning world. Neither flesh nor fleshless;
> Neither from nor towards; at the still point, there the dance is,
> But neither arrest nor movement. And do not call it fixity,
> Where past and future are gathered. Neither movement from nor
>   towards,
> Neither ascent nor decline. Except for the point, the still point,
> There would be no dance, and there is only the dance.
> I can only say, *there* we have been: but I cannot say where.
> And I cannot say, how long, for that is to place it in time.
>   (15; lines 62–69; original emphasis)

It appears that life is a dance without movement at an indeterminate location out of time. Even more radically than with Wordsworth's "something" and "elsewhere", all markers of conventional orientation are reduced to an empty deictic gesture, which figures the metaphysical homelessness of human beings. At the same time, the very consciousness of this is acknowledged to be inhuman, because "only in time can the moment in the rose-garden [. . .] / Be remembered; involved with past and future" (15; lines 85, 88). Moments of being which throw into relief the limitations of the ordinary framework of consciousness must yet again be framed by those very expanses of half-consciousness they seek to transcend—a state of things which awareness cannot remedy. Thus, human beings are confounded by their own cleverness, which concerns poets more than most, since language must also obey this principle:

> Words move, music moves
> Only in time; but that which is only living
> Can only die. Words, after speech, reach
> Into the silence. Only by the form, the pattern,
> Can words or music reach
> The stillness, as a Chinese jar still
> Moves perpetually in its stillness. [. . .]
> And all is always now. Words strain,
> Crack and sometimes break, under the burden,
> Under the tension, slip, slide, perish,
> Decay with imprecision, will not stay in place,
> Will not stay still. (17; lines 137–43, 149–53)

Eliot seems to be in dialogue with Keats here, with an interesting twist, because instead of saying 'only that which is living can die', or 'only that which can die can also live', he elects to say "but that which is only living / Can only die", which belittles the human condition in a way Keats had not done, and neither had Wordsworth, although they both ultimately acknowledge human beings' limitations in realizing their own ontological situation. For the moment, Eliot rejects *negative capability*.

Regarding language, he says explicitly what the others had implied: since mortals' words, or mortal words, cannot come within close range of the ineffable, they must—another spatialization via an image schema—"reach / Into the silence". Silence figures the mystery of existence, and form, pattern, chanting, rhythm, i.e. the musical quality of language rather than the content, offers the only chance to get further, to the "stillness" which appears to lie beyond the silence, where the absence implied by silence has evaporated along with the need for expression. Traversing "the silence" in order to reach "the stillness", a nihilistic state of grace, we have entered what will become Beckett territory. Annoyingly, "one has only learnt to get the better of words / For the thing one no longer has to say" (26; lines 176–77), as the speaker puts it in "East Coker". Eliot is at his most querulous here, but he passes through this mood, in the succession of the poems in *Four Quartets*, by a kind of baptism similar to that at the end of *The Waste Land*. In "Dry

Salvages", he conjures up first the river, "a strong brown god" (31; line 2) and then the sea, as Wordsworth had also done: "The river is within us, the sea is all about us" (31; line 15). Water imagery—recalling Wordsworth's "and hear the mighty waters rolling evermore"—introduces a rhythm which carries the poem forward again. The river figures time: "Time the destroyer is time the preserver, / Like the river with its cargo of dead negroes, cows and chicken coops" (34; lines 115–16). For a moment, it looks as if the water imagery could express life's mystery by capturing its basic rhythm.

However, as the conventions of the sea voyage as a conceptual metaphor for life assert their power, the poem appears to acknowledge the futility of trying to circumvent metaphor:

We cannot think of a time that is oceanless [. . .]
Or of a future that is not liable
Like the past, to have no destination.
We have to think of them as forever bailing,
Setting and hauling, [. . .]
Not as making a trip that will be unpayable
For a haul that will not bear examination. (33; lines 69, 71–74, 77–78)

Once thinking about life as a sea voyage, the particulars of such a voyage come into focus. The sea is contaminated; humans drift about amidst wreckage, breakage and wastage in a "boat with a slow leakage" (33; line 74), and there are rocks in the water concealed by fog. Noting the emphasis on wreckage, it is perhaps well to remember that the poem was written in wartime. The apparent compulsion to think of life in terms of a (sea) voyage is triggered by a mysterious "voice", which speaks no language and cannot be heard, the "murmuring shell of time" (35; line 48), saying "'Fare forward, you who think that you are voyaging; / You are not those who saw the harbour / Receding, or those who will disembark" (35; lines 149–51). With the image of a perpetual voyage Eliot shifts the emphasis from the individual to the life of the species.

Ultimately, life gains meaning only in the succession of generations. Here, Eliot introduces a notion of collective consciousness, which can also be found in essays like "Tradition and the Individual Talent" (Eliot 1957) and which can be seen as a variant of the GREAT-CHAIN METAPHOR (Turner 1991: 167–71). In the chain of generations, the past is the future, and the future is the past. This involves evolutionary assumptions about how the species fits into the general scheme of things including an animalistic prehistory of existential fear and awe at the "dawn" of civilization:

not forgetting
Something that is probably quite ineffable:
The backward look behind the assurance
Of recorded history, the backward half-look
Over the shoulder, towards the primitive terror.
(Eliot 1983: 34; lines 99–103)

The terror of a sublime universe which threatens to overwhelm the human mind is interpreted along the lines of Romantic philosophy both as an assurance of continuity and as proof of the presence of "something" beyond the grasp of human understanding—"High instincts before which our mortal Nature / Did tremble like a guily thing surprised—as Wordsworth puts it in the "Ode on Immortality" (lines 147–48).

The submission of the soul to a higher principle then becomes the predictable response to the ineffable experience of sublime terror, so that it appears only logical that the journey of the *Four Quartets*, now reconfigured as a pilgrimage, should end in the chapel of Little Gidding.

> You are here to kneel
> Where prayer has been valid. And prayer is more
> Than an order of words, the conscious occupation
> Of the praying mind, or the sound of the voice praying.
> And what the dead had no speech for, when living,
> They can tell you, being dead: the communication
> Of the dead is tongued with fire beyond the language of the living.
> Here the intersection of the timeless moment
> Is England and nowhere. Never and always. (Eliot 1983: 42; lines 45–53)

The ineffable is communicated through dialogue with the dead, whose language is at last adequate to the need for expression. In an ironic move on the level of form, the whole sequence of poems as Eliot published it, which starts with a radical unravelling of every meaningful structure or pattern, turns out to have a Christian trajectory. Eliot begins by shaking the very foundations, so to speak, of the cognitive processes involved in thinking with images, deconstructing all customary assumptions about space and time, only to discover in this poetic quest that it is neither possible nor desirable to move beyond the images, because "[w]e cannot think of a time that is oceanless" (33; line 69). In keeping with this insight, *Four Quartets* culminates in a mystical incantation with echoes of Julian of Norwich, which reaches back beyond my starting point in John Donne:

> And all shall be well and
> All manner of thing shall be well
> When the tongues of flame are in-folded
> Into the crowned knot of fire
> And the fire and the rose are one. (48; lines 255–59)

Eliot turned back where Beckett would soldier on, back from the void, and towards the speaking silences of Christian mysticism. Due to its violent turn from radical deconstruction to mystical revelation in the image "the fire and the rose are one", Eliot's poem embraces the hyperessentiality inherent in the discourse of negative theology. Before the silence of the *apophasis* there must be a prayer (Derrida 1989: 41) to ensure the proper communion with God, and that prayer is the poem. *Four Quartets* begins and ends with two different kinds of ineffability, moving from the iconoclastic to the redemptive—from a de(con)struction of the metaphors we live by to a sacralized literality of the image.

6   SUMMARY

In Donne's "Extasie", the ineffable is love's mystery, and the silence surrounding it is resignified in a metaphysical conceit as soul's language in a transformative out-of-body experience. Expanding the scale of the poetic project, both Wordsworth and Keats grapple with huge, ineffable abstractions like eternity and immortality. Wordsworth reaches beyond silence, or the "immortal sea", to divine presence, signalled by signposts into the void, while Keats takes the work of art to symbolize beauty, truth and eternity, thus imparting a culturally specific meaning to these abstract concepts. Both Romantic poets do not employ figurative speech in terms of the metaphysical conceit, but as an intellectual tool in their exploration of ineffability—Wordsworth taking a necessary "tropic detour" and Keats drawing back, in a spirit of *negative capability*, from the 'outer reaches', so to speak, of the ineffable. Finally, Eliot seeks deliberately to destroy the conceptual groundworks of space and time in order to move beyond the figurative in his exploration of the mystery of life, only then consciously to return to the images. Conceding and indeed highlighting their heuristic and ontological inevitability, he finally elevates them to vehicles of mystic revelation where "the fire and the rose are one" (48, line 259).

NOTES

1. Thanks go to Ralf Schneider for extremely helpful comments on an earlier draft of this chapter.
2. For a neoplatonic reading of the poem, which discounts the sexual element, see Spitzer (1949).
3. Cleanth Brooks (1947) also notes this in an early close reading of the poem, but since he is mainly interested in figures of ambiguity and paradox as a gauge of the poem's quality, he does not offer a detailed analysis of the metaphorical structure.
4. Echoes like these could be responsible for the fact that the Christian orthodoxy of the poem has repeatedly been questioned. For a discussion of *khora* in the context of negative theology, see Derrida (1989: 34–41).
5. Scholars have searched in vain for the object Keats describes; I like to think that it existed and that he brushed it off its pedestal in a fit of absent-mindedness.

WORKS CITED

Blumenberg, Hans (1989) *Paradigmen zu einer Metaphorologie* [1960]. Frankfurt: Suhrkamp.

Benthien, Claudia (2006) *Barockes Schweigen: Rhetorik und Performativität des Sprachlosen im 17. Jahrhundert.* München: Fink.

Brooks, Cleanth (1947) "Wordsworth and the Paradox of the Imagination". *The Well Wrought Urn: Studies in the Structure of Poetry.* Ed. Cleanth Brooks. New York: Harcourt, Brace & World. 124–50.

Budick, Sanford, and Wolfgang Iser (1989) Eds. *Languages of the Unsayable: The Play of Negativity in Literature and Literary Theory.* New York and Oxford: Columbia University Press.

Derrida, Jacques (1989) "How to Avoid Speaking: Denials". *Languages of the Unsayable: The Play of Negativity in Literature and Literary Theory.* Eds. Sanford Budick and Wolfgang Iser. New York and Oxford: Columbia University Press. 3–70. [Original (1987) "Comment ne pas parler: Dénégations". In: *Psyché: Inventions de l'autre.* Paris: Galilée].

Donne, John (1912) "The Extasie" [1633]. *The Poems of John Donne*, Vol. 1. Ed. Herbert J. C. Grierson. Oxford: Clarendon. 51–53.

Eliot, T. S. (1957) *The Sacred Wood: Essays on Poetry and Criticism* [1919]. London: Methuen.

———. (1983) *Four Quartets: Burnt Norton, East Coker, The Dry Salvages, Little Gidding* [1944]. London: Faber & Faber.

Fauconnier, Gilles, and Mark Turner (2002) *The Way We Think: Conceptual Blending and the Mind's Hidden Complexities.* New York: Basic Books.

Hartman, Geoffrey H. (1964) *Wordsworth's Poetry, 1787–1814.* New Haven and London: Yale University Press.

Keats, John (1942) *The Letters of John Keats.* Ed. Maurice Buxton Forman. Oxford: Oxford University Press. 70–2.

———. (1956) "Ode on a Grecian Urn" [1819/20]. *The Poetical Works of John Keats.* Ed. H. W. Garrod. Oxford: Oxford University Press. 209–10.

Kelley, Theresa M. (2001) "Keats and 'Ekphrasis'". *The Cambridge Companion to Keats.* Ed. Susan J. Wolfson. Cambridge: Cambridge University Press. 170–85.

Lakoff, George, and Mark Johnson (1980) *Metaphors We Live By.* Chicago: University of Chicago Press.

Lakoff, George, and Mark Turner (1989) *More than Cool Reason: A Field Guide to Poetic Metaphor.* Chicago and London: University of Chicago Press.

Michaud, Philippe-Alain (2007) *Aby Warburg and the Image in Motion.* Transl. Sophie Hawkes. New York: Zone Books. [Original (1998) *Aby Warburg et l'image en mouvement.*]

Ricoeur, Paul (1975) *La Métaphore Vive.* Paris: Editions du Seuil.

Shakespeare, William (1997) "The Tragedy of Hamlet, Prince of Denmark" [c. 1602]. *The Norton Shakespeare.* Eds. Stephen Greenblatt et al. New York and London: Norton. 1659–1759.

Spitzer, Leo (1949) *A Method of Interpreting Literature.* Northampton, MA: Smith College.

Turner, Mark (1991) *Reading Minds: The Study of English in the Age of Cognitive Science.* Princeton: Princeton University Press.

———. (1996) *The Literary Mind: The Origins of Thought and Language.* Oxford: Oxford University Press.

Wordsworth, William (1883) "Ode: Intimations of Immortality from Recollections of Early Childhood" [1807]. *The Poetical Works of William Wordsworth*, Vol. 4. Ed. William Knight. Edinburgh: William Paterson. 47–55.

———. (1936) "Lines Composed a Few Miles Above Tintern Abbey, on Revisiting the Banks of the Wye During a Tour. July 13, 1798". *Complete Poetical Works.* Eds. Thomas Hutchinson and Ernest de Selincourt. Oxford: Oxford University Press. 163–65. [Originally published in *The Lyrical Ballads* in 1798 with S. T. Coleridge].

5 Literary Criticism Writes Back to Metaphor Theory

Exploring the Relation between Extended Metaphor and Narrative in Literature

Bo Pettersson

1 INTRODUCTION

The relation between extended metaphor and narrative in literary studies has not received as much attention as it deserves. Elsewhere, I have called for a rapprochement of the figural and narrative trends in cognitive literary studies and proposed possible ways of achieving this end in theory (Pettersson 2001, 2005). By analysing some poetry and fiction, I here aim to explore what literary-critical practice might suggest about the relation between extended metaphor and narrative. As such, this project is nothing new in cognitive metaphor studies (consider, for instance, the work of Donald and Margaret Freeman). However, many practitioners have concentrated on a top-down search for cognitive metaphors, despite the emphasis on the body-related basis of meaning. As we shall see, some conclusions to be derived from a bottom-up literary-critical practice are rather far-ranging. I will suggest that broad hermeneutic-generic circles with attention to the specifics of each literary work are best suited to produce lasting literary-critical contributions. Thus, I argue that literary-critical practice and its recognition of the richness of sense and sensa (sensuous qualities, as discussed in Hester 1967: 76 and *passim*) in literature should inform cognitive literary theory.

Since this volume thematizes the development of metaphor theory after the cognitive turn, let me note that some applications of cognitive metaphor theory have entailed a number of shortcomings. First, applying cognitive metaphor theory is often not even understood as an interpretive move in the first place, which it evidently is (see Johansen 2005 for a critique of Lakoff & Turner 1989). Second, such applications often reduce much of the literary work to surface manifestations of cognitive metaphors, at times questionably interpreted as such. Third, cognitive readings do not seem to be able to deal with the complexity and specificity of literature or with how it is read (see Pettersson 2005). Fourth (as we shall see), cognitive literary criticism at times displays a disregard of other literary theory and criticism, which may lead to thwarted results or false claims of critical novelty.

The single most important recent contribution to metaphor theory is Raymond Gibbs's *The Cambridge Handbook of Metaphor and Thought* (2008a). In his introduction, Gibbs notes that "[t]here is now much greater attention to the ways that context shapes metaphor use and understanding" (2008b: 3) as well as "greater recognition of the complex ways that metaphor arises from the interaction of brains, bodies, languages, and culture" (4). This is not only true of many of the chapters in Gibbs's volume but also of those in the present collection. That is, metaphor is now studied in relation to other tropes and text-types, which is crucial to understanding the many shapes metaphor takes. The present chapter aims to contribute to that development by analysing how (lyrical) poetry may include narrative features and, in turn, how fiction, even novels, may be based on extended metaphor. The chosen test cases suggest that cognitive literary studies could well be a useful starting-point for literary analysis, if pursued by bottom-up literary-critical analysis and if it broadens its view of blending to include various tropes, text-types, and contextual features. Important foundations for this work were laid by Paul Werth (1999: 317–29), who showed how literary works can make use of sustained metaphor or mega-metaphor in ways that are cumulative. First, however, let us briefly consider a few other central theorists who have pointed the way towards broadening our understanding of the relation between metaphor and narrative.

2   RECENT THEORISTS ON METAPHOR AND NARRATIVE

Some of the most important recent advances stressing the affinity between metaphor and narrative come from three scholars: Mark Turner, Jørgen Dines Johansen and particularly Paul Ricoeur. In *The Literary Mind,* Turner discusses conceptual blending, including the kind of narrative blending he terms *parable*, defined as "[t]he projection of one story onto another" (1996: v, cf. 7). But he does not study the interrelation of analogy (such as metaphor) and narrative at any length, except, for instance, when noting that proverbs often consist of "a condensed, implicit story to be interpreted through projection" (ibid.: 5–6). These views are expanded in Fauconnier and Turner's *The Way We Think* (2002). In the context of presenting his semiotic-pragmatic model of literature, Johansen argues that "poems are truncated narratives", representing "the peak moment, as it were, of a narrative made autonomous—or rather relatively autonomous" (2002: 203). Thus, the reader supposedly contextualizes the poem by inscribing it "in a minimal narrative". When discussing how a literary text acquires an iconic dimension, Johansen defines the notion of allegorization as a "metaphoric reading", which entails going from the *sensus litteralis* to the *sensus plenior* and which attunes the text to "important aesthetic, moral, or epistemological issues" (2002: 334). Thus, both Turner and Johansen imply that narrative plays a key role in all kinds of literature, not just fiction.

Ricoeur is even more explicit about seeing a connection between metaphor and narrative. In fact, he stresses that his trilogy *Time and Narrative* and *The Rule of Metaphor* "form a pair" and "were conceived together" (1984: ix; see also Pettersson 2007: 36). According to Ricoeur, both metaphor and narrative make use of productive imagination, since they generate *predicative assimilation* (see ix–xi). Extending his theorizing on the basis of Aristotle, Ricoeur asks "whether the secret of metaphor, as a displacement of meaning at the level of words, does not rest in the elevation of meaning at the level of *muthos* [plot]" (2003: 46). On this view, he goes on to say that "metaphor would not only be a deviation in relation to ordinary usage, but also, by means of this deviation, the privileged instrument in that upward motion of meaning promoted by *mimêsis*" (46). Thus, in literature at least, metaphor can be viewed as a mechanism akin to the second, configuring sense of Ricoeur's mimesis, which "opens the kingdom of the *as if*" (64, original emphasis). It is important to note that Ricoeur's view of mimesis is referential in the broader sense of combining imitation and imagination—which is why, in his view, metaphorical discourse, like narrative, can both discover and invent new ideas (see 79–80, 283).

In short, Ricoeur, Turner and Johansen view metaphor from their respective theoretical background—the figural branch of hermeneutics, cognitive literary theory and semiotics—and point to various kinds of interrelation between metaphor and narrative. However, they provide only few examples of such affinity in literary-critical practice, although Turner (1996) offers a number of literary instances of cognitive blending.

Perhaps the most fruitful approach for analyzing extended metaphors in relation to narrative is Ricoeur's hermeneutic account, since it draws in part on the tradition that views metaphor not primarily as a figure of speech but as symbolic activity (see Schön 1993: 137).[1] Symbolic activity refers to an elaboration of one central meaning of the term *symbol*: "a word, phrase, image, or the like, having a complex of associated meanings" (definition 3 in *Webster's*, 1989). In this nearly forgotten tradition of symbol studies the main names are those of Ernst Cassirer and his foremost student Susanne K. Langer, who both focus on the proximity of metaphor and narrative (primarily in the form of myth). Cassirer emphasizes that "[l]anguage and myth are near of kin" and that the former is "by its very nature and essence, metaphorical" (1974: 109). Langer goes on to develop this view in relation to the work of art, which she considers "a single symbol" and, more precisely, "a metaphorical symbol" (1988: 40, 47). Although Ricoeur's oeuvre includes only passing references to this tradition (notably to Cassirer), I think Richard Kearney's note about "the common project" of Ricoeur's entire oeuvre is right to the point; Kearney characterizes this project as "the retrieval of thought in symbolic mediation and the extension of symbolic mediation into thought" (Kearney 2004: 15).[2] In other words, symbolic and cognitive aspects are interlinked throughout Ricoeur's works—and this will prove a useful starting-point for studying the relation between extended metaphor and narrative in literary-critical practice.

Viewing metaphor as a kind of conceptual representation as well as a figure of speech may make us more apt to recognize the dynamism inherent in the uses of metaphor, especially its extensions. Even before Ricoeur, Northrop Frye had regarded the symbol as an image (as against a sign, an archetype or a monad); famously, he goes on to claim that "all [literary-critical] commentary is allegorical interpretation, an attaching of ideas to the structure of poetic imagery" (1973: 82–84, 89). Frye's definition of allegory is general but still specific enough to be helpful: "A writer is being allegorical whenever it is clear that he is saying 'by this I also (*allos*) mean that.' If this seems to be done continuously, we may say, cautiously, that what he is writing 'is' an allegory" (ibid.: 90). This definition tallies with the etymology of *allegory* as the combination of Greek *allos* (other) and *agoreuein* ('to speak openly, as in the assembly or market') (see Fletcher 1964: 2, n1). What is more, Frye's view of allegory as constructed on a continuous or sustained use of symbol is also in line with Madeleine Kasten's definition of allegory in the *Routledge Encyclopedia of Narrative Theory*. She claims that allegory achieves its "effect [of multiple meaning] through the use of sustained [. . .] metaphor" (Kasten 2005: 10 s.v. allegory). Such definitions show an affinity with Werth's "double-vision" account of sustained metaphor, which could well be regarded as related to allegory (1999: 318).

Some promising work along similar lines has also been done more recently, for instance in the tracing of various kinds of affinities between metaphor and narrative. Gibbs and Matlock (2008) study how readers can simulate the bodily actions suggested by both metaphorical language and extended narratives in order to understand what they are reading. Semino and Steen (2008: 238–41) present recent research on the relation between metaphor and narrative and show what uses various genres have made of metaphor. Forceville (2008: 478) broadens the perspective by considering metaphor in relation to various multimodal representations and suggests that metaphor should be defined in relation to the mode in which it is represented. In this volume, Biebuyck and Martens, Kimmel, Sinding and Yacobi also discuss the relation between metaphor and narrative.

What I aim to do in this chapter is to present some instances of the affinity between extended metaphor and narrative. I want to do so by analysing three brief lyrical poems, where imagery usually is considered central, as well as one novel, the most extensive of narratives. By discussing some instances of the diverse relations between extended metaphor and narrative in William Blake's lyrical poetry and the contemporary British author Magnus Mills's fiction, I try to show what is distinctive in the way that metaphor and narrative combine in different kinds of literature. The two case studies seem to suggest that there is a wide variety of ways in which metaphor and narrative can be combined by fleshing out the symbolical dimension through various kinds of allegory.

3   FROM METAPHOR TO NARRATIVE AND FROM NARRATIVE TO ALLEGORY IN BLAKE'S *SONGS OF EXPERIENCE*

Brief lyrical poems, which are often simply metaphorical or descriptive, may make use of multiple text-types. Take William Blake's famous short poem "The Sick Rose" from *Songs of Experience*.

THE SICK ROSE

O Rose thou art sick.
The invisible worm,
That flies in the night
In the howling storm:

Has found out thy bed
Of crimson joy:
And his dark secret love
Does thy life destroy. (Blake 1977: 123–24)

The first sentence simply states that the rose is sick, by apostrophizing it. The second sentence (that is, the rest of the poem) gives a longer description of how this came to be. But, as the fact that the tense moves from the present to the perfect to the present tense suggests, the second sentence is a brief narrative of how a flying "worm" has found the rose and is killing it through his "love". From the subtitle of the collection in which it is included, *Songs of Innocence and of Experience*, we know that the collection aims to show "the Two Contrary States of the Human Soul" (Blake 1977: 104), and we can thus gather that the sick rose is a symbol for the plight—or one kind of plight—of man. By depicting the rose's bed as one of "crimson joy" and calling the worm's action "dark secret love", Blake strengthens the anthropomorphic dimension implied in the title and suggests that a symbolic reading is plausible. In terms of Seymour Chatman's useful view of text-types "at each other's service" (1990: 8–12), we can see that the second sentence of "The Sick Rose" is a brief narrative, which forms a more detailed presentation elaborating on the short descriptive first sentence. At the same time, the two sentences of the poem expand its title by depicting an actual rose that is languishing because of a worm, and its descriptive and narrative features supply a deeper symbolic sense that has a bearing on human life.

So far I have only explicitly considered the classic aspect of narrative in "The Sick Rose", the chronological sequencing of events as suggested by the perfective aspect of the present perfect tense. But further features of narrative can be observed in the poem. In his recent encompassing textbook of narrative studies, *Basic Elements of Narrative*, David Herman singles out four elements typical of narrative: (1) *situatedness*, (2) *event sequencing*, (3) *worldmaking/world disruption* and (4) *what it's like* (2009: 9 and *passim*). "The Sick Rose" fulfils all these requirements. Besides displaying event sequencing (2), the poem features generic situating (1) in terms of displaying communicative discourse in the form of a poem (in a book of poems, an anthology, or, as here, in a literary-critical chapter). "The Sick Rose" also represents an imaginative story world (in which roses can be sick and worms can be invisible, fly and love roses). In this world, previously healthy rose has fallen ill after being contaminated by a worm's love (3). And this sequence of events would not be of any particular interest without the symbolical anthropomorphizing import (that Herman terms *what it's like*): flowers are not usually "sick" (but are infested or wilted) and worms cannot feel love (4). In other words, much of what, according to Herman (2009), prototypically characterizes narrative can be applied to a typical lyrical poem. The vague and apparently symbolic metaphor of the ailing rose appears in a poem that has many features in common with narrative. In terms of Chatman's hierarchical view of text-types, what we have in "The Sick Rose" is an apostrophe followed by a narrative at the service of a description (of how the rose has been infested and is dying). This as such would not be enough to make it a classic poem, if the description did not seem to be at the service of some sort of symbolic level, which, in terms of text-types, could be termed an argument.

But what about the poem's symbolic features? Blake criticism indulges in sweeping statements such as: "The symbolism of the red rose for corporeal love and of the worm (or flesh) for the source of the sickness is plain. [. . .] The 'howling storm' in which the worm comes is a symbol of materialism" (Keynes in Blake 1982: 147). Apart from the questionable reading of the poem (the colour of the rose is not given, although the illustration suggests it), such specific interpretations are dubious. To be sure, reading the symbolic import of the poem as that of heterosexual love or corrupting materialism is a rather common strategy, but the hundreds of hits in Google Scholar show that there is a plethora of other readings. One of the most interesting recent ones is by Jon Mee (1998), who in a political interpretation claims that the rose referred to George Rose, a corrupt statesman and journalist. According to Mee, George Rose personified corruption in contaminating the English Rose, that is, England. Again, the double meaning of the rose in this reading is rather dubious: if this had been Blake's (however veiled) point, should not the worm in some sense be identified with George Rose (whereas, on the contrary, as a statesman, George Rose stands for the English Rose)? If the illustration is taken into account when interpreting the poem, the caterpillar in it in fact traditionally symbolizes destruction and Blake often equates it with the clergy (see Keynes in Blake 1982: 147)—another aspect that should be considered in a political reading of the poem. Apparently Blake meant to leave "The Sick Rose" open for multiple possible readings, not least by his use of a suggestive illustration (including a human figure lying on the stem of the rose). Even Blake's drafts of the poem (1977: 149) imply that no easy equation of the rose with woman and of the worm with man is possible, since Blake wavered about the gender of the worm.[3]

The evocative nature of Blake's use of metaphor can take quite different shapes in the other songs of experience. Most famously, "The Tyger" asserts nothing about the tiger so apostrophized (except that it is, clearly metaphorically, "burning bright"); the poem consists almost entirely of rhetorical questions that seem to be designed to stimulate readers' imagination. Despite its questioning mode, the poem obliquely describes the tiger and various ways of relating to it. There is progression to a climax in which the creator's view of the tiger is in focus, from the open question "Did he who made the Lamb make thee?" to a query likely to suggest an answer in the negative: "What immortal hand or eye / *Dare* frame thy *fearful* symmetry?" (Blake 1977: 125, 126, emphases added). The implication that the creator might be frightened by his creation conveys much of its considerable symbolical import to the tiger in Blake's poem. Even though, formally, there is no narrative as such, the poem shows narrative-like progression in the creation of the tiger (which reaches its climax in the questions quoted from the end of stanzas 5 and 6); stanzas 2 to 5 portray the creation of the tiger: from fire for its eyes to the sinews of his heart, from the blacksmith's tools and materials used in forming a live animal to the creation completed. Thus, the symbolical meaning of the tiger is extended by a series of questions implying the act of creating the tiger.

The existing drafts suggest how careful Blake was in weeding out pointed and exaggerated expressions, such as "The cruel fire of thine eye" and the suggestion that the creator would "laugh" [original emphasis] (rather than "smile") "his work to see" (1977: 146). In trying to come to grips with the imagery of "The Tyger", it is not far-fetched to read this poem in conjunction with *The Book of Los*, which Blake composed roughly contemporaneously with *Songs of Experience*. "The Tyger" seems to be connected to the imaginative cosmology that Blake was creating at the time.[4] In making use of both the drafts of the poem and other poems in dealing with the imagery of "The Tyger", such a critical effort evidently goes beyond the final version of the poem, but the help extratextual sources are able to offer in terms of interpretation might be worthwhile—as long as their status as extraneous hermeneutic tools is kept in mind. The juxtaposition between the fierce imagery of the poem and the most famous illustration of the tiger as a rather tame big cat could be viewed as central in interpreting the poem, but it should be noted that among Blake's versions of "The Tyger" there are also much fiercer tigers. Thus, in both "The Sick Rose" and "The Tyger" the symbolic meaning brought about in part by narrative or narrative-like progression seems evocative, if intentionally vague.

Having considered the use of extended metaphor and narrative in two Blake poems, we are now ready to discuss a recent cognitive reading of a third poem, "A Poison Tree", focussing on metaphor and allegory (Crisp 2008). Here is Blake's final version:[5]

A POISON TREE

I was angry with my friend:	[1]
I told my wrath, my wrath did end.	[2]
I was angry with my foe:	[3]
I told it not, my wrath did grow.	[4]
And I watered [sic] it in fears.	[5]
Night & morning with my tears:	[6]
And I sunned it with smiles.	[7]
And with soft deceitful wiles.	[8]
And it grew both day and night.	[9]
Till it bore an apple bright.	[10]
And my foe beheld it shine.	[11]
And he knew that it was mine.	[12]
And into my garden stole.	[13]
When the night had veild the pole;	[14]
In the morning glad I see;	[15]
My foe outstretchd beneath the tree.	[16] (1977: 129–30)

As against a rather persistent line in literary criticism of viewing allegory as a continued or extended metaphor (see Fletcher 1964: 3; Murrin 1969: 205; Johansen 2002: 334; Kasten 2005: 10), Peter Crisp in his analysis attempts a firm separation between metaphor and allegory: "Extended metaphors create a conscious, and rather strange, experience of metaphorical blended spaces, while allegories refer to and characterize fictional situations functioning as their metaphorical sources" (2008: 293). He argues that there must be a particular point at which this change from extended metaphor to allegory occurs (although it may differ from reader to reader), and locates it in line 10 between "Till it" and "bore an apple bright" (302). However, since what Crisp terms a fictional situation remains rather vague, it is difficult to draw such lines. I think Crisp is right in suggesting that "grow" in line 5 is still a conventional, though metaphorical, verb signalling increasing anger (300), and only "waterd" (the edition I use misspells it "watered") and "sunned" in the rest of the second stanza (not "verse" as Crisp has it throughout) signal an innovative metaphor by extending and developing the cognitive metaphor EMOTIONS ARE PLANTS. But I cannot see that there is a particular cut-off point at which this extended metaphor becomes an allegory, nor that in reading the poem's third stanza "the conscious awareness of a blended space" gives over "to conscious awareness of a *fictional situation*" (Crisp 2008: 303).

On the contrary, in my own view Angus Fletcher, one of the leading traditional allegory theorists, may be right in portraying the move from metaphor to allegory:

> Surprise [which for Fletcher is typical of metaphor[6]] diminishes as the analogy is extended, because we see more and more clearly the meaning of the hidden tenor. In most cases allegories proceed toward clarity, away from obscurity, even though they maintain a pose of enigma up to the very end. (Fletcher 1964: 81–82)

In the case of "A Poison Tree", however, there is little surprise, since, as Crisp notes, it starts with the conventional metaphor of anger growing (Crisp 2008: 299). I would say that the last two lines drive home the allegorical import by describing the speaker's reaction to seeing his enemy dead (lines 15–6). But throughout, the fictional situation is constructed in tandem with the extended metaphor, and even at the end of the final stanza there is no radical change from metaphor to allegory: the allegory builds on an extended metaphor based on EMOTIONS ARE PLANTS. What is more, it should be noted that the polysyndeton (And . . . And . . . And . . .) used from the second to the fourth stanzas is a traditional way of signalling event sequencing. Thus, the speaker's relation to his foe is developed as a narrative culminating in the foe's death: the metaphor of increasing wrath viewed as growing a poison tree is extended by narrative, which, by implying that the foe when stealing into the garden has devoured the poisoned apple, finally becomes an allegory.

As for the ending of the poem, it drives home the allegory but seems to ironize both the speaker and his foe: the former since he has acted rather immorally by poisoning his enemy, the latter since he was rather easily fooled. The final title does not guide the reader's interpretation, whereas the original title "Christian Forbearance", its original capitalising of "Glad" and the later omitted line "And I gave it [the apple] to my foe" in the second stanza (all of which Crisp fails to mention), suggest that by the allegory's irony, Blake, at least originally, primarily targeted the speaker and his allegedly Christian virtue.[7] What is rarely noted is that even though "A Poison Tree" may be read as an allegory, its form is primarily that of a parable, which Gerard Steen defines as an "anecdote that is meant to be understood as a [. . .] metaphor for a moral or spiritual aspect of life, in particular good behaviour" (2005: 418). In "A Poison Tree", Blake simply turns the parable on its head by suggesting that foregoing overt aggression is not Christian behaviour. What is more, as in the cases of "The Sick Rose" and "The Tyger", Blake took great care not to make his moral too explicit or simplistic. Painting the tree in his illustration as rather barren and leafless was apparently Blake's way of pointing to an ironic condemnation of the poem's speaker (1982: 49).

Crisp's (2008) reading has its merits but it shows some of the dangers of literary criticism based on cognitive metaphor theory, if the theoretical and critical basis is not as firm as in, say, Margaret Freeman (2005): a theoretical point is made on rather shaky grounds without using previous literary criticism, other theory or even an established edition of the source text.[8] Such a reading, although in other respects rather different from the now rather obsolete theory-driven readings of the 1980s and 1990s (see Pettersson 2008), runs into similar problems: straightforward reliance on one particular theory and disregard of existing literary criticism, textual criticism and literary theory (other than the one espoused) may lead to rather untenable results. As I have noted, a cognitive reading of Blake's poem can stand on firmer ground if the extant drafts are compared to the established final version; if allegory theory is taken into account; if the allegorical, narrative, parable-like and ironic features are recognized in the poem, which shows no clear-cut move from extended metaphor to allegory; in short, if literary-critical and text-critical practice is more firmly wedded to both cognitive metaphor theory and cognitive narratology. It is precisely the fact that "A Poison Tree" by its use of various literary techniques retains its allegorical "pose of enigma" that makes it so intriguing.

4 EXTENDED METAPHORS IN NOVELS: MAGNUS MILLS'S *ALLEGORICAL FABLES*

Before I move on to discuss Magnus Mills's fiction, let me note the rather self-evident fact that summarizing a book by its title—be it fiction, poetry or non-fiction—is a well-established convention. Nils Enkvist discusses the use of titles in literary works as "the semantic equivalent of priming the pump: it is one of the most economical devices of starting the contextualization and scenario-building" (1994: 55).[9] However, in literature this is most likely done in more multifarious ways than elsewhere. Titles can metaphorically epitomize the entire narrative in all sorts of ways. *The Odyssey* stands for the adventurous and fantastic journey by the protagonist, and by allusion to it Joyce's *Ulysses* invites readers to interpret a rather realistic portrayal of some Dubliners metaphorically in terms of that epic. An intertextual allusion in the title can also suggest how to read a novel, as in Jay McInerney's *Bright Lights, Big City*, which, by evoking the title of Jimmy Reed's blues song that thematizes the dangers of the city, implies that the portrayal of cocaine-addled yuppies in New York City should be understood as having a moral undercurrent. But there are rather different kinds of symbolic novel titles. A title may refer to the name of the protagonist (Flaubert's *Madame Bovary*), the theme (Chopin's *The Awakening*), or it may form an ekphrastic pointer to the main character and hint at how she is depicted (James's *Portrait of a Lady*). In less realistic literature, it may be more usual to have ironic titles (Beckett's *Happy Days*) and titles achieving greater symbolic breadth by remaining enigmatic (Kafka's *The*

Castle). It is well-known that some novels—especially modern and post-modern ones—summarize the plot in the first paragraph, so that the rest of the novel forms an elaboration of it.[10] In *The Castle*, the symbolic plight of the protagonist is similarly presented in the first lines, as there is not "even a glimmer of light to show that the castle was there" and K. stands "for a long time gazing into the illusory emptiness above him" (Kafka 2005: 9). The subsequent narrative can be read as an extended description of this plight, whose symbolic dimension grows as K.'s attempts at entering the castle are thwarted.

Magnus Mills is one of the most prominent contemporary British authors of allegorical fables, if *fable* is understood in the general sense of "a brief narrative told in order to provide moral instruction" (Tate 2005: 157). In some of his novels, especially *The Restraint of Beasts* (1998), *All Quiet on the Orient Express* (1999) and *The Scheme for Full Employment* (2003), the society depicted is recognizably British, even though in *The Restraint of Beasts* and *The Scheme for Full Employment* there are speculative features that suggest these may be future versions of Britain. In *Three to See the King* (2001) and *Explorers of the New Century* (2005), desolate areas are inhabited and explored, respectively, by a handful of people. In all five novels, except *Explorers of the New Century*, an unnamed first-person male narrator tries to deal with characters whose motivations he struggles to understand; like the narrator, these characters are rather tight-lipped, and their simple words and actions seldom betray the strange and at times sinister intentions they harbour. The phrases in the titles of the novels serve as central symbols for the action by which the allegorical fables are constructed.[11] How the fables form allegories can perhaps best be understood from Deborah L. Madsen's view of twentieth-century forms of allegory:

> Modern allegories, such as Kafka's, treat interpretation as valid only in terms of subjective individual perception. Postmodern allegories, however, question the authenticity of this personal identity in relation to the invisible cultural systems of value which may be projected through the individual consciousness and into the world. (Madsen 1996: 144)

Those of Mills's novels which are set in Britain may seem to focus on the narrator-protagonists and their experiences, but these narrators are in fact lost in a cultural system that they should be familiar with. The vagueness of the allegory of Mills's latter-day fables could thus be viewed as a postmodern feature. In fact, in an early short story, "Only When the Sun Shines Brightly", Mills (2004a) explicitly rewrites Aesop's well-known fable about the wind and the sun that compete as to which of them can make a man take off his coat (with the sun finally prevailing). In this story, the first-person narrator-protagonist is disturbed by a plastic sheet fastening itself onto a neighbouring building, and even though the wind blows like a fury, only when three men tug at it does it finally come off. Mills's point seems to be that age-old morals—such as those of Aesop—do not hold anymore. In order to drive home his point of the lack of a clear-cut moral to his story, Mills retells Aesop's original story of the wind and the sun and leaves his Kafkaesque protagonist just as disturbed by the silence after the sheet has been removed as he was by the noise it made before (2004a: 34).

In *The Restraint of Beasts*, the full import of the metaphor of the title—that which turns the novel into an allegory—is gradually revealed. First it is noted that fences are being built for "the restraint of beasts" (the non-metaphorical sense of herding cattle) (Mills 1999: 10), but on the following pages the fencers Tam and Richie are compared to "wild men, head-bangers with long Viking hair", who by "a prolonged stare" from their boss are rendered "meek and mild" (11–12). In this way, men are early on compared to beasts that are to be restrained (in the metaphorical sense). The beastly quality of men emerges in various ways during the course of the novel, through arguments, such as those between the Scots and the English (27, 51, 68, 80), fights between men (26–27, 82), between men and women (105), between father and son (161–62, 175, 184), and the clash between personal identity and company identity (employees complain when the company uniform is to be worn day and night) (172). These disputes finally lead the contracting company to segregate genders (202), not pay wages to employees (208) and incarcerate them (214). Similarly, the metaphorical sense is strengthened towards the end of the novel as the fencers' employer calls the electric fence "[t]he final solution to the problem of the restraint of beasts" (159) and makes the connection between man and beast explicit by "forever talking about 'rounding us up' and 'shipping us off' as though we were being transported to some sort of penal colony or corrective camp" (183).

In this way, Mills gradually extends the metaphor of MAN IS A BEAST, in two senses: (1) man is a beast that needs to be restrained for what he does to other men, and (2) in restraining and incarcerating other men, man acts in beastly ways. For about three fourths of the novel, the former sense is prevalent. Men must indeed be restrained because of their violent disposition and carelessness (Tam, Richie and the narrator each accidentally kill a man). The institutionalized violence of (2) is in focus at the end of the novel as the fencers' contractor makes them build the electric fence of their own jail—rather pen, since they will most likely end up as meat for the contractor's factory. At the end of the novel, Mills has established both senses (1) and (2) as well as their allegorical moral that man must be restrained and that such restraint (especially when enforced by incarceration) can become institutionalized violence. Thus, the allegorical import of the novel proceeds in Fletcher's sense towards a clear allegorical meaning, which still retains "the pose of enigma" (1964: 82). Here, the word *pose* is apposite, since Mills seems to be suggesting that there is some truth in both (1) and (2): men can act beastly, but the restraint of such action can

become even more beastly. This is signalled by the phrase "the final solution" (ibid.: 159).

For Mills, then, Ricoeur's view of myth (equated with plot) as "subordi-
nated to the symbol" is apt (Ricoeur 2004: 28). The titles of his novels are
phrases that are allegorized by "metaphoric reading", as Johansen has it (2002:
334). In fact, *The Scheme for Full Employment, Three to See the King* and
Explorers of the New Century could be read as a trilogy representing Mills's
allegorical visions of, in turn, politics, religion and (social) philosophy. Mills
may eschew simplistic moral teachings, such as those in Aesop's fables, but
despite his black humour plots and strange, even deranged protagonists, he
does make serious moral points. For instance, *The Scheme for Full Employment* shows that, despite the lack of viability in the instituted full employment
scheme, the hierarchical strife within it, and the envy it may cause, humans
have a deep-seated need to be of use and to belong to social groups.

Mills's novels demonstrate how long narratives can have symbolic titles
as starting-points and then go on to develop them into extended metaphors
by way of plot as well as how the morals add mimetic dimensions to the
allegories. In Ricoeur's terms, metaphor thus extended is indeed "the privileged instrument in that upward motion of meaning promoted by *mimêsis*"
(2003: 46). By means of their morals, Mills's novels, although at times
displaying features of alternative history or science fiction in imaginative
worlds discontinuous with the one readers know, clearly comment on that
world by the moral views they advocate. These views are corroborated by
the characters' psychology and the colloquial dialogue he uses. That is,
however strange the plot, settings or characters in these novels, the way in
which the characters react and speak makes them recognizable, even possible to empathize with. In this manner, Mills's allegorical fables go beyond
the fictional worlds portrayed and question the values in contemporary
British society and beyond—perhaps even more so than does much realist
fiction (see Pettersson 2007).

5   CONCLUSIONS AND IMPLICATIONS
FOR COGNITIVE LITERARY STUDIES

Before considering the implications of such literary-critical readings for
cognitive literary studies, I would like to draw some conclusions as concerns the interpretation of Blake's poetry and Mills's fiction.

"The Sick Rose" exemplifies how metaphor and narrative, description
and argument, even in a brief poem can work together and be at each
other's service. "The Tyger" illustrates how questions, even if they do not
seem to assert anything, may intimate a highly symbolic description of their
object of reference. Such descriptions may display a kind of metaphorical
and narrative-like progression that serves to extend the symbolic import.
The relationship between the rose and the worm and the depiction of the
tiger are so evocative because they are not rendered by straightforward

portrayal but are given vague allegorical meanings. In "A Poison Tree", the inhumanity of the speaker is evident (his foe has apparently not done anything to deserve being poisoned) and Christian hypocrisy is implied—at least for readers familiar with the drafts of the poem or with Blake's other poems which ironically expose Christianity, from "The Marriage of Heaven and Hell" to "The Everlasting Gospel". Mills's fiction, on the other hand, develops the metaphors suggested by the symbolical phrases of their titles into narratives that turn into allegories displaying an interpretive openness similar to that found in Blake. Both authors tend to use irony, even multiple irony, which makes their moral hard to pinpoint. Both seem adamant in not spelling out their moral.

In sum, the two case studies have proven that both extended metaphor and narrative must be taken into account when interpreting fiction as well as poetry. Blake's poems and Mills's novels suggest that titles can be symbolic and develop their central metaphor by means of narrative into various kinds of allegory. Of course, one can discuss extended metaphor without discussing narrative and the other way round, but total neglect of either is bound to lead to a thwarted view of the poem or novel studied. I would suggest that this is also true of other tropes and text-types that are centrally employed in literary texts. Thus, the contextual study of metaphor that Gibbs (2008b: 3) detects in contemporary cognitive studies should continue to be pursued. What my test cases indicate is that such work should be interpretively and text-critically attuned and that it should ask questions such as: What edition is being used? What is the work's manuscript and/ or editing history? What light can other works by the author throw on the one studied? What theory and methodology are the most useful ones in interpreting the work? How does the literary form and genre influence the reading of the theme and motifs of the work? What tropes and text-types are used, and how are they combined?

Needless to say, such questions are basic ones in critical and text-critical practice, even though some of them have at times been neglected. But, as I see it, metaphor studies after the cognitive revolution have not always bothered to do the critical legwork that in serious literary studies is part and parcel of accounting for the fusion of sense and sensa in literature. In other words, the practice of literary criticism should write back to cognitive metaphor theory, since literary theory should not be applied in a top-down manner that disregards how crucial formal and thematic features are combined in texts (see also Pettersson 2008).

Of course, this is no revolutionary insight for literary studies, although some quarters have recently tended to forget it. In an idealistic presentation of the Russian formalist method, Boris Eichenbaum makes the point quite succinctly:

> We [Russian formalists] speak and may speak only about theoretical principles suggested to us not by this or that ready-made methodology, but by the examination of specific material in its specific context. [. . .]

> We posit specific principles and adhere to them insofar as the material
> justifies them. If the material demands their refinement or change, we
> change or refine them. (Eichenbaum 1965: 102, 103)

What the above readings suggest is precisely that no simple or ready-made
theoretical frameworks suffice and that each literary work must be understood in relation to its contexts. As James Phelan recently put it when arguing
for the study of hybrid forms of fiction, "there is no theoretical or practical
reason why, in any specific text, the relationships among events, character,
attitude/thought/belief, change, and audience activity need to stay within the
boundaries of narrativity, lyricality, and portraiture" (2007: 23–24). If this is
so, where does that leave cognitive literary theory, which in much of its efforts
has centred on either narrative or on cognitive tropes and their blends?

Finally, let us see in what ways extended metaphor and narrative can
profitably be combined in theory. Above I mentioned that the configurating
sense of Ricoeur's mimesis "opens the kingdom of the *as if*" and is thus
closely related to metaphor. In fact, in his treatise on metaphor, Ricoeur
also states: "'Seeing X as Y' encompasses 'X is not Y'; seeing time as a
beggar is, precisely, to know also that time is not a beggar. The borders of
meaning are transgressed but not abolished" (2003: 253). Thus, by drawing on Wittgenstein's notion of seeing-as by way of Marcus Hester's (1967)
literary application of it, Ricoeur is able to come to a cognitively-informed
view of metaphor that need not do away with traditional metaphor theory.
In fact, Hester stresses that "metaphor is a *fusion* of sense and sensa" and
that in poetic metaphor "thought and sensation are inseparable because
the object of reading is a *sensuous object interpreted*" (1967: 188, original
emphases). In terms of cognitive literary theory, this means that one ignores
essential thematic and formal qualities if one reduces literary works to
cognitive patterns or techniques.

As regards extended metaphor and narrative, what cognitive literary studies could go on to study is: What features are included and
excluded in the use of metaphor? How is metaphor extended or changed
when combined with other tropes and text-types? What is included and
excluded by particular uses of narration and focalisation? In what ways
are metaphor and narrative combined and to what effect? In what ways
can metaphors be extended into allegories? This chapter indicates that
extended metaphor and narrative are so intertwined that readers seldom
focus on their combination. Furthermore, elsewhere I have suggested
that the juxtaposition in cognitive studies and cognitive literary studies
between figural and narrative modes should be rejected and that various
combinations of tropes and text-types should receive more analysis (see
Pettersson 2005).

As has so often been the case in literary studies in the last few decades,
one of the problems with cognitive literary studies could be argued to consist in its having to some extent been conducted in top-down ways. The
above literary-critical exercise, like the volume *Cognition and Literary*

Interpretation in Practice (Veivo, Pettersson & Polvinen 2005), points to the fact that cognitive literary theory—like all literary theory—, if it is to be of use in literary-critical practice, must have a firm grounding in the practice it is supposed to theorize.

NOTES

1. At roughly the same time, Kenneth Burke employed the term *symbolic action* even more broadly for "poetry, or any verbal act" (1961: 8).
2. It is worth noting that Ricoeur (1984: 57) develops his term *symbolic mediation* expressly on the basis of Cassirer's *Philosophy of Symbolic Forms*.
3. May these few notes on "The Sick Rose" suffice, since my point here is merely to show the affinity between metaphor, description and narrative in the text. Like all poems in *Songs of Innocence and of Experience*, its evocative symbolical character gains additional depth by forming ironies, both within itself and with other songs of innocence and experience.
4. For a similar act of creation, see chapter 4 of *The Book of Los* (Blake 1977: 271–72), and for a suggestive reading of "The Tyger" in the light of possible sources, see Ackroyd (1996: 147–49).
5. Unfortunately, there is no space here for a wholesale interpretation of "A Poison Tree" (or indeed "The Sick Rose" and "The Tyger"), which of course should discuss Blake's illustration in some detail. For a more thorough cognitive reading of "A Poison Tree", see Herman (2010).
6. Cf. Ricoeur's view that the metaphorical utterance is based on "predicative impertinence" that produces "a shock between semantic fields" (2008: 168).
7. For an informed discussion of Blake's double-edged view of allegory, see Frye (1949: 9–11).
8. The version edited by Keynes, a reputed Blake scholar also quoted in this chapter, includes a number of questionable minor editorial changes (see Blake 1982).
9. Enkvist also includes an illuminating analysis of taxonomies of literary titles on the basis of work done by Harry Levin and Laurence Lerner (Enkvist 1994: 55–56).
10. A famous instance is the opening of Vladimir Nabokov's novel *Laughter in the Dark*. Elsewhere, I have termed this *metafictional determinism* (see Pettersson 1994: 138–42).
11. The most complex title is *All Quiet on the Orient Express* in that it is a portmanteau phrase referring to the narrator's (ultimately defeated) dream of taking the Orient Express to Turkey (see Mills 2004b: 3), to the antagonistic social interaction in the village in which he is an outsider by alluding to Erich Maria Remarque's famous World War I novel *All Quiet on the Western Front* (originally *Im Westen nichts Neues*) and possibly to Agatha Christie's novel *Murder on the Orient Express*.

WORKS CITED

Ackroyd, Peter (1996) *Blake* [1995]. London: Minerva.

Blake, William (1977) *The Complete Poems*. Ed. Alicia Ostriker. London et al.: Penguin.

———. (1982) *Songs of Innocence and of Experience* [1967]. Introduction and commentary by Sir Geoffrey Keynes. Oxford: Oxford University Press.

Burke, Kenneth (1961) *The Philosophy of Literary Form: Studies in Symbolic Action* [1941]. New York: Vintage.

Cassirer, Ernst (1974) *An Essay on Man: An Introduction to a Philosophy of Human Culture* [1944]. New Haven and London: Yale University Press.

Chatman, Seymour (1990) *Coming to Terms: The Rhetoric of Narrative in Fiction and Film*. Ithaca and London: Cornell University Press.

Crisp, Peter (2008) "Between Extended Metaphor and Allegory: Is Blending Enough?" *Language and Literature* 17.4: 291–308.

Eichenbaum, Boris (1965) "The Theory of the 'Formal Method'". *Russian Formalist Criticism: Four Essays*. Eds. Lee T. Lemon and Marion J. Reis. Lincoln and London: University of Nebraska Press. 99–139. (Original in Ukrainian in 1926)

Enkvist, Nils Erik (1994) "Context". *Literature and the New Interdisciplinarity*. Eds. Roger D. Sell and Peter Verdonk. Amsterdam and Atlanta: Rodopi. 45–60.

Fauconnier, Gilles, and Mark Turner (2002) *The Way We Think: Conceptual Blending and the Mind's Hidden Complexities*. New York: Basic Books.

Fletcher, Angus (1964) *Allegory: The Theory of a Symbolic Mode*. Ithaca: Cornell University Press.

Forceville, Charles (2008) "Metaphor in Pictures and Multimodal Representations". *The Cambridge Handbook of Metaphor and Thought*. Ed. Raymond Gibbs. Cambridge et al.: Cambridge University Press. 462–82.

Freeman, Margaret H. (2005) "Poetry as Power: The Dynamics of Cognitive Poetics as a Scientific and Literary Paradigm". *Cognition and Literary Interpretation in Practice*. Eds. Harri Veivo et al. Helsinki: Helsinki University Press. 31–57.

Frye, Northrop (1949) *Fearful Symmetry: A Study of William Blake* [1947]. Princeton: Princeton University Press.

———. (1973) *Anatomy of Criticism: Four Essays* [1957]. Princeton: Princeton University Press.

Gibbs, Raymond W., Jr. (2008a) Ed. *The Cambridge Handbook of Metaphor and Thought*. Cambridge et al.: Cambridge University Press.

———. (2008b). "Metaphor and Thought: The State of the Art". *The Cambridge Handbook of Metaphor and Thought*. Ed. Raymond Gibbs. Cambridge et al.: Cambridge University Press. 3–13.

Gibbs, Raymond W., Jr., and Teenie Matlock (2008) "Metaphor, Imagination, and Simulation: Psycholinguistic Evidence". *The Cambridge Handbook of Metaphor and Thought*. Ed. Raymond Gibbs. Cambridge et al.: Cambridge University Press. 161–76.

Herman, David. (2009) *Basic Elements of Narrative*. Malden, MA, et al.: Wiley-Blackwell.

———. (2010) "Directions in Cognitive Narratology: Triangulating Stories, Media, and the Mind". *Postclassical Narratology: Approaches and Analyses*. Eds. Jan Alber and Monika Fludernik. Columbus: Ohio State University Press. 137–62.

Hester, Marcus B. (1967) *The Meaning of Poetic Metaphor: An Analysis in the Light of Wittgenstein's Claim That Meaning Is Use*. The Hague and Paris: Mouton.

Johansen, Jørgen Dines (2002) *Literary Discourse: A Semiotic-Pragmatic Approach to Literature*. Toronto: University of Toronto Press.

———. (2005) "Theory and/vs. Interpretation in Literary Studies". *Cognition and Literary Interpretation in Practice*. Eds. Harri Veivo et al. Helsinki: Helsinki University Press. 241–66.

Kafka, Franz (2005) *The Castle* [1930]. Transl. Willa and Edwin Muir; additional material transl. Eithne Wilkins and Ernst Kaiser. London: Vintage.

Kasten, Madeleine (2005) "Allegory". *Routledge Encyclopedia of Narrative Theory*. Eds. David Herman, Manfred Jahn and Marie-Laure Ryan. London and New York: Routledge. 10–12.

Kearney, Richard F. (2004) *On Paul Ricoeur: The Owl of Minerva*. Aldershot and Burlington, VT: Ashgate.

Lakoff, George, and Mark Turner (1989) *More than Cool Reason: A Field Guide to Poetic Metaphor*. Chicago and London: University of Chicago Press.

Langer, Susanne K. (1988) *Mind: An Essay on Human Feeling*. Abridged Edition. Baltimore and London: Johns Hopkins University Press.

Madsen, Deborah L. (1996) *Allegory in America: From Puritanism to Postmodernism*. New York: St. Martin's Press.

Mee, Jon (1998) "The 'Insidious Poison of Secret Influence': A New Historical Context for Blake's 'The Sick Rose'". *Eighteenth Century Life* 22.1: 111–22.

Mills, Magnus (1999) *The Restraint of Beasts* [1998]. London: Flamingo.

———. (2002) *Three to See the King* [2001]. London: Flamingo.

———. (2004a) "Only When the Sun Shines Brightly". *Only When the Sun Shines Brightly* [1999]. Tadworth, Surrey: Acorn. 25–38.

———. (2004b) *All Quiet on the Orient Express* [1999]. London: Harper Perennial.

———. (2004c) *The Scheme for Full Employment* [2003]. London: Harper Perennial.

———. (2006) *Explorers of the New Century* [2005]. London: Bloomsbury.

Murrin, Michael (1969) *The Veil of Allegory: Some Notes toward a Theory of Allegorical Rhetoric in the English Renaissance*. Chicago and London: University of Chicago Press.

Peer, Willie van, and Seymour Chatman (2001) Eds. *New Perspectives on Narrative Perspective*. Albany: State University of New York Press.

Pettersson, Bo (1994) *The World According to Kurt Vonnegut: Moral Paradox and Narrative Form*. Turku, Finland: Åbo Akademi University Press.

———. (2001) "On LIFE IS A JOURNEY as a Link between Analogy and Narrative". *Language, Learning, Literature: Studies Presented to Håkan Ringbom*. Eds. Martin Gill et al. English Department Publications 4. Turku, Finland: Åbo Akademi University. 199–214.

———. (2005) "Afterword. Cognitive Literary Studies: Where to Go from Here". *Cognition and Literary Interpretation in Practice*. Eds. Harri Veivo et al. Helsinki: Helsinki University Press. 307–22.

———. (2007) "The Real in the Unreal: Mimesis and Postmodern American Fiction". *The European English Messenger* 16.1: 33–39.

———. (2008) "Procrustean Beds and Strange Bedfellows: On Literary Value as Assigned by Literary Theories". *Journal of Literary Theory* 2.1: 19–33.

Phelan, James (2007) *Experiencing Fiction: Judgments, Progressions, and the Rhetorical Theory of Narrative*. Columbus: Ohio State University Press.

Ricoeur, Paul (1984) *Time and Narrative*, Vol. 1 [1983]. Transl. Kathleen McLaughlin and David Pellauer. Chicago and London: University of Chicago Press.

——— (2003) *The Rule of Metaphor: The Creation of Meaning in Language* [1977]. Transl. Robert Czerny with Kathleen McLaughlin and John Costello. London and New York: Routledge. (Rev. ed. of the French original from 1975.)

———. (2004) "Structure and Hermeneutics". *The Conflict of Interpretations: Essays in Hermeneutics* [1974]. Ed. Don Ihde. London and New York: Continuum. 27–60.

———. (2008) "Imagination in Discourse and Action". *From Text to Action: Essays in Hermeneutics, II* [1991]. London and New York: Continuum. 164–83.

Schön, Donald A. (1993) "Generative Metaphor: A Perspective on Problem-Setting in Social Policy". *Metaphor and Thought*. Ed. Andrew Ortony. Second Edition. Cambridge et al.: Cambridge University Press. 137–63.

Semino, Elena, and Gerard Steen (2008) "Metaphor in Literature". *The Cambridge Handbook of Metaphor and Thought*. Ed. Raymond Gibbs. Cambridge et al.: Cambridge University Press. 232–46.

Steen, Gerard (2005) "Parable". *Routledge Encyclopedia of Narrative Theory.* Eds. David Herman, Manfred Jahn and Marie-Laure Ryan. London and New York: Routledge. 418–19.

Tate, Aaron (2005) "Fable". *Routledge Encyclopedia of Narrative Theory.* Eds. David Herman, Manfred Jahn and Marie-Laure Ryan. London and New York: Routledge. 157.

Turner, Mark (1996) *The Literary Mind.* New York: Oxford University Press.

Veivo, Harri, Bo Pettersson and Merja Polvinen (2005) Eds. *Cognition and Literary Interpretation in Practice.* Helsinki: Helsinki University Press.

Webster's Encyclopedic Unabridged Dictionary of the English Language (1989). New York: Portland House.

Werth, Paul (1999) *Text Worlds: Representing Conceptual Space in Discourse.* Harlow, Essex: Longman.

6   Metaphors in Context
The Communicative Structure of Figurative Language[1]

Tamar Yacobi

1   WHY A FIGURE'S WHOLE DISCOURSE CONTEXT MATTERS

In both life and fiction, metaphors are produced and understood in context. Such contextualizing reaches beyond "the surrounding verbal text" (Forceville 1995: 697). This verbal context, or co-text, almost goes without saying, though sometimes forgotten or minimized in examples cited by theorists. Generally, it is both available and extendible in concentric circles (from the sentence that frames a metaphor through the utterance to the discourse whole). However, the non-verbal contextual parameters involved—or their very involvement—are anything but manifest, and so far less known. They still need to be mentioned, and often even to be redefined, uncovered, established, sorted out: adequately theorized, in short. Thus, Forceville suggests that context

> may also consist of the perceptual environment in which the metaphor is used, of the (sub)cultural context, and, in the case of persuasive or didactic communication, of the intentions that the utterer of the metaphor has. In the broadest sense, these intentions always are the triggering of some sort of effect in the addressee's cognitive environment. (ibid.)

Three frameworks arise here, whose implications are to some extent nicely illustrated by Forceville, yet not pursued to their operational end. For example, analysing a metaphor that originated in a demonstration of pit bull owners and offended its addressees—PIT BULLS ARE JEWS—he invokes "[t]he whole situation (that is, context)" (Forceville 1995: 703). This largely resides in the juxtaposition of *two* legal contexts: a new law directed against pit bulls and the infamous past legislation concerning Jews under the Nazi regime. Various other dimensions also play a role: some are duly foregrounded by Forceville, especially the problem of tenor/vehicle (in)appropriateness, others are less articulated, if not absent altogether.

Above all, note how Forceville's analysis of the cited controversial metaphor implies the centrality of the communicating subjects. Thus, the emotional involvement of the metaphor-makers (pit bull owners) in the tenor collides with a comparable involvement in the vehicle "Jew" on the part of the addressees (some of whom may be Nazi victims, or their descendants) and gave rise to their objections. So the judgment that an incongruity between tenor and vehicle subsists depends on which party you belong to; in fact, the polarization in emotional load crucially arises from the viewpoints and contexts involved. Moreover, as will emerge throughout, the communicators—metaphor producers and receivers—are closely linked with all other contextual aspects, from the immediate, textual-linguistic to the broadest historical and cultural frames.[2] Unlike many scholars, Forceville does bring the non-verbal contexts to the fore. Yet he limits their range. Thus his reference to the communicators focuses only on the "intentions" of an "utterer" to "trigger [. . .] [an] effect in the addressee's cognitive environment", and only with regard to "the case of persuasive or didactic communication" (Forceville 1995: 697). As we shall see throughout, when communicated, all figures, regardless of discourse type, imply a communicator's intention to affect an addressee. In this sense, they all necessarily work for a rhetorical ("persuasive or didactic") purpose as well. The special case is in fact the rule.

This orientation towards an addressee has far-reaching consequences for both the making and the reading of figures, in life and fiction alike. Figures of speech never come out of the blue, nor are they simply part of a text. Some speaking/thinking subject is responsible for choosing, shaping and contextualizing the figure, which in the speaker's case includes transmission (with an eye) to a receiver, who will need to 'figure it out'. The anchorage of figuration in the discourse act (or utterance) as a whole only assumes greater importance the more we appreciate the range of variables, hence composites, open to it and the difference their play makes to the figure's production, transfer, understanding and effect. Here are some meaningful typological lines of convergence and divergence to consider.

To begin with, figure-making entails at least one subject, and usually involves more than one. When subjects create figures in the privacy of the mind, they need not worry whether or how their intention is understood. Once they communicate the figure to an addressee, another subjectivity enters the scene and the success of the verbal transaction is put at risk. Among other variable factors, the personality, ideology, linguistic competence and intertextual horizon of the respective participants determine how a figure is created by one discourser, received by another, or, if either repeats it, even (mis)understood by a third, who possibly (mis)uses it in turn, and so forth. Such variables can evidently produce a variety of differences, all along the line of transmission, regarding the figure's meaning and impact. A real-life case in point arose when a student of mine referred in a working paper to "analogies like spider webs", and added, "please forgive the simile". Why the apology? Receiving her message shortly after the Israeli-Lebanese war of 2006, I immediately understood the intertextual and communicative background for her discomfort. The figure became imprinted on our national memory when Hassan Nasralla, the leader of Hezbolla, announced that the state of Israel was weaker than a spider web. The figure, as first voiced by Nasralla, expressed both his ideology and his rhetoric.[3] My student's need for apology reflected the effectiveness of the figurative insult. As both of us were originally cast in the role of the metaphor's target and oblique addressee, she felt obliged to beg indulgence for reapplying its vehicle to a totally unrelated, poetic tenor and within a totally different context.

If a figure's communicative context bears on its meaning and effect in the real world, how much more so in fiction?[4] Whether in poetry or prose, both the figure of speech and its surrounding fictional context gain significance and complexity from their interaction. This is due, I believe, to the complex structure of communication typical of fiction. Fictional discourse as such represents a world, while its figures of speech re-present the quoted discourse (or self-discourse) of fictive subjects, who may themselves echo others. The discourse, as well as the plot, will then form a chain. This built-in, possibly enchained re-presentation, set within the fictionalizer's frame, maximizes the resources and practices of figuration. Let me, therefore, proceed to explain and subdivide this exemplary range of complexity.

2 COMMUNICATION AND QUOTATION IN FICTION: AN OUTLINE[5]

Fictional communication is always hierarchical and mediated. Between the two extra-fictional parties—the implied author and reader—there is at least one fictional speaker who transmits the discourse to his/her addressee, and so mediates the author's implicit discourse to us readers. Consider Robert Browning vis-à-vis his monologist, the Renaissance painter Andrea del Sarto. Andrea wishes to appease his wife Lucrezia, who is impatient to meet her current lover. So he idealizes her appearance, and his praise for her "serpentining beauty, rounds on rounds!" (Browning 1951: 344; line 26) culminates in another, lunar metaphor:

> My face, my moon, my everybody's moon,
> Which everybody looks on and calls his,
> And, I suppose, is looked on by in turn,
> While she looks—no one's. (lines 29–32)

The figures thus simultaneously signify two viewpoints on two parallel communicative levels. Whereas Andrea is mainly concerned with the complimentary side of his ophidian and lunar metaphors, the author ironically implies (in English) the serpent in the one and inconstancy in the other.

As this simple example shows, the discourse of the fictional mediator is quoted, hence contextualized and controlled, possibly countered, within the silent authorial frame. Yet the author's quotee may in turn play the quoter, vis-à-vis the dramatis personae. This is often the case, especially in narrative fiction. The inset primary teller then quotes the discourse of other subjects in their capacity as speakers and thinkers, uttering figures while engaged in dialogue and monologue. Thus, in Conrad's *Heart of Darkness*, the overall anonymous narrator first describes, and thus frames, the situation in which Marlow tells his adventure to a circle of listeners; and then he quotes Marlow's figure-laden tale. Marlow, in his turn, quotes the voices not only of his past fellow agents but also of his own experiencing self: both as a speaker in various dialogue scenes and as a thinking subject whose confused perception is translated into figures of speech. The fictive text accordingly becomes a hierarchical quote-within-quote discourse, with metaphors possibly enunciated by any of the speaking/thinking agents along the chain of transmission.

But note the radical difference—in what Meir Sternberg terms (un)self-consciousness—between a speaking and a thinking agent.[6] The concept of *self-consciousness* opposes a discourser who communicates with others (e.g. a narrator, a dialogist) to one who is unself-conscious or self-communing: for example, a perceiver (or Jamesian "reflector") who confronts the world in his/her mind, without transmitting his/her secret life to any outsider. This public/private, communicative/secret opposition bears on figurative discourse, as on everything else, and across narration levels—from the authorial frame, all the way down to the last inset and quote. For a figure of speech that arises in communication is rhetorically oriented to, say, the knowledge, interests, tradition, ideology and taste of the addressee(s) involved, as, for example, is Andrea's "my moon, everybody's moon" above. On the other hand, when a self-communing thinker enunciates a figure of speech within the privacy of the mind, this figuration, unmindful of any outsider, is above all true to the subject's hidden character, mood, experience, viewpoint: true *because* hidden, inaccessible to others, or so the self-communer believes (in giving free rein to the cruel, biased, hyperbolic metaphors of his heart, for example). In real life, indeed, we cannot gain access to a privately created metaphor; yet fiction can always grant us this privilege, by way of omniscient inside-view, authoritatively quoting from within.

Further, granting a communicator this privilege of mind-reading entails a notable dissymmetry in self-consciousness. Elsewhere, whenever one public discourser quotes another, the two share an orientation to an audience, no matter how different these speakers are in the rest of their narratorial features: in informational range, in value scheme, in control, in language, or in the very audience envisaged. This common denominator holds across levels of communication: from the author quoting the primary narrator, to that narrator quoting a secondary narrative or dialogic voice (e.g. Marlow relaying Kurtz's figurative clichés) and so forth. Again, from the reader's side, this affects the way we approach and interpret the perspectival composite (or montage) presented by quotation as discourse about discourse, discourse within discourse. We may not find it easy to disentangle one component voice from another, but it helps to know that both voices, the quoting and the quoted, are those of communicators in touch with their respective addressees.

By contrast, when an omniscient narrator reports to us readers what goes on in the mind of some fictive agent, we encounter a montage between two participants, or perspectives, who are very unlike in terms of discourse orientation as well as of knowledge itself. Of the two, the narrator alone is self-conscious or aware of the act of transmission to another—including communicative goals and needs and abilities—and will proceed accordingly: means adapted to ends, rhetorical effect kept in view. After all, it is the communicative goals of the teller (narrative, persuasive, ideological, etc.) that determine what and how s/he quotes from within the mind of the agent (secret figuration included). On the other hand, the non-communicating character, privately thinking, is in touch with no outsider to the self. So, throughout the goal-directed communication of fiction, the character remains unself-conscious, i.e. unaware of the fact that his/her private thought is conveyed and exposed by the all-knowing teller (as well as the fictionalizing author) to an audience: quoted or inset, that is, within a higher discourse frame. An example would be Emma Bovary's cliché-ridden day-dreams as quoted by the Flaubertian narrator. This polarity in awareness builds irony into all mind-quotation. Specifically, though not exclusively, all mental figures are ironized in quoted communication, whatever their claims to empathy otherwise.

But then, how do we identify a given figure *as* mental? Maybe it has been produced by the teller in person, rather than transmitted at second hand? This problem actually attaches to all quoted figures in fiction, especially in narrative. Take again *Heart of Darkness*: Which given simile, or metaphor or metonymy, is whose? How to distinguish the figurations produced and addressed by the self-consciously telling Marlow from those internal to the unself-conscious experiencing self? Which figures arise in Marlow's public speech, now or then, which originated in his past thought? And in either case, where does their transmission retain, and where replace, or even reverse, the original forms, meanings, effects? As irony is inherent to the quoted mental figure, so is ambiguity in source and viewpoint endemic to quoted, and thus to fictional, figures at large.

Regarding ambiguity, figuration as quoted discourse conforms to a set of universal rules, long theorized by Meir Sternberg and applied since on a wide front.[7] While quoter and quotee remain distinct in principle, practice always complicates the dividing line—by the very nature of quoted discourse. The text or segment in which the narrator possibly transmits (i.e. quotes) an agent's metaphor is ambiguous, if only because we can never be absolutely sure where the quoter's own "frame" ends and the "inset" geared to the quotee begins: what belongs to whom, in short.

According to Sternberg's universals of quotation, moreover, to quote is to re-present, so that the "original" discourse becomes a part within a new discourse whole, which frames it in a different key and structure. Quoting thus subordinates the quote to the communicative aims of the quoter, through recontextualizing, and often also retextualizing strategies, of various kinds. Interference by the quoter can take the form of ellipsis, addition, reordering, commentary, summary, or that of the mixture of voices and viewpoints entailed by direct, indirect or free indirect discourse. The result is a *perspectival montage* between the voices and/or views apparently involved, which we as readers have to disentangle as best we can.

Now, when a metaphor or simile appears within such perspectival montage, the built-in ambiguity of quotation is a challenge, but it can also serve as a guide to making sense of the text. For our attempt to infer who is responsible for what (e.g. for the choice of vehicle, its elaboration, syntactic structure, link to the tenor, etc.) may yield a better understanding of the participants in question, with their respective motives and goals. In our simple example from Browning, disentangling the communicative contexts reveals the monologue quoter's ironic intent behind the quotee's straight metaphor of the wife as a moon. What we thus figure out about the division of labour between the quoting teller and the quoted speaker or reflector is often a key to the rich functionality of fictive figuration in narrative, in both poetry and prose.

3 HOW ENTITIES (AGENTS, EXISTENTS, SUBJECTS) RELATE TO METAPHORS IN FICTION

Addressing the complexities of quoted figuration involves a larger circle or network of participants. Again, it does so more crucially in fictional narrative's discourse about discourse than in the rest of discourse or even of quoted discourse. Fiction constitutes the most inclusive case of all. For fiction multiplies not only the kinds and numbers of entities (agents as well as existents and subjects) relatable to figuration but also their relations to the figure (e.g. to the metaphor or simile).

A fictive entity can thus be associated with metaphorical figures in a variety of communicative roles:

(1) as discourser (e.g. Flaubert's author-like narrator; a dialogic speaker like Andrea; an internal monologist like Eliot's Prufrock);
(2) as addressee and receiver generally (whether in a frame, like Marlowe's listeners, or an inset, like Andrea's wife);
(3) as the object of figuration or tenor (the way Lucrezia inspires Andrea);
(4) as vehicle, whereby one entity figuratively signifies another belonging to the same reality (as the moon signifies Andrea's wife);

(5) as party to a perspectival montage, where the dividing line between the quoter and the quotee in speech or thought becomes ambiguous. In extreme cases (as in passages of what may possibly be unmarked free indirect discourse, e.g. in Marlowe's narrative or in Faulkner's "Barn Burning", discussed below), we cannot even clearly distinguish the discourse roles named in (1);

(6) as various combinations of the above.

Moreover, the participants' multiple involvement in the figure of speech goes with a corresponding multiplicity or plurality in how even a simple figure relates to them. In fiction, a metaphor is often simultaneously associated with a set of narrative agents: originating in one, referring to another, received by a third, reported by one of these to someone else or by a fourth to a fifth, or equivocally hovering between quoter and quotee in perspectival montage. Let me then illustrate various manners of agent/figure association, so that we may see how the agents' communicative roles affect the figurative language, how the figures affect or reflect the agents in their communicative negotiations, and what functions are served by these interplays.

3.1 The Discourser vis-à-vis the Figure

The most direct relationship occurs between an enunciator and the figure of his/her choice. In Robert Browning's "The Bishop Orders His Tomb" (1951: 112–15), the dramatic monologist entreats his sons to adorn his planned effigy with a semi-precious stone:

> Some lump, ah God, of *lapis lazuli,*
> Big as a Jew's head cut off at the nape,
> Blue as a vein o'er the Madonna's breast . . .
> (lines 42–44; ellipsis in the original)

This double simile presents an odd mixture, for the vehicles both accord and clash with the tenors. The dying Bishop, who has hidden the stone, instructs his sons how to recognize it by size and colour. But why, of all possible figurative equivalents, liken the bigness of the stone to a decapitated Jew's head and the colour to a vein on the Madonna's breast? The shock effect produced by the first is immediately followed by the jolt of sacrilege in the second, and the juxtaposition of the two polar religious extremes compounds the incongruity.

That the similes originate in the words of a dying Bishop highlights their oddity, but also leads us from the tenor/vehicle relationship per se to its dramatic source. Simile-makers are responsible for the implications of their figural choices.[8] Here, a church dignitary on his deathbed, expected to think and speak in accordance with his status and circumstances, demonstrates his blindness to the multilevel outrageousness of his figurative discourse.

We are thus encouraged to motivate the incongruities of the double simile by appeal to the aesthetic materialism and moral callousness of the monologist, the dying Bishop who is all too worldly to the last.

But this mimetic motivation covers only the fictive speech that is reported to us within Browning's dramatic monologue. It is ultimately the poet's choice to make the Bishop choose, voice and enjoy these figures, and he does so with a view to another, obliquely communicative goal. The self-exposure of the fictive monologist, then, implies in turn the irony and rhetorical aims of his author vis-à-vis us readers. So the parallel responsibility of the two communicators—the fictive Bishop expressing the similes, the author manoeuvring him and his text from behind the scenes—illustrates how both author and Bishop simultaneously use the same figurative couplet for distinct purposes and audiences, yet with the author in ultimate control.[9]

3.2   The Addressee's Linkage to the Figure

When we read the Bishop's shocking double simile, the convention of the monologic genre denies us access to his own addressees' response. By contrast, given a dramatized encounter within dialogue, an internal addressee can approve or question a speaker's choice of metaphor. Thus, in Henry James's story "The Beldonald Holbein", Mrs. Munden explains to the narrator—a painter who is about to draw the portrait of Lady Beldonald—that the lady is "[n]o longer even a little young; only preserved—oh, but preserved, like bottled fruit, in syrup!" (James 1964b: 284). This sounds rather unkind. But, in reporting his own first impressions of the lady, the addressee not only approves of the figure but appropriates it. In his role as teller, he begins by echoing the original simile, with due attribution ("If she is 'preserved', as Mrs Munden originally described her to me"), and then proceeds to develop the kernel vehicle:

> [I]t is her vanity that has beautifully done it—putting her years ago in a plate-glass case and closing up the receptacle against every breath of air. How shouldn't she be preserved, when you might smash your knuckles on this transparency before you could crack it? And she *is*—oh, amazingly! Preservation is scarce the word for the rare condition of her surface. She looks *naturally* new, as if she took out every night her large, lovely, varnished eyes and put them in water. The thing was to paint her, I perceived, *in* the glass case—a most tempting, attaching feat; render to the full the shining, interposing plate and the general show-window effect. (ibid.)

We thus encounter a multiple and progressive elaboration of the figure by an addressee turned speaker. Among other things, he details the process whereby Lady Beldonald was figuratively preserved: its agent ("her vanity"), its locus ("a plate-glass case"), its finishing touch (the receptacle closed up "against every breath of air"). He proceeds to cast the extraordinary product in analogous, complementary figurative terms ("the rare condition of her surface", on which "you might smash your knuckles"). Then he piles another, "synecdochic" simile onto the already extended, emplotted figure by redescribing the mechanism of preservation by reference to one item ("as if she took out every night her large, lovely, varnished eyes and put them in water"). And he ends with the fantasy of painting her "in the glass case" to reproduce the "show-window effect" that—as his figuration suggests—is the lady's hallmark.

Throughout, the painter's profession helps to explain (or motivate) why he resumes and how he elaborates Mrs. Munden's figure of speech in artistic terms (as opposed to the originator's dietary domain, "preserved, like bottled fruit, in syrup"). But, even for a painter, does not this reduction of the lady to an object or, worse, a mere surface, go too far? Does the figurative description correspond to her real nature?

3.3   The Subject as Object/Target of Figuration

This question brings out the fact that, along with the dialogists, who, in their roles as *speaker* and *addressee*, exchange and evolve the metaphor between them, Lady Beldonald is centrally linked to the figure as its unwitting *object* and tenor. Quoting the cruel figure out of context leaves the question of its (in)appropriateness open, insistently so. It highlights the direct responsibility of the parties concerned, and with it the issue of their (un)reliability (bias, interest, insight, kindness, etc.) in ascribing this vehicle to Lady Beldonald as tenor.[10] In its turn, the (un)reliability issue (as happened in the case of Browning's monologists) brings to the fore yet another viewpoint, the most privileged of all—that of the implied Jamesian author. Does he endorse or reject, or perhaps qualify, the figurative attribution that he delegates to his creatures? Whatever the answer, it is the emergence and relevance of the question that primarily matter: they extend the operative context to the limit. The figure thus involves a network of participants—variously associated with it as speaker, addressee, echoer, object, implied author and reader; this network activates, and its understanding must coordinate, the discourse as a whole.

3.4   Quoter/Quotee Ambiguity in Perspectival Montage

In Faulkner's "Barn Burning" (1960), the built-in ambiguity of perspectival montage hovers between an audience-oriented (i.e. self-conscious) teller and a self-centred (unself-conscious) subject, namely, a child who is himself caught in a dilemma between his innate moral sense and his loyalty to his father. Here is the figure that represents how the boy feels when the justice of the peace waits for the plaintiff to decide whether he will insist on eliciting evidence from the boy against his father. In the expectant silence of the crowded room,

> it was as if he [the boy] had swung outward at the end of a grape vine, over a ravine, and at the top of the swing had been caught in a prolonged instant of mesmerized gravity, weightless in time. (Faulkner 1960: 5)

Where does this striking and extended figure come from? Doubtless, the unlettered boy cannot have generated Faulkner's high linguistic register, but he does feel the sudden unwelcome attention centred on him by all these strangers and the constraint to testify against his father. So it is *his* fear and inner conflict that are presumably analogized ("as if") to his swinging in the air, "mesmerized [. . .] weightless in time". The simile, then, gives the appearance of an inside-view, to which the quoted child has contributed the matter, or mind-stuff, and the quoting teller the verbal manner. But a closer look complicates this binary unpacking of the montage. While the verbal choices are indeed beyond the boy's ken, the semantic field of the "as if . . ." (the ravine, the vine, the swinging) is quite familiar to him from the lifestyle of his family. The world-items, or referents, chosen for the vehicle again suit the character's mind. But, regardless of language, does the child now *think* of himself as swinging from a vine? We cannot tell. So the montage of perspectives certainly reflects the subject's felt experience and emotional involvement and horizons of reference, but apparently leaves to the narrator their translation into the discourse of hypothetical similitude ("as if"), for our benefit.[11]

These examples (3.1–3.4) of the linkage between figuration and fictive agents already indicate how the *communicative parameters of figuration* bring new questions to the fore. Who originates, who expresses, who transmits, who receives, who echoes, who provokes or endures the figure? Who in the world, or what, gets otherwise associated with it, as either tenor or vehicle? Does the vehicle and/or the tenor match their respective associates within the network? Who is responsible for which part of the figure? What does the choice and make-up and (in)congruity of the figure tell us about these various participants? What functions does it serve, and how does the communicative structure affect, entangle, explain them, especially in the fictive context?

As illustrated above, communicated figures of speech in fiction always relate to at least two subjects, the fictive speaker/thinker and the implied, fictionalizing author. Yet a *thinking* figure-maker is also mediated by a narrator who transmits the discourse: a trio of expressers, as in Faulkner. More often, figures relate, one way or another, to an assortment of enunciators, addressees, quoters, quotees, objects of figuration and so forth. We have already met such pluralities. Thus, while Browning's dramatic speakers (Andrea, the Bishop) choose a figure within the fictive world to affect their immediate audience, the author implies, behind the monologists' back, and through the same figures, another message to his own, larger readership. A quartet of agents thus participates in a double (inset/framing) communication. James's tale illustrates an even more complex and dynamic assortment, with Mrs. Munden as the dialogic speaker, and the painter as addressee, of the figure, vis-à-vis Lady Beldonald as the object of figuration. The painter's relation even multiplies, because he shifts roles: from addressee and perceiver within the dialogue to a re-speaker (quoter) and a figure-maker in his own right as narrator after the event. This plurality within the fictive world is ironically manipulated by the implied author from without, for our benefit (as addressees).

Yet these examples do not begin to exhaust the possibilities. In still more complex cases, the circle of discourse participants associated with the figure widens again, and the communicative network grows more intricate yet, enriching the figure's meaning and effects in and through the fiction. But whatever perspectives added, changed, disclosed and reconfigured, with whatever specific contextual implications, their unravelling and interpretation brings into the process the inset (dramatized, immediate) and the outside (framing) addressees, who need to read the figure and understand it. Their perspective is the topic of the next section.

4   ADDRESSEE-SENSITIVE FIGURATION AND ITS RHETORICS

Among the figure's perspectival relations, that with the receiving end is the least obvious and appreciated, just as the connection with the producer, transmitter or (re)quoter almost suggests itself, if only in context. At the receiving end, in turn, the metaphor's orientation to the dramatized or fictive receiver has most often escaped notice, even compared with that to "the reader".

Thus, our earlier examples variously show how figurations (e.g. the choice of vehicles) are motivated, even in causal terms, by reference to their makers: to psychological or emotional state (Madame Bovary's daydreams, Andrea's unrequited love), life experience (the boy in Faulkner's tale), profession and bias (the painter in James's "Beldonald Holbein") and so forth. But, unless we are dealing with unself-conscious producers of metaphors, like the interior monologist, figure-makers are in principle (and to some extent in practice) sensitive to their addressees or target audience, whether authorial or dramatized.

Addressee-friendly metaphors often show an addresser who endeavours to fit the figuration to the abilities, constraints and preferences of a target audience. But a writer may also wish to puzzle some or all readers, and contextualize the figuration accordingly: choosing an incongruous vehicle (as with the Browning similes), or withholding relevant information with a view to our temporary misunderstanding and late discovery. Similarly with the rest of the devices, local and global, available for confusion, ambiguity, guidance, enlightenment and so forth. It all ultimately depends on the perspective (either more or less familiar, informed, dynamic) in which the author places the reader (or some readerly group, e.g. the one implied as against others), in relation to the metaphor, with a view to a specific effect. John Fowles's *The French Lieutenant's Woman* thus opens by dividing past from present standpoints. On the one hand, the postmodern knowledge and ideology, shared by the implied author, omniscient narrator and readers of the novel (first published in 1969); on the other hand, the dramatis personae (living in 1867), who represent the Victorian world, public and worldview.

One early figure dramatizes this incongruity in perspective. The sea rampart at Lyme Regis, the narrator observes, is "as full of subtle curves and volumes as a Henry Moore or a Michelangelo" (John Fowles 1971: 7). By the logic of simile, the double comparative term is assumed to be known, and so to make known the tenor likened to it. But known and made known to whom? While the "curves" of the Renaissance sculptor are celebrated among all the subjects and perspectives involved, fictive and real, past and present, the opening reference to Moore (born in 1898) draws an impassable epistemic line between Fowles's contemporary audience and all Victorian subjects. His implied readers alone, aware of the modern break with previous artistic models, can envisage the compared shore-line through the two visual frames: Michelangelo's "subtle curves and volumes" of fleshly allure juxtaposed with Moore's more abstract opulence of bronze. As a matter of fact, the reader-oriented choice of the vehicle's domain here gains salience from the ironic, exclusionary contrast. Moreover, the perspectival division miniatured in this ekphrastic simile nicely introduces us to the special discourse world of the novel.

Unlike the reader-oriented choice of the vehicle's domain in the Fowles example, the rhetorical effect of figuration grows more complex when it works and, in sequence, evolves in two parallel communicative frames, each with its own audience. Thus, analysing the simile "Politics is like prison" in *A Prison Diary* by Jeffrey Archer, Monika Fludernik notes that

> [t]he most interesting aspect of this passage is the choice of source and target domains. It would have been less unexpected to have encountered a metaphor of imprisonment ("prison is [like] politics"), since, from the reader's perspective, prison is the unknown that needs to be explained by recourse to a more familiar area of life (politics). Significantly, in this exchange, Jeffrey Archer is talking to a lifer and assumes that prison is what his addressee knows about and that politics for him is a mysterious sphere. (2005: 234)

The example illustrates more than the diversity of recipients. As in Browning or in James's "Beldonald Holbein" (2, 3.1–3.4), the reader receives a figure when and as it is directed to a specific addressee within the narrative world. Archer's figure, however, suggests the inverse relation (though not, as in Fowles, the incompatibility) in knowledge and experience between the two audiences, the "lifer" in prison and the general public that reads the simile addressed to him. Between "politics" and "prison", the one addressee's unknown is the other's known, and vice versa. So these two components may change figurative roles as "source" and "target", but must and do compose to suit the figure's immediate addressee. This exemplifies how an inset, dialogic figure can further manipulate (entangle, pattern, adjust) the differences between its receivers, original vs. authorial, and how, given the twofold communicative structure, a relatively simple "basic" metaphor can produce an intricate effect.

Fiction can proceed to complicate the doubling of addressees, within and outside the world, along with the double effect. In Isak Dinesen's *Ehrengard* (1963), a Grand Duchess is looking for a reliable maid-of-honour, one that will help to cover up the embarrassingly premature birth of the Duchess's first grandson and future heir to the Grand Duchy. Herr Cazotte, an influential society painter, recommends a candidate, Ehrengard, in whom the Duchess sees "nothing much to look at". So the painter reinforces his proposal by describing the young lady's presentation "at court":

> In a white frock. A young Walkyrie. Brought up in the sternest military virtues, in the vast and grim castle of Schreckenstein, the only daughter of a warrior clan. An almost unbelievably fitting white-hot young angel with a flaming sword to stand sentinel before our young lovers' paradise! (Dinesen 1963: 27–28)

The pair of intertextual metaphors here, alluding to Norse mythology and to Genesis 3 (a "Walkyrie" and an "angel with a flaming sword", like the one who guarded the entrance to the Garden of Eden), are meant to commend the girl. But soon, when confiding in an old friend, Cazotte's figuration changes values or at least value-frames:

> I saw at a court ball, a girl in a white frock, the daughter of warriors, in whose universe art, or the artist, have never existed. And I cried with Michelangelo: "My greatest triumph hides within that block of marble". (34–35)

Juxtaposing Cazotte's two figurative descriptions, one is struck by their difference amid unity. The speaker, court occasion, "warrior" descent, even the synecdoche of "white frock"—all repeat themselves to underline the identity of the tenor. For extra continuity, the second description appears shortly after the first. Against this unitary background, it would appear that he picks the different vehicles ("Walkyrie . . . angel . . ." as against "block of marble") to suit his goals vis-à-vis the respective addressees. So the rhetoric of Cazotte's vehicles varies with his own immediate (to us fictive) addressees, and with the effects for the authorial audience (ourselves) that he and they unself-consciously mediate or motivate. Thus the variety in his appeal to affective allusions: to the high status of the source-text (the Bible, Norse mythology) or the source-speaker (Michelan-gelo). In the earlier cluster of figures, addressed to the doubtful Duchess, the war-like mobile walkyrie and the sword-wielding angel "to stand sentinel"—both with superhuman associations—join persuasive forces. The angel also suggests the young lady's purity, as does the recurrent epithet "white . . . white-hot" subtly transferred to or extended from the literal colour of her "frock" to the figurative colour of her temperament. So the vehicles co-operate to project a character and a scenario loaded with positive value, as desired.

In writing to his confidante, however, Cazotte leaves out all these persua-sive measures, while his new figure reveals his secret motives for recommend-ing Ehrengard. Quoting Michelangelo, he transforms the literal (or idiomatic) statement, about the "block of marble" where the sculptor's art lies hidden, into a vehicle for the art-less Ehrengard. Instead of praising Ehrengard in the way he did in his voice as courtier, he reduces her to inert material for his future "triumph" as artist. In retrospect, however, this variant, incongruous-looking figure makes sense. It recalls, activates, and newly patterns a cluster of expositional antecedents describing Cazotte as "the irresistible Don Juan of his age" (10), whose credo is that "the whole attitude of the artist towards the Universe is that of a seducer" (11). All orders of beings, inanimate ("an earth-enware pot"), animate ("lemons"), human ("women"), are equally reduced to artistic material in the painter's eyes (12–13). By retrospective linkage, then, Ehrengard as "a block of marble" is now envisaged as the latest addition to the objects "seduced [. . .] into yielding their inmost being" to Cazotte—here, seduced into blushing—with her own obliviousness to art promising the ulti-mate challenge and glory.

The Michelangelesque figure's surprising realignment may accordingly appear to involve yet another shift: from the earlier addressee-oriented figuration to the addresser's self-exposure. But the confidante as recipient still functions here, though less simply than the Duchess. From within the fictive world, as our inset dramatic counterpart, she motivates the early disclosure of Cazotte's hidden intention, along with his self-disclosure, for the benefit of the readers. And what is disclosed runs to nothing less than a secret artistic plot within the overall secret aristocratic plot. For good mea-sure, the two plots are erotic, the one intended to elicit a revealing "blush", the other to camouflage a premarital conception. Both are engineered by Cazotte, with different goals, scenarios, roles, role-players, characteriza-tions and figurations to match.

The artistic plot with all its elements indeed advances in the guise of its counterpart throughout, unknown to the rest of the co-plotters, least of all the Duchess or Ehrengard herself. But, ironically, it does not generate the triumphant ending nor the related effects forecast by the would-be manipu-lator of fates and figures in the name of art. Behind, or below, the secret plot itself, there runs accordingly a still deeper, authorial (counter)plot. Starting from Cazotte's avowal of his designs on Ehrengard, his hidden project in turn motivates the implied author's art of communication, which alludes to yet another field of reference. As Robert Langbaum has shown long ago, Cazotte is Dinesen's counter-version of Kierkegaard's seducer in *Either/Or*, the aesthete intent on awakening woman's eroticism, so that she will desire to give herself freely (1965: 274–83). Besides implying its own key analogy, the author's art has its own favoured sharer: it gives the reader a superior insight into all the represented plots and characters, hence into the re-presented figures.

From this vantage point, our perception of the contrastive figurations also generates dramatic tension and narrative interest. Once we cast Cazotte and Ehrengard as antagonist vs. protagonist, there arises suspense about the outcome of the struggle between them. Who will prevail, the seducer or his chosen victim? Figuratively speaking, which of Cazotte's opposed metaphors for Ehrengard will prove true and in effect realize itself? Our suspense is the narrator's distinctive aim in juxtaposing the painter's *two* figures of Ehrengard. And the suspense thickens owing to conflicting reinforcements or entanglements of either hypothesis. On the one hand, Cazotte seems to miss the implications of his own reference to the guarding angel as "white-hot" and armed with "a flaming sword". The suggestion of a fiery Ehrengard predicts trouble for the seducer, diametrically opposing and questioning his reduction of her to cold lifeless marble. On the other hand, the text's recurrent allusion to Kierkegaard's *Either/Or* highlights the danger threatening the innocent victim at the hands of the experienced Don Juan.

In the event, neither of the scenarios, or the figures embodying them, neatly materializes. Their actual crossing, with surprises and ironies on the way to the end, would take too long to trace here. But our example does illustrate how the aims of fictive agents for using figuration may themselves vary (e.g. between rhetoric and self-expression) and how they may variably relate to authorial aims implied for our readerly eyes, behind the agents' backs.

5 FIGURATION IN THE LARGER NARRATIVE CONTEXT: BETWEEN THE AUTHORIAL COMMUNICATOR'S FRAME AND THE REFLECTOR'S PRIVATE INSET

The Dinesen-type rhetoric behind rhetoric of figuration has its complement in the perspectival set-up that is almost unique to fiction and canonized by Henry James, namely: authorial rhetoric operating behind an unself-conscious as well as otherwise limited reflector. Amid the radical difference in audience awareness, that limited perspective motivates, *inter alia*, the subject's comparable, if only temporary, blindness to the figures he or she originates, and so motivates a developing incongruity with the omniscient frame. The sphinx metaphor in James's "The Beast in the Jungle" (1964a: 380) throws rich light on this point of contact between the two narrative strategies. At the same time, in the process, it integrates the immediate figurative context with the movement of the narrative as a whole—orchestrating all the participants in terms of the riddle thematized by the sphinx.

But the story opens, as early as the title, with another and, on the face of it, unrelated metaphor. The reflector cum protagonist, Marcher, believes that some undefined calamity will befall him one day, without fore-warning, like the jump of a beast in a jungle. He therefore abstains from any career or responsibility and devotes his life to waiting for the beast to jump. During his lifelong suspended animation, an acquaintance, May Bartram, supports him by serving as his only confidante. After years of wait-ing with him, May assures Marcher on her deathbed that his fate has *already* overtaken him. He accepts her judgment, though he feels bitter about hav-ing failed to "experience" his catastrophe. After her death, which height-ens the aridity of his existence, the protagonist mourns the loss of his only confidante. But then Marcher chances to observe authentic grief in a fellow mourner, which leads him to the painful understanding that his fate was to be "the man, to whom nothing on earth was to have happened" (James 1964a: 401). Too late he realizes that he might have escaped his fate had he accepted May's love for him. As usual with James, the tale is transmitted by following Marcher's perspective, from ignorance to belated knowledge.

The sphinx metaphor appears in mid-tale, when Marcher realizes that May is going to die and leave him all alone. It is important to note that, at this point, the omniscient teller and the reticent May alone know and fully understand the meaning of Marcher's ordeal. Both the protagonist and the reader are still ignorant. Marcher is still expecting his beast; the reader is still trying to figure out where all this waiting will land the protagonist. As he and we wait, though, May suddenly falls ill. Coming to visit her, Marcher observes the fireless hearth, and then shifts focus to May herself:

> May Bartram sat, for the first time in the year, without a fire, a fact that, to Marcher's sense, gave the scene of which she formed part a smooth and ultimate look, an air of knowing, in its immaculate order and its cold, meaningless cheer, that it would never see a fire again. Her own aspect—he could scarce have said why—intensified this note. Almost as white as wax, with the marks and signs in her face as numerous and as fine as if they had been etched by a needle, with soft white draperies relieved by a faded green scarf, the delicate tone of which had been consecrated by the years, she was the picture of a serene, exquisite, but impenetrable sphinx, whose head, or indeed all whose person, might have been powdered with silver. She was a sphinx, yet with her white petals and green fronds she might have been a lily too—only an artificial lily, wonderfully imitated and con-stantly kept, without dust or stain, though not exempt from a slight droop and a complexity of faint creases, under some clear glass bell. (Ch. IV; James 1964a: 380)

Regarding the sphinx figure, two communicative facts are certain: that it is transmitted by the self-conscious omniscient teller, and that May is its object. But to what extent does Marcher generate or share this view of her, as given, with all that it implies? How exactly to divide the givens ("the perspectival montage") between the quoting omniscient and the quoted thinking subject? The whole passage develops an ambiguous answer to this question. Appropriately so where the key vehicle's main feature is its literal as well as hermeneutic impenetrability: a double sphinx.

On the one hand, the quoted passage apparently refers the metaphoric imagery to Marcher's ongoing thought process. To begin with, there is a marked difference between his confident inference regarding the surrounding physical scene and his uncertain reading of the woman in the centre. Thus, the observed fireless setting becomes "to Marcher's sense" a configured metonymic prediction of her approaching death. But he is less sure of his ground when he tries to understand how "her own aspect [. . .] intensified [the] note" of the last scene, for "he could scarce have said why". And his uncertainty is revealed afresh in the series of figures that read like an attempt on his part to find figurative vehicles for his sense of her mysteriousness. Instead of penetrating the mystery, in short, he tries to capture its impenetrability, if only via metaphor.

This attempt culminates in the sphinx metaphor, since it embodies an enigma beyond his ken, one transformed immediately after to the lily beyond his touch. Moreover, since in the past he has already suspected May of knowing something about his fate that she will not share with him, her figuration as an enigmatic mythological being suits his conception of her, just as her approaching death matches with her removal beyond touch.

Linguistic signs of free indirect style further confirm his involvement in the two sentences that elaborate the sphinx figure. Marcher's hesitant process of perception is implied in the local change of mind ("or indeed") and modal verbs ("might have been . . . might have been . . ."), perhaps even in the "as if" form of one earlier simile, and the various serial qualifications that signify a mind in action ("yet . . . only . . . though"). These little self-qualifying moves parallel, punctuate and reinforce the overall transformation of the sphinx metaphor into the artificial lily under the glass bell. The constant changes in representing the woman jointly betray the perceiver's inability to define her, even metaphorically.[12]

Yet, as in many (in principle all) cases of quoted figuration, so with the combined discourse here between the self-conscious omniscient teller and the unself-conscious subject: the ambiguity regarding Marcher's share in the figuration is not fully resolvable. For example, has he thought through the sphinx allusion, and how it bears on the present analogue? What we can do, however, is to look more closely into the figure's communicative structure, which may throw a sharper light on the relative share of either participant and on the larger narrative functions served by the given montage.

To this end, the figure has to be read not just in its immediate context (cited above) but also in the larger context of the tale as a whole.

To begin with, from his vantage point of omniscience, the Jamesian narrator is at this juncture the only participant aware of the full ironic appropriateness of the sphinx figure: it merges May and the monster, thus highlighting May's role in Marcher's story. In the Oedipus myth, the sphinx is a winged monster with a woman's head and a lion's body, who devours those who cannot solve her riddle. When Oedipus provides the true answer, she kills herself. Oedipus's solving of the mystery, however, leads to his tragic end when he discovers another secret, familial and criminal. In James's story, May has already solved Marcher's riddle through her secret love for him. She is also dying because of the secret that she cannot share with him. The present chapter dramatizes her last attempt to help Marcher to discover the truth for himself. And the end of the tale dramatizes his painful discovery, after her death.

Unlike our cases of vehicle/tenor dissonance (e.g. the lapis lazuli in Browning) or of equivocal suitability (e.g. Lady Beldonald and Ehrengard as objects of figuration), May Bartram perfectly matches the chosen vehicle. In her deep understanding of Marcher, which surpasses his self-knowledge, she corresponds to the secret-holding sphinx. Marcher's realization at the end that his love might have saved her life (as well as his own, in a way) causally links her death to her knowledge of the secret, a variation on the mythological monster's suicide. Other variations likewise highlight May's secret knowledge, especially of Marcher. Thus, the Greek riddle concerns the three stages of Man; here it concerns the stages in the life of one man. There, the stages differ in the freedom of movement; here, they display a persistent emotional and actional paralysis.

So at this moment in Marcher's ordeal, when, baffled, he resorts to figuration, the participants are divided through the sphinx figure between those in the know and those who are still groping. In contrast to the all-knowing narrator, Marcher and the reader are epistemologically disprivileged relative to May: neither can as yet see much in the metaphor beyond its general sense of an enigma. The reader is in fact limited to the protagonist's own order of discovery. To both, May now appears a "sphinx" indeed, in this minimal idiomatic sense—a dead allusive figure for opacity. So both stand opposed, and exposed, to the full ironic intent of the self-conscious yet taciturn narrator in reviving the allusion into new metaphorical, perspectival life.

Taking into account these differences among the various participants—in knowledge, in understanding and in the *time* of discovery—we can make out some of the figure's narrative functions. These extend, or evolve, from the local to the global context. Among other things, as we review the cited passage vis-à-vis the end of the tale, we can learn whose position remains stable, whose is dynamized, and how, when and in what direction it moves, due to what, in relation to which other participants and so forth. Let me, then, outline this functional network converging on the figure.

(1) The sphinx metaphor not only suggests an analogous mythic plot, but also captures a pivotal point in Marcher's own plot. He is about to lose his companion and his ordeal alike: the one dying and the other, as she will soon assure him, already behind him. As May's solving of the riddle leads to her death, so will her death eliminate the possibility of his salvation. She knows the alternative plot scenarios, then, and her own fate eventually tips the balance between them.

(2) According to the Jamesian ideal of unity, Marcher doubles as centre of narration and of interest. The sphinx, however, foregrounds May's role in the tale—as an enigma, as the keeper of the secret, as the one in the know and, more concretely, as the woman who secretly loves Marcher and dies of unrequited love and of the burden of her secret. She knows he could have been saved, she knows even the way to his salvation, but he must discover on his own what might have been. In this sense, from an early stage in the action she also carries the burden of his tragedy in addition to her own, as the sphinx does its secret. For all her knowledge, she cannot prevent either tragic end. Marcher begins to shoulder the burden of it all only as late as the final agonized retrospect, which newly highlights by contrast his lifelong earlier self: blind, passive, evasive, egocentric—to his own loss along with May's, or, rhetorically, to her gain as his mirror-image.

(3) The metaphor also encapsulates the tale's main thematic irony. While Marcher dreams of exotic beasts in the jungle, he cannot see his missed opportunity so near home. The "dull woman" (369) who has accompanied him embodies all his exotic dreams. Yet even in their last encounter, when his blindness casts her as a legendary monster, he falls short of identifying her as the beast of his desire. He learns too late, i.e. after her death, that he has wasted his whole life on idle dreams, in face of the real thing, now vanished beyond reach. Only at the end, therefore, will Marcher and through him the reader come to appreciate the thematic irony implied in the sphinx (as, less covertly, in the titular beast-in-the-jungle).

(4) Here also lies the final twist in their respective processes of change from ignorance to painful discovery—one within the told world, the other along the telling sequence—and in the tale's perspectival configuration as a whole. From the viewpoint of the reader, the enigma of the sphinx, linked with May's secret knowledge, heightens narrative interest. It thus plays on our curiosity: What is the secret she refuses to share? It also builds up suspense concerning the narrative future: Will Marcher ever learn the secret? The viewpoints polarize the readings of the metaphor accordingly. At this moment along the text continuum, these gaps oppose those in the know, the narrator and May, to those who are in the dark, Marcher and the reader. But the narrative movement will eventually close the plot gaps, redress the perspectival imbalance. At the end, Marcher will come to understand the meaning of the present scene; the

reader will gain a better understanding of the text, including the figures. So, in sequence, the perspectival opposition itself shifts: our and Marcher's present ignorance will contrast with the knowledge jointly achieved at the end. But even so, the juncture is not complete, if only because of a difference in figurative retrospection. Marcher's own discovery naturally centres on the beast of the jungle whose latent irony escaped him throughout life. The one-off sphinx figuration is in effect subsumed in the process. Yet the reader can at last also work out the full intertextual bearing of Sophocles' monster. Rather than a generalised term for impenetrability, the figure now reads as a miniature vignette both of what happened (or failed to happen) in the action and of how and why it all emerges in the discourse, notably regarding the mobile play of perspectives.

To sum up: the analysis of figures *in context* shows the centrality of the perspectival framework to all figuration and the basic rhetorical orientation of all self-conscious, communicative (as opposed to private) figure-making. As we have seen, the question of who transmits a figure to whom and about whom may affect its meaning and impact no less than the nature of tenor/vehicle relationship. This is true in real life and in fiction alike. However, due to fiction's peculiar communicative complexity, fictional figures are always quoted, and the multiplicity of participants involved allows for a greater manoeuvrability as well as multifunctionality of figuration. Thus, on the transmitting side, we saw the typical incompatibility between quoter(s) and quotee(s)—above all, when the self-conscious omniscient teller enables us readers to eavesdrop on figures made in the privacy of a character's mind. In turn, when figures are self-consciously addressed by fictive speakers to affect their addressees, while the same figures are quoted to us in the wider, narratorial frame, the circle of communication expands accordingly. Each participant, whether transmitter or receiver, may thus enrich the functionality of the figure, along such lines as (self-)characterization, rhetoric, irony, plot dynamics, semantic density, emotional and ideological impact. Moreover, beyond such rich but local effects, a metaphor's very linkage to the communicating agents in their respective worlds or frameworks enables it to serve global narrative roles. Thus, whenever assimilated to the action's narrative interest(s), the figure's effect unfolds and develops along the global sequence, often to the very end.

NOTES

1. I wish to thank Monika Fludernik for her helpful comments and uncommon editorial attention. I also thank my student Nomy Bornstein for her pertinent simile and her evocative thesis on the artist-tales of Henry James and Isak Dinesen.
2. A terminological note. In an argument based on referring figures to communication, I. A. Richards's pair of terms "tenor" and "vehicle" (1971[1936]:

96) seems to me the least ambiguous, hence the most useful. Tenor rather than subject, which is needed (and liable to be mistaken) for designating the participants in their subjective capacity, vocal or mental. Target, which other analysts prefer to tenor, appears to qualify better, except that its complementary term source is again liable to be mistaken for subject (e.g. as source of information). Wishing to bring in a neglected key-dimension, my main point is the necessity of the dimension regardless of either terminology or theoretical model.

3. A Google search indicates the extent of the references and responses to the figure. Cf. the title of a recently published book, *Spider Webs: The Story of the Second Lebanese War* (2008), by Amos Harel and Avi Issacharov.

4. As explained in Sternberg (1983: 177–78), real life "imposes constraints on fictionality that affect both speaker and addressee", e.g. in the courtroom. In contrast, fiction, in verse and prose alike, presupposes a double communicative framework, so that "the literary speaker is in principle as fabricated and his speech as mediated as any other textual component".

5. The outline and the terminology are based on Tel Aviv narrative theory: see especially the references to Sternberg and Yacobi listed here.

6. On the self-conscious/unself-conscious distinction see Sternberg (1978: 254–305; 2005) and Yacobi (1981, 2000), with various follow-ups.

7. See Sternberg (1982, 1991, 2001), with further references there. From a related standpoint, Fludernik (1993) extensively reviews the situation in reference to free indirect discourse.

8. No wonder self-characterizing is so often singled out as the function of metaphors in fiction. E.g. Semino and Swindlehurst (1996: 147): "the systematic use of a particular metaphor (or metaphors) reflects an idiosyncratic cognitive habit, a personal way of making sense of and talking about the world: in other words, a particular mind style" (with earlier references there).

9. For a pinpoint counterpart, recall the shock effect of the "PIT BULLS ARE JEWS" slogan: produced in a real-life demonstration, it is not so intentional, far less multilevel and multifunctional. This comparison newly opposes in miniature life's immediate to fiction's quoted (author-mediating, subject-mediated) discourse, with their respective figure-constructions.

10. On this narrator's unreliability in blurring the distinction between (sur)face and depth see Yacobi (2006: 280–81).

11. Cohn (1978: 21–59) ascribes figurative language in "psycho-narration" to the narrator, who alone thereby expresses what the subject's mind does not and cannot articulate. The Faulkner example (or the "Beast in the Jungle" below) reveals a more complex picture (including a spectrum of quoter/quotee montage).

12. The lily figure, with its subtle ekphrastic aspect, and as a metonymy for the virgin, deserves a separate analysis.

WORKS CITED

Browning, Robert (1951) *Selected Poetry*. Ed. Kenneth L. Knickerbocker. New York: Modern Library.

Cohn, Dorrit (1978) *Transparent Minds: Narrative Modes for Presenting Consciousness in Fiction*. Princeton: Princeton University Press.

Dinesen, Isak [Karen Blixen] (1963) *Ehrengard*. London: University of Chicago Press.

Faulkner, William (1960) "Barn Burning". *Selected Short Stories*. New York: Modern Library. 3–27.

Fludernik, Monika (1993) *The Fictions of Language and the Languages of Fiction*. London and New York: Routledge.

———. (2005) "The Metaphorics and Metonymics of Carcerality: Reflections on Imprisonment as Source and Target Domain in Literary Texts". *English Studies* 86.3: 226–44.

Forceville, Charles (1995) "(A)symmetry in Metaphor: The Importance of Extended Context". *Poetics Today* 16.4: 677–709.

Fowles, John (1971) *The French Lieutenant's Woman* [1969]. London: Panther.

Harel, Amos, and Avi Issacharov (2008) *Spider Webs: The Story of the Second Lebanese War*. Tel Aviv: Yediot Books.

James, Henry (1964a) "The Beast in the Jungle". *The Complete Tales of Henry James*, Vol. 11. Ed. Leon Edel. Philadelphia and New York: J. B. Lippincott. 351–402.

———. (1964b) "The Beldonald Holbein". *The Complete Tales of Henry James*, Vol. 11. Ed. Leon Edel. Philadelphia and New York: J. B. Lippincott. 283–306.

Langbaum, Robert (1965) *The Gayety of Vision*. New York: Random House.

Richards, I. A. (1971) *The Philosophy of Rhetoric* [1936]. London: Oxford University Press.

Semino, Elena, and Kate Swindlehurst (1996) "Metaphor and Mind Style in Ken Kesey's *One Flew Over the Cuckoo's Nest*". *Style* 30.1: 143–66.

Sternberg, Meir (1978) *Expositional Modes and Temporal Ordering in Fiction*. Baltimore: Johns Hopkins University Press.

———. (1982) "Proteus in Quotation-Land: Mimesis and the Forms of Reported Discourse". *Poetics Today* 3: 107–56.

———. (1983) "Mimesis and Motivation: The Two Faces of Fictional Coherence". *Literary Criticism and Philosophy*. Ed. Joseph P. Strelka. University Park and London: Pennsylvania State University Press. 145–88.

———. (1991) "How Indirect Discourse Means: Syntax, Semantics, Pragmatics, Poetics". *Literary Pragmatics*. Ed. Roger Sell. London: Routledge. 62–93.

———. (2001) "Factives and Perspectives: Making Sense of Presupposition as Exemplary Inference". *Poetics Today* 22: 129–244.

———. (2005) "Self-Consciousness as a Narrative Feature and Force: Tellers vs. Informants". *Blackwell Companion to Narrative Theory*. Eds. James Phelan and Peter Rabinowitz. Oxford: Blackwell. 232–52.

Yacobi, Tamar (1981) "Fictional Reliability as a Communicative Problem". *Poetics Today* 2: 113–26.

———. (2000) "Interart Narrative: (Un)Reliability and Ekphrasis". *Poetics Today* 21: 708–47.

———. (2006) "'The Beldonald Holbein': The Artist's Power and Its Risks as Narrative Center". *The Henry James Review* 27.3: 275–84.

Part II

Cognitive Metaphor Theory and Literary Analysis

7 Conceptual Metaphor and Communication

An Austinian and Gricean Analysis of Brian Clark's *Whose Life Is It Anyway?*

John Douthwaite

1 INTRODUCTION

1.1 Conceptual Metaphor: Advent, Nature and Functions

Since the ground-breaking work of Reddy (1979) and of Lakoff and Johnson (1980), conceptual or cognitive metaphor theory (CMT) has taken over metaphor analysis,[1] displacing both classical theories of rhetoric (Cameron 2003) and the pragmatic account of metaphor (Sadock 1979; Searle 1979; Levinson 1983) as the 'dominant' research paradigm in the field.

CMT analysts argue that metaphor is pervasive in thought and communication (Gibbs 1994; Kövecses 2002, 2005; Knowles & Moon 2006) and not simply an attached 'ornament' as theorised in classical rhetoric.[2] Secondly, they maintain that it is a cognitive phenomenon—a mode of thought which pre-exists in cognitive structure and by means of which an abstract concept is made more readily comprehensible by mapping certain pertinent characteristics[3] from a concrete source domain onto an abstract target domain.[4]

For instance, the conceptual or cognitive metaphor (CM) LIFE IS A JOURNEY makes sense of the abstract concept 'life' by 'comparing' it to the concrete concept 'journey' through specific "metaphorical linguistic expressions" (Kövecses 2002: 4), or "linguistic metaphors" (Kövecses 2002: 30) which realize that CM, such as those on which Christina Rossetti's poem "Uphill" (quoted below) and Emily Dickinson's poem "Because I could not stop for Death" are constructed:[5]

> Does the road wind uphill all the way?
> > Yes, to the very end.
> Will the day's journey take the whole long day?
> > From morn to night, my friend.
>
> But is there for the night a resting place?
> > A roof for when the slow, dark hours begin.
> May not the darkness hide it from my face?
> > You cannot miss that inn.

Shall I meet other wayfarers at night?
>Those who have gone before.
Then must I knock, or call when just in sight?
>They will not keep you waiting at that door.

Shall I find comfort, travel-sore and weak?
>Of labour you shall find the sum.
Will there be beds for me and all who seek?
>Yea, beds for all who come. (Rossetti 2001: 59)

In this poem, there are manifold correspondences between the concrete source domain ("journey") and the abstract target domain ("life"), including, respectively, the traveller representing human beings, the road representing 'events' in life, the distance covered representing the progress made in time, with the obstacles encountered representing the difficulties encountered (a road going uphill requires greater physical effort than a flat road, and if the road is a winding one, then that increases the distance to be travelled before reaching one's destination, again augmenting the effort required). The starting point represents birth and the destination death and heaven.

Classic Lakoffian CMT tends towards a one-to-one mapping between source and target domains. Despite the fact that Lakoff and Johnson (1980: 7; 52) claim that CMs are systematic (cf. Kövecses 2002: 7), the two scholars also acknowledge that not all of the source domain features are mapped onto the target domain (the invariance hypothesis; ibid. 52–55). One obvious issue requiring explication is what aspects of the source domain are mapped onto the target domain and why are these aspects mapped and not others, a full answer to which has yet to be provided.

A second issue, closely connected to the first, concerns the fact that a metaphorical linguistic expression might actually be a complex metaphor, i.e. a composite, or blend, of two or more underlying CMs or linguistic metaphors. (See 1.2 below. Examples will be analysed in section 2.2.) Furthermore, a given (abstract) concept may be 'explained' by more than one CM.[6] The specific CM deployed will thus avail itself of certain source features and will therefore highlight only certain aspects of the target CM.

Given the hypothesized systematicity of CMs and the fact that they highlight certain aspects while masking other possible features of a target domain, CMs are said to be ideological in nature—selecting a given CM in a given context by definition reveals the speaker's (conscious or unconscious) point of view. As Lakoff and Johnson (1980) point out, using a CM to structure the account of an experience can only be partial, since one's selection of which features to transfer from source to target domain implies that a CM will necessarily highlight certain aspects of the target domain while hiding other aspects.[7] The classic instance quoted is the CM ARGUMENT IS WAR. This necessarily expresses a negative view of argument, leaving out of the account those aspects and arenas of argumentation which have positive valences, such as cooperation, as in (i) parliaments and courts of law in a democratic society and (ii) scientific debate in the furtherance of knowledge.

Blending theory—in one sense an offshoot of CMT[8]—attempt to parry these objections. Fauconnier and Turner (2002) argue that in processing language, the mind creates four mental spaces: one where it activates the pertinent features of the target (input space 1), one for the pertinent features of the source (input space 2) and another generic space for world knowledge relevant to the interpretation of the CM. The combination of these three yields a fourth mental space, termed the "blended" space, where the pertinent features come together to produce the interpretation of the specific linguistic expression being processed (Grady, Oakley & Coulson 1999). More specifically, Fludernik (2010: 10) has pointed out that metaphors may be "semantically enriched construct[s]" creating "new meanings not contained in either the source or target domains", an aspect which "the original [CM] model by Lakoff, Johnson and Turner did not yet fully bring out". In particular, given the numerous connections ("proliferations of meaning" in Fludernik's [2010: 11] terms) that might in theory be made between source and target domains, the introduction of the generic space "determines the structure of the analogies" (Fludernik 2010) between the two domains. Fludernik provides a cogent illustration by analysing a cartoon depicting Obama and McCain in cowboy gear shooting at each other with pistols during the presidential campaign, showing how the cartoon "could be read conservatively as an implied denigration of Obama (qua villain cowboy or Indian), or ironically and liberally as a criticism of McCain's subconsciously racist attitude towards his antagonist" (Fludernik 2010: 10–11).

With regard to processing, a distinction has been drawn between conventional metaphors and novel or creative metaphors (Lakoff & Turner 1989; Kövecses 2002; Deignan 2005; Knowles & Moon 2006). The former are claimed to be relatively automatic and unconscious, since they are stored in long-term memory and retrieved therefrom as single, pre-fabricated units having a conventional meaning (e.g. "He's a chip off the old block", a conventional implicature in Gricean terms). As Goatly (1997: 35) points out, such conventional meaning may be classified as the 'literal' or 'surface' meaning of the expression.[9] By contrast, the latter require greater processing effort both for their production and for their comprehension, since they have to be (re)constructed through a process of pragmatic inferencing (e.g. Goatly 1997: 137–45). This is the major point of the present chapter. It will be developed in theoretical terms in section 1.3 and then 'demonstrated' in practical terms in section 2.

In addition to facilitating comprehension, CM is claimed to perform other functions related to communication. Gibbs (1994: 124–25) discusses (a) the inexpressibility hypothesis: "metaphors provide a way of expressing ideas that would be extremely difficult to convey using literal language", as in "the thought slipped my mind like a squirrel behind a tree"; (b) the compactness hypothesis: the complexity of the preceding example would require a high number of words to unpack it when employing literal language; (c) the vividness hypothesis: the compactness and complexity of metaphors enable rich, suggestive messages to be succinctly formulated, often having emotional appeal. Further functions posited include: (d) (in part related to the previous point) suasion: Charteris-Black (2004) states that metaphor is "typically used in persuasion [...] because it represents a novel way of viewing the world that offers some fresh insight"[10] (7) and also because of "its potential for moving us" (11; see also Goatley 1997); (e) conveying ideology (Charteris-Black 2004: 1–2; 28): at one remove from persuasion is ideology, for convincing someone means convincing them of a given viewpoint or worldview. However, ideology is not merely a function of suasion, but a general phenomenon in social life. All texts are ideologically situated. Charteris-Black (2004: 28) identifies a sixth function, that of evaluation, which may, however, be considered inherent to ideology, since expressing a worldview necessarily entails value-judgments about the world being predicated of.

1.2 Research in CMT

Two major strands may be identified in CM research. The first is the identification of (1) CMs, (2) metaphorical linguistic expressions and (3) the features that are mapped from the source to the target in creating/exploiting a CM. The excellent work by Kövecses (2000, 2002, 2005), for instance, is exemplary in this sense.

The second major strand seeks to identify CMs at work in texts. Not only are the individual CMs been singled out, but some researchers offered middle- to high-level accounts of the communicative effects of the deployment of CMs, showing also how CM patterning across a work is the carrier of ideology and point of view.

Donald Freeman analyses the role of CMs in Shakespearean plays such as *Macbeth* (Freeman 1998) and *Antony and Cleopatra* (Freeman 1999). He demonstrates that each play deploys a different set of CMs, each set being functional to the underlying message. Thus, *Macbeth* is dominated by the PATH and CONTAINER image schemas. Macbeth sees life as a journey culminating in success, hence avails himself of all means—legal and illegal—to achieve that success. The CONTAINER image schema sees Macbeth violating Duncan's body by penetration though stabbing. Furthermore, the two image schemas interact to create a multidimensional image of Macbeth's downfall. In *Antony and Cleopatra*, on the other hand, the shift in deployment of CMs enables Freeman to hypothesize a three-part structure of that play, as well as identify the different characters and worldviews of Antony and Cleopatra.

1.3   Critiques of CMT

Although various criticisms have been levelled at CMT and blending theory by supporters, as well as by its detractors (Eubanks 1999; Coulson & Oakley 2000; McGlone 2001; Charteris-Black 2004; Deignan 2005; Moreno 2007; Crisp 2008; Tendahl & Gibbs 2008), here I want to direct attention to the exclusion of the role of pragmatics from analyses of CM and to its consequences for communication and creativity theory. Stated differently, the basic claim is that CMT does not provide a full account of the knowledge base and of the actual mental processes involved in the production and comprehension of metaphors and, above all, of their role in communication.[11]

First of all, the feeling is conveyed in some analytical texts on metaphor that the single instantiations of metaphorical realizations in texts can be understood by referring only to the 'system' of metaphors itself, e.g. by referring to a list of CMs and their possible linguistic realizations, as if the meaning of a metaphor could be read off in a void without any reference to text, context and general mechanisms of mental processing. Or, as Moreno (2007: 63) puts it, "metaphor comprehension cannot be based solely on the identification of common properties unconstrained by general cognitive or pragmatic mechanisms".

The second and most fundamental point is that the impression is gained in many works on CM that once one has identified the CM behind the metaphoric linguistic expression, one has understood the text.[12] In other words, a regression almost to de-contextualized sentence-level-like analysis appears to have taken place. What often fails to be noted is that identifying and comprehending the CMs and their realizations in a text is only the first stage in interpretation. Full comprehension of Christina Rossetti's "Uphill", for example, comes about only when each word, line and metaphor are understood both singly and in relationship to the entire text, against the background of its context—Christian culture. And such comprehension will require complex mental processing involving, primarily, pragmatics. A return to the Gricean cooperative principle (Grice 1989) or to Sperber and Wilson's (1995) theory of relevance (Goatly 1997; Tendahl & Gibbs 2008[13]) seems warranted.

Third, given the multiplicity of symbolising patterns which go into the construction of even the simplest utterance (Douthwaite 2000: 205–66) and the diversity of communicative functions generally performed by any single utterance, one additionally has to note the variety of levels of meaning that such functions cover (ideational, emotional, psychological, social, textual [in the Hallidayan sense of the term]). A further aspect neglected on occasion by CMT treatments is the frequent existence of 'mixed forms', in which the mechanisms explaining the metaphorical expression are intertwined with other linguistic mechanisms accounting for additional non-literal meanings produced by an utterance.[14]

The following example is intended to illustrate the complexity of communication:

> *PETER:* Where's my box of chocolates?
> *BILL:* I saw John in your room this morning.

Calculating the conversational implicature 'John may well have taken the chocolates' conveyed by Bill through his utterance "I saw John in your room this morning" requires the working of the inferential machine as described, for instance, in Sperber and Wilson (1995, using relevance theory) and in Douthwaite (2000, using the Gricean approach). Reconstruction of the line of reasoning leading to the recovery of the illocutionary force of accusation conveyed by Bill's utterance will identify several steps (S) in the inferential process. The starting point of the line of reasoning, (S1), is the context— Peter and Bill are talking in Peter's room when the former utters "Where's my box of chocolates?" From the context and from Peter's utterance we can infer that there was a box of chocolates in Peter's room (S2); we can also induce (S3) that those chocolates are ostensibly no longer there, and infer (S4) that Peter has not eaten the chocolates himself or has not forgotten what he did with them (e.g. given them to Mary). All these steps are based on the exploitation of (i.e. respect for) the Gricean Quality and Relevance maxims: that is, we are presupposing that Peter is telling the truth and that Peter wants to eat his chocolates or has suddenly discovered they are missing (i.e. his utterance is relevant to the achievement of a goal; it has perlocutionary force). The following four steps are based on encyclopaedic knowledge of the world: (S5) people like chocolates; (S6) people try to obtain the things they like; (S7) some people may steal to obtain the things they want; (S8) chocolates cannot move on their own. Steps 1–8 constitute the premises for the (intermediate) conclusion (S9): someone stole Peter's chocolates. The next two steps in the line of reasoning are based on idiosyncratic (or personal) knowledge of the world in reference to John (S10: John likes chocolates; S11: John has taken chocolates without permission before). S12 returns us to "encyclopaedic knowledge": people who have stolen before can steal again. Note that S12 is actually an instance of prejudice—folk linguistic knowledge—but it is an essential step in the reasoning, revealing how simple it is for fallacies to slip into chains of reasoning without being readily detectable. Steps 10–12 thus constitute another set of premises which team up with the conclusion in S9 to yield the conversational implicature, S14, accusation: 'John probably took your chocolates'.

For a variety of reasons, CMT does not appear to account for the complexity outlined above. The unpacking of the intricate chain of reasoning behind Bill's utterance can be achieved through the deployment of Gricean maxims[15] (or relevance theory, depending on one's preferences).[16]

Now consider an alternative, metaphorical expression that Bill could have employed to create the same conversational implicature, such as "I saw a little birdie in your room this morning", an ambiguous expression which could be variously interpreted as conveying: (i) I took them but am not telling you; (ii) I know who took them but am not telling you; (iii) a real bird took them. Exactly the same type of complex processing would have to occur, but in cases (i) and (ii), the metaphor would also have to be priorly unpacked.

The central tenet expounded in this chapter is similar to the position taken by relevance theory: "[W]e see metaphors as simply a range of cases at one end of the continuum that includes literal, loose and hyperbolic interpretations. In our view, metaphorical interpretations are arrived at in exactly the same way as these other interpretations" (Sperber & Wilson 2008: 84; see also 95; cf. Moreno 2007: 93).

This chapter will therefore concentrate on demonstrating the complexity of mental processing involved in communication and the role of metaphor in the process. It will do so by providing an in-depth scrutiny of the opening scene of a play (tantamount to one complete speech event). The main theoretical orientation is based on Gricean Conversational Implicature combined with speech act theory, but the analysis of the selected text will also make use of conversation analysis, politeness, culture, text and context, and all the other analytical frameworks employed in text analysis.

2 CONCEPTUAL METAPHOR AND COMMUNICATION

2.1 Brian Clark's Play *Whose Life Is It Anyway?*

Whose Life Is It Anyway? (1978) by Brian Clark may be defined as a 'pièce à thèse', for it is a play specifically written to dialectically argue the case for euthanasia. Suasion thus lies at the heart of the text.

A man, an artist and a teacher, has had an extremely serious accident which has ruptured his spinal column. Ken is thus completely immobile and will never recover. He thus decides that his life is meaningless and undignified, and so he wishes to die. The head doctor in the clinic opposes this wish. The patient takes the hospital to court in order to achieve his goal.

Two basic types of "argumentative genre" may be identified in the play. One type consists in an exchange of views and of arguments supporting those views with the aim of persuading the interlocutor. It thus displays a gamut of rhetorical strategies, including "illicit" emotive arguments and *ad hominem* attacks. It is characterized by a great amount of humour and word play. In this type of speech event one encounters an extensive use of CMs and indirect language in general. The second type of discourse situation is more formal. It is concentrated mainly in the 'trial scene' in Act II where the judge hears the case and takes his decision, but is also to be found in some of the speech events in which the hero, Ken, argues with the Consultant Physician over his decision to die. This type of subgenre is more 'rational', deploys few CMs and the language is generally more explicit (i.e. consisting mainly of direct speech acts). Such linguistic behaviour veers towards the subgenre of 'legalese'.

My analysis will concentrate on the opening lines of the play, which belong to the first subgenre.

2.2   Utterances One to Six

TEXT 1

Sister: [U1] Good morning Mr Harrison. [U2] A new face for you today.
Ken: [U3] That's nice.
Nurse: [U4] Hello.
Ken: [U5] Hello, I'm afraid I can't offer you my hand. [U6] You'll just have to make do with my backside like all the other nurses.
They lower the bed.
Ken: [U7] Going down—Obstetrics, Gynaecology, Lingerie, Rubber wear.
They roll KEN over and start to massage his back with spirit and talc.
Ken: [U8] It's funny you know. I used to dream of situations like this.
Sister: [U9] Being injured?
Ken: [U10] No! [U11] Lying on a bed being massaged by two beautiful women.
Sister: (mock serious): [U12] If you go on like this Mr Harrison I shan't be able to send my young nurses in here.
Ken: [U13] They're perfectly safe with me, Sister.
The phone rings outside.
Sister: [U14] Can you manage for a moment Nurse?
Nurse: [U15] Oh, yes Sister.
Sister: [U16] Wipe your hands and put the pillows behind Mr Harrison; we don't want to have him on the floor.
Ken: [U17] Have me on the floor Sister please. [U18] Have me on the floor.
Sister goes out. (Clark 1989: 1–2)

The play opens with a metonymy: "a new face for you" (U2). Given that the metonym has a conventional meaning, following the greeting in U1 (i.e. the co-text), the implicature of U2 may be readily comprehended as an introduction. However, since these are the first two utterances in the play, there is as yet insufficient co-text and insufficient context—hence insufficient knowledge shared by audience and playwright—for the audience to comprehend the total, i.e. both local and global (Douthwaite 2000: 201–5), illocutionary and perlocutionary effects of this instance of foregrounding.

What is common knowledge in linguistics is thus confirmed immediately: shared knowledge of text and context is required to comprehend fully any utterance in a 'real' communicative event, including those cases of an utterance being constituted by a (conventional) cognitive metaphor.[17] More importantly, simply understanding the 'immediate' or 'surface' meaning conveyed by the metonym yields only a minor part of the wide-ranging effects the deployment of that metonym produces in that determinate linguistic and non-linguistic context—a general principle which is true of any utterance, not simply those utterances employing a metaphorical expression.

That only limited comprehension of the full effects of U2 can be achieved at this point in the play may be confirmed by employing our knowledge of the entire drama (viz. co-text) to explicate this metonym as well as U3–U6. In U2, the part for the whole does not simply perform a referential function ('pointing to' the new participant in the context) and initiate the speech act of introducing the interlocutors to one another; it is also symbolic at a macro-level, for it highlights the fact that Ken is 'disembodied': one part (his "face") 'works', and the rest of his body does not. This symbolic meaning is arrived at not through unwrapping a metaphorical expression, i.e. not through mapping features of entity A onto entity B, but through an inferential process which is triggered by having first identified the surface meaning of the metonym and then relating this surface meaning to the entire play (i.e. to contextual and co-textual information). This, of course, can occur only at second viewing/reading, with text and context having been 'fully established'.

Thus, after the first utterance (U1)—an obligatory, canonical greeting—, at the level of deep structure the second utterance immediately draws attention to the human condition, or plight, of the main character and anticipates the viewpoint he will take: Ken will argue that he is only 'part' human, and that that part is so 'small' that he cannot possibly consider himself human, hence he wants to cease living. He will thus do everything in his power to get the doctors to stop keeping him alive. The metonymy thus encapsulates the theme and foreshadows the 'action' of the play. The metonym has global as well as local significance.

The same metonym realises two further textual functions. First, given Ken's 'condition', a pretty, young nurse will constitute a 'weapon' in the Sister's fight trying to 'save' Ken from 'mental strife' and alleviate his suffering to the best of her abilities, because she cares for her patients. Secondly, however, in deploying the metonym, the Sister concurrently, albeit unintentionally, draws attention to Ken's 'human condition' by 'offering' something that Ken unlike a 'normal' male cannot try to avail himself of, as female beauty. She thereby inadvertently causes Ken pain, since he is a highly sensitive and intelligent person and fully aware of the potentialities of language, as his repartee will show.

A second instantiation of foregrounding immediately follows the deep communicative functions realised by the metonymy "face". In taking his turn (U3), Ken seemingly provides a polite conventional social response to Sister's introductory utterance: "That's nice" (observing Leech's Approbation maxim: "maximise praise of other"—Leech 1983: 132). However, turn-taking and politeness rules demonstrate that Ken is actually verging on rudeness, for after Sister's introductory utterances, Ken should have at least[18] reciprocated the greeting by acknowledging the presence both of Sister with for instance a "Good morning", and of the new nurse, with a "Pleased to meet you". Instead, with U3 Ken fails to reciprocate the greeting prompted by U1 and even goes so far as to ignore the new nurse in U2 by failing to address her! Furthermore, if one examines the utterance "That's nice" more deeply, then praise is not actually being maximized for the nurse, for she is soon to be insulted (U6). Rather, Ken is violating Leech's Generosity maxim (1983: 132) by maximizing benefit to self, for it is he who will benefit from the fresh stimuli provided by a new nurse, given his highly circumscribed access to the external world, hence to new, invigorating stimuli which humans require if they are not to fossilize. Additionally, Ken is being ironic, for despite the fact that Sister deploys all means in her power to provide new stimuli to get Ken to fight for his life, the circumstances nevertheless severely limit her action, objectively allowing her little efficacy given the enormity of Ken's problem. Finally, Ken has in fact no intention of cooperating with Sister since he wishes to die. Hence his "That's nice" is doubly ironic. A further function of the metonym is therefore to stimulate 'symbolic' (i.e. deeply significant) repartee.

The nurse is thus obliged to repair on Ken's behalf, which she does by pursuing the interrupted canonical turn-taking ritual of 'introductions' by saying "hello" (U4). She pretends that Ken has greeted her and she takes her legitimate turn without the floor having been officially given to her by the current speaker. The nurse, in other words, 'covers up' for Ken's deliberate 'blunder'. This is another manifestation of irony and the third instantiation of foregrounding in four utterances as it is the 'offender' who should repair a faulty utterance and not the offended party.

U5–U6 exploit the metonym introduced in U2 by extending the figurative possibilities of that metonym to create novel meanings through contiguity ("hand" and "face" belonging to the same semantic field). U5 appears to return to social 'normality' when Ken first greets the nurse with "hello", and then, in the remaining part of the utterance, in addition to realizing the direct speech act of apologising, he performs the multiple indirect speech acts of informing, explaining and justifying the fact that his mode of greeting is limited to the purely verbal without the standard accompanying symbolic gesture.

However, the expansion following the greeting is merely the first token or 'presequence' (Schegloff 2007: 28) of a two-stage conversational strategy which Ken will deploy on several occasions in an attempt to achieve a set of short- and long-term objectives. He first produces the presequence utterance U5, which creates expectations through triggering 'normal' schemas, thereby creating the impression of a return to normality, only to defeat those expectations with his subsequent utterance to produce an 'extreme' and 'unpleasant' perlocutionary effect. Thus, at the first stage the information/explanation/justification, which is rendered even more polite by the deployment of the conventional metaphor "offer you my hand", he merely lulls the unsuspecting receiver into tranquillity (perlocutionary effect). While it first appears as if Ken is being polite, he is actually preparing for the crushing 'punch line' in U6: "You'll have to make do with my backside". This is a pointedly vulgar face-threatening act (Brown & Levinson 1987). Through an unexpected clash of styles, namely through Hymesian inappropriacy to context (Hymes 1971; Cortese 2001), he thus foregrounds his rejection of the establishment of an interpersonal relationship, viz. the putative aim of an introduction. The offensiveness of the remark is intensified by the negative rider "like all the other nurses", which has a downward 'levelling' effect, thus redoubling the insult. The perlocutionary intention is to insult and to shock, and the utterance is extremely effective in realizing this intent.

On the other hand, if we delve below the surface, we again find that the deep communicative intent is not principally the obvious one of offending the addressee, which at the surface level could be taken as a psychologically understandable reaction, given Ken's situation, of working off pent-up anger and frustration. More importantly, Ken's "backside" still 'works', whereas his hand does not. In drawing attention to this crucial fact through an arresting utterance (foregrounding), Ken implies two points. First, Ken's hands constitute a metonym for his being a sculptor, thus suggesting his 'death' as an artist and a teacher leading to his desire for physical death. Secondly, Ken is exploiting the classic orientational image schema BAD IS DOWN: one's backside and its physical functions are socially reputed as being low down in our scale of values (CHAIN OF BEING CM; Kövecses 2002: 126). Hence, by contiguity, Ken employs a CM to evaluate his life negatively. Furthermore, by playing the metonym "backside" off against the metaphor "offer [. . .] my hand" Ken underscores how much more limited his life is, since (a) backsides can perform far fewer tasks than hands, and (b) for people to have to come into contact with another person's backside rather than his hands may be a demeaning act.

On a more general level, Ken's use of CM is a key strategy in his battle to convince others of the highly 'diminished' value of his existence, hence of the correctness of his decision to fight for his being allowed to die. Stated differently, CMs have an ideological function in Ken's discourse. Of course, as my analysis demonstrates, working out the implicatures listed above and identifying the ideological function of his strategic use of metaphor requires much more mental processing than simply mapping features from source onto target domains.

Thus, the first 'mini' speech event in the play (U1–U6) begins with a metonym and then exploits that metonym in a novel fashion. In order to comprehend what is really happening, the way the metonym is intertwined with other metaphors and other linguistic dimensions and devices, such as context, co-text, style, sequencing, turn-taking, exploitation and violation of Gricean and Leechian maxims, one must also be familiar with Brown and Levinson (1987) and their politeness theory. Furthermore, both low-level and high-level effects of the utterances can and must be identified, even in this mini-segment. The short-term effects here include: (a) shocking the new nurse, (b) attacking Sister indirectly through showing her that her strategy to keep Ken happy is not working and (c) making verbal play which highlights Ken's (in)human condition. At a higher level of generalisation, Ken's goal is to engage in conflict in order to 'dominate the scene'. Domination is not, however, an end in itself, for by engaging in a dialectic process—realised both in serious debate and in repartee—Ken wishes in the long term to establish that he is the 'dominator', the 'authority' on his 'case'. This specific middle- to high-level perlocutionary force has itself a further, higher-level perlocutionary force, that of trying to get the others to accept his viewpoint and eventually achieving the ultimate goal of persuading them to allow him to die.

A final general point to be noted regarding Ken's novel manipulation of the metonyms "hand" and "backside" in U5–U6 is that Ken exploits the opportunities offered by the context and co-text to make repartee a constant feature of his behaviour, one which shows he is a highly intelligent person, gifted verbally as well as artistically. Hence one global function of Ken's verbal artistry, including his consistent deployment of cognitive metaphor, is to build up a positive character portrait of himself so that the accusation of depression and/or madness that the Consultant Physician, Doctor Emerson, will level against him at the hearing will be disproven. Consequently, Ken's ability to manipulate language communicatively (especially figuratively) and argumentatively will convince the judge of Ken's sanity, i.e. the 'soundness' of his reasoning—a major fact which will induce the judge to allow Ken's petition.

Thus, at the highest level of generalisation, Ken's deployment of non-literal language (of which metaphor is only a part) represents merely one weapon in a rich armoury of linguistic (and non-linguistic) tools employed in enacting the strategy of attack he has selected to achieve his ultimate goal of being allowed to die.

2.3   Utterance Seven

Over and beyond the locutionary/illocutionary force of setting the scene, the stage directions "They lower the bed" has a dual textual function. First, it brings to an end the first 'mini'-speech event, and second it again provides Ken with the contextual input for his creative invention of a novel metaphor (parallelism), U7, again based on the image schema DOWN IS BAD. The functions of this calculated deployment of parallelism—the constancy of his creative wordplay—include establishing Ken as an intelligent, rational, controlled person who is capable of deciding for himself.

U7 in its entirety is a complex metaphor requiring intricate, conscious processing for its comprehension. The utterance is divided into two parts. The first part—realised by the non-finite clause "going down"—performs the direct speech act of describing the event of the nurses lowering Ken's bed. This use is thus, in the first instance, non-metaphorical. The assertive illocutionary force would not appear to have a transparent perlocutionary force because it flouts the Quantity maxim: the nurses do not need someone to inform them of what they are doing. Hence, communicatively speaking, the utterance may be hypothesized as performing a social and turn-taking function: Ken avoiding silence while passing the time of day with his interlocutors.

However, U7 also has a deeper set of functions. First, it constitutes a metaphoric reference to death. Such an association in the context of this utterance is not mapped automatically, for it has not been cued by a conventional metaphorical linguistic expression, such as 'going downhill', nor by preceding linguistic items in the preceding verbal and non-verbal context. In addition, prior general knowledge of the play is of itself unlikely to be sufficient to instantly trigger in the audience's mind the image schema DOWN IS BAD and associated connotations since no 'death' schema has yet been activated. On the other hand, the 'literal' interpretation is 'naturally' triggered by the visual context. Indeed, it is the remaining part of the utterance (co-text) that cues the three indirect speech acts which derive from the orientational image schema: 'my health is deteriorating' and 'I am dying' (morally and spiritually and not simply physically),[19] speech acts which also foreshadow Ken's death through euthanasia, his ultimate goal in the play. Through the speech acts performed in the scene, "going down" thus constitutes the linguistic embodiment of another classic CM, LIFE IS A JOURNEY. The three indirect speech acts performed by "going down" (informing of impending physical, moral and spiritual death) are the result of the blending of two CMs: the image schema DOWN IS BAD and the CM LIFE IS A JOURNEY (Ken's journey to 'hell'). Yet again, however, working out the meaning of the first part of U7 cannot be achieved exclusively through the unravelling of the blend (i.e. the mapping of two sets of source and target features and blending them).

More importantly, the interpretation of "going down" is crucially modified by the subsequent co-text. The full import of the metaphorical meaning of a verb phrase can be calculated only after the utterance has been completed. Although the utterance continues with the naming of four locations which switch the context of reference away from the immediate context—the hospital room—by adding information specifying the preceding clause, these locations do not appear to have any transparent, immediate, direct connection with the concept 'death'. Indeed, the first impression is that the addition of these four locations infringes the

Gricean maxim of Manner by making the utterance even vaguer. A much wider knowledge base (several input spaces in blending theory terms) and much more complex processing are required in order to retrieve the illocutionary force of U7 and, consequently, for the understanding of the CMs embodied in "going down".

The key to comprehension lies, of course, in the four 'locations' ("Obstetrics, Gynaecology, Lingerie, Rubber wear") which represent an embodiment of the EVENT STRUCTURE CM, and, specifically, EVENTS/STATES ARE LOCATIONS. What is crucial to note, however, is not the nature of the CM itself, but the actual details—the specific locations—that realize the CM (tying in with Gricean Relevance) and the order of presentation of those details (Gricean Manner, the sub-maxim: be orderly). To understand that U7 is actually a metaphor the receiver must employ Gricean maxims. He cannot simply map source features onto target features for he must first work out which metaphors are being employed.

The first two locations evoke the hospital context, while the latter two lexemes conjure up the context of a large department store of bygone times where the lift was operated by a lift-boy who called out the name of the department on each floor as the lift reached it. Only if we conjure up such a context can we realize that the actual locations are metonymies of 'stages' in life representing the physical capacities possessed and the 'activities' engaged in at each specific stage.

Obstetrics metonymically stands for conception and birth. Gynaecology also stands for the female reproductive apparatus physical love and conception; as does lingerie, which evokes the idea of foreplay in lovemaking. By contrast, rubber wear is a metonym of old age or babyhood. Thus the specific pathway of the LIFE IS A JOURNEY CM implied by U7 evokes first birth, then gestation, followed by conception, and finally by death (here pre-life tantamount to non-life). In other words, the utterance describes an inversion of the standard cultural symbolism of a left-to-right event/time sequence of life to death—regression, not progression, to a state of 'non-existence', hence Ken's quip "going down". Such a creative metaphor encapsulates Ken's view of his own situation: the 'direction' of his life has been reversed. It again underscores Ken's impotence, his present condition of 'spiritual' death, yielding the illocutionary force "I'm dying and nothing can be done about it" as hypothesized at the outset. In other words, the negativity does not lie simply in the conventional meaning of the metonym per se.

Turning to the relevance of this analysis to CMT, what is therefore interesting about U7 is that the first part of the utterance ("going down") stands upon its own, creating a first meaning which is literal: Ken's bed is indeed "going down". Then it unites with the second part of the utterance (itself divided into two on the semantic level, though forming one unit on the graphological level, the one unit indicating the continuous movement) to produce two further effects. First, it constrains a return to the first clause and its reinterpretation as being concurrently literal and metaphorical (i.e. an image schema). Secondly, it creates a novel metaphorical linguistic expression with ulterior meaning (the reversal of direction of the CM LIFE IS A JOURNEY). To accomplish the latter it calls upon not one, but (at least) three input spaces—the physical space of generic downward movement, the hospital and the department store. What should further be noted is that standard connotations, such as the positive connotation of eroticism 'normally' evoked by "lingerie", conjuring up the foreplay preceding the act of making love (hence conception), is negatively value-laden here, since it constitutes part of the regression which Ken painfully and powerfully feels he is undergoing.

This inversion of the conventional schema thus goes against Lakoff's Invariance Principle, which is central to his theory of CM and which states that "metaphorical mappings preserve the cognitive topology (that is the image schema structure) of the source domain, that is consistent with the inherent structure of the target domain" (1993: 215). Instead, the present example would suggest that in communication it is possible to go against the constraints on the possible mappings imposed by our knowledge of the target domain. The negativity (or irony) of the reference to "lingerie" here is just one of the many references to love-making that Ken makes as part of his strategy to persuade his audience that he is no longer 'a man', as he can no longer engage in 'manly' activities. Going against the standard constraints on potential mappings is possible because mapping per se is an insufficient condition both for the creation and for the comprehension of meaning. Indeed, the mapping process as described in classic or early CMT appears at times to be as mechanistic as the positivist and structuralist views of encoding and decoding as consisting of one-to-one relationships between form and meaning.

This raises the familiar problematic issue in CM theory of what exactly is transferred from source to target domains and the less debated issue of what mental processes account for the transfer. This is a question that CMT cannot answer satisfactorily if it overlooks pragmatics, as the analysis of the above examples suggest (see also Charteris-Black 2004: ch. 1 *passim*).

Thus, with regard to matching target and source domains in U7 we have, first, a complex, partial overlap of at least three input spaces; and second, a most particular matching of features between spaces where, as the "lingerie" example bears out, 'standard' equivalences are negated (and foregrounding occurs yet again).

The key to working out these equivalences lies, as argued above, in Gricean maxims. Change the nature of the items (Quality)—e.g. to 'electronics, lingerie, endocrinology, gynaecology'—or their order (Manner)—e.g. 'gynaecology, lingerie, rubber wear, obstetrics'—and the novel metaphor is lost! As Charteris-Black (2004: 10) emphasizes, "metaphors are not a requirement of the semantic system but are matters of speaker choice". They must therefore be accounted for in the same way that any speaker choice (viz. any communicative act) is accounted for, using the inferential machine. Mapping features from source to target is not enough, and selection of relevant features and their specific effects (especially when in contrast to 'standard effects') depends on factors 'external' to the metaphor itself, and, in the first instance, on pragmatic maxims. Indeed, the wary reader will have noted that in my synthetic variants I omitted to employ capital letters, as does the source text, when referring to the four locations. I thereby eliminate the additional graphological (hence pragmatic) 'clue' provided by Clark to indicate that these nouns are intended to refer to proper names, that they constitute a reference to wards in a hospital and to departments in a store.

It may thus be concluded that linguistic metaphors in texts are not simply independent, self-referential entities; otherwise, a code view of language (Douthwaite 2000: 10–12) would be sufficient to work out the meaning(s) conveyed by a metaphor. To extend an insight from Charteris-Black (2004: 11), one could say that the 'traditional' or 'early' cognitive approach limits metaphor explication to the "underlying experiential basis" conjured up by the source domain.

2.4   Utterances Eight to Seventeen

The remaining utterances in the opening scene confirm the points outlined above. In U8 ("I used to dream of situations like this"), Ken reiterates the strategy of deliberately proferring an utterance which creates expectations in the addressee—expectations which, in this case, are verbalized by Sister in U9 ("Being injured?")—only to defeat them in U10–11 ("No! Lying on a bed being massaged by two beautiful women"). Ken does this by exploiting the Gricean maxim of Manner (sub-maxim 'avoid obscurity'). Since demonstrative "this" has opaque reference, Sister is obliged to have recourse to her manifest cognitive environment, hypothesizing the present physical location as constituting the most readily available context. This allows her to recover an interpretation of the utterance (Sperber & Wilson 1986). Ken thus creates a mismatch between the context 'naturally' referred to by Sister (the hearer) and the one he (the speaker) then refers to in U11.

Turning from technique to content, we can note that this 'mini speech event' (U8–11) again aims at highlighting Ken's impotence through sexual banter. Standard cognitive environment would classify U11 as evoking an erotic scene, yet Ken's (ironic) message through that evocation is that eroticism is precisely what he cannot engage in physically. At the highest level of generalisation the final outcome of 'sex' is birth—viz. life, the thing Ken asserts he no longer possesses. Sexual repartee is thus simply a symbolic means to an end, though a highly persuasive one as it goes to the heart of the matter. U8 to U11 thus constitute the first of three 'jokes' which are all based on polysemy rather than on metaphor.

U12 sees Sister taking her turn and continuing the make-believe in a game of 'one-upmanship', which I prefer to call 'domination' here, for in this dialectic play it represents a struggle for power through the use of language. Her retort is indirect, but does not deploy metaphor. It rather creates the implicature that, as Ken puts it in the following utterance (U13), the nurses won't be "safe" if left alone with Ken. Since Sister's reply is based on a marked reduction in explicitness, it leaves room for Ken to 'put her down' by explicating the implicature via a conventional metaphor, "perfectly safe" (see below). This remark is sadly ironic because Ken once more implies that he is impotent, undermining the standard socially value-laden presupposition implicit in the text that MEN ARE SEXUAL PREDATORS (a subdomain of the CM MEN ARE ANIMALS). The third joke (U16–U18) plays on the multiple (conventional metaphorical) meanings of "have", exploiting the associations of transgressive and passionate sex by invoking a 'typical' location on which such acts are consumed—"on the floor".

Four further points can be made regarding this bantering scene. First, joking for Ken is a way of making light of the situation, of trying to come to terms with his predicament. Second, it also provides a topic for conversation, for there is little you can talk about to a total invalid. Third, the deployment of sexual innuendo underscores not simply Ken's sexual impotence, but his general, and especially his creative, artistic impotence, which is the main reason he provides for wishing to have his life terminated. (This wish will be adumbrated on several occasions, for instance through the reiterated use of the CM PEOPLE ARE MACHINES.) Thus, it is no coincidence that all five of Ken's opening linguistic puns (U6, U7, U8, U11, U13, U17–U18) are erotic[20] in the widest sense of the term for sex implies joy and creativity, precisely what Ken can no longer obtain from life. One can also conclude that the deployment of metaphor is not a chance, local affair but is patterned, a form of foregrounding. It helps not simply to highlight the experience that Ken is going through, but to emphasize Ken's ideological meaning at the global level.

The fourth point concerns the nature of metaphor and metaphorical processes. The use of the linguistic metaphors "go on" (U13), "perfectly safe" (U14) and "have (me on the floor)" (U17) are lexemes which, to my knowledge, are not generally treated as metaphors in CM literature. Presumably, they have been so conventionalised as to be no longer treated as metaphors, but as denotations of the lexemes. However, *go on*, meaning 'continue', exploits the CM ACTIVITY IS MOTION (*go*) and the orientational CM embodied by the preposition *on* (motion forward). Together they form a blend realizing the CM LIFE IS A PATH, which in turn is a superordinate metaphor of LIFE IS A JOURNEY. *Safe* corresponds to 'no danger of sexual aggression', which may embody the CMs MENTAL WELL-BEING IS PHYSICAL WELL-BEING and PEOPLE ARE INDUSTRIAL PRODUCTS (*safe* = 'undamaged'), as well as MEN ARE SEXUAL PREDATORS. *Perfectly* as an intensifier may also be hypothesized to be a metaphorical linguistic expression realizing the CM PEOPLE ARE INDUSTRIAL PRODUCTS (an undamaged product is perfect). The same CM is used in the expression *have me on the floor*, where Ken becomes a (sexual) consumer product.

What these examples show is the pervasiveness of cognitive metaphors and the difficulty of recognising them, since, as stated above, items such as the ones we have examined are generally considered as non-metaphorical lexemes with purely denotational value.

3   CONCLUDING REMARKS

In 1999 Eubanks complained that too little attention had been devoted to the way in which metaphors were used concretely in communication (421). Since then more textually-oriented studies on corpora (Deignan 2005) and discourse analysis (Charteris-Black 2004) have appeared, but again, attention has focussed more on the definition, identification and general functions of metaphor rather than on the specific use a given linguistic metaphor is put to in a given text and how this creates meaning in relation to the entire text. Texts, or significant extracts of texts, are not examined in their entirety but (contextualized) examples are selected illustrating specific theoretical points and showing the usefulness of a particular approach.

The objective of the present analysis has been to take the opposite direction by analysing an extract which in some meaningful way is complete in itself (as far as this is possible, namely by taking into account the entire text and context when examining the extract). This was done to demonstrate how meaning is produced in the text and then to evaluate the contribution made by cognitive metaphors in the meaning-making process. This procedure has not only enabled me to identify how cognitive metaphors work concretely in communication, but also to scrutinise hypotheses concerning the nature of cognitive metaphors, highlighting the inadequacies of the standard model. It is therefore to be hoped that more studies employing pragmatic theories will be undertaken to delve further into such matters.

NOTES

1. I wish to thank Monika Fludernik and Beatrix Busse for their valuable suggestions on previous versions of this chapter, and the former also for having brought to my attention Moreno's (2007) important study.
2. Although Aristotle did deal with metaphor as a theory of composition and style, and as a theory of argumentation, it should not be forgotten that he also drew attention to the cognitive dimension which CM theorists now focus on (Cameron & Low 1999; Mahon 1999).
3. Lakoff and Turner (1989: 63–64) classify the "correspondences" or "mappings" which are transferred from the source domain to the target domain as consisting of "slots", "relations", "properties" and "knowledge".
4. It has now been demonstrated that mapping is not 'uni-directional', but may be from abstract to abstract (TIME IS MONEY), from concrete to concrete and from one element to another within the same domain (as in the case of metonymy; Kövecses 2002: 145).

5. For an analysis of Rossetti's poem in terms of CM, see Gibbs (1994), and of that by Dickinson, together with an extended discussion of the CM LIFE IS A JOURNEY, see Lakoff and Turner (1989).

6. In both cases, then, there will be more than two input spaces in terms of blending theory.

7. Or of the *Weltanschauung* embodied in the culture the speaker belongs to, since his language is a result of the culture he has 'inherited' socially, depending on his accident of birth place. As Eubanks (1999: 421) puts it: "[W]hen we speak of argument as war, we reveal not just mental processes but also something of our culture".

8. For it is a general theory of mental processing rather than 'simply' an account of metaphor processing.

9. In strict Austinian terms, these meanings cannot be classified as having locutionary force.

10. Note that while persuasion goes back to classicism, the embellishment theory of metaphor has been largely abandoned.

11. Such a criticism can be found at least as early as Gibbs (1994: 245)

12. Exceptions to this are those studies in which pragmatic patterning in the deployment of CMs in a text lead to the discovery of high-level meanings, as in Freeman (1998, 1999). (On pragmatic patterning, see Douthwaite 2003.) However, Jakobsonian parallelism is only one, albeit important, of a myriad of devices creating indirectness, hence the need for pragmatic inferencing and stylistic analysis.

13. Indeed, in their article Tendahl and Gibbs (2008) argue that CMT and relevance theory are compatible and not antithetical approaches. To state the matter differently, CMT should be integrated with pragmatics to yield an exhaustive interpretation of communicative events.

14. In claiming that "ordinary everyday English is largely metaphorical", Lakoff (1993) is one of the many who lay the foundation for the sacrifice of pragmatics. Such a neglect of pragmatics benefits cognitive linguistics in CMT research, since non-literal language becomes almost equated with metaphorical language, which is actually far from being the case. This trend is noticeable, for instance, in Coulson and Oakley's (2000) introduction to CMT.

15. Paul Grice claims that human interaction is governed by the cooperative principle, which can be divided up into four maxims: the maxim of Quantity (*Be [exactly] as informative as required.*); the maxim of Quality (*Be truthful.*); the maxim of Relation (*Be relevant.*); and the maxim of Manner (*Be clear.*) (1989: 22–40, esp. 26–28).

16. At least tentatively, since our knowledge of mental processing remains extremely circumscribed.

17. Or assimilated phenomena. CMT includes the study of metonymy (e.g. Kövecses 2002; Knowles & Moon 2006), although some scholars treat metaphor and metonymy as different phenomena (e.g. Glucksberg 2001; Haser 2005).

18. One might further note that Ken employs a minimal response. He makes no effort at expansion. This should warn the audience that all is not what Ken seems to make it appear—i.e. "nice" might not mean 'nice'.

19. An utterance such as "I've come to the end of the road" constitutes a conventional linguistic realization of the CM SOURCE-PATH-GOAL (which, in turn may be taken as a sub-category of the CM LIFE IS A JOURNEY); unlike "going down", in this context it would therefore be processed unconsciously, automatically and effortlessly, as conveying an announcement of impending death.

20. Indeed, Ken will deploy this semantic field over and over again to underscore the fact that he is physically useless and can therefore have no purpose in life. Thus, one evening he says to the beautiful Doctor Scott, while he is being shaved: "I was just making myself beautiful for you Doctor".

156   *John Douthwaite*

WORKS CITED

Brown, Penelope, and Stephen C. Levinson (1987) *Politeness: Some Universals in Language Usage*. Cambridge: Cambridge University Press.
Cameron, Lynne (2003) *Metaphor in Educational Discourse*. London: Continuum.
Cameron, Lynne, and Graham Low (1999) Eds. *Researching and Applying Metaphor*. Cambridge: Cambridge University Press.
Charteris-Black, Jonathan (2004) *Corpus Approaches to Critical Metaphor Analysis*. Houndmills: Palgrave.
Clark, Brian (1989) *Whose Life Is It Anyway?* [1978]. Oxford: Heinemann.
Cortese, Giuseppina (2001) "Introduction". *Textus* 14.2: 193–230. Special issue *'Languaging' in and Across Human Groups: Perspectives in Difference and Asymmetry*.
Coulson, Seana, and Todd Oakley (2000) "Blending Basics". *Cognitive Linguistics* 11.3–4: 175–96.
Crisp, Paul (2008) "Between Extended Metaphor and Allegory: Is Blending Enough?" *Language and Literature* 17.4: 291–308.
Deignan, Alice A. (2005) *Metaphor and Corpus Linguistics*. Amsterdam: John Benjamins.
Douthwaite, John (2000) *Towards a Linguistic Theory of Foregrounding*. Alessandria: Edizioni dell'Orso.
——— (2003) "Pragmatic Patterning as Foregrounding: Albert Camus' *L'Etranger*". *Il testo: meccanismi linguistici e strategie retoriche*. Ed. Ines Loi Corvetto. Rome: Carocci. 101–20.
Eubanks, Philip (1999) "The Story of Conceptual Metaphor: What Motivates Metaphoric Mappings?" *Poetics Today* 20.3: 419–42.
Fauconnier, Gilles, and Mark Turner (2002) *The Way We Think: Conceptual Blending and the Mind's Hidden Complexities*. New York: Basic Books.
Fludernik, Monika (2010) "Naturalizing the Unnatural: A View from Blending Theory". *Journal of Literary Semantics* 39: 1–27.
Freeman, Donald C. (1998) "'Catch[ing] the Nearest Way': *Macbeth* and Cognitive Metaphor". *Exploring the Language of Drama: From Text to Context*. Eds. Jonathan Culpeper, Michael H. Short and Peter Verdonk. London: Routledge. 96–111.
——— (1999) "'The Rack Dislimns': Schema and Metaphorical Pattern in *Anthony and Cleopatra*". *Poetics Today* 20.3: 443–60.
Gibbs, Raymond W. (1994) *The Poetics of Mind*. Cambridge: Cambridge University Press.
Glucksberg, Sam (2001) *Understanding Figurative Language: From Metaphors to Idioms*. New York: Oxford University Press.
Goatly, Andrew (1997) *The Language of Metaphors*. London: Routledge.
Grady, Joseph E., Todd Oakley and Seana Coulson (1999) "Blending and Metaphor". *Metaphor in Cognitive Linguistics*. Eds. Raymond W. Gibbs and Gerard J. Steen. Amsterdam: John Benjamins. 102–24.
Grice, Paul (1989) *Studies in the Way of Words*. Cambridge, MA: Harvard University Press.
Haser, Verena (2005) *Metaphor, Metonymy and Experientialist Philosophy: Challenging Cognitive Semantics*. Berlin: de Gruyter.
Hymes, Dell (1971) "On Communicative Competence". *Sociolinguistics: Selected Readings*. Eds. John B. Pride and Janet Holmes. Harmondsworth: Penguin. 269–93.
Knowles, Murray, and Rosamund Moon (2006) *Introducing Metaphor*. London: Routledge.

Kövecses, Zoltán (2000) *Metaphor and Emotion*. Cambridge: Cambridge University Press.

—— (2002) *Metaphor: A Practical Introduction*. Oxford: Oxford University Press.

—— (2005) *Metaphor in Culture: Universality and Variation*. Cambridge: Cambridge University Press.

Lakoff, George (1993) "The Contemporary Theory of Metaphor". *Metaphor and Thought*. Ed. Andrew Ortony. Second Edition. Cambridge: Cambridge University Press. 202–51.

Lakoff, George, and Mark Johnson (1980) *Metaphors We Live By*. Chicago: University of Chicago Press.

Lakoff, George, and Mark Turner (1989) *More than Cool Reason*. Chicago: University of Chicago Press.

Leech, Geoffrey N. (1983) *Principles of Pragmatics*. Burnt Mill: Longman.

Levinson, Stephen C. (1983) *Pragmatics*. Cambridge: Cambridge University Press.

Mahon, James Edwin (1999) "Getting Your Sources Right: What Aristotle *Didn't Say*". *Researching and Applying Metaphor*. Eds. Lynne Cameron and Graham Low. Cambridge: Cambridge University Press. 69–80.

McGlone, Matthew S. (2001) "Concepts as Metaphors". *Understanding Figurative Language: From Metaphors to Idioms*. Sam Glucksberg. New York: Oxford University Press. 90–107.

Moreno, Rosa E. Vega (2007) *Creativity and Convention: The Pragmatics of Everyday Figurative Speech*. Amsterdam: John Benjamins.

Poetics Today 20.3 (Fall 1999). Special issue on *Metaphor and Beyond: New Cognitive Developments*.

Reddy, Michael J. (1979) "The Conduit Metaphor—A Case of Frame Conflict in Our Language about Language". *Metaphor and Thought*. Ed. Andrew Ortony. Cambridge: Cambridge University Press. 284–324.Rossetti, Christina (2001) *The Complete Works of Christina Rossetti*. Ed. Rebecca W. Crump. London: Penguin.

Sadock, Jerrold (1979) "Figurative Speech and Linguistics". *Metaphor and Thought*. Ed. Andrew Ortony. Cambridge: Cambridge University Press. 46–63.

Schegloff, Emanuel A. (2007) *Sequence Organization in Interaction: A Primer in Conversation Analysis*. Volume 1. Cambridge: Cambridge University Press.

Searle, John (1979) *Expression and Meaning: Studies in the Theory of Speech Acts*. Cambridge: Cambridge University Press.

Sperber, Dan, and Deirdre Wilson (1995) *Relevance: Communication and Cognition* [1986]. Oxford: Blackwell.

—— (2008) "A Deflationary Account of Metaphors". *The Cambridge Handbook of Metaphor and Thought*. Ed. Raymond W. Gibbs. Cambridge: Cambridge University Press. 84–108.

Tendahl, Marcus, and Raymond W. Gibbs (2008) "Complementary Perspectives on Metaphor: Cognitive Linguistics and Relevance Theory". *Journal of Pragmatics* 40: 1823–64.

8 The Role of Metaphor in Poetic Iconicity

Margaret H. Freeman

INTRODUCTION

Contemporary theories of metaphor in cognitive linguistics present a challenge to literary scholars who believe that metaphor differentiates poetry from prose (Brooks 1965). If the same cognitive metaphors can be shown to structure both literary and everyday language, then wherein does the difference lie? If there is a difference, is it linguistic or conceptual? A matter of kind or degree? Of entrenchment or innovation? Of communicative (conventional) discourse or expressive (aesthetic) utterance? Or is it the case that all these questions miss the mark, that to understand poetic metaphor, one needs to probe more deeply into the nature of poetry itself?

Poetry has been defined variously as a vision, an illusion, an imitation, a semblance of reality. Philosophically, the word *image* refers to impressions of all five senses in the conceptual mind. That poetry can create in our minds an image of the world's reality makes it iconic in the semiotic sense of "a verbal sign which *somehow* shares the properties of, or resembles, the object which it denotes" (Wimsatt 1954: x). Peirce identifies the icon as being composed of image, diagram and metaphor. Iconicity studies fall mainly into two categories: iconography—the representation of reality through material signs (Tseng 1999), and iconology—the placing of signs within an ideological (social, political, cultural) environment (Miller 1993). These procedural and functional categories result in an icon's ontology, a state of being or "essence" (Freeman 2007). How image and diagram might iconically interrelate with metaphor was not explored until Masako Hiraga's (2005) ground-breaking studies on applying blending theory to the role of iconicity and metaphor in poetic texts. Hiraga suggests that "grammatical metaphor" is the bridge that links Peirce's image to diagram. In Fauconnier and Turner's (2002) original blending model, the generic space "contains" the structural elements that the two input (image) spaces have in common, thus enabling the blend to emerge. I propose that in art forms the emergent meaning of the blend becomes iconic when the relationship between concept and structure in an expression is metaphoric. In other words, when a metaphorical relation exists between image and diagram, iconicity may occur (Figure 8.1).

Missing from this model is the role of emotion. Although some attempts have been made to model emotional integration on the basis of blending theory (Brandt & Brandt 2005; Deacon 2006), the implicit claim that conceptual and emotional integration processes are the same has not as yet been empirically tested. In poetry, as in all the arts, metaphorical schemas may be the structuring principle that links forms and images through feeling to create *poetic iconicity*, or what Susanne K. Langer (1953: 40) calls the semblance of felt life through "forms symbolic of human feeling". Reuven Tsur (2008), for example, throughout his extensive research, explores the ways in which one might identify the emotional qualities of a literary text. In my own work, I have argued that feeling (emotions/sensations) motivates the creation of iconicity (Freeman 2007, 2008, 2009).

Underlying the question of literary metaphor is the question of a theory of art, itself a complex and difficult notion to address. The question

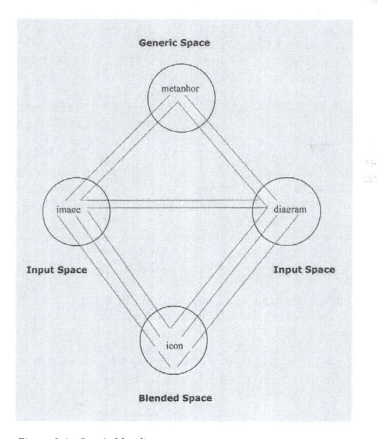

Figure 8.1   Iconic blending.

of art is not resolved by claiming "it is art if you say it is". The problem remains: what determines "good" or even "great" art? The good and the great seem to transcend the boundaries of language, culture or time. Art critics—musicologists, art historians, literary theorists and the like—have developed expertise in distinguishing the great and the good from the bad and the indifferent. What is it that they know? Cognitive science is still far from generating a scientific explanation or model of the cognitive processes of aesthetic evaluation. But one small step to establish a foundation in this direction might be to explore the ways in which metaphor structures art. I suggest that poems may be judged aesthetically successful when they achieve poetic iconicity.

POETIC ICONICITY: A COMPARISON OF TWO SONNETS

To explore the iconic role of literary metaphor, I examine prosodic effects in two sonnets by Percy Bysshe Shelley and Horace Smith on the same theme, one of which achieves poetic iconicity through a structuring metaphoric schema, and one which does not. Both sonnets originally bore the same title, "Ozymandias".[1] Although Smith's sonnet certainly has poetic virtues, the lack of any structuring metaphorical schema to create a coherence of formulated feeling, drawing the reader into emotional engagement with the text, prevents the poem from achieving poetic iconicity. In contrast, Shelley's poem is structured by the metaphoric schema of ENTROPY THROUGH TIME IS CHANGE THROUGH SHIFT.[2] Entropic movement can take many forms. The change may be metamorphic, catastrophic or a barely perceptible shifting or displacement of forces. I use the term *shift* in this latter sense. Shelley's poem creates a metaphoric relation between its shifting forms and the theme of entropy, giving the reader an ironic sense of the futility of man's hubris in assuming the permanence of his own achievements. Try as I would, I could discover no structuring metaphorical schema in Smith's poem that would create iconicity.

1   Contextual Background

Shelley and Smith wrote their sonnets in friendly competition at Marlowe, England, on December 26, 1817, perhaps inspired by an announcement of the imminent arrival in 1818 of the head of Ramesses II that Giovanni Belzoni had acquired for the British Museum (Rodenbeck 2004).

Both sonnets share the theme of the disappearance of what was once a great empire. The requirement of a turn or *volta*, classically at the sestet but manipulated to serve the purposes of the verse, establishes the sonnet's formal frame. Shelley focuses on Ozymandias's statue, Smith on Ozymandias's works. Thus Shelley's turn in line 12 ironically compares the physical statue and its inscription with what is no longer there, whereas Smith's turn

Shelley's Sonnet[3]	Smith's Sonnet[4]
1 I met a traveller from an antique land,	In Egypt's sandy silence, all alone,
2 Who said—"Two vast and trunkless legs of stone	Stands a gigantic Leg, which far off throws
3 Stand in the desert ... Near them, on the sand,	The only shadow that the Desart knows:—
4 Half sunk a shattered visage lies, whose frown,	"I am great OZYMANDIAS," saith the stone,
5 And wrinkled lips, and sneer of cold command,	"The King of Kings; this mighty City shows
6 Tell that its sculptor well those passions read	"The wonders of my hand."— The City's gone,—
7 Which yet survive, stamped on these lifeless things,	Nought but the Leg remaining to disclose
8 The hand that mocked them, and the heart that fed;	The site of this forgotten Babylon.
9 And on the pedestal, these words appear:	We wonder,—and some Hunter may express
10 My name is Ozymandias, King of Kings,	Wonder like ours, when thro' the wilderness
11 Look on my Works, ye Mighty, and despair!	Where London stood, holding the Wolf in chace,
12 Nothing beside remains. Round the decay	He meets some fragment huge, and stops to guess
13 Of that colossal Wreck, boundless and bare	What powerful but unrecorded race
14 The lone and level sands stretch far away.	Once dwelt in that annihilated place.

in line 9 introduces a comparison of Ozymandias's works with contemporary London, which will be likewise seen at some future time as "an annihilated place". It is not the choice of focus that determines whether or not each poem achieves poetic iconicity, but the way in which each poet uses the cognitive strategies available to him in establishing the reader's emotional engagement in the poem's semblance of felt life. Only Shelley's poem has a metaphorical schema that governs those cognitive strategies.

Shelley's and Smith's versions of the inscription on the statue paraphrase somewhat differently the inscription on the base of the statue, provided in Booth's (1814) translation of Diodorus Siculus as "I am Osymandias, king of kings; if any would know how great I am, and where I lie, let him excel me in any of my works", and indicate the very different purposes the poets have.[5] Neither Shelley's nor Smith's version includes reference to where Ozymandias might lie. Diodorus's translation of the original inscription (if indeed there were one) focuses on Ozymandias's challenge to discover his greatness by surpassing his achievements. Smith's version loses the sense of challenge by simply naming the "works" as "this mighty City" which existed as a testimony to the "wonders" wrought by Ozymandias. Shelley turns the challenge into a direct command, "Look," and reinforces Ozymandias's greatness by having him address not just anyone, but "ye Mighty". By collapsing the challenge into the one word "despair!" Shelley sets up the irony that exists between what the inscription was originally meant to mean and what it actually does to the nineteenth-century observer and subsequently to contemporary readers of his poem. Smith's inscription misses both the challenge of the original and the irony that Shelley captures. This contrast raises the question: what precisely are the cognitive strategies that Shelley successfully manages and Smith fails to apply in creating both a sense of the real and an emotional engagement with the text that would indicate the achievement of poetic iconicity?

2   The Metaphoric Schema of ENTROPY
THROUGH TIME IS CHANGE THROUGH SHIFT

One schema that links diagram (form) and image (concept) is CHANGE. *Change*—the alteration in state, condition, time, place, etc.—takes many forms (often indicated by the Latinate prefix *trans-*: *transform*, *transpose*, *translate*, etc.). It may be abrupt or gradual, whole or partial. It may involve a movement in place or time, or a transmutation of matter. *Entropy* in its popular sense indicates a negation of energy. The schema of NEGATION is a mental construct. It does not exist in the real world. It is only in our minds. That is, humans are able to conceive of absence, lack, something that is not there. NEGATION is, therefore, the least embodied of all our mental schemas. It also entails an emotional response. Our automatic reaction to what is not there is either positive or negative: relief—the absence of what we fear (an airplane crash, cancer), or despair—the lack of what we desire (success, money). Negation is conditioned by our perception of space and time, it is dependent upon past memory and future expectation, and it is grounded in potentiality.

Both poems focus on change from existence to non-existence through time. In Smith's sonnet, change is represented at two points in time: the present moment, in which "we wonder" at the disappearance of Ozymandias's city some time in our past, and some future moment, when a hunter similarly wonders at the disappearance of London at some point in his past. Smith's time is past and imperfective, with Ozymandias's story never resolved. Shelley's time is past and perfective, with Ozymandias's story ending in disappearance into nothingness.[6] In Shelley's poem, change takes on the metaphorical schema of ENTROPY THROUGH TIME IS CHANGE THROUGH SHIFT or, more briefly, ENTROPY IS SHIFT. *Shift* implies a slight, not major, adjustment of position, as in both the literal and metaphorical meaning of "shifting gears". It is not surprising that literary critics have used the term *shift* to refer to several features in Shelley's poem (e.g. Austin 1994; Tsur 2008: 595–622). Shifting manifests itself in the interrelationships of all the macroscopic and microscopic features of the poem, such as prosody, rhyme, sound pattern, repetition, point of view. In each case, shifting occurs from an expected "position", as in deviation from the standard sonnet form or a change in point of view. In Shelley's poem, shifting takes on the negative connotations of slipping, crumbling, deterioration, decay from forces within rather than from some exterior power, a movement from more to less, thus suggesting movement of entropy from stability to instability, security to insecurity, invulnerability to vulnerability. By linking the poem's forms to its images, the metaphor ENTROPY IS SHIFT enables us to feel the force of the inevitable processes of decay that bring men's work to nought.

Smith attempts to capture the idea of disappearance, but he focuses on what is there rather than what is not, by using words with negative connotations but positive effects, such as *silence* (the absence of noise), *alone* and *only* (the absence of others). In line 7 the *nought but* construction results in focus on the leg rather than on the absent body. By contrast, Shelley captures, in the scene depicted, the *feeling* of what is not there. Consider, for example, his use of the suffix *-less*. The suffix implies that the root to which it is affixed once existed but does no longer, another significant example of the perfective aspect in Shelley's poem. It occurs three times in the poem in three strategic places. The first and last lines of the sonnet evoke both space and time:

> I met a traveller from an antique land,
> *where*
> The lone and level sands stretch far away.

Within this frame, *-less* occurs at the beginning, end and in the exact middle of the interior lines in "trunkless" (line 2), "lifeless" (line 7) and "boundless" (line 13). Each occurrence falls toward the end of the line in which it appears, a suggestion of loss toward the end. The meaning of the suffix shifts subtly with each noun, and the order of the three words creates a progression of abstraction from the missing body of the statue, to the oxymoronic survival of passions stamped on non-living "things", to the concept of unlimited vistas, just as the city as the "body" of Ozymandias's works is now missing, lost forever in the entropy of the shifting sands that have reduced Ozymandias's achievements to nought.

Following is a brief summary of the ways in which the theme of entropy in Shelley's poem is conveyed metaphorically through its shifting forms, compared with the forms of Smith's sonnet.

3   Shifting Prosody

Prosody carries a poem's emotional weight. The sonnet's underlying form—the two quatrains of an octet and a sestet—and the rhyme schemes of the Petrarchan, Shakespearian and French variations establish a basis from which individual poets may deviate. Both Smith and Shelley employ irregular rhymes that interact with stress placement, caesura and syntax to create specific prosodic effects, but only in Shelley's poem are these effects governed by an overarching metaphorical schema.

Syntax may confirm or complicate prosodic metre. When intonation patterns and phrasal units converge with metrical position and grouping, then syntax and metre converge, as in the opening line of Thomas Gray's "Elegy Written in a Country Churchyard":

The cúrfew tólls the knéll of párting dáy (Gray 1973: 61)

Just as the stress patterns of nouns, adjectives and verbs each fall on the even position in this iambic pentametre line, so does the phrasing of the main clause followed by a prepositional phrase fall in the region of the prosodic caesura, and sentence end coincides with line end.[7] Gray's line is thus perceived as a perceptual whole with no tension, contributing to a tone of peacefulness. If, however, linguistic syntax deviates from prosodic metre, certain degrees of tension occur depending on where and how the displacement takes place. When syntactic caesurae occur towards the end of the line, there is a strong "requirement" for prosodic completion (Tsur 2008: 143). In line 4 of Shelley's poem, syntax overrides prosodic caesura in positions 3–7: "a shattered visage"; and the syntactic break after position 8, "lies, whose frown", raises a strong expectation for closure, which is both provided by prosodic completion and denied by two shifts: syntactic enjambment and the off-rhyme of the words *stone/frown*. This shifting of continuity against expectation of closure, and discontinuity against expectation of continuity is the first indication of the poem's ironic stance, and carries with it the force of emotive feelings, reflected in the "passions" that are all that remain of the human agency that both fed the heart of Ramesses II and guided the hand of the sculptor who traced them on the stone. The term "mocked" captures the feelings that guided the hand, and anticipates the mockery of the words transcribed on the pedestal.

Sentences that coincide with line endings are "released"; enjambments are "arrested" (Sinclair 1966). In Smith's sonnet, the octet ends with a period, followed by the turn, confirming the conventional division of the sonnet form. The end of Shelley's octet appears to be released, but the sentence is continued, marked by both the punctuation and the conjunction that follows, and does not close until the end of line 11, which ends the description of the statue and its inscription. Shelley's turn therefore does not occur until line 12, on the poem's shortest sentence that carries the entropic force of the poem in its perfective aspect: "Nothing beside remains". The fact that the turn comes after one long sentence comprising eleven lines and marks a caesura boundary rather than a line end gives it extra weight. It stops continuity. On the macrolevel, then, entropic shift occurs with a diagrammatic reduction in the ratio of lines as the sonnet moves from a vertical to horizontal image schema.[8] The conceptual metaphor MORE IS UP governs the vertical to horizontal move, first with the image of the legs that "stand" to the head that is "half sunk" and then from the inscription "on the pedestal" to the "level(ing)" sands. MORE is also GREATER. By delaying the turn to line 12, Shelley overweights the sonnet's proportional ratio from 8:6 to 11:3, so that MORE becomes LESS as the immense weight of the statue collapses at the poetic climax, "Nothing beside remains". The equivalent sentence in Smith's sonnet, "The City's gone", to the contrary, appears parenthetically at line end in the middle of the second quatrain, and, though it appears to be released, the sentence continues across the next two lines. Thus the force of the statement is weakened, not reinforced, by the lack of closure, in both its imperfective aspect and its placement. Smith's turn focuses not on the disappearance of the city but on our "wonder".

The tension created in the split between syntax and prosody contributes to a tone of emotional suspense. In the opening quatrain of Smith's sonnet, no clear split creates tension. The second quatrain deviates from the closed rhyme scheme of the Italian sonnet form, with which the sonnet opens, by switching to an open rhyme scheme. This switch would support the disruption of closure at the end of the first quatrain were it not for the fact that Smith continues the *a b* rhyme scheme (with only a slight shift in vowel assonance from *alone/stone* to *gone/Babylon*), and repeats the pattern of using transitive verbs for all the *b* rhymes, which forces enjambment over the line breaks, resulting in a neat division into two units of two lines each. These regularities override the deviations of rhyme and enjambment so that there is no suspensive quality to create an emotional tone. The sestet comprises one long sentence, which means that each line is syntactically enjambed. The only prosodically marked line occurs in line 12, whose tension is increased by the intransitive verb "stops", creating a strong requirement for prosodic completion, offset by the enjambment provided by the transitive verb "guess". The suspense set up by the continuing sentence of the sestet is, however, narrative telling, not emotional feeling. Two additional factors contribute to lack of emotional suspense in Smith's sonnet: the predominance of transitive verbs which establish clear logical relationships, and the conclusive tone that narration provides over description (Tsur 2008: 108).

Shelley's use of the arrest-release strategy is quite different. The introduction of the deictic "those passions" in line 6 suggests an anaphoric reference to the frown, lips and sneer of the preceding lines; however, the reader must shift in line 7 to adjust to a cataphoric reference to "Which yet survive". Another shift occurs immediately afterwards, as the continuation of the sentence in line 8, "The hand that mocked them and the heart that fed", causes an adjustment in the reading of "survive" from intransitive to transitive mood and a shift from imperfective to perfective aspect, from the survival of Ozymandias's passions to the fact they have in fact not survived, except through the sculptor's art. The tension in this line caused by the caesura after position 5 (see note 7) is realized in the feeling at the end that something is missing syntactically. Austin (1994: 149–54) discusses the truncated syntax of line 8 and provides a structural analysis of this nonstandard coordinate structure, where the final clause "and the heart that fed" lacks an object. He notes that the entire sentence, beginning with "Near them, on the sand" is comprised of five levels of sentential structure whose vertical structure is mimetic of the passage of time.

Austin's description provides syntactic reinforcement for the prosodic weight of the entropic collapse I mentioned earlier. His comment on the final clause, "and the heart that fed", invokes the idea of the structuring metaphor for Shelley's poem: "Syntactically incomplete, the only clause that could have expressed how Ozymandias's [*sic*] own heart actually contributed to the production of the monolith crumbles to syntactic dust before our very eyes" (153). The sentence thus culminates in the loss of something at a climactic prosodic moment, a something that is also "tenuous" (to use Austin's term), since that which is not there could either be the repeated pronoun, "them" or a prepositional phrase "on them".[9] Either way, syntax reinforces prosody since both interact to reflect ENTROPY IS SHIFT.

4   Shifting Sounds

Changes in sound signal change in meaning. The greater the change, the further apart the words appear. Conversely, when sounds repeat, the tendency is greater to bring the words into relation, a psychological phenomenon literary critics have noticed in rhyme equivalence. When words with similar but not identical phonetics appear in a formal pattern or near each other, tension is set up between sameness and difference, resulting in the impression that shifting has occurred. In Shelley's poem, the most obvious shifts of sound occur in the rhyme scheme, where assonantal vowels shift from pure rhyme equivalence, as in *stone/frown, appear/despair*. But shifting also occurs in patterned repetitions, as in *trunkless legs*, where the unvoiced consonant /k/ which precedes /l/, /e/, /s/ transmutes to its voiced equivalent /g/ and moves to a position between /e/ and /s/. Another example immediately follows in *stone/stand*, where the vowel shifts between the identical /s/, /t/, /n/ consonants, which themselves shift in the following phrase in both placement and voicing, from the /s/, /t/, /n/, /d/ of *stand* to /n/, /d/, /z/, /t/ in *in the desert*. The effect is one of continuous phonetic shiftings, creating a sense of instability. These shiftings culminate in the rhyme scheme, as /t/ disappears altogether in the word *sand*, a phonetic image of the disappearance of Ozymandias's city in the desert sands.

The word *frown* that is stamped on the *stone* with which it is made to rhyme mocks the stone in its not quite perfect vowel assonance, as *command* (in its standard English pronunciation, [kə'ma:nd]) might mock the "sand" ([sænd]) as well as the inscriptional name "OzyMANDias".[10] Mockery is associated with turning's one's nose up or "cocking a snoot at",[11] so that the word *sneer* resonates with the *sn-* sound that marks many of the words associated with the nose (*snort, snore, snout*, etc.) as well as the mimicry that occurs with the tense frontal vowel [i:] that forces lip stretching. Interactive mimicry also occurs in the phrase "frown and wrinkled lips", as Tsur (personal communication) notes: "the diphthong in *frOWn* and the rounded /r/ in *WRinkled* force you to contract your lips into wrinkles". The sound-image of the "wrinkled lips", with its clipped vowel repetition closed by the plosive /ps/ and the /k/ of "wrinkled", is picked up in the repetition of the hard sound in "cold" and "command", all three words ending with the voiced /d/. The employment of these phonetic features marks the way Shelley is using his sound palette to express the feelings he ironically attributes to the statue, ironic because these passions "survive" on "lifeless" stone, their continuity outlasting the discontinuous lives of the long dead humans that felt and invoked them, just as, one might say, the phonetic patterning of the poem's words evoke those passions centuries later.

The pure rhymes of Smith's sonnet show no such repetitions of subtle sound patternings. In the first three lines of Smith's poem, the low back rounded sound repeats in "al<u>o</u>ne", "thr<u>o</u>ws", "<u>o</u>nly", "shad<u>o</u>w", and "kn<u>o</u>ws", continued in the following four lines in "st<u>o</u>ne", "sh<u>o</u>ws", "discl<u>o</u>se". Six of these eight occurrences are at line end, thus linking the internal vowel sound of both the *a* and *b* rhymes. The two remaining occur in the phrase "only shadow" in line 3, coinciding with a prosodic and syntactic caesura on position 5. Such repetition creates a feeling of monotony, but monotony is not utilized metaphorically to create a structural schema for the poem. The semantic relation of "only" to "alone", in line 1, shows Smith treading on his own words: if the leg is alone, then it would logically be the only shadow cast (and where, then, is the observer?). This back rounded sound then disappears altogether from the rest of the poem, so that no sound link is made between the description of Egypt's desert and London's wilderness. Compare this lack of sound repetition with just one line from Shelley's sonnet: "Tell that its sculptor well those passions read" (line 6). As Austin (1994: 101–3) cogently explains, the sound patterns of "tell", "well" and "read" cohere to create metrical balance (the prosodic caesura occurring before the "well" that also rhymes with "tell"), semantic complementarity ("tell" and "read" occurring at line onset and line end) and metrical congruence (the "well" linking the sculptor that "read" to the passions that "tell"). By foregrounding the sculptor's "pivotal position" (Austin 1994: 101), the sound patterning also interrelates with the distancing of the narrative framing that simultaneously occurs, from the speaker's "I" to the traveller to the sculptor to Ozymandias, and, I would argue, with the ultimate metaphorical blending of the poem's three creations: Ozymandias's works, the sculptor's statue and the poet's poem.

5 Shifting Words and Meanings

In Shelley's poem, the deflection of the value term *cold* from the physical expression "sneer" to the abstract concept of "command" is characteristic of the phenomenon Tsur refers to as thematized predicates, where the stable shape of an otherwise concrete image is rendered diffuse. These transpositions weaken control to create an emotive impression. A similar process may be seen in lines 12–13, where the wreck decaying is transposed to "the decay / Of that colossal Wreck" so that attention is focused on the decay rather than on the concrete object of the wreck. This focus is reinforced by the placement of *decay* at the end of the line in rhyming position, first as a shifted rhyme with *despair/bare* and then pure rhyme with *away*. The association of "Wreck" and "sunk" with the sea echoes in the word *boundless*, stereotypically used in conjunction with the word *main* to refer to the ocean. The fact that the phrase "boundless and bare" may be first read to describe the decay, before the last line shifts it to refer to the "lone and level sands", reinforces the sense of destabilization.

In Smith's poem, there is no diffusion of stable shape, no tension set up in the formal patterning of the lines or the repetitions of words. The one place where Smith attempts anything approximating a topicalized attribute occurs at the beginning: "In Egypt's sandy silence". By reversing the relationship of sand and silence, Smith creates an unsuccessful blend, since no topology for SAND structures SILENCE (compare "silent sands"). Although poets may violate topology, I suggest that such violation is successful when supported by an alternative topology that is sustained in the gestalt of the poem as a whole. In Smith's case, no such gestalt exists.[12]

Smith's sonnet is marked by a pattern of agency ascribed to inanimate objects. The human activities of knowing, saying and revealing are attributed to the inanimate: the silent "Desart knows", the stone "saith", the "City shows" and the "Leg" discloses. This pattern is reversed in the sestet; human activity is now attached to human agency, since it is "we" who wonder, "some Hunter" who expresses, meets and guesses, and a "race" that once dwelt. In Smith's subsequent title (see note 4) appear "discovered" and "inserted"; in the poem itself, "forgotten", "unrecorded" and "annihilated". All these are human activities, though the agents are unmentioned. I can find no metaphoric schema that links, ironically or otherwise, the active and passive constructions to the images of people and things in Smith's poem.

Naming reduces diffuseness, creating stability of reference. Whereas Shelley nowhere identifies location by naming, Smith does it three times, in "Egypt's" (line 1), "Babylon" (line 8) and "London" (line 11). Babylon is presumably inserted between Egypt and London as a possible reference to the prophecy in the Book of Isaiah (14: 4–23) against the king of Babylon for his overweening pride and of the future destruction of "the golden city".[13] Babylon's great downfall is compared with London's future, but no emotionally motivated schema structures the comparison. The lexical item alone is made to convey the allusion to Babylon's king, and only the parallel structures of "this forgotten Babylon" / "that annihilated place", links Ozymandias's works to the City of London. The presumed emotional force behind words like *forgotten*, *unrecorded* and *annihilated* dissipates in the lack of connection with any agency (who has forgotten? who has not recorded? who has annihilated?), and the intrusion of people rather than objects in the word *race* seems egregious and there only to serve the demands of rhyme. One wonders what possible connection "some Hunter" chasing a wolf in the wilderness (or is it London that is "holding the Wolf in chace"?) has to the events of the poem.[14]

In his title, Smith names granite as the stone used for the statue. Shelley makes no reference to it. As a result, Shelley's sound echoes of "stone", "stand" and "sand" in lines 2–3 suggest not the solid impermeability of granite but the crumbling permeability of sandstone. A sleight of hand guides the poet's skillful juggling here. The word *vast* suggests enormous magnitude of dimension, more suited to the sands that stretch far away. In ascribing the word to the legs themselves, Shelley is "mocking" (in both senses) the greatness of Ozymandias's works that the size of the Colossus is attempting to capture.[15] The "trunkless legs of stone" and the "shattered visage" become the "lifeless things" while "Nothing beside remains".

The original inscription from Diodorus includes not only the invocation to greatness but also a reference to the king himself: "if any would know how great I am, and *where I lie* [. . .]" (my emphasis). Where, then, in Shelley's poem is Ozymandias's body? It has disappeared, from both the scene and the inscription, exemplifying the fear of all tyrants, namely the fear to be without memorial. The great city over which the Colossus originally looked has also disappeared, not appearing at all except by inference in the ironic inscription, "Look on my Works, ye Mighty, and despair!" Both Colossus (body) and City (works) as iconic manifestations of Ozymandias's greatness have suffered ultimate entropy of disintegration into nothingness.

6   Shifting Points of View

Deixis is the process by which point of view is established. One of the most remarked upon features of Shelley's poem is its deictic shifting. Austin (1994: 96–125) provides a detailed and complex analysis of the poem's narrative framing through deictic strategies that reveal the unreliability of its ostensible "historical transmission". Shelley's poem shifts its deictic centre five times: from the speaker "I" at the beginning, to the traveller who "said", to the expressions on the sculpture that "tell", to the "words" of Ozymandias himself and finally back to the traveller's observations. None of these roles, Austin notes, stabilize into specific identities.

Shelley's setting is grounded in the present as its speaker, "I", addresses a presumed listener (the reader of the poem). This present is immediately distanced by the aspectual schema of perfective tense as the speaker refers to a time prior to the present when he "met" a traveller who "said" something to him (thus shifting the speaker's role to that of addressee). The traveller has come "from an antique land", distant in both time and space. The word "from" makes "an antique land" ambiguous in scope. Is the traveller someone who lived in or someone who was simply visiting the antique land? The difference lies in deictic distancing, whether the travel-ler is more closely identified with the land or not. The fact that Shelley frames his sonnet with the traveller's story suggests a comparison with Coleridge's *Rime of the Ancient Mariner.* Coleridge's poem, first pub-lished in 1798, had just appeared in the fall of 1817 in a revised version, and may very well have been in Shelley's mind when he was writing his sonnet. The framing of Coleridge's poem is set by the ancient mariner who corners a "wedding guest" (line 14) as captive audience for his tale of the sea. Unlike Coleridge's poem, which returns to the wedding frame at the end, Shelley's traveller's tale ends in the desert. Being drawn into the perspective of the here and now of the experience, and being left in the boundless desert, we feel the emptiness of the shifting sands and the loneliness of entropic decay.

Within the story the traveller tells are two further communicative situ-ations: the expression on the statue's face that "tells" the observer (who may or may not be the traveller) that the sculptor "well those passions read", and the "words" that "appear" on the inscription itself, which, in its use of the present tense, makes us present in the scene. This aspectual schema in moving from the present of the poem through the past of the report to the timeless present of the inscription grounds the reader in a blended space, in which the command "Look on my Works, ye Mighty, and despair!" carries the force of immediate address, so that the reader participates in the despair, not as the inscription meant it (a despair that we could never match or surpass such greatness), but in recognizing the irony that Ozymandias's greatness is over, past, long disappeared without trace in the desert sands.

In Smith's sonnet, no deictic grounding of the reader or even the poem's speaker occurs until the final sestet, with the shift to the perspective of "some Hunter" in future time from the present space of "We wonder". Temporal reference throughout the poem is predominantly the present, representing both Egypt's past and London's future. Three notable exceptions—"The City's gone", "Where London stood" and "Once dwelt"— create a per-spective of contemplating the past from a present space, a viewpoint that remains incomplete and unresolved. Unlike Shelley's deictic use of "those" (line 6) and "these" (lines 7 and 9), drawing the reader into the immediacy of the remains, Smith represents the lost past as "this" for Babylon (line 8), followed immediately by "We wonder" (line 9), thus putting 'us' in the scene. He then refers to his own time as "that" for London (line 14). These deictic terms distance the past colossus from the present hunter-observer who is simultaneously located in the past of the reader's future. Smith might have intended this distancing to invoke the idea that the "powerful but unrecorded race" is his own contemporary society, but why "unre-corded"? There is no deictic grounding of the reader in Smith's sonnet. It is propositional telling, not imaginative creativity. As Langer notes:

There is, of course, a great deal of poetry in our literary heritage that is ruined by unimaginative report of emotion. But it is neither the moral idea nor the mention of feelings that make such passages bad; it is the lapse from creativity, from creating the illusion of a moral illumination or a passional experience, into mere discourse about such matters; that is, the fallacy of using the poem simply to state something the poet wishes to tell the reader. (1953: 255)

7   The "Real" Story

If ENTROPY THROUGH TIME IS CHANGE THROUGH SHIFT is the metaphorical schema that structures Shelley's sonnet, what is the nature of the iconic blend that emerges? I suggest that it is not simply the story of foredoomed hubris, of Ozymandias's downfall and the natural processes that destroy his mighty constructions. Rather it is the fusion or blending of the shifting between "works" and "words", between "wrought" and "wrote". Shelley's use of terminology such as *say, tell, read, words, name, works,* and those of description, in *stand, lies, survive, appear, despair, remains, stretch,* fuse in the blend that is the poem to provide an unsettled feeling of mutability and decay. As Austin has shown in his extensive analysis, the narrative structure underlying the sonnet involves many layers of identity attributions. Beginning beyond the poem itself to the narrative you are (now) reading that I am (now) writing, the narrative structure of Shelley's poem is like "The House That Jack Built" (a nursery rhyme that also metaphorically equates the telling of story with the construction of building):

[You are reading
What I am writing in the twenty-first century
What I read]
What Shelley wrote in the nineteenth century
What he read
What Diodorus Siculus wrote in the first century BC
What he read
What Hekataios of Abdera wrote in the third century BC
What he read
What some earlier Arab historian wrote
What he read
What the sculptor Memnon of Sienitas wrote
What he heard (or imagined)
What Ozymandias said in the thirteenth century BC
What works he [Ozymandias] wrought.

Shifting thus occurs in the transmission of story as well as in the image of the material reality of human construction. Shifting also noticeably occurs in transmission through translation, as both Smith's and Shelley's rewritings of Diodorus's Greek translation show. Both Shelley and Smith would have been well aware of the Rosetta Stone, discovered in 1799 and on view at the British Museum since 1802, which contains a text in three languages: Classical Greek, Egyptian Demotic and hieroglyphic. The hieroglyphics that appear on the statuary remains of ancient Egypt were not decoded by Champollion until 1822, five years after Shelley wrote his poem (Rodenbeck 2004). What was wrought becomes only what was written.

CONCLUSION

My comparison of the two sonnets focuses on the role of literary metaphor in governing the poetic strategies that create an iconicity of form and feeling. Approached from this point of view, literary metaphor may thus be distinguished from other uses of metaphor that occur in general and conventional cognitive processes. In fusing form and feeling in its complex blending through the ENTROPY IS SHIFT metaphor, Shelley's sonnet creates the semblance of felt life and thus becomes an icon of reality. No such complex blending is at work in Smith's sonnet. No structuring metaphoric schema creates the semblance of felt life, no emotion informs or responds either to the discovery of the "Leg" and the words of the inscription, or to the idea that London, too, may go the way of Ozymandias's city.

Both the prosodic features and the deictic and narrative framings of Shelley's artistic creation, in their shiftings across person, space and time, are semblances of the reality of the inherent nature of Ozymandias's hubristic creations that contain within themselves the instability, slippage and deterioration of entropy, and engage the reader in feeling the results. Shelley's metaphorical structuring of ENTROPY THROUGH TIME IS CHANGE THROUGH SHIFT makes the poem iconic of a felt reality.

NOTES

1. Rodenback (2004) notes: "The name Ozymandias is a Greek rendition of 'User-macat-rec', the first element in the praenomen or throne name of the ancient Egyptian king now usually known instead by his Ra-name as Ramesses II (1279–1212 B.C.)".
2. *Entropy* is not meant as conservation of energy as in physics, but in disintegration of energy to nothingness. This definition may have its source in Tait's (1868: 29) statement that "[w]e shall use the excellent term Entropy in the opposite sense to that in which Clausius has employed it; viz., so that the Entropy of the Universe tends to zero" (*OED*).
3. The original text is in the Bodleian Library MS Shelley e.4, fol. 85r. The poem, titled "Ozymandias", was first published January 11, 1818, under the pseudonym Glirastes in *The Examiner*, no. 524. The following changes were made between the original manuscript and its subsequent publication in *Rosalind and Helen: A Modern Eclogue; with Other Poems* (London: C. and J. Ollier, 1819): line 5] lip *Bod. Shelley MS e.4*; lips *1819*; line 9] this

legend clear *Bod. Shelley MS e.4*; these words appear *1819;* line 12] No thing remains besides *Bod. Shelley MS e.4;* Nothing beside remains *1819*. (Online text copyright © 2005, Ian Lancashire for the Department of English, University of Toronto. Published by the Web Development Group, Information Technology Services, University of Toronto Libraries. http://rpo.library.uto-ronto.ca/poem/1904.html.)

4. Smith's sonnet appeared in *The Examiner* on February 1, 1818, with the same title, "Ozymandias", under the initials H. S. When the poem was reprinted in *Amarynthus, The Nympholet: A Pastoral Drama, In Three Acts. With Other Poems* (London: Longman, Hurst, Rees, Orne, and Brown, 1821), it was given the following title: "On a Stupendous Leg of Granite, Discovered Standing by Itself in the Deserts of Egypt, with the Inscription Inserted Below". The text remains the same in the two publications.

5. The poets would have read Diodorus Siculus in Greek. Rodenbeck (2004) comments: "Mrs. Shelley's note on the year tells us that in fact Shelley's reading throughout 1817 was 'chiefly Greek.' She mentions specifically the Iliad, Aeschylus and Sophocles, the Homeric Hymns, Plato, and Arrian, and it is possible that he and Horace Smith found themselves reading Diodorus at the same time".

6. I thank Donald C. Freeman (personal communication) for noting this perfective-imperfective contrast.

7. Tsur notes that in iambic pentametre prosodic caesura may fall anywhere between the fourth and sixth positions. If it falls after the fifth, the unequal prosodic structure of the two segments creates tension.

8. I thank Ewa Chrusciel (personal communication) for pointing out the sonnet's vertical-to-horizontal movement.

9. All the critics, including Austin, assume the missing syntax is a direct object of *fed.* I argue that it is the passions that feed the heart, which would call for the prepositional phrase.

10. Reuven Tsur (personal communication) noted the hidden rhyme in *command* and *Ozymandias*. Several commentators have discussed the ambiguity of the verb *to mock*, meaning either to make a mockery of or to imitate or make a model of (as in "mock-up"). Although the latter meaning goes back to the sixteenth century as a noun, its verbal usage was not recorded by the *OED* until the twentieth century. Shelley may have been playing with the meaning of the noun in making it verbal (in which case this perhaps marks the first recorded usage of the term in its model-making meaning), but the negative connotations of imposture, deceit and ridicule that predominate in all uses of the word in its verbal, noun and adjectival forms since the fifteenth century suggest that it is this emotional force of the word that is guiding Shelley's choice.

11. The origins of the phrase "cocking a snook" (American) or "cocking a snoot" (British) are unknown, though the British form is more suggestive in this context. The *OED* provides an etymological history for the word *mock*, all of which are related to the wiping of the nose in derision.

12. Peer Bungaard (Aarhus University, October 9, 2008) noted that poets do indeed violate topology. One avenue for research would be an analysis of what makes such poetic violations successful.

13. I am grateful to Jacob Lunddahl Pedersen at Aarhus University for pointing out the reference to Babylon's king in the Book of Isaiah.

14. Smith's spelling of the word *chace* reflects its older spelling, following the British practice of using *s* for verb forms and *c* for nouns.

15. The word *vast* was used in specific reference to the colossus statue of ancient times (*OED*): "1603 Holland *Plutarchís Mor.* 294 Unskilfull cutters are of opinion that the enormous and huge statues, called Colosses,

which they cut, will seeme more vast and mightie if they frame them stra-
dling with their legs".

WORKS CITED

Austin, Timothy R. (1994) *Poetic Voices: Discourse Linguistics and the Poetic Text*. Tuscaloosa and London: University of Alabama Press.

Booth, G. (1814) *Diodorus Siculus: Historical Library*, Book 1, Chapter 4. Retrieved January 23, 2008, from http://en.wikisource.org/wiki/Historical_Library/Book_I#Chapter_4

Brandt, Line, and Per Aage Brandt (2005) "Making Sense of a Blend: A Cognitive-Semiotic Approach to Metaphor". *Annual Review of Cognitive Linguistics* 3: 216–49.

Brooks, Cleanth (1965) *Modern Poetry and the Tradition* [1939]. New York: Oxford University Press.

Coleridge, Samuel Taylor (2001) "The Rime of the Ancient Mariner" [1798]. *The Collected Works of Samuel Taylor Coleridge: Poetical Works I*. Ed. J. C. C. Mays. Princeton: Princeton University Press. 372–419.

Deacon, Terrence (2006) "The Aesthetic Faculty". *The Artful Mind: Cognitive Science and the Riddle of Human Creativity*. Ed. Mark Turner. Oxford: Oxford University Press. 21–53.

Fauconnier, Gilles, and Mark Turner (2002) *The Way We Think: Conceptual Blending and the Mind's Hidden Complexities*. New York: Basic Books.

Freeman, Margaret H. (2007) "Poetic Iconicity". *Cognition in Language: Volume in Honour of Professor Elžbieta Tabakowska*. Eds. Wladislaw Chlopicki, Andrzej Pawelec and Agnieska Pojoska. Kraków: Tertium. 472–501.

———. (2008) "Revisiting/Revisioning the Icon Through Metaphor". *Poetics Today* 29.2: 353–70.

———. (2009) "Minding: Feeling, Form, and Meaning in the Creation of Poetic Iconicity". *Cognitive Poetics: Goals, Gains, and Gaps*. Eds. Geert Brône and Jeroen Vanaele. Berlin: de Gruyter. 169–96.

Gray, Thomas (1973) "Elegy Written in a Country Churchyard" [1751]. *The Complete English Poems of Thomas Gray*. Ed. James Reeves. London: Heinemann. 61–65.

Hiraga, Masako K. (2005) *Metaphor and Iconicity: A Cognitive Approach to Analysing Texts*. Houndsmill, Basingstoke and New York: Palgrave Macmillan.

Langer, Susanne K. (1953) *Feeling and Form: A Theory of Art*. New York: Charles Scribner's.

Miller, David C. (1993) Ed. *American Iconology: New Approaches to Nineteenth-Century Art and Literature*. New Haven and London: Yale University Press.

Rodenbeck, John (2004) "Travelers from an Antique Land: Shelley's Inspiration for 'Ozymandias'". *Alif: Journal of Comparative Poetics*. American University of Cairo. Retrieved July 24, 2007, from http://www.accessmylibrary.com/coms2/summary_0286-18298891_ITM

Shelley, Percy Bysshe (1818) "Ozymandias". *The Examiner*, January 11, No. 254.

Sinclair, John M. (1966) "Taking a Poem to Pieces". *Essays on Style and Language*. Ed. Roger Fowler. New York: Humanities Press; London: Routledge and Kegan Paul. 68–81.

Smith, Horace (1818) "Ozymandias". *The Examiner*, February 1. 73.

———. (1821) "On A Stupendous Leg of Granite, Discovered Standing by Itself in the Deserts of Egypt, with the Inscription Inserted Below". *Amarynthus, The*

Nympholet: A Pastoral Drama, In Three Acts. With Other Poems. London: Longman, Hurst, Rees, Orne and Brown.

Tseng, Ming-yu (1999) "The Iconic Quality in Verbal Patterning". *Dong Hwa Journal of Humanistic Studies* 1: 147–64.

Tsur, Reuven (2008) *Toward a Theory of Cognitive Poetics.* Second Edition. Brighton and Portland: Sussex Academic Press.

Wimsatt, W. K. (1954) *The Verbal Icon: Studies in the Meaning of Poetry.* Lexington: University of Kentucky Press.

9 "One should never underestimate the power of books"
Writing and Reading as Therapy in Paul Auster's Novels

Beatrix Busse

1 INTRODUCTION

This chapter takes a cognitive stylistic approach (Stockwell 2002; Semino & Culpeper 2002; Gavins & Steen 2003; Burke 2005),[1] and applies Fauconnier and Turner's (2002) theory of blending to Paul Auster's *The Brooklyn Follies* (2006) and *The Book of Illusions* (2002). To explore a central aspect of the two novels and the main characters' mental lives as well as of the readers' inference processes, I will show how the blend WRITING IS MEDICINE is foregrounded (Douthwaite 2000; Leech 2008) in the novel, how it structures *The Brooklyn Follies* (Auster 2006) and *The Book of Illusions* (Auster 2002) and how it addresses the reader's cognitive processing. I will examine how the narrators of the novels not only play with the more conventional associations and ideas of writing and medicine, but also allude to metaphorical meanings, among which are the ideas that writing is a disease (WRITING IS ILLNESS) and that imagining may function as medicine (IMAGINATION IS MEDICINE).

David Zimmer's comparison in *The Book of Illusions* between writing and medicine, for instance, is one of the most obvious examples illustrating the connection between writing and medicine in Paul Auster's work. David, who has lost his entire family in a plane crash, and who is writing a book about Hector Mann, a famous comedian and silent filmmaker, sees parallels between writing and medicine because writing has helped him to come to terms with the deaths of his wife and children. This "odd form" of medicine is considered to be a more unconventional cure than the customary intake of pills or liquids. He explains retrospectively that writing "about comedy had been no more than a pretext, an odd form of medicine that I had swallowed every day for over a year on the off chance that it would dull the pain inside me" (Auster 2002: 5). My analysis of the blend WRITING IS MEDICINE focuses on the reader whose mind has to arrive at an interpretation. It therefore participates in the cognitive turn and highlights the reader's mechanisms of psychological processing during the act of reading.

Certainly, a textual *and* reader-oriented base should not sidestep the important role of political, social and cultural background of the story and of the author. They are all part of the interpretation process. For example, Toolan (2009) stresses that reading is also influenced and guided by readers' encyclopaedic knowledge, personal values, their information about the author of a narrative and so on: "Every literary narrative episode is susceptible to a 'colouring in' by the reader", which allows the reader to draw implicatures (7).

If we were to collect some of the material that a reader might draw on in relation to both writing and medicine, we could argue that the equation of writing with medicine is probably a familiar (almost well-worn) trope; writing is seen as therapeutic, healing and curative. Yet this trope may certainly also have to be understood as culture-specific because, in its narrow sense, it would not be valid for oral cultures or communities. Conventional literal associations for both medicine and writing suggest that they are non-life-threatening. Medicine can be a solid or a liquid consumable, whose function is to combat minor illnesses and diseases (see also *OED* 1.a and 1.b). When referred to as a science, medicine evokes associations with scientific research and medical progress for the good of humanity. In these contexts, doctors or medical authorities are involved as agents. Medicine, however, may also have more general associations with healing. Cultural history tells us that medicine was used as a metaphorical attribute in the Middle Ages for various not exclusively physical activities like making love or to characterize the enjoyment derived from art. In a metaphorical sense, medicine then involves a change in well-being, which can be either positive or negative. It can be sweet or bitter; it can alleviate and heal but also provoke painful purgation.

Writing, in its turn, is readily associated with writing with a pen, typing on a sheet of paper or a computer screen or writing an email, and also with the production and the reception of writing, i.e. with the reading of documents, books and so on—and also of fiction. It is connected with the concepts of a writer, a reporter, a narrator or a story-teller. The process of writing may have the function of reporting, informing, narrating, etc. Though writing may merely be a private coming to terms with one's own thoughts, it also communicates an intentional reaching out to a recipient. In relation to the production of fiction, the writing process can be located on several fictional levels. Both characters and extradiegetic narrators write and thus call attention to the process of narration itself. Dietrich von Engelhardt (1991; 2004: 39) touches on the multiplicity of interdisciplinary links between literature and medicine. For example, he notes the intersection of writing and medicine in fiction in which medicine contributes to the interpretation of literature; he also describes the scientific function of literature in which literature helps broaden the medical scope in research and teaching and may serve as a therapeutic instrument and as a source for medical history; finally, he stresses the genuine function of "literalised" medicine which describes how outside the framework of medicine and literary criticism literary (re-)presentations of decease influence the public evaluation of illness and of a patient (see also von Jagow & Steger 2009).

Paul Auster's novels display a preoccupation both with writing and with characters who have experienced personal crises. As Auster himself points out in an interview published in German with *Neue Zürcher Zeitung* on October 4, 2008:

> Ich versuche stattdessen, zu der Realität des inneren Lebens vorzudringen, Antwort auf die Frage zu finden, was es an einem beliebigen Ort und zu jeder beliebigen Zeit bedeutet, am Leben zu sein.

> I try to reach the reality of one's inner life, to find answers to the question of what it means, at a given place or a given time, to be alive. (my translation)

What is called bibliotherapy or poetry therapy (Burr-Nevanlinna 2005: 129–30), i.e. the therapeutic method of healing with the help of literature, is one expression of these interrelationships between writing and medicine. I will return to bibliotherapy towards the end of my chapter. My main focus in this chapter concerns the metaphorical blending of writing and reading in Paul Auster's novels, of which poetry therapy could be said to be a real-world equivalent. Since I am using blending theory as my main framework, the following section is meant to ease those readers who are not specialists into the theory.

2   FAUCONNIER AND TURNER'S (2002) THEORY OF BLENDING

According to Fauconnier and Turner (2002), human beings create concepts by drawing on different sources of knowledge and experience and by integrating these domains with one another. Language and communication are major pieces of evidence that reflect and create this integration. Forceville (2004: 83) stresses that similar ideas to Fauconnier and Turner (2002) had been proposed by a variety of scholars and that this observation had already been appropriated by artists such as, for example, Russian film-makers of the 1920s in their artistic expression of a collage. A new aspect which Fauconnier and Turner (2002) add is that the ability of blending or combining domains of knowledge is not only an artistic phenomenon, but also strikingly typical of everyday thinking (Forceville 2004: 83).

A minimal conceptual integration network consists of four spaces: two input spaces, a generic space, which links the input spaces, and the blend. We construct meaning by creating "mental spaces" (Fauconnier and Turner 2002: 40, 102), which are temporary representations that recruit structure from many conceptual domains during the online process of meaning creation. Each mental space contains different meaningful elements, but also relations between these elements. In contrast to conceptual metaphor theory as outlined by Lakoff and Johnson (2003), there is no hierarchical distinction between source and target domain, because both input spaces (democratically) take on the same role or part. In conceptual metaphor theory, the target is always understood "in terms of" the source. The blend, on the other hand, arises from the fusion or blending of the material from both input spaces. It contains what each of the elements in the input spaces share, but it may also contain additional structures projected from neither of the inputs (Evans & Green 2006: 403). It is creative because it contains more than the sum of the parts of the input spaces. The result is a new blended space which has its own conceptual structure, and it is not uni-directional or one-dimensional. It is in the entire blend that meaning is generated.

Brandt and Brandt (2005) criticise Fauconnier and Turner's model because of its lack of attention to context. They add two spaces to their more semiotically based model: a base space for the immediate or situational context, and a relevance space "that provides relevant thought content for the construction of the blend and, ultimately, for the emergence of reasonable inferences" (Brandt & Brandt 2005). Brandt and Brandt's base space is also adopted by Coulson and Oakley (2005) as a "grounding box". Fauconnier and Turner (2002) have also come in for criticism from Forceville (2004), who faults *The Way We Think* for not establishing the obvious links between blending theory and other models, or including pragmatic and contextual factors, for example as outlined by Brandt and Brandt (2005). The need for an inclusion of pragmatic factors is probably most obvious in the three processes that Fauconnier and Turner (2002: 48–9) propose and claim to be involved in the emergent meaning of the blended space. These processes are *composition, completion, elaboration* and *compression. Composition* is always involved in the process of blending, because conceptual content from two or more mental spaces is projected into the blended space (Ungerer & Schmid 2006: 259). In the process of *completion*, information is always recruited subconsciously, and background frames are also projected subconsciously from the inputs. The process of *elaboration*, which is often dynamically seen as "running the blend" (Ungerer & Schmid 2006: 260), creates the unique structure of the blend.

As regards *compression*, Fauconnier and Turner (2002: 89–111) distinguish between the compression of relations within the input space and the compression of relations between mental spaces: "Compression is in fact the ultimate goal of the whole blending process. The crucial effect of compression is that the conceptual complexity of the inputs from several sources is reduced considerably" (Ungerer & Schmid 2006: 260). Input spaces are moreover mapped onto each other through various cross-spaces, which are based on what Fauconnier and Turner (2002: 89–111) call "vital relations". These additional matching specifications, or "vital relations", can be relations of identity, space, time, representation, change, role value, cause and effect or part-whole.

To summarize, although blending theory has affinities with several other paradigms (see Forceville 2004), which are not always explicitly stated, it is an innovative theory that helps explain emergent structures and how human beings create concepts by integrating information from different inputs.

3 THE BLEND WRITING IS MEDICINE IN AUSTER'S *THE BROOKLYN FOLLIES* (2006) AND *THE BOOK OF ILLUSIONS* (2002)

The preceding contexts play an important part in the cognitive processing of the blend of WRITING IS MEDICINE and in developing it. To illustrate, let us look at the beginning of Auster's *The Brooklyn Follies*. The reader encounters Nathan Glass and immediately learns that he is a bitter solitary man who has just been divorced and who seems to expect his death, despite a successful cancer operation and good prospects for his survival. The parallelism between writing and medicine is construed implicitly in a metaphorical elaboration of medicine as causing a positive mental or physical change and of medicine functioning as a pleasurable drug. Nathan Glass begins to create the integrational network of WRITING IS MEDICINE in the process of thinking about and preserving past events (Auster 2006: 7). The physicality and hypnotic force of the parallelism between writing and medicine is explained almost iconically through recurrent parataxis and the repetition of the preposition *by*:

> Every time I sat down to write, I would begin by closing my eyes and letting my thoughts wander in any direction they chose. By forcing myself to relax in this way, I managed to dredge up considerable amounts of material from the distant past, things that until then I had assumed were lost forever. (Auster 2006: 7)

Nathan's passion for reading books is also one reason why he starts to write:

> [. . .]—but I had never lost my interest in books. Reading was my escape and my comfort, my consolation, my stimulant of choice: reading for the pure pleasure of it, for the beautiful stillness that surrounds you when you hear an author's words reverberating in your head. (Auster 2006: 7)

The enumeration of noun phrases with a similar structural amplification— deictic element and head noun (as, for example, visible in "my escape" or "my consolation")—emphasizes the force of the process of reading. Nathan's aims are illustrated at length in the following quotation:

I called it *The Book of Human Follies* and in it I was planning to set down in the simplest, clearest language possible an account of every blunder, every pitfall, every embarrassment, every idiocy, every foible, and every inane act I had committed during my long and checkered career as a man. [. . .] I called the project a book, but in fact it wasn't a book at all. [. . .] I was compiling what amounted to a collection of random jottings, a hodgepodge of unrelated anecdotes that I would throw into a cardboard box each time another story was finished. There was little method to my madness. (Auster 2006: 5–6)

In Auster's novels, the equation of writing with medicine includes the stress of both a physical and mental process. It emphasizes the holistic religious-spiritual aspect of the alignment, featuring the individual as a reader or a writer who only subconsciously realises that he/she, by the act of writing/reading, interacts with another (with no explicit mentioning of a physician or a medical authority) and is thereby transformed.

In contrast to *The Brooklyn Follies* (2006), *The Book of Illusions* (2002) uses the blend of WRITING IS MEDICINE much more overtly. David Zimmer is a devastated man. He has lost his family in a plane crash. Because, as a professor, all his work has been "connected to books, language, the written word" (Auster 2002: 13), he secludes himself in that world. He writes about the allegedly disappeared comedian and filmmaker Hector Mann, and this act is seen as an "odd form of medicine". *The Book of Illusions*, which the reader holds in his/her hands, tells his long story about writing this book, and describes his encounter with Hector and his wife, and his relationship with Alma, the woman who writes a biography about Hector. The fragmentary character of Nathan's book is also stressed in *The Book of Illusions* when David Zimmer calls it "a book of fragments, a compilation of sorrows and half-remembered dreams" (Auster 2002: 316).

The integrational network WRITING IS MEDICINE captures Nathan's, David's and the other characters' complex developments towards finding new identities. They encourage the reader to go through the various stages of their transformations and of the act of "artistic creation" (Peacock 2006: 56). Auster's work is famous for its multiplicity of narratological levels and its preoccupation with the process of writing fact and fiction. Based on an analysis of reader involvement construed by narrative passages of his first-person narrators, Nathan Glass in *The Brooklyn Follies* (2006) and David Zimmer in *The Book of Illusions* (2002), and on the analysis of the various forms of discourse presentation, the blend of WRITING IS MEDICINE is foregrounded.[2] The reader is capable of understanding the blend because of his/her familiarity with elements of the input spaces, which, in the blend, result in new meaning structures that may be divergent from the input spaces.

Figure 9.1 illustrates the blend of WRITNG IS MEDICINE in Auster's two novels. It also exemplifies the four spaces usually attributed to blending

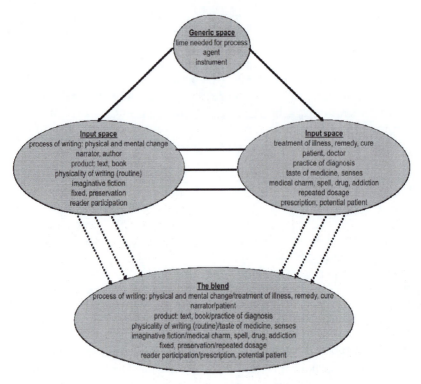

Figure 9.1   The blend of WRITING IS MEDICINE.

theory. There is (1) the input space which is writing, (2) the input space which is medicine, (3) a generic space which shares the entities referred to and the time of the process[3] and (4) a blend where writing is medicine. The connections are established by matching (represented by the dotted lines). The result is a double-scope network (Evans & Green 2006: 431), because both inputs contain distinct frames, and the blend is organised by a structure taken from each frame. The meanings reside in the entire network of this blend, with all the four spaces contributing to them.

For the interpretation of the two Auster novels, the use of a base space which captures contextual information cannot be underestimated. It is through the way context construes the specific blend of WRITING IS MEDICINE that meaning can be created. This creation includes pragmatic meanings and effects deduced from the texts as such as well as encyclopaedic knowledge—similar to that outlined in the introduction about writing and medicine. It is in this space that the textual base of each meaning inference process is also stressed.

Nathan and David both write their stories retrospectively. In their roles as controlling narrators, the process of healing and recovering—the blend of WRITING IS MEDICINE—is actively construed in their stories. In their roles as characters, on the other hand, they 'tell' their story subconsciously and they also undergo this process of change without being aware of it.

Having read the novels, the reader creates the mental space MEDICINE. This cognitive model features the treatment of illness, a remedy and a cure, a patient, the practice of diagnosis, the taste of medicine, and its consequences for the senses. Medicine figures as a medical charm, a spell or drug, as addiction. There may be a repeated dosage, a prescription. The scenario moreover contains a potential patient and a doctor or medical authority.

Parallel to the medicine space, Nathan's and David's initial references to writing and their high proliferation[4] trigger the second mental space, that of WRITING. It is an online conceptual representation, which taps stored information like the process of writing, physical and mental change, the narrator and the author, the product as a text or a book, the physicality of writing (routine), imaginative fiction, something which is fixed and may be preserved, and reader participation.

To prove this line of argumentation further, it should be argued that Nathan's initial subconscious desire to produce and preserve his story results from both his physical and mental struggle: "I'd suffered the long bouts of nausea and dizziness, the loss of hair, the loss of will, the loss of job, the loss of wife" (Auster 2006: 3). So the source of the input space reflects his experience with medicine and his general schematic knowledge of medicine and its effects. Notice how here, as well as in other examples, he describes the negative experience in his life by means of a list of noun phrases, which, in general, according to Halliday (1994: 342–43; Halliday & Matthiesen 2004: 637–42), construe unchangeable and static facts or commodities. In addition, the enumeration, as an example of diagrammatic iconicity,[5] suggests how drastic his situation is.

The processes involved in the emergent meaning of the blended space are realized in the following manner. *Composition* is involved in the sense that writing, like taking medicine, ideally has the power to improve the health of its writer and his general well-being or generally to transform it. The process of *completion* through the reader is needed because the reader will subconsciously and continuously draw on additional information to complete the structure of the blend online. For example, writing and reading are also seen as a routine with additional specific physical qualities. The dynamic process of *elaboration* is the actual "running of the blend". Initially, Nathan, for example, describes in detail the process of writing and the routines used to prepare for it: closing his eyes, relaxing and moving to past events. In *The Book of Illusions*, David routinely "swallow[s]" (Auster 2002: 5) his medicine hoping that "it would dull the pain inside" (Auster 2002: 5). Writing is therefore alluded to as a process of regaining events from the past and preserving them, or as a means of suppressing these memories.

Notice the physical and solitary qualities, but also the sensuality attributed to reading and writing. Thus, in *The Brooklyn Follies*, reading is described as a "stimulant" and as "pure pleasure" (Auster 2006: 7), which may be restricted to the individual's experience and may also function as a routine for both reading and writing. The doctor schema from the medicine space is not overtly mentioned, but Nathan realizes that only in interaction with a "You" can he recover his health. In *The Book of Illusions*, David explicitly denies the help of a doctor, and it is only through the book (but not until after the actual completion of writing the book about Hector Mann) that he meets Alma, who draws him back to life.

Input spaces are also mapped onto each other through various cross-spaces, which are based on what Fauconnier and Turner (2002: 89–111) call "vital relations". To begin with identity relations in *The Brooklyn Follies*, there are mappings between the actions of writing a book and taking one's medicine, because these can be seen as having an, admittedly rather optimistic, effect, such as recovery, distraction from pain, and healing. The result of the compression of this identity relation is a new combination of actions, the emergent structure described as "writing and medicine taking" and the goals of the two actions are fused in "writing a book as improving health". But the agent of the input space "writing" turns out to be the patient in need of medical treatment in the blended space, and, at the same time, he is also the physician, "the actor", because no other authority is mentioned. In addition, by writing down their own stories and those of others, Nathan and David (and Alma) are life preservers and healers of others.

Although the narrators in the two novels initially intend to collect their own stories for their own personal needs (David writes about Hector Mann because he made him laugh), it becomes obvious that there is a further— initially subconscious— aim for him. The reader learns that the blend construes not only Nathan's and David's search for new identities, but also that of other characters in the novels. For example, in *The Brooklyn Follies*, "hodgepodge" (Auster 2006: 6) relates to a magical potion, which at this stage of the novel still alludes to a supernatural rather than a self-willed change of life. Similarly, the reference to writing as an obsession in Nathan's "There was little method to my madness" (Auster 2006: 6) points to the connection between writing and therapy only subconsciously. In *The Book of Illusions*, Alma, towards the end of the novel, describes her endeavour to write about Hector as "whether it comes out or not, writing the book has been the biggest experience of my life" (Auster 2002: 217).

The blend WRITING IS MEDICINE structures the processes of identity construction in which the psychological issues of healing, mental disorders, of transformation, of pleasure, but also purely physical experience, are involved. It moreover structures the process of narration, that is the activity of writing. Finally, it also structures the product of writing which relates to the reader.

The space that results from the blending of the target and the source input is highly creative and idiosyncratic because of the polysemy of meanings of both writing and medicine. Both the production and the reception processes of writing and medicine are construed and also portrayed with complex properties. The blend develops its own structure and creates a rich narrative scenario. It corroborates that narrative is what Fludernik (1996) has called "experientiality"; that is, narrative corresponds to the projection of the consciousness and subjective experience of both Nathan and the reader. WRITING IS MEDICINE projects an intramental construct (Palmer's [2004] term, describing individual cognitive functioning) that is limited to Nathan as narrator, author or patient, but WRITING IS MEDICINE is also an intermental phenomenon that connects the interdependent cognitive functioning of groups of characters in the novel (Semino 2006: 57).

The sub-features of the source-and-target-input spaces contribute to the blend some of the affinities that Nathan in *The Brooklyn Follies* perceives in writing and medicine, or wishes to attribute to them. The blend alludes to the stories told, to the process of writing, to the process of taking medicine as a physical experience; it also alludes to the product of writing and to that of taking medicine as, respectively, introspection for the writer/narrator and healing of the writer/narrator. The blend moreover features the creation of a different reality and the preservation/immortalisation of life, personality and identity, especially in the stories Nathan writes down and in his wish at the end of the novel to preserve individual people's lives by writing down their biographies and internalising/preserving their follies:

> My idea was this: to form a company that would publish books about the forgotten ones, to rescue the stories and facts and documents before they disappeared—and shape them into a continuous narrative, the narrative of a life. (Auster 2006: 303)

In *The Book of Illusions*, David sees one function of Alma's biography about Hector as preserving Hector's life: "but at the same time Hector gets to live on through you. Not because of his films—which won't even exist anymore—but because of what you have written about him" (Auster 2002: 217). But Alma herself is not able to survive. She commits suicide because Frieda destroyed her book. By doing so, Frieda routs Alma's process of finding her identity by means of re-writing Hector's life. David understands the physical and mental strains she must have undergone when writing about Hector's life and reading David's book about Hector, as well as in this process reflecting her own life. Due to his reverence for Alma, he therefore decides that her identity of being a writer should be engraved on her gravestone: "ALMA GRUND 1950–1988 WRITER" (Auster 2002: 313). David also stresses that:

> Except for the twenty-page suicide note she sent me on the last night of her life, I had never read a word she had written. But Alma had died because of a book, and justice demanded that she be remembered as the author of that book. (Auster 2002: 313)

In this constellation, writing is seen as medicine beyond life. The writing space provides the difference between fact and fiction, and the chance of introspection, as well as the spell or addiction to books/medicine as expressed in Nathan's and David's passion for books, and the physical and mental effects they attribute to them. The medicine space provides the patient-medicine schema, which is generally assumed to be successful (the patient generally gets better). The blend partly enables Nathan and David as well as Alma to transform reality into a schema that they can cope with, to keep reality alive and permanent; it helps them to create another fictional/artificial reality (they are the narrators).[6]

Nevertheless, the subconscious healing or transformation of the power of writing also expresses Nathan's and David's subjective experience with the society around them and the people close to them. Hence, several of the other "vital relations" prevail, such as the compression of time and space, and the relation of books and biographies to fact and fiction. The author (or Nathan as both the narrator and author) cannot capture everything, but the reader understands that writing is one way of preserving other people's lives. Also, the "vital relations" of representation and part-whole are construed here, as books may present real lives and may stand for real lives. As such, the blend WRITING IS MEDICINE is further enhanced in *The Brooklyn Follies* by the introduction of more conventional metaphors (Fauconnier & Turner 2002: 279ff.), such as LIFE IS A JOURNEY or UNDERSTANDING IS SEEING (Lakoff & Johnson 2003).

The "vital relation" of analogy is created through various intertextual relations in both novels. For example, in *The Book of Illusions* David's translation of Chateaubriand's *Memoirs* is crucial in its parallelism with David's life. One of Chateaubriand's statements quoted in the novel is "Moments of crisis produce a redoubled vitality in men" (Auster 2002: 238). David's vitality seems to return only towards the very end of the novel after he completes the book on Hector Mann, which leads to his relationship with Alma and his meeting with Hector. All of this helps him to overcome the loss of his family. In *The Brooklyn Follies*, the collocation of method and madness in "There was little method to my madness" (Auster 2006: 5–6) is a reverberation of Shakespeare's *King Lear*, where Edgar finds "Reason in [Lear's] Madness" (IV, vi, 175). In *The Brooklyn Follies*, Lessing's play *Nathan the Wise* serves as an important intertext. Note the choice of names for both the narrator Nathan and his daughter Rachel (alluding to biblical figures in the Old Testament and to Recha, Nathan's daughter in Lessing's play). There is also an overt reference to *Nathan the Wise*. In Lessing's play, Nathan proposes an enlightened humanity by means of his parable of the three rings which represent the three major religions. In Auster's novel, Nathan is turned into a counsellor of the people he loves, and in his writing he reflects his and their situations. He thereby becomes a medieval knight who protects his women, for example, Rachel, Rory and Joyce:

[B]ut she [Aurora] said no [to consulting a psychologist], she'd rather just talk to me. Me. The bitter, solitary man who had crept home to Brooklyn less than a year earlier, the burnout who had convinced himself there was nothing left to live for—knuckleheaded me, *Nathan the Unwise*, who could think of nothing better to do than quietly wait to drop dead, now transformed into a confidant and counsellor, a lover of randy widows, and a knight errant who rescued damsels in distress. (Auster 2006: 286, my emphasis)

To sum up, in the two novels, writing is described as medicine in the sense that it causes a positive physical and mental change. The blend of WRITING IS MEDICINE structures the process of narration. Because both Nathan and David write their stories retrospectively, their roles as controlling first-person narrators construe the process of healing and recovering for the reader who reads their stories. The creation of the blend of WRITING IS MEDICINE is more implicit in Auster's *The Brooklyn Follies* (2006) and more directly created in *The Book of Illusions* (2002). The mental space of medicine allows the reader to conceptualize, for example, the treatment of illness, a remedy and a cure, a patient, the practice of diagnoses and so on. The mental space of writing conceptualizes information like the process of writing, the product as a text, the physicality and sensuality of writing and reader participation. The emergent meaning in the blended space fuses those associations but also carries new meanings not necessarily related to the input spaces. Once a blend is at work it may also be expanded into related directions. The following two sections will show how in *The Brooklyn Follies* WRITING IS DISEASE and IMAGINING IS MEDICINE represent elaborations on the blend of WRITING IS MEDICINE.

4 WRITING IS A DISEASE—ELABORATION OF THE BLEND WRITING IS MEDICINE

In *The Brooklyn Follies*, further running of the blend is done by Tom, Nathan's nephew. This is also based on contextual and situational information provided by the text. At first, Tom extends the blend WRITING IS MEDICINE in partly negative terms. At the beginning of the novel, Nathan illustrates Tom's attitude to his job as a taxi-driver, and makes it clear that due to his experience with, or failures in the world of literature, he detests the written word and the lifeless character of any book or fictional story. To Tom, writing and the consumption of fictional worlds, which he used to like when he started his studies, is not medicine, but a disease that makes him sick. This negation of the blend WRITING IS MEDICINE can be incorporated because Fauconnier and Turner (2002) argue that mental spaces are online mental constructions prone to include the individual mental representations of a particular input space. Similar to *The Book of Illusions*, where David describes his book/autobiography (which the reader holds in his/her hands) as "a book of sorrows, of half-remembered dreams", and therefore illusions (Auster 2002: 315), Tom's preference for real life over fictional stories appears in the following quotation from his direct speech: "No book can duplicate those things. I'm talking about real transcendence, Harry. Leaving your body behind you and entering the fullness and thickness of the world" (Auster 2006: 31). Nathan reports Tom's outburst in indirect speech and free indirect speech:

> There were no rules when it came to writing, he said. Take a close look at the lives of poets and novelists, and what you wound up with was unalloyed chaos, an infinite jumble of exceptions. That was because writing was a disease, Tom continued, what you might call an infection or influenza of the spirit, and therefore it could strike anyone at any time. (Auster 2006: 149)

Later in the novel, however, Tom seems to have been healed by the events in his life. These include his working in a bookshop and the re-intensified relations to his family through his uncle and the arrival of two people: Lucy, Tom's niece, the daughter of Tom's lost sister; and his future wife Honey. Tom still describes writing as a disease, but now refers to it as an addiction that demands introspection and requires the disclosure of individual and existential deficiencies. Therefore, he praises Nathan for taking the risk: "You are a writer, Nathan. You're becoming a real writer" (Auster 2006: 149). Tom even acknowledges the healing power of writing and the creation of a new, valuable reality, for instance when he expresses his fascination with Kafka and Kafka's attempt to save a sad little girl who had lost her doll. It is said of Kafka that he wrote fictional letters from the doll addressed to the little girl he met in a park in Berlin in order to prepare the girl for the separation from her doll. What we get is one of the most moving elaborations of WRITING IS MEDICINE and WRITING IS DISEASE in Tom's direct speech:

> He isn't about to cheat the little girl. This is real literary labor, and he's determined to get it right. If he can come up with a beautiful and persuasive lie, it will supplant the girl's loss with a different reality—a false one, maybe, but something true and believable according to the laws of fiction. (Auster 2006: 155)

Hence, Tom not only introduces a further input space (WRITING IS A DISEASE), which is an extension to WRITING IS MEDICINE because disease and the taking of medicine are conventionally interdependent, but he also further modifies it in a more positive direction by arguing that as long as a serious task underlies the production of the written, even fictional writing can have a useful purpose. In addition, Tom seems to suggest that although a writer may be said to be ill, addicted or insane, he may still heal others. This elaboration on the blend leads to another contextual framework in which the blend works and that is IMAGINING IS MEDICINE.

5 IMAGINING IS MEDICINE AS AN ELABORATION OF THE BLEND WRITING IS MEDICINE: THINKING OF THE UTOPIA OF "THE HOTEL EXISTENCE"

In both novels, the act of writing and imagining more or less rapidly leads to the foundation of a non-fictitious re-creation of identity and the coming to terms with devastating past events. The quoted example from Kafka is one of the many cases in point. IMAGINING IS MEDICINE as an elaboration on the blend WRITING IS MEDICINE is extended even further in both novels.

In *The Book of Illusions*, the process of writing and the actual product represent an imaginative retreat for David to cope with the world:

> I was in the book, and the book was in my head, and as long as I stayed inside my head, I could go on writing the book. It was like living in a padded cell, but of all the lives I could have lived at that moment, it was the only one that made sense to me. I wasn't capable of being in the world. (Auster 2002: 55)

He also stresses: "All through the writing of the book, I intentionally put off thinking about the future" (Auster 2002: 56). As mentioned, it is only much later in time that he is able to write his story.

During a meal with Tom and Nathan at a French restaurant, Harry in *The Brooklyn Follies* introduces to them his childhood dream of a happy society, what he then called the "Hotel Existence". This conversation is transferred to the recipient in direct speech, in the form of a play text. These modes of speech presentation not only strengthen the immediacy and authenticity of what is being said, but also, for the recipient/reader, broaden the role of the reader to that of the audience.

As a small child passing by a hotel during the war, Harry at first sees life and his existence as a hotel, which provides its guests with a comfortable refuge and shelter to make them happy.

> HARRY: (closing his eyes; pressing his forefingers against his temples): It's all coming back to me now. The Hotel Existence. [...] The sole purpose of a hotel was to make you happy and comfortable [...] A hotel represented the promise of a better world, a place that was more than just a place, but an opportunity, a chance to live inside your dreams.

> NATHAN: That explains the hotel part. Where did you find the word
>   existence?
> HARRY: I heard it on the radio that Sunday afternoon. I was only
>   half listening to the program, but someone was talking about
>   human existence, and I liked the way it sounded. The laws of
>   existence, the voice said, and the perils we must face in the
>   course of our existence. Existence was bigger than just life. It
>   was everyone's life all together, [. . .]
> TOM: I still don't follow. You invent a place called the Hotel Exis-
>   tence, but where is it? What was it for?
> HARRY: For? Nothing, really. It was a retreat, a world I could visit
>   in my mind. That's what we're talking about, no? (Auster
>   2006: 102–03)

Due to his war experience, Harry then modifies his idea of the "Hotel Existence" and turns it into a refuge for lost children, and he sees his own role
as a saviour of the lost and starving boys (Auster 2006: 103–04). Harry's
somewhat pathetic, altruistic and noble idea of himself as a hero, of what
he calls "the product of a rich inner life", is destroyed by his own super-
ficialities, betrayals, eccentricities and sexual encounters—all features of
his early life as a husband and a father. He is as stranded as Nathan and
Tom. There is his frantic daughter, then the time he spent in prison for having forged the paintings of a dead painter, and finally the betrayal of his
great love. Tom criticises Harry's dream as "adolescent jerk-off material"
(Auster 2006: 106) and describes his own vision of his "Hotel Existence"
as a community of people he loves, has lost during his life of crisis, but is
still related to:

> TOM: [. . .] What's my Hotel Existence, Harry? [. . .]
> HARRY: A commune.
> TOM: No, not a commune—a community. There's a difference.
> HARRY: And where would this little utopia of yours be?
> TOM: Somewhere out in the country, I suppose. A place with a lot
>   of land and enough buildings to accommodate all the people
>   who wanted to live there. (Auster 2006: 106)

The image of the "Hotel Existence" reappears in an even more dreamlike form in the Chowder Inn in Vermont. The narrator tells the reader,
this time in the present tense, that "[t]he sign at the edge of the driveway
says THE CHOWDER INN, but a part of me already understands that
we have come to the Hotel Existence" (Auster 2006: 169). Harry turns
out to be the real human hero, and his "Hotel Existence" becomes alive
when Nathan realizes that Harry has given all his money to his lover
Rufus and to Tom. Despite Harry's own deficiencies as a human being,
he rescues Tom:

For all his wisecracking irreverence, for all his peccadilloes and false-hoods, he had never stopped believing in the principles of the Hotel Existence. Good old Harry Brightman. Funny old Harry Brightman. (Auster 2006: 215)

IMAGINING IS MEDICINE then functions as an elaboration of the blend of WRITING IS MEDICINE. Harry does not write anything but he takes refuge in his thoughts, which he later shares with Tom and Nathan, and which Nathan writes down. Although Harry's idea of the "Hotel Existence" is, as he calls it, "a retreat, a world I could visit in my mind" (Auster 2006: 103) and therefore not as visible a product as is a book, Harry's idea has strong resemblances with writing because both acts include processes of thinking and imagining.

6 CONCLUSION

Nathan's advice "One should never underestimate the power of books" (Auster 2006: 304) echoes the creative and reflective force of both writing and reading in the two novels discussed. Following a cognitive stylistic approach in general and Fauconnier and Turner's (2002) concept of blending in particular, this chapter has illustrated how the blend of WRITING IS MEDICINE structures the characters' mental and even physical lives as well as serves as guidelines for a reader to infer meanings. The blend of WRITING IS MEDICINE embraces some of the more conventional associations of both mental spaces, that of writing and medicine, and also includes more creative elaborations, such as WRITING IS ILLNESS and IMAGINING IS MEDICINE.

The blend of WRITING IS MEDICINE expresses the protagonists' writing as both a physical and mental experience. It describes a healing process that is not initiated and conducted by any outward medical authority but by the individual in relationship with a "You". This integrational network also captures the characters' complex process of finding new identities. As such, it alludes to ways how literature and writing can be therapeutic (von Engelhardt 2004: 39). At the same time, the practice of bibliotherapy and poetry therapy, which use literature (both its reception and its production) as a method of healing diseases (Burr-Nevanlinna 2005), can implicitly be seen. Yet, although Auster in an interview with Céline Curiol (2006: 18) from 2006 stresses that "[w]riting can certainly be dangerous. Dangerous for the reader—if something is powerful enough to change his view of the world—and dangerous for the writer", such a therapeutic method is only implicitly construed in the two Auster novels analysed here. The effect on the characters presented in the novels, however, seems to be the same, despite the much stronger critical stress on the success of writing a story as an illusion in *The Book of Illusions* (Auster 2002) than in *The Brooklyn Follies* (Auster 2006).

Moreover, it is difficult to determine and test whether the effect that the blend notes for the narrator in general and Nathan and David in particular applies equally to the reader, but it is through the blend that the readers' cognitive processing is activated. Yet, the focus on the reader certainly demands to include "the colouring in" (Toolan 2009: 7) by the reader (that is, the inclusion of online associations a reader might have when reading about WRITING and MEDICINE and when reading the novels). In the already quoted interview with *Neue Zürcher Zeitung* on October 4, 2008, Auster emphasises the fictionality of language and literature:

> Aber mir ist beim Schreiben stets sehr bewusst, dass die Sprache die Wirklichkeit immer verzerrt. Selbst wenn sie die Realität einerseits erschafft, verzerrt sie diese zugleich, und das ist eine der grossen Paradoxien des Schreibens. Sprache schenkt uns die Welt und nimmt sie uns zugleich, weil sie Kategorien schafft, während die Welt der Erfahrung keine festen Kategorien kennt und immer im Fluss der Bewegung bleibt.

> When writing I am always aware of the fact that language always distorts reality. Although it creates reality, it distorts it at the same time, and that is one of the great paradoxes of writing. Language presents the world to us, but at the same time takes it away, because it creates categories, while the world of experience does not know any fixed categories and always remains in the flux of movement. (my translation)

This "flux of movement" seems to echo an essential part in Fauconnier and Turner's (2002) theory of conceptual blending: the fact that human beings constantly conceptualize by drawing on various domains of information, renewing those and giving them shape and expression through language. Therefore, resorting to Fauconnier and Turner (2002) to explain the interaction between the mental spaces of WRITING and MEDICINE seems to be particular useful because both input spaces take on an equal role (that is, the two spaces are not expressed one through the other). Also, the blend is creative; it arises from the fusion of the two input spaces and may contain additional material. The blend functions both on the intratextual level of the novel and also, extratextually, addresses the reader who is the potential patient-participant. It serves as an anchor-point for the reader in the processing of these two novels. As such, the cognitive stylistic aim of highlighting the cognitive aspects of reading which consumers of literature operate when they process a piece of literature (Stockwell 2002: 1) could be shown.

NOTES

1. Within the research field of cognitive stylistics, the theory of blending has been applied to literature by Turner (1996, 2003, 2006), Semino (2002,

2006) or Dancygier (2006). Conceptual blending theory has not been applied to Paul Auster's novels, although some studies approach Auster's work with psychoanalytic theory (Bennett, Luksic and Huidobro 2007).

2. In this chapter, foregrounding is not understood to be synonymous with emphasizing. It should be related to the theory of foregrounding, which is crucial to stylistics and, among others, has its base in Russian Formalism (see Short 1996 and Douthwaite 2000).

3. This will not be further pursued here because it does not provide any new information (see also Ungerer & Schmid 2006: 259).

4. As a further step, Busse (forthcoming) will fuse a cognitive stylistic approach with a corpus stylistic approach and test whether the blend of WRITING IS MEDICINE has a textually foregrounded base, that is, whether there are ways of proving linguistically, textually and/or stylistically as well as empirically that the blend WRITING IS MEDICINE actually features in the text through keywords, foregrounded syntactic structures and so on.

5. Diagrammatic iconicity refers to an "arrangement of signs, none of which necessarily resembles its referent but whose relationships to each other mirror the relationship of their referents" (Nänny and Fischer 2006: 462).

6. But as Toolan (2001: 130) points out: "[T]he appearance or illusion of character control should not be overstated: behind all the fictional individuals, however reported, stands the controlling teller".

WORKS CITED

Auster, Paul (2002) *The Book of Illusions*. London: Faber and Faber.
———. (2006) *The Brooklyn Follies*. New York: Henry Holt.
———. (2008) "Sprache schenkt uns die Welt". *Neue Zürcher Zeitung* October 4, 2008. http://www.nzz.ch/nachrichten/kultur/literatur_und_kunst/sprache_schenkt_uns_die_welt_und_nimmt_sie_uns_zugleich_1.1019111.html (accessed January 2, 2009).

Bennet M., Carlos, Yerka Luksic, and Consuelo Huidobro M. (2007) "The Mirror of Emptiness: Post Traumatic Stress Disorder and Dissociative Phenomena in the Literature of Paul Auster" [El espejo del vacío: Trastorno por Stress Post Traumático y fenómenso disociativos en la narrative de Paul Auster]. *Revista Chilena de Neuro-Psiquiatria* 45.1: 51–58.

Brandt, Line, and Per Aage Brandt (2005) "Making Sense of a Blend". *Annual Review of Cognitive Linguistics* 3. http://www.hum.au.dk/semiotics/docs2/pdf/ brandt&brandt/making_sense.pdf (accessed January 2, 2009).

Burke, Michael (2005) "How Cognition Can Augment Stylistic Analysis". *European Journal of English Studies* 9.2: 185–95.

Burr-Nevanlinna, Anja (2005) "Was ist Poesie- und Bibliotherapie? Eine Einführung". *Literatur und Medizin*. Eds. Peter Stulz, Frank Nager and Peter Schulz. Zürich: Chroves. 129–37.

Busse, Beatrix (forthcoming) "Blending cognitive and corpus stylistics in Paul Auster's *The Brooklyn Follies* (2006) and *The Book of Illusions* (2002)". *Bi-Directionality in the Cognitive Sciences: Examining the Interdisciplinary Potential of Cognitive Approaches in Linguistics and Literary Studies*. Eds. Marcus Callies, Wolfram Keller and Astrid Lohöfer. Amsterdam: John Benjamins.

Coulson, Seana, and Todd Oakley (2005) "Blended and Coded Meaning: Literal and Figurative Meaning in Cognitive Semantics". *Journal of Pragmatics* 37: 1510–1636.

Curiol, Céline (2006) "The Making of *The Inner Life of Martin Frost*: Céline Curiol in Interview with Paul Auster". *The Inner Life of Martin Frost*. Paul Auster. New York: Picador. 1–19.

Dancygier, Barbara (2006) "What Can Blending Do for You?" *Language and Literature* 15.1: 5–15.

Douthwaite, John (2000) *Towards a Linguistic Theory of Foregrounding*. Torino: Edizioni dell'Orso.

Evans, Vyvyan, and Melanie Green (2006) *Cognitive Linguistics: An Introduction*. Edinburgh: Edinburgh University Press.

Fauconnier, Gilles, and Mark Turner (2002) *The Way We Think: Conceptual Blending and the Mind's Hidden Complexities*. New York: Basic Books.

Fludernik, Monika (1996) *Towards a 'Natural' Narratology*. London: Routledge.

Forceville, Charles (2004) "Book Review: *The Way We Think. Conceptual Blending and the Mind's Hidden Complexities*". *Metaphor and Symbol* 19.1: 83–89.

Gavins, Joanna, and Gerard Steen (2003) Eds. *Cognitive Poetics in Practice*. London and New York: Routledge.

Halliday, Michael A. K. (1994) *An Introduction to Functional Grammar*. Second Edition. London and New York: Arnold.

Halliday, Michael A. K., and Christian Matthiesen (2004) *An Introduction to Functional Grammar*. Third Edition. London and New York: Arnold.

Lakoff, George, and Mark Johnson (2003) *Metaphors We Live By*. Second Edition. Chicago: University of Chicago Press.

Leech, Geoffrey (2008) *Language in Literature: Style and Foregrounding*. London: Longman.

Nänny, Max, and Olga Fischer (2006) "Iconicity: Literary Texts". *Encyclopedia of Language and Linguistics*. Ed. Keith Brown. Amsterdam: Elsevier. 462–72.

Palmer, Alan (2004) *Fictional Minds*. Lincoln and London: University of Nebraska Press.

Peacock, James (2006) "Carrying the Burden of Representation: Paul Auster's *The Book of Illusion*". *Journal of American Studies* 40: 53–69.

Semino, Elena (2002) "A Cognitive Stylistic Approach to Mind Style in Narrative Fiction". *Cognitive Stylistics: Language and Cognition in Text Analysis*. Eds. Elena Semino and Jonathan Culpeper. Amsterdam: John Benjamins. 95–122.

———. (2006) "Blending and Character's Mental Functioning in Virginia Woolf's 'Lappin and Lapinova'". *Language and Literature* 15.1: 55–72.

Semino, Elena, and Jonathan Culpeper (2002) Eds. *Cognitive Stylistics: Language and Cognition in Text Analysis*. Amsterdam: John Benjamins.

Short, Mick (2006) *Exploring the Language of Poems, Plays and Prose*. London and New York: Longman.

Stockwell, Peter (2002) *Cognitive Poetics: An Introduction*. London: Routledge.

Toolan, Michael (2001) *Narrative: A Critical Linguistic Introduction*. Second Edition. London: Routledge.

———. (2009) *Narrative Progression in the Short Story: A Corpus Stylistic Approach*. Amsterdam and Philadelphia: John Benjamins.

Turner, Mark (1996) *The Literary Mind: The Origins of Language and Thought*. New York: Oxford University Press.

———. (2003) "Double-Scope Stories". *Narrative Theory and the Cognitive Sciences*. Ed. David Herman. Stanford: CSLI Publications. 117–42.

———. (2006) "Compression and Representation". *Language and Literature* 15.1: 17–27.

Ungerer, Friedrich, and Hans-Jörg Schmid (2006) *An Introduction to Cognitive Linguistics*. Second Edition. London: Longman.

von Engelhardt, Dietrich (1991) *Medizin in der Literatur der Neuzeit I: Darstellung und Deutung*. Hartgenwald: Guido Pressler.

———. (2004) "Vom Dialog der Medizin und Literatur im 20. Jahrhundert". *Literatur und Medizin: Ein Lexikon.* Eds. Bettina von Jagow and Florian Steger. Göttingen: Vandenhoeck & Ruprecht. 21–40.

Von Jagow, Bettina, and Florian Steger (2009) *Was treibt die Literatur zur Medizin? Ein kulturwissenschaftlicher Dialog.* Göttingen: Vandenhoeck & Ruprecht.

10 Metaphor Sets in *The Turn of the Screw*
What Conceptual Metaphors Reveal about Narrative Functions

Michael Kimmel

1 INTRODUCTION

Literary scholars of a more classical bent have critically questioned why cognitive stylistics is so much in the thrall of conceptual metaphors, the generative thought patterns that underlie metaphoric expressions with similar meanings or imagery.[1] To these critics, bypassing a traditional stylistics through a generalising approach risks the neglect of aesthetics, context-specificity and ultimately "literariness" (Downes 1993). Although it has been convincingly argued that a cognitive linguistic analysis can avoid reductionism (Danaher 2007), it has gone unnoticed that the defence of conceptual metaphor can be taken up from the opposite angle by asking what it contributes to genuinely narrative functions. Before entering into this agenda, it will be helpful to reiterate the general framework and possible criticisms it is faced with.

1.1 Background and Aims

Cognitive metaphor theory goes beyond a view of metaphors as linguistic entities. It aims at reconstructing conceptual patterns and connects superficially dissimilar linguistic expressions as manifestations of a single underlying logic. This allows analysts to cast their nets widely and retrieve similarities that readers, most often subconsciously, make sense of while reading. The soon to emerge cognitive literary movement began to capitalise on conceptual metaphor theory for describing recurrent motifs/themes. In doing so, they also corrected the long-standing research bias towards particularly creative linguistic usage and called into question the assumption that the lion's share of conventional metaphors does not matter because they are 'un-literary'. Few will gainsay that a focus on conceptual patterns constitutes a significant advance over views that see metaphor as a locus of linguistic ornament or style. What is, by degrees, less recognized is that the theoretical move sensitises us to how novels unfold their conceptual coherence and draws our gaze to an author's cognitive-cultural resources. The book that set the tone, Lakoff and Turner's *More than Cool Reason* (1989), claims that literary metaphor frequently manifests culturally conventional mappings in creative garb. Besides evaluating literary metaphor against the backdrop of the standard repertoire of English speakers, cognitive literary studies have established a model for delineating and sub-categorizing metaphor. They have also proposed a testable theory of metaphor processing, specified the elements of metaphorical mappings and discovered recurrent image schemas that scaffold most metaphors.

Of late, we have seen demonstrations of image schemas like FORCE, CONTAINER, LINK or BALANCE being constitutive of novels or plays at large (i.e. across different mappings) or examinations of key conceptual metaphors in the narrower sense. If traditionalist critics have felt that these renderings are decontextualized, this is in part due to their unwillingness to accept the cognitive research agenda that explores story-telling as a generic human feat. However, the cognitive poetic approach has more momentous causes for a critical self-examination. First, the approach tends to conceal interesting differences beneath some overly unitary terminology. What is cognitively effective is not always ideally captured through 'standard cognitive linguistics'. We frequently find metaphors with non-identical narrative functions, despite their instantiating the same conceptual metaphor. Likewise, image schemas are not 'embodied' *tout court*, but invite different degrees of bodily participation by the reader. At both levels, necessary gradations have not been highlighted enough.

Second, a cognitive stylistics that only varies the theme "image-schematic structures X, Y or Z underlie the motif so-and-so" stagnates in an important sense. It needlessly limits the scope of the approach. We need to sensitise ourselves to analytic loci for metaphor that connect to broader narratological topics, e.g. its role in creating character "mind-styles" (Semino & Swindlehurst 1996) or in defining different levels of a plot model (Kimmel 2005, 2008).

With this aim in mind, my chapter systematically explores a text from a broader narratological angle. I shall identify narrative effects cued by conceptual metaphor at the following five levels: (1) theme-setting and foregrounding (*"What is important?"*), (2) the enrichment of motifs and creation of symbolic nodes (*"How does it interrelate?"*), (3) the generation of plot and character models (*"What drives the action and what is the nature of the agents?"*), (4) the creation of unique literary effects such as ambiguity (*"Why does ontological multiplicity arise?"*) and (5) reader involvement at an affective and embodied level (*"How is the reader engaged in what she reads?"*). My case study is Henry James's *The Turn of the Screw*, a psychological ghost story that is exceptionally rich in patterned metaphors and also noted for its irresolvable ambiguity and complex effects.[2] Previous studies of the novella have variously addressed some of the above research questions (Miall 1984),[3] except for the embodiment issue, but no-one has managed to show that metaphor ties in with them all. My present purpose, then, is to illustrate the broad analytic possibilities that systematic metaphor analysis gives to cognitive literary studies.[4]

1.2   Method

The data for this rather extensive research agenda comes from a project that weds cognitive literary practice with tools typically used by discourse linguists.[5] Specifically, a full-scale analysis of metaphor and imagery was applied to six English and American (short) novels, aiming to gain insight into metaphor frequency, diversity, types of metaphor and their literary functions (cf. Kimmel 2008). I followed a procedure that brackets a heavily contextual literary reading in the first step in favour of a close linguistic description, which is only gradually raised to higher analytical levels. Note that each step remains thoroughly hermeneutic; i.e. what the applied annotation software (here *Atlas.ti* 6) adds requires contextual validation by the researcher:

(1) At the lowest level, annotation software is used to systematically code all imagistic phenomena in a sentence-by-sentence manner. First, a general type is chosen from a list of phenomena (metaphors, idioms, metonymy, synaesthesia, extended metaphor, etc.), after which the sources and targets of each metaphoric phenomenon are specified.

(2) Next, metaphors are grouped by conceptual metaphor or, alternatively, by shared sources and targets, thus retracing what Goatly (1997) calls metaphor diversification and multivalency. The filter and pattern search options of the software make these and other kinds of data retrieval easy.

(3) Then, all conceptual metaphors are listed and probed for possible connections, with the aim of reconstructing similarities *between* patterns that do not meet the eye. This makes the method suitable for demonstrating the sheer number of cross-connections that readers may exploit in a metaphorically rich text.

(4) Finally, an author's general (often genre-related) rhetoric strategies of using metaphor are analysed by integrating all the former descriptive levels. These strategies refract the story's specific 'literariness' through the prism of metaphor.

This bottom-up procedure hands the researcher a powerful heuristic that guides the study itself and later allows systematic comparisons between texts at several levels. The present chapter follows this stepwise structure. First, I shall survey James's recurrent conceptual metaphors and discuss their relation to the main story themes. Then, the above-mentioned narrative functions are explored by cross-connecting related data. Finally, I will turn to the emerging "modes of metaphorization".

2   BASIC-LEVEL ANALYSIS—THE MAIN CONCEPTUAL METAPHOR SETS

The full-scale coding of metaphor with Atlas.ti software yielded 1,021 expressions. Target and source domains were coded separately with the intention of later reconstructing conceptual metaphors from their overlap. Here, I shall report on conceptual metaphors with at least six tokens, while discarding all less systematic ones. The more than fifty patterns are grouped by six target domains, many of which split into several subgroups, as summarized in Table 10.1. Under each specific heading I discuss the relevant source domains and give a representative example for each mapping.

Table 10.1   Conceptual Metaphor Sets

(1) cognition	(1a) knowledge as visual or tactile sensing (1b) realizations as forces and paths (1c) psychological states/processes as forces and paths
(2) emotion	(2a) emotions as force dynamics (2b) emotional forces and containers (2c) emotions/realizations as force contours (2d) emotions as verticality
(3) protagonist interaction	(3a) protagonist perception: the children are bright/sweet creatures (3b) protagonist enthrallment and control as force dynamics (3c) protagonist communication as object transfer (3d) protagonist interaction as force (e.g. vying forces)
(4) protagonist action	goals of discoveryas paths/verticality
(5) morality	moral abjectness and the corruption of the innocent as verticality/lostness
(6) external appearance	settings as animate/brightness/a fairytale world

(1a)   Knowledge as Sensing

Metaphors for knowledge reflect *the* ultimate suspense-generating question "Are the ghosts real or not?" and the governess's disputable reliability in her reports about seeing Quint and Jessel. Ignorance, suspicion and attempted disclosure recur as metaphors of sight and touch. The frequency of KNOWING IS SENSING shows that sensory evidence is a major theme and something that drives the plot forward.

> KNOWING IS GRASPING OR TOUCHING → "Of what other things have **you got hold?**" (James 1999: 47)

> ALARM IS BEING TOUCHED / HIDDEN PRESENCE IS SOFT TOUCH → "a small shifty spot on the wrong side of it all still sometimes **brushed my brow like the wing of a bat**" (34)

> KNOWING IS SEEING / IGNORANCE IS BEING BLOCKED FROM SEEING → "I felt the importance of **giving the last jerk to the curtain**" (34)

> KNOWLEDGE IS LIGHT / IGNORANCE IS DARKNESS → "deep **obscurity** continued to cover the region of the boy's conduct at school" (18)

> POSITIVE COGNITIVE STATES ARE BRIGHT / NEGATIVE STATES ARE DIM → "and if I once more **closed my eyes it was before the dazzle**" (41) / "the two or three **dim elements of comfort**" (34)

The tactile metaphors are related both to the governess's attempt to know and to the eerie effect of a hidden presence. The visual metaphors are mostly specific to the governess's search for (and comfort in) truth, whereas the light-dark polarity points to the governess's ambivalence. She is partly in the obscure and wants to shed light on the enigma, but partly recoils (e.g. "shut my eyes"—77) and takes herself to task for this. These metaphors also pronouncedly contribute to a Gothic mood and a sense of the uncanny.

(1b)   Realizations as Forces and Paths

Concerning the governess's recurrent efforts to understand the events, the following metaphors again reflect the plot-related importance of sudden realizations, which typically create sudden turns.

> REALIZATIONS ARE FORCES → "If so much had **sprung to the surface**" (77)

> REALIZATION IS A LEAP ON A PATH → "the wildness of **my veritable leap**" (84)

REALIZATION IS MOVING ALONG A PATH → "It was as if, at moments, we were perpetually **coming into sight of subjects**" (49)

CONSIDERING SOMETHING IS PASSING OVER IT → "The more I **go over it**" (30)

PERCEPTION IS TAKING IN (INTO THE MIND-CONTAINER) → "I **took it in** with a throb of hope" (79)

(1c)   Psychological States/Processes as Forces and Paths

The following two conceptual metaphors instantiate a familiar *metaphor dual*, a figure-ground reversal between a trajector (mover) and a landmark (space) (Lakoff & Johnson 1999). Both imply a strong emphasis on closure and opening.

PSYCHOLOGICAL STATES ARE CONTAINERS → "I've been living with the miserable truth, and now it has only too much **closed round me**" (James 1999: 70)

MINDS/SOULS ARE CONTAINERS FOR PSYCHOLOGICAL STATES → "but I shall **get it out of you** yet!" (35)

We will see that this converges with metaphors in which the governess manipulatively plants ideas into Mrs. Grose's mind.

(2a)   Emotions as Force Dynamics

Emotion-related metaphors occur with astonishing frequency and high elaboration. They almost exclusively draw on the source domain of forces and refer to the governess's intense emotional experience that runs the gamut from anxiety, horror and fear, via sadness, elation, mustering of courage and resolve to warmth and devotion. The metaphors depict the heroine as a heavily troubled woman struggling for self-control. Despite her permanent agitation, she has to brace herself to save the children and therefore imposes taboos on herself, especially not to ask the children directly about the ghosts and not to disappoint their unapproachable uncle by sending a letter to solicit his help.

AFFECTS ARE IMPULSES → "I was taken with an **impulse** that might **master** me" (56)

ANXIETY IS AN ASSAILING FORCE → "so **assailed** with apprehensions" (76)

CONTROLLING EMOTION IS VYING WITH A COUNTERFORCE → "at the renewed touch of her kindness my **power to resist broke down**" (32)

EMOTIONAL RELEASE IS LETTING GO / STRONG EMOTIONS ARE OUT-
BREAKS → "There are directions in which I must not for the present **let
myself go**" (36) / "excite suspicion by the little **outbreaks** of my sharper
passion for them" (37)

As described by Kövecses (2000), emotion metaphors involve a dynamic interaction between a force Agonist and Antagonist. The heroine is caught in a
quasi-Freudian dynamic between her own impulses, the self-imposed impulse
to perform her duty to resist the (mental or real) influences and the impulse
towards emotional release. We shall later see further control-related metaphors
converging with these, concerning both her manipulation of others (she is skil-
fully using Mrs. Grose for her purposes) and being manipulated herself.

(2b)   Emotional Forces and Containers

Force metaphors are frequently combined with container image schemas.
Emotional dynamics are conceptualized as scripts involving forces on path
trajectories moving out of containers.

VENTING OR SHOWING EMOTIONS IS LETTING THEM OUT → "she took
me to her motherly breast, and my lamentation **overflowed**" (James
1999: 32)

BEING SUBJECT TO AN EMOTION IS BEING CAUGHT IN IT / ESCAPING AN
EMOTION IS MOVING OUT OF IT → "It was the idea, the second movement, that **led me straight out, as I may say, of the inner chamber of
my dread**" (24)

At the basis of this group of metaphors we find another metaphor dual:
EMOTIONS ARE SUBSTANCES IN BODY-CONTAINERS is the reverse of EMO-
TIONAL STATES ARE CONTAINERS PEOPLE ARE IN. Overall, it is noteworthy
that the in-out dimension is so much emphasized, perhaps due to the governess's conscious decision to feign imperviousness in the children's presence while needing frequent outlets when alone.

(2c)   Emotions (and Realizations) as Contours

To bestow a rich and empathy-engendering quality on a character's emotional experience or perception, authors frequently use *contour expressions*
which encode a temporal gestalt pattern and thereby specify the emotion's
"event shape" (cf. Parrill 2000). Contours concretize the general idea of
emotional force by creating felt imagery of its manner, modality and temporal dynamics. Bodily feelings thus come as waves, throbs, pangs, flashes,
vibrations, snaps, etc.

QUALITY OF SUBTLE EMOTIONS IS SUBTLE FORCE → "a little seesaw of
the right **throbs** and the wrong" (James 1999: 6)

QUALITY OF STRONG EMOTIONS IS INTENSE FORCE → "a sudden **vibration** of duty and courage" (20)

SUDDEN REALIZATIONS ARE FLASHES → "The **flash** of this knowledge" (20)

SUDDEN REALIZATIONS ARE SUDDEN FORCES → "The change was actually **like the spring of a beast**" (14)

SUDDEN EMOTIONS ARE SUDDEN IMPACTS → "it was only the relief that a snap brings to a strain or the burst of a thunderstorm to a day of suffocation" (52)

GRADUAL EMOTIONS ARE THE GRADUAL FLOW OF A LIQUID → "the strange, dizzy **lift or swim**" (51)

SUDDEN, INTENSE EMOTIONS ARE FLOODING LIQUIDS → "on a **great wave** of infatuation and pity" (14)

Metaphors like "drop" or "heave" may enrich such contours by adding a vertical dimension (UP-DOWN) of intensity to the temporal change. A special case of this is emotional intensity metaphorically depicted as flames that go up (not unlike the force of emotional outbreaks).

CHANGING EMOTIONAL INTENSITY IS UP-DOWN → "beginning as a succession of **flights and drops**" (6)

CHANGING EMOTIONAL INTENSITY IS A FLAME'S INTENSITY → "I had to shade, as it were, my **flame**" (82)

(2d)   Emotions as Verticality

Besides "event shapes" overtime, verticality metaphors are also found in the simpler function of expressing the governess's waxing and waning fortitude.

DEJECTEDNESS IS DOWN → "the **deeper depths** of consternation that had opened beneath my feet" (71)

COURAGE IS UP → "the extraordinary **flight of heroism**" (27)[6]

(3a)   Protagonists: The Children are Bright/Sweet Creatures

We can move now to the target domain of protagonist interaction. The first sub-group here concerns how the governess evaluates her wards. The children evoke strong positive connotations and an image of perfection. They are sensitive, charming and innocent, but threatened by evil forces. Non-metaphorical words like *beauty* and words of endearment frequently reinforce this.

THE CHILDREN ARE ANGELS → **"one of Raphael's holy infants"** (8)

THE CHILDREN ARE BRIGHT CREATURES → **"radiant image** of my little girl" (7)[7]

THE CHILDREN ARE SWEET → "Miss Flora was **too sweet"** (58)

Sweetness and brightness are sensory poles with a cross-modal likeness, converging at the super-schema level (Grady 2005) and involving a bipolar scale. The children almost always sit at the positive pole in the governess's mindset, whereas the ghosts (**"dark"**, "the **devil"**) occupy the negative pole. This attribution pattern sits uneasily with her occasional admission that the children are not what she takes them to be (Miles as "the **dark prodigy** I knew"—James 1999: 63), thus hinting at the state of denial the governess lives in.

(3b)   Protagonist Interaction: The Force Dynamics of Enthrallment and Control

How the protagonists affect each other appears in force-related metaphors of two types. First, the children's loveliness has enthralled and captivated the governess, creating a force that moves or constrains her.

ENTHRALLMENT IS A MOVER → "You WILL be **carried away** by the little gentleman!" (8)

ENTHRALLMENT IS BEING SEIZED → "He '**had' me** indeed, and in a cleft stick" (48)

ENTHRALLMENT IS A SPELL → "Of course I was **under** the **spell"** (19)

Second, the governess perceives the ghosts as interacting with the children by force logic and herself as competing with them for control over (or possession of) the children. As Lyndenberg has it, "[s]haring is impossible; the children must be either hers or theirs" (1957: 49). Opposing the ghosts' desire, the governess thinks of herself as a screen, shield or saviour.

THE GHOSTS' CONTROL IS POSSESSION/SEIZING → "They're not mine— they're not ours. They're his and they're hers!" (James 1999: 47)

PROTECTING THE CHILDREN IS SHIELDING → "I was **a screen—I was to stand before them"** (27)

PROTECTING THE CHILDREN IS CATCHING → "**catching him in his fall"** (85)

(3c)   Protagonist Communication as Transfer

Henry James bases communication acts on the conventional conduit metaphor in which objects are transferred between mind-containers or, inversely, communicators move towards topic-containers. Whether the emphasis lies on the origin, the endpoint or the transfer itself, forces and paths are always implied.

COMMUNICATION IS OBJECT TRANSFER BETWEEN MIND-CONTAINERS → "She offered her mind to my disclosures as, [...] she would **have held out a large clean saucepan**" (44)

COMMUNICATION / STORYTELLING IS MOVING TOWARDS TOPICS → "he repeated **as if retreating for a jump**, yet leaving his thought so unfinished" (54) / "I find that I really **hang back**; but I must **take my horrid plunge**" (38)

COMMUNICATION IS EXTRACTING AN OBJECT FROM ANOTHER OR ONE-SELF → "Miles **had got something out of me**" (55) / "she [...] **brought out** the rest" (74)

The first scenario relates to communicated meanings flowing effortlessly (i.e. without counterforce) mostly between the governess and Mrs. Grose. The second scenario targets the governess's more laborious communication with the children that never quite goes all the way (and is mirrored in the story-teller's effort). A third scenario suggests an outright struggle between them, as they try to wrest information from each other's minds or bring it out from their own. This boundary is resistant, making communication very strained in the majority of cases.

(3d) Protagonist Interaction as Force and Conflict

A next group of metaphors suggests violent communication directly, i.e., a struggle with the children and occasionally with Mrs. Grose. The first pattern suggests vehement emotionality, while the others implicate an outright struggle.

COMMUNICATION IS FORCE → "I heard myself **throw off with homely force**" (84)

COMMUNICATION BETWEEN GOVERNESS AND MRS. GROSE IS FIGHTING → "Mrs. Grose took it **as she might have taken a blow in the stomach**" (29)

COMMUNICATION GOVERNESS-CHILDREN IS STABBING → "each of her **stabbing little words**" (70)

COMMUNICATION GOVERNESS-CHILDREN IS WAR → "his **supreme surrender** of the name" (85)

(4)   Goals of Discovery

The governess's efforts to lay open Bly's mystery are another major target. It is organised in terms of DISCOVERY IS MOTION and implies that the enigma is a taboo subject, especially as concerns Miles's behaviour at school, for which he got expelled (and which was possibly related to sexual acts).

> DISCOVERY IS REACHING A PATH ENDPOINT / TABOOS ARE BLOCKAGES → "we were perpetually **coming into sight** of subjects **before which we must stop short**" (49)

> DISCOVERY IS REACHING A DEEPEST (OR CENTRAL) POINT → "I should never **get to the bottom**" (37)

These metaphors foreground an "action style" of frenzied and frustrated goal pursuit that is characteristic of the governess.

(5)   Moral Abjectness and the Corruption of the Innocent

A further key theme is the corruption of the innocent. The ghosts, especially Quint, the instigator and seducer of Ms. Jessel, are evil creatures from whom the children need to be protected. The governess, a Puritan parson's daughter, couches this in biblical terms of the Fall of Man and being lost.

> IMMORAL IS DOWN → "my predecessor's **abasement**" (32)

> IMMORALITY IS THE 'FALL' FROM GRACE → "he uttered the cry of **a creature hurled over an abyss**" (85)

> CORRUPTING THE CHILDREN IS LOSTNESS → "Of the **lost**. Of the damned" (58)

(6)   External Appearance

Various metaphorical descriptions of the appearance of the place give the Gothic scenery great prominence and the effect of a hidden agency that the governess is subject to, but also mark the place as one of great romance and sensorial impact.[8]

> THE SURROUNDINGS ARE ANIMATE → "The rooks stopped **cawing** in the golden sky" (16)

> UNCORRUPTED IS BRIGHT → "The **gold** was still in the sky, the **clearness** in the air" (16)

BLY IS A FAIRYTALE WORLD → "I had the view of a **castle of romance** [...] which would take all colour **out of storybooks and fairytales**" (9)

The latter two conceptual metaphors convey the governess's idealization of Bly. I shall later discuss how this flips over to dark and eerie images, which are very memorable, though often not metaphoric.

Intermediary Summary

The Turn of the Screw relies massively on metaphor to create literary themes and stylistic effects (albeit not to the exclusion of other cueing devices). Conceptual metaphors are far from arbitrary and reflect key themes like the incertitude of the governess's knowledge, her complex psychodynamics and dilemmas. She herself conveys to us her inner feelings and predicaments through metaphor, i.e. her devotion and compulsive preoccupation with knowledge, discovery and 'truth'. From a more psychologizing viewpoint, the ambivalent patterns of holding vs. pushing that are evident in both action and emotion point to sexual anxiety, obsession and the presence of taboos, while a combative quality in the dialogues hints at manipulative violence. Throughout, a metaphysical show-down between good and evil is created, implicating the Christian motifs of corruption of the innocent and salvation of the damned. A Gothic mood with a hidden menace is foreshadowed, then sustained.

Previous scholarship has often focused on one or a few of these conceptual metaphor sets, especially the symbolic ones. What is more commonly overlooked are metaphors which do not feel especially 'literary' (e.g. for communication and goal-directed actions) and which subtly realize narrative effects. Moreover, as we shall see next, complex interaction effects occur regarding the metaphors.

3 HIGHER-LEVEL ANALYSIS

If the cognitive literary studies are to explain how general narrative *functions* are realized, what can metaphor analysis contribute? First, quantitative trends in metaphoric themes prove insightful. Second, many important functions become evident when we move beyond the basic patterns and look at conceptual metaphors in their interaction with others (partly patterns that join forces, partly antithetical relations between them).

3.1 Key Themes and Frequent Target Domains

Metaphor is a recognized foregrounding device. Thus, when patterned metaphors for a story theme are numerous, this foregrounds the theme itself. The predominant metaphoric themes may even reflect trends typical of a whole genre. Recurrent target domains offer indicators for this,

Table 10.2   Metaphor Frequencies by Target Domain

Target Domain Group	Hits
Knowing or not	160
Psychological dynamics	165
Emotional dynamics	154
Interaction and communication	202
Characteristics of persons	104
External appearance of persons and things	45
Action goals (such as discovering the secret)	87
Event descriptions more generally	67
Morality, abjectness, seduction	28
Diverse other cognition-related	45

somewhat independently of specific mappings. The following quick-scan was done by compacting target domains into groups and counting the metaphors for each. In comparing the numbers we need to bear in mind where metaphor is optional (e.g. settings and people) and where the English language employs metaphor almost obligatorily (e.g. for abstract goals, emotions, inner states, knowing, realizing and morality).

The fact that the novella is so rich in psychological and emotion metaphors relates directly to the psychological genre and the intense character narration that draws the reader into the governess's inner world. Knowledge and ignorance-related metaphors and a great number of action metaphors reflect the governess's plot-driving aims to uncover the enigma and obtain a confession. Metaphorical descriptions of persons and things tie in with the Gothic mood and a symbolically imbued characterization of the protagonists. Finally, the tremendous number of interaction metaphors seems less genre-specific; it simply relates to the presence of several protagonists and frequent direct speech.

3.2   Motif Enrichment through Nodal Source Domains

In a next step, we must go beyond sheer frequency counts and the generalising logic of targets only, and consider the more specific metaphoric mappings. My particular interest is to examine how they interact and cross-buttress (or undercut) each other. I will begin with a look at how different, yet related mappings create symbolic nodes and enrich story motifs. This most often happens through what Goatly (2007: ch. 5) calls *multivalency*, i.e. different targets taking on the same image-schematic or sensory source domain.

For example, light maps not only on knowledge, but also on the children, and, as clarity and purity, on Bly House itself. In all these cases, a shared pattern of GOOD IS LIGHT/BRIGHT emerges, encapsulating all that the governess desires. In addition, brightness stands for intensity and connects 'throwing light onto the mystery', the intensity of realization (e.g. "**flashes** of succession"—James 1999: 39) and the intensely enthralling children (e.g. "**radiant** image of my little girl"—7). Inversely, the dark pole connects the obscurity of the enigma, the governess's mood, exposure to something evil and the sombre aspects of Bly. IGNORANT IS DARK, DESPERATE IS DARK and THREATENING IS DARK converge in NEGATIVE IS DARK. Beyond metaphor, this is further heightened by a sombre mood and darkness suffusing Bly.[9] Note that we may often consider words from different sensory source domains as similar in this context.[10] Such cross-modal correspondences depend on a similar axiological organisation (Krzeszowski 1993). On an evaluative scale, the children's brightness and sweetness both belong to the pole of positive/high intensity. Tactile and visual attributes expressing the same pole are even found in text clusters, e.g. in "It was a **crisp, clear** day, the first of its order for some time; the night had brought a touch of frost, and the autumn air, **bright** and **sharp**, made the church bells almost gay" (James 1999: 52). The boldfaced vehicle words constitute a cross-modal set of high intensity. More generally, the governess's enthrallment almost always has *some* sort of intense sensorial quality to it (e.g. "a castle of romance inhabited by a **rosy sprite**"—9), arguably a Gothic genre effect that depends on cross-modal matching.

In another case of multivalency, the UP-DOWN schema connects the governess's mood swings between elation and despondency, the abjectness of Quint and Jessel and the children's imminent fall (DESPONDENCY IS DOWN and DEPRAVITY IS DOWN). The 'despondent governess', 'spiritually lost children' and 'depraved Quint/Jessel' receive the same negative evaluation. There is a binary opposition between a positive pole (the ideal of childhood innocence, the angelic children and the governess's fondness of them) and a negative one ('Quint, the devil', sexuality).[11] The children are angelic, beautiful and perfect. They sit at the top, in sharp contrast to the 'low' morals of Quint and Jessel and their 'fall'. The mapping GOOD IS UP/BAD IS DOWN thus interrelates the governess's radical mood swings and the evaluations of good and evil. We repeatedly see how moods and evaluations move in tandem; whenever the governess thinks she can protect her wards from the fall, her courage mounts.

Another important multivalency pattern relates to a binary view of the IN-OUT dimension.

COMMUNICATION IS EXTRACTING AN OBJECT FROM ANOTHER/FROM ONESELF

COPING WITH EMOTIONS IS LETTING THEM OUT

COPING WITH EMOTIONS IS ESCAPING FROM THEM

The shared motif here is that of great strain. A container initially resists breach, yet must be breached. In her emotions, the governess experiences a strained

Table 10.3   Multivalencies

LIGHT	knowledge, charity, purity, children, goodness
UP-DOWN	despondency, depravity, evil
IN-OUT	communication, emotions, non-metaphoric spatial boundaries

demarcation. In communication too, wresting information from a counter-force produces tension. Both lend an almost visceral feel of taboo to the novella, rather than a free flow (cf. 3.6). This reflects the Victorian preoccupation with imposed sexual, social and emotional boundaries (Harrell 1982), while also creating narrative interest through a plot-driving complication. A different, yet similar container results from PROTECTING THE CHILDREN IS SHIELDING THEM. The governess treats good and evil as Manichaean spheres. Hence, the children must be enclosed and kept in a fairy-tale world.[12] The governess herself is always at the threshold, the maintainer of the sharp boundary, acting to "save and shield" them. In scene descriptions too, Bly House appears as a dangerous enclosure (Lustig 1994: 130–34),[13] again emphasizing 'liminality' and an ambiguous interface. Long corridors and doors that are opened or closed appear recurrently (133), as do edges and borders the interface between day and night in setting scenes at dawn or dusk (134–35). The novel "focuses with such intensity on the way in which thresholds simultaneously divide and connect borders that borders seem to occupy the whole field, to prevent simple oppositions between the outer and the inner rather than making them possible" (133–34). I summarize this section in Table 10.3.

3.3   Protagonist Characterization

Explicit characterization metaphors like THE CHILDREN ARE BRIGHT may be found on occasion. More pervasively, however, characterization depends on how the protagonist's action tendencies are described. Action tendencies are implemented around emotion descriptions and psychological processes, which, as we have seen, are metaphorically conceived in force-dynamic terms. Together, these give rise to a complex schema defining the governess's character disposition, notably when we examine the numerous introspective passages that testify to her constant dilemma. In these passages, she persistently oscillates between fear and resignation on the one hand and a fighting spirit, Victorian decorum and duty. Emotional forces are freed, held back and released again, in an alternation between impulsivity, her self-imposed duty of resistance and her need for venting her feelings or tensions.

REALIZATIONS ARE FORCES

DESIRES ARE IMPULSIVE FORCES

PSYCHOLOGICAL PRESSURE IS A FORCE

CONTROLLING EMOTION IS VYING WITH A COUNTERFORCE

EMOTIONAL RELEASE IS LETTING GO / STRONG EMOTIONS ARE OUTBREAKS

VENTING OR SHOWING EMOTIONS IS LETTING THEM OUT

ESCAPING AN EMOTION IS MOVING OUT OF IT

These force-dynamic emotion metaphors collude to describe an inner struggle. In fact, a full script-like 'action chain' can be reconstructed from these patterns, in which the governess is first subject to forceful impressions; this produces emotional impulses; she is striving to control or escape these, but then ultimately needs a periodical outlet (the subtext being that her own strong ideas and desires create the conflict). What the various metaphors share is the image-schematic idea that the governess's inner dynamic moves back and forth between an 'enclosing' and an 'outbreak mode' of emotion, as restraint alternates with sudden release or self-abandon. The qualitative descriptions of the governess's affects through imagistic *contour words* reinforce this, as they alternate between "**passionate throb**" and "**finest little quiver**" (James 1999: 45, 80).[14] Furthermore, various non-metaphoric descriptions of physical actions in the storyworld amplify this rhapsody of moods. Rigid forces ("**clutching**"—76; "**spasm**"—28, 41; or "**holding on to**"—47) alternate with suggestions of loosening. All these means bring about a sustained back-and-forth motion and let narrative disequilibrium, suspense and uncertainty mount.

The master metaphor EMOTIONS ARE FORCES explains the psychological impact of the novella in more than one way. One may take a distanced view on the governess's neurotic compulsiveness and use the force-dynamic metaphors to infer repressed desires, an urge to control and a defensive projection in a depth-psychological reading. For those readers who immerse themselves fully in the narration and sympathize with the governess's predicament, the force metaphors' intensity, frequency and imagistic detail are gripping. Besides implicating the reader in the heroine's tornness, her intensifying emotions constitute a major plot engine. The governess's urge to save the children and to extract a confession are the ultimate grounds of her emotional dynamic,[15] which in turn sets her actions into motion. What 'tightens the screw' is the sheer ambivalence underlying her plot-driving emotions. Her ultimate goal is to "**trace it—follow it all up**" (47), "to **shorten the distance** and **overcome the obstacle**" (48), in the conviction that "the **straightest road out** is doubtless to advance" (38) (DISCOVERY IS REACHING A PATH ENDPOINT). Yet, her inner ambivalence lets her hold back (TABOOS ARE BLOCKAGES ON A PATH). While proclaiming resolve, the governess mitigates this by saying "we were perpetually **coming into sight of subjects** before which we must stop short" (39). (The reasons for Miles's expulsion from school and her silent accusations of a collusion with the ghosts remain off-limits.) However, the heroine's marked inner restraint continuously dwindles. One is brought to ask "when will the woman crack from the tension?", something that can be ignited any minute, but is deferred repeatedly until the climactic finale. Faced with the woman's tortuous inability to resolve her conflict, a mood of tension and mounting suspense grips us as readers. The plot dynamic we come to feel through the main character's goals is like a rubber band stretched until it snaps.

3.4   Actants and Protagonist Interaction

We can now extend the previous analysis, relating to the fact that the action tendencies in the heroine's character are embedded in a wider actant configuration (Greimas 1966, following Propp 1968). In the structuralist tradition, the notion of actant roles describes story functions performed by characters vis-à-vis other characters and include *subject*, *object*, *sender*, *receiver*, *helper* and *opponent*. Although they may be stable throughout a novel, actants are relationally defined by the ongoing action. The roles are filled out by a protagonist at a given moment; any protagonist can change from helper to opponent or be entangled in different actor relations vis-à-vis various other protagonists. Actants were postulated to describe basic possible story configurations and, by extension, story dynamics.

I propose that Talmy's (2000) analysis of force dynamics contributes to a deeper cognitive understanding of actancy, while also supplying a linguistic method anchored in the text. Actancy becomes tangible both by looking at forces in physical storyworld interactions and by studying force metaphors. Basically, Talmy posits that when we build representations of causality we conceive an Agonist interacting with an Antagonist. Any such interaction involves (a) the Agonist's and the Antagonist's inherent tendencies towards rest or motion, (b) a force distribution between them that is balanced or not and (c) a resulting action. Examining these three aspects in detail extends our understanding of how actancy works conceptually, especially when we allow for more than one character aim, examine whether the protagonists adapt their force tendencies over time and look at how forces can be tilted or shifted by third parties.

Here is a slightly simplified view of the characters' inherent action tendencies. The governess's inherent tendency is one of strong active force that surfaces as pushing ahead, controlling or restraining. The inherent force tendency of the children is to follow their activities undisturbed and later on to stay away from the governess, an avoidance of force interaction. The inherent force tendency of the ghosts, in the heroine's perception, is to keep or augment their power over the children. Mrs. Grose's force tendency is to help the governess, a converging force, although with some hesitation towards the end.

Various actant configurations result from this. A first model is about *main character goals*. The governess's inherent tendency is her strong drive towards discovery, an attempt of FORCE BLOCKAGE REMOVAL. In one sense her thrusts ahead just vaporize, as her goal of getting a confession is undercut by the children's naïve charm. The children inhabit a strange position of "dispersers" of her force. It remains utterly unclear if they are mischievously thwarting her or really playfully innocent. In another sense, her own self-restraint obstructs her progress. The governess as Agonist is subject to an Antagonist counterforce not from her ghost opponents, but from her own Puritan ideals. This involves a kind of actant relation that current theory does not envisage. The idea that only ordinary agents can be actants evidently proves too limited and must be augmented to include intra-personal force dynamics. If we allow for this, the governess's inner vying tendencies (curiosity/duty vs. fear/taboo) constitute quasi-actants.

Another actancy model concerns the *control of one protagonist over another*. This surfaces in the governess's manipulative attempts to make others do something (FORCE COMPULSION). The governess's perceived struggle with the ghosts shows the same active force tendency (VYING FORCES) and soon spills over to her interaction with the children in conversations that increasingly resemble violent acts (either PENETRATING FORCES or FORCED OBJECT EXTRACTION). In some sense, this model of actancy can, again, be augmented to include *control over the self* if we add conceptual metaphors that describe self-manipulative acts of object extraction and containing one's emotions.

A third actancy model is inherently triadic and concerns the *governess's aim to shield her wards from the ghost's seizing grasp* in an (unsuccessful) act of FORCE BLOCKAGE. In the triad governess/ghosts/children, the perceived apparitions are Antagonists thwarting her control over the children. It is striking how this control aim parallels her urge to keep her Antagonist emotions in check. Even more strikingly, her abovementioned mood swings (enclosing vs. outbreak mode) create the same dynamic of a cyclic boundary transgression. In the present actancy model we find something almost analolgous: a 'shielding' mode when she succeeds in protecting the children and a 'permeation' mode when she fails. The rigid boundaries of her protective self repeatedly turn permeable whenever the ghosts demonstrate their influence and seductive force. Enclosing her emotions is different from shielding the children in that dangerous emotional forces issue from within, not from an external threat. Yet, the deeper parallelism is evident. In both cases the governess's strong self is upheld as a boundary in opposition to what she fears. Her personality dictates an overarching need to contain forces, be it her own or external ones, and to be in control of both. The following figure captures this common image-schematic aspect between the emotions/self dyad and the protagonist triad.

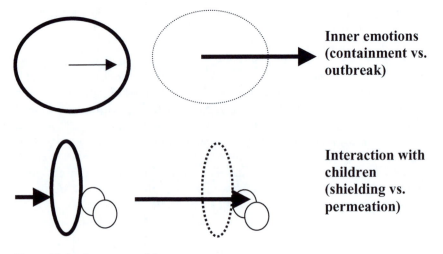

Inner emotions (containment vs. outbreak)

Interaction with children (shielding vs. permeation)

Figure 10.1   Actancy models.

3.5   Literary Ambiguity Effects

Complex literary tropes can also benefit from cognitive linguistic analysis (Popova 2002). The Jamesian master trope of *ambiguity* accounts for much of the tale's fascination. Conceptual metaphors substantially contribute to ambiguity. While the intricate ploys that James uses to deny the reader ontological clarity ("Is the governess hallucinating or not?") are only indirectly grounded in metaphor, mood-related ambiguity is pronouncedly reflected by various incompatible metaphor sets.

First, ambiguity results from person- or place-related metaphors that alternatively take on both poles of the same axiological source domain (i.e. opposite attributes attached to the same target domain). One implied ambiguity lies in the governess's oscillation between positive and negative states, a going to and fro between GOOD IS UP and BAD IS DOWN. Another ambiguity stems from the colour symbolism that contrasts GOOD IS BRIGHT with BAD IS DARK.[16] The initial positive projections of the governess characterize the children as having "the **great glow of freshness,** the same positive fragrance of purity" (James 1999: 13) and describe Bly as being "inhabited by a rosy sprite" (9). Later, her view of the children oscillates between idealization and dark speculations, paralleled by Bly's change between brightness and darkness, sometimes with sinister states of dusk, twilight or grayness and decay. Many of these descriptions constitute *extended metaphors* (Werth 1999), rather than linguistic metaphors. If we wish, we can therefore understand them literally, without any semantic tension arising. Yet, an additional non-literal layer suggests itself with respect to the recurrent innuendo and previous metaphors that have prepared the ground.

Another ambiguity device results from rather incompatible entailments of different conceptual metaphors. Through such clashing inferences the state of denial in which the governess finds herself, is revealed as well as her manipulative character. Frequent terms of endearment for the bright and sweet creatures and for Mrs. Grose clash with their increasingly antagonistic communication (wresting knowledge from each other, using words as weapons) and her general strategizing attitude. The way that the polar opposites of bright and dark attach to different, albeit metonymically connected, targets tells of a similar ambivalence. While the governess holds the children to be bright creatures, they leave her in a state of dim knowledge and dark premonitions.[17]

Third, how the governess perceives her predecessor Ms. Jessel has a deep metaphoric ambiguity to it. The inferential clash owes to the source domain DOWN, which connects the target domains of Jessel's morality and happiness. Ms. Jessel's 'fall', her presumed disgrace by getting pregnant from Quint makes her morally low in the prurient governess's judgment, but also a dejected woman who has left in shame and died shortly thereafter. Here, one is struck by a scene where the governess seems to empathize with Jessel's tragedy.[18] Both the double value of DOWN and this scene leads to an inherently ambiguous evaluation of Jessel. A similar uneasy placement on the up-down scale applies to Quint. It appears as an extended metaphor where he makes his appearance high above the Gothic setting. This involves a strange inversion of the lowliness with which he is otherwise depicted.

> They're seen only across, as it were, and beyond—in strange places and on **high places, the top of towers, the roof of houses,** the outside of windows, the further edge of pools; but there's a deep design, on either side, to shorten the distance and overcome the obstacle; and the success of the tempters is only a question of time. (James 1999: 47–48)

A fourth type of ambiguity comes about because James switches the agent-patient roles in otherwise similar metaphors. Here, the issue of control involves two inverse seizing scenarios (PROTECTING THE CHILDREN IS SEIZING and ENTHRALLMENT BY THE CHILDREN IS BEING SEIZED/IS A SPELL). In one scenario, the governess is trying to protect the children from the grasp of the ghosts, notably by holding them herself ("**catching him in his fall**"—85), up to the final scene where she presses Miles to her body in a smothering embrace. In the inverse scenario, the governess herself is in the grip of the children's spell. Thus, the question "Who has whom?" is answered by ironical inversion.[19] Another connection suggests itself to the reader concerning the story's key image of the tightening screw. The pattern already appears in the framing tale with regard to the 'gripping' effect on the listeners, which converges with the obsessive emotions seizing the governess. The common metaphoric denominator between what the tale does to the reader and what emotions do to the heroine is that both have a tense, strained and obsessive quality, something that can arguably be felt in a bodily way (see next section).

Finally, ambiguity arises from metaphorically expressed character goals, depending on the degree to which the actions in a given metaphoric frame or scenario are spun out. The governess wants something badly, moves ahead and then recoils again. Her character dynamic is reflected in two alternative states that occur within a path scenario (DISCOVERY IS REACHING A PATH ENDPOINT, TABOOS ARE BLOCKAGES). So whenever one or the other metaphor foregrounds the governess's inner split this produces a sensed ambivalence of character against the background of the other.

3.6   Embodied and Perceptual Simulation

As one might expect from the title, *The Turn of the Screw* triggers an intense, embodied reader involvement. To examine how this happens, some prior theoretical considerations are needed. Cognitive linguistic authors tend to see metaphor as embodied phenomenon per se whenever image-schematic source domains are involved. Lakoff and Johnson (1999) convey the impression that because the archetypical container schema originates in the proprioceptive body boundary all container metaphors are equally 'embodied'. Against orthodoxy, I believe that treating metaphors so indiscriminately will not do. This results in the most unhelpful idea that when one strikes upon a random metaphor in literature, 'embodiment' will accompany it. This definition would make the present novella highly embodied merely due to its extraordinary metaphor frequency and overlooks that other similarly metaphoric texts may invite much less bodily immersion. A purely quantitative analysis thus leads us off track when we are interested in *imagistically rich and phenomenally accessible* levels of embodiment that are *felt* by the reader as a specific kind of immersive state. We carefully need to select the focal metaphorical embodiment cues, rather than equating the whole category with embodiment.

Most notably, the phenomenological quality of embodiment depends on the ontological locus of the target into which the source domain's imagery is projected (Kimmel 2008). This locus can be body-internal, body-external or wholly abstract. Metaphors like "I'm about to **explode**" have a proprioceptive locus, because emotions are inherently conceived as something body internal. This contrasts sharply with metaphors like "the ship's **belly**" which are imagined in an external locus. The metaphor "**body politic**" is situated in a wholly abstract target locus.[20] As a consequence, in literature, metaphoric image schemas can variously be situated

(a) in the body schema and affects of a character with whom we empathize (e.g. the governess's inner pangs),
(b) in external storyworld activity that the reader simulates as visual or auditive imagery with somewhat less emotional saturation, or

(c) in abstract metaphors that might not invite much visceral response at all (and appear disembodied with respect to the imagined physical storyworld).

To which category the metaphor belongs can influence the degree to which the reader may vicariously experience and thereby "simulate" a protagonist's experience (Pecher & Zwaan 2005). In some cases this happens at a merely cognitive level, i.e. 'knowing what she knows'. In other cases the simulation will additionally arouse muscular tension-release patterns or preparation for action, bioenergetic flow, blood pressure, respiratory rhythm and hormonal response. Activated proprioception tends to create a stronger inner sense of "being there" for the reader.

Which metaphors are then particularly prone to embodied simulations in our case? First, emotion metaphors produce intense embodied involvement. They constitute the source *par excellence* from which the reader develops an empathic feel for the heroine's inner experience. The reason why emotion metaphors inherently create a strong simulation effect is their metonymical motivation in the bodily affects that typically accompany the emotion. In cases like "get cold feet" or "seething with rage" this is fairly obvious. Does the same apply to emotion metaphors of a force-dynamic nature like our AFFECTS ARE IMPULSES, CONTROLLING EMOTIONS IS VYING WITH A COUNTERFORCE, or BEING SUBJECT TO AN EMOTION IS BEING CAUGHT? My answer is yes, since all images in which emotion and reason vie for dominance are rooted in an inner muscular feeling of tensing and releasing. We do not only speak of letting go, venting emotions or bottling them up. Emotional force metaphors have the genuine power of evoking this felt inner quality.

One particular sub-category of emotion metaphors arguably creates the richest embodied simulations. So-called 'contour words'—emotional flashes, throbs, see-saws, quavers, etc.—evoke a dynamic proprioceptive image with enormous qualitative detail about the felt event (e.g. QUALITY OF SUBTLE EMOTIONS IS SUBTLE FORCE, SUDDEN EMOTIONS/REALIZATIONS ARE FLASHES, GRADUAL EMOTIONS ARE GRADUALLY FLOWING LIQUIDS). Contour words create rich scenario-like imagery that is prone to evoke vicarious embodied experiencing in the reader.[21] *The Turn of the Screw* continuously deploys contour imagery specifying the manner of the governess's emotions, thereby making embodied simulation in the reader likely. By this means James fosters empathy with the heroine. He also heightens the literary effect of ambivalence, because vicariously 'slipping into the governess's shoes' makes it quite difficult to dismiss her state of mind as psychotic. Seeing the event her way lets the question of what is 'real' become equally pressing and tantalizing.

A third kind of strong embodiment effect stems from tactile and visual metaphors for knowledge (KNOWING IS GRASPING, ALARM IS TOUCH, KNOWING IS SEEING, KNOWLEDGE IS LIGHT, POSITIVE COGNITIVE STATES ARE BRIGHT). They are not only theme-creating in the sense that sensory evidence is a strongly foregrounded issue in a story about ghost sightings. They also evoke distinctly sensorial images of a rich and forceful kind. Tactile imagery evokes a proximal embodied simulation (e.g. "roused like if **an arm had shaken me**"—James 1999: 42; "still sometimes **brushed my brow like the wing of a bat**"—34). Visual imagery is more distal than tactile or proprioceptive imagery, but is equally attention-grabbing through its detail. The effect comes about through rich event contours ("**giving the last jerk to the curtain**"—34), through highly intense percepts ("if I once more **closed my eyes it was before the dazzle**"—41) or through the opposite ("deep **obscurity**"—18; "two or three **dim elements of comfort**"—34). Thus, the bright-dark metaphors tune the reader to a persistent sensory mood. This effect is probably reinforced through the reader's simulation of bright and dark originating in the governess's perception of the Gothic estate. This kind of extended metaphor amplifies surrounding linguistic metaphors.

We have seen that the empathy-engendering character narration and its enhancement through metaphor produce a strong affective reader involvement. The reader's tantalizing urgency to find out what is 'real' is conditional on the fact that the governess's perspective is so highly simulable and her account, at some level, plausible. Slipping into her Puritan saviour role and her imperative of pressing a confession from the children, while never daring to address matters directly, lets the reader re-experience the governess's torments and relate to a kind of 'emotive logic' in her. I would conjecture that if an authorial narrator had told the same events from a remote perspective, most readers would simply put down the governess as an unstable personality. James's many cues for simulating her emotions and motives give her some subjective credibility, thus heightening the reader's ambivalence. An ultimate reading of what is 'real', however, is just what James denies the reader with some consequence. A trace of suspense is left even after one has finished reading.

4   MODES OF LITERARY METAPHORIZATION

Taking stock, it would seem that metaphors are James's stylistic device *par excellence*, with more than a thousand occurrences and several dozen systematic conceptual patterns among them. With the story themes of emotional dilemma, psychodynamics and evidentiality, all of which elude literal English lexis, this wealth is to be expected to some degree. Yet beyond this, deliberate stylistic effects are aimed at, notably an imagistic quality, embodied immersion, symbolic evocativity and polyvalence. For summary purposes it is therefore worthwhile to discern what I call 'modes of literary metaphorization'. These allow us to understand the literary functions created by metaphors in *The Turn of the Screw* in a broader comparative perspective. (We might even conjecture that the genre itself is partly defined through the metaphorization strategies employed.)

A first general observation is that James, while creating novel linguistic realizations like "She offered her mind to my disclosures **as, had I wished to mix a witch's broth and proposed it with assurance, she would have held out a large clean saucepan**" (James 1999: 44), hardly uses unfamiliar conceptual metaphors. This *conventionality mode of metaphorization* is characteristic of much literature (Lakoff & Turner 1989),[22] but this clearly does not mean that literary specificity is lacking. Besides emerging from creative linguistic realizations, specificity also arises from the novel ways in which conceptual elements are interrelated. We have seen how the appeal to the deep cultural frame of the Manichaean battle between absolute good and evil is undercut through moments of pity for Jessel and attraction to Quint. We have seen how rather conventional metaphors of human interaction and psychodynamics manage to create ambiguity. Although I have had little space to treat this, literary specificity also accrues from the richly evocative fields of imagery found in metaphor clusters which interweave sensory and metaphors into something more complex.

Second, in view of both the high diversity of conceptual patterns and the imperfect coherence between them, one may plausibly speak of a moderately high *multiplicity mode of metaphorization*. Instead of presenting a completely rounded off or consistent metaphor field, James invites his readers to interweave metaphors that characterize the protagonists, their actions or the setting in unfamiliar ways. This can happen through either complementary or antithetical patterns. A similar creativity is invited by the rich possibilities for reading extended metaphors and cultural symbols into the literal events. Both literary strategies create polyvalence and an openness of meaning.

Third, the frequency of metaphors used to depict feelings and inner states points to an *introspection mode of metaphorization*. This allows the reader to create a complex image of the narrator's psyche and vicariously allows us to share in the emotions. This mode also leaves us free to ponder depth-psychological readings or identify with the governess, but in any case it blocks a facile rejection of her tale as hysterical. The compelling 'inside view' creates reader immersion and with it a great deal of suspenseful uncertainty. Heightening this effect, an *imagistic simulation mode of metaphorization* lets the reader empathize with the governess's somatic states and rhythms. James thus lends an added visceral dimension to the merely introspective. Finally, the reader is encouraged to imagine settings and interactions in richly perceptual ways, thus intensifying this sense of 'being there' while also focalising the possible symbolic value of darkness, depth and thresholds.

5 CONCLUSION

My study has brought to the fore several genuinely narrative functions that may be cued through patterned metaphor deployment. It has been shown that metaphor directly impacts on literary characterization, interaction, plot-driving character goals, as well as on complex tropes and immersive reading. The more common first level of analysis was to examine how recurrent conceptual metaphors create themes or motifs. The next level attempted something less common, namely to scan for similarities and antithetical relations between different conceptual metaphor patterns. The last section elevated this more complex analysis to a new, topmost level by considering work-defining trends in metaphor use that might in part be characteristic of Henry James's art or the entire genre. I believe that this more integrative viewpoint, always based on sound empirical groundwork, provides comparative literary studies with an important new tool to be honed in the future.

NOTES

1. I would like to thank Wolfram Aichinger, Inge Kimmel and Monika Fludernik for their feedback on previous versions of the chapter.
2. *The Turn of the Screw* is situated in the nineteenth-century 'Gothic' estate Bly where a young governess is hired by the uncle of a boy of ten, Miles, and his eight year old sister, Flora. Although a framing tale exists—an old gentleman reads the story out loud from the governess's diary decades later—, the story itself is told from the perspective of the governess with a focus on her intense feelings and perceptions. At first, the governess is fascinated by her precocious, sweet and enthralling wards. Soon, ghost apparitions of the 'fallen' Ms. Jessel and her seductor, the house teacher Quint, begin challenging the governess, although no one else admits to seeing them. She becomes convinced of a secret collusion between the children and their former guardians. Struggling to save the children from the perceived immoral influence and aided by the housekeeper Mrs. Grose, she carefully keeps her countenance, while scanning desperately, even obsessively, for corroborative signs. In her mounting turmoil she confronts Flora with an explicit question. When the girl reacts hysterically, she is taken to town for recovery. In the story's culminating scene, the governess pressures Miles to confess to Quint's presence, upon which Miles breaks down and dies (whether of possession by the ghosts, of fear or by smothering in the governess's embrace remains unanswered).
3. Many studies discuss whether the ghosts are real or a figment of a compulsive and hysterical narrator. Recent *opinio communis* tends to identify a 'stylistics of ambiguity' rather than focusing on the issue of ontology.
4. The intent is similar to previous studies of mine on image schemas, which include many kinds of metaphor (Kimmel 2005; forthcoming).
5. A deficit that cognitive stylistics shares with more traditional approaches is a largely unquestioned bias whereby researchers select the metaphors for analysis they happen to find most striking. The discourse linguist's systematicity counteracts this tendency.
6. A single exception instantiates COURAGE IS DIVING ("but I must take my horrid plunge"—James 1999: 38).
7. The same pattern occurs in literal descriptions of Miles's appearance, e.g. in "I can still see his wonderful smile, the whites of his beautiful eyes, and the uncovering of his little teeth shine to me in the dusk" (45).
8. Colour symbolism plays an equally important role in characterizing the ghosts and Miles, ranging from "the white face of damnation" (84) to "Dark

as midnight in her black dress" (57). However, the effects are too complex and ambiguous to report as a single pattern here.

9. In a depth-psychological reading, the governess dissociates evil from the children to idealize them, which, split off from a clear object, returns atmospherically in more subtle form.

10. Technically, this exemplifies *diversification* after Goatly (1997), because the sources are not really identical, but at least the targets are.

11. This shapes a wider *iconographic reference frame* (Hawkins 2001).

12. The logical coherence between BLY IS A FAIRYTALE WORLD and PROTECTING THE CHILDREN IS SHIELDING THEM illustrates that motif enrichment also works via shared general inferences, rather than shared image schemas only.

13. At the same time that the governess attempts to contain herself, she produces the opposite effect of being in 'full exposure' and 'in a trap' (paraphrased from the text).

14. The kindred but not force-based shift between DESPONDENCY IS DOWN and FORTITUDE IS UP creates a matching alternation pattern.

15. This illustrates Oatley's (1992) claim that emotions issue from character goals.

16. This becomes possible by virtue of the master trope ESSENCE IS EXTERNAL APPEARANCE. The metaphors map evaluative and emotional images associated with bright and dark.

17. We may note that conceptual metaphors may simply be incompatible with *non-metaphoric* aspects of the tale in their suggested inferences. For example the "brightness" and "angelic" nature of the children becomes increasingly ambivalent as the governess becomes suspicious of their (non-metaphoric) conspiracy. Although darkness metaphors for the children are rare and reserved for the external evil (Quint in particular) the same effect arises as if it had been metaphorically induced.

18. James here subtly hints at a Freudian projection. The governess splits off the sexual element from herself due to her inability to fulfil her longing towards the children's uncle whom she is in love with. At one point she is even engrossed in romantic fantasies when she encounters the handsome apparition of Quint who flows directly into her fantasies.

19. Readers might additionally fill in the conventional conceptual metaphor SEARCH FOR TRUTH IS GRASPING.

20. Even lesser embodied activations occur for non-image-schematic metaphors. The mapped attributes of "the poor chicks" (James 1999: 4) or "the fellow was a hound" (32) (A PERSON IS AN ANIMAL) at best create a visual, but no proprioceptive image. The mapping might not even rely much on image-schematic scaffolds.

21. Felt temporal patterns like rising, subsiding or ostinato have been described as *vitality affects* by Stern (1985). Similar imaginative patterns have been shown to underlie lexical and grammatical verb aspect in its imperfective and ongoing forms (Parrill 2000).

22. Exceptions testify to the rule. For instance, a recent case study I did on Anaïs Nin's *Spy in the House of Love* (1954) dominantly creates novel conceptual patterns.

WORKS CITED

Danaher, David (2007) "Cognitive Poetics and Literariness: Metaphorical Analogy in *Anna Karenina*". *Perspectives on Slavistics*. Eds. Kris van Heuckelom and David Danaher. Amsterdam: Pegasus. 183–207.

Downes, William (1993) "Reading the Language Itself: Some Methodological Problems in D. C. Freeman's '"According to My Bond": King Lear and Recognition'". *Language and Literature* 2.2: 121–28.

Goatly, Andrew (1997) *The Language of Metaphors*. London: Routledge.

———. (2007) *Washing the Brain: Metaphor and Hidden Ideology*. Amsterdam and Philadelphia: John Benjamins.

Grady, Joseph (2005) "Image Schemas and Perception: Refining a Definition". *From Perception to Meaning: Image Schemas in Cognitive Linguistics*. Eds. Beate Hampe and Joseph Grady. Berlin: de Gruyter. 35–56.

Greimas, Algirdas. J. (1966) *Semantique Structurale*. Paris: Larousse.

Harrell, Bill J. (1982) "The Social Basis of Root Metaphor: An Application to *Apocalypse Now* and the *Heart of Darkness*". *The Journal of Mind and Behavior* 3.3: 221–40.

Hawkins, Bruce (2001) "Ideology, Metaphor and Iconographic Reference". *Language and Ideology*. Eds René Dirven, Roslyn Frank and Cornelia Ilie. Philadelphia and Amsterdam: John Benjamins. 27–50.

James, Henry (1999) *The Turn of the Screw* [1898]. Eds. Deborah Esch and Jonathan Warren. New York and London: Norton.

Kimmel, Michael (2005) "From Metaphor to the 'Mental Sketchpad': Literary Macrostructure and Compound Image Schemas in *Heart of Darkness*". *Metaphor & Symbol* 20.3: 199–238.

———. (2008) "Properties of Cultural Embodiment: Lessons from the Anthropology of the Body". *Body, Language and Mind, Vol II: Interrelations between Biology, Linguistics and Culture*. Eds. René Dirven et al. Berlin and New York: de Gruyter. 77–108.

———. (forthcoming) "Analyzing Image Schemas in Literature". *Cognitive Semiotics*.

Kövecses, Zoltán (2000) *Metaphor and Emotion: Language, Culture, and Body in Human Feeling*. Cambridge and New York: Cambridge University Press.

Krzeszowski, Tomasz P. (1993) "The Axiological Parameter in Preconceptual Image Schemata". *Conceptualizations and Mental Processing in Language*. Eds. Barbara Rudzka-Osztyn and Richard Geiger. Berlin and New York: de Gruyter. 307–29.

Lakoff, George, and Mark Johnson (1999) *Philosophy in the Flesh: The Embodied Mind and Its Challenge to Western Thought*. New York: Basic Books.

Lakoff, George, and Mark Turner (1989) *More than Cool Reason: A Field Guide to Poetic Metaphor*. Chicago and London: University of Chicago Press.

Lustig, T. J. (1994) *Henry James and the Ghostly*. Cambridge: Cambridge University Press.

Lyndenberg, John (1957) "The Governess Turns the Screws". *Nineteenth-Century Fiction* 12.1: 37–58.

Miall, David (1984) "Designed Horror: James's Vision of Evil in *The Turn of the Screw*". *Nineteenth-Century Fiction* 39: 305–32.

Oatley, Keith (1992) *Best Laid Schemes: The Psychology of Emotions*. New York: Cambridge University Press.

Parrill, Fey (2000) *Hand to Mouth: Linking Spontaneous Gesture and Aspect*. BA Thesis. University of Chicago.

Pecher, Diane, and Rolf A. Zwaan (2005) *Grounding Cognition: The Role of Perception and Action in Memory, Language, and Thinking*. New York: Cambridge University Press.

Popova, Yanna (2002) "The Figure in the Carpet: Discovery of Re-Cognition?" *Cognitive Stylistics*. Eds. Elena Semino and Jonathan Culpeper. Amsterdam and Philadelphia: John Benjamins. 49–71.

Propp, Vladimir (1968) *Morphology of the Folktale*. London: University of Texas Press.

Semino, Elena, and Kate Swindlehurst (1996) "Metaphor and Mind Style in Ken Kesey's *One Flew Over the Cuckoo's Nest*". *Style* 30.1: 143–66.

Stern, Daniel N. (1985) *The Interpersonal World of the Infant: A View from Psychoanalysis and Developmental Psychology*. New York: Basic Books.

Talmy, Leonard (2000) *Toward a Cognitive Semantics: Language, Speech, and Communication*. Cambridge, MA, and London: MIT Press.

Werth, Paul (1999) *Text Worlds: Representing Conceptual Space in Discourse, Textual Explorations*. Harlow: Longman.

11 Hyperliteralist Metaphor

The Cognitive Poetics of Robert Musil in His Novella "Die Portugiesin"

Ralph Müller

Robert Musil (1880–1942) is a fascinating writer for anyone interested in the grounding of cognition in bodily, respectively embodied, experience. This is not to say that Musil was exactly some kind of cognitive poetician *avant la lettre*; rather, that he was very much interested in issues that are currently of great interest in the field of cognitive poetics: issues such as the relation between experience ("Erleben") and rational cognition ("Erkennen", cf. Musil 1978d: 1218). The aim of this chapter is to show how Musil's aesthetical reflections can be understood in the context of cognitive poetics and how he uses metaphors to convey experience via literature. In addition, this chapter will deploy corpus analyses to investigate the particular use of metaphors found in Musil's historical novella "Die Portugiesin" ("The Lady from Portugal", Musil 1999).

1 EXPERIENCE AND COGNITION

Musil, who held a PhD in philosophy, was well acquainted with proto-cognitivist theories, and he used these theories to explore the differences between propositional thinking and non-propositional experience. He based his aesthetical reflections on contemporary psychological insights such as early cognitivist gestalt theory. Gestalt theory explicates phenomena of perception (for instance, the recognition of the pattern of a melody) in terms of so-called "gestalts" (whole forms) in which a sequence or co-occurrence of sensory elements combine to form an emerging whole that cannot be expressed by the elements themselves (Ehrenfels 1960; Musil 1978d: 1218). It is precisely this conception of gestalt that underpins George Lakoff's development of the theory of conceptual metaphor (Lakoff 1977). Lakoff describes conceptual entities as gestalts for which the whole is simpler than its parts and in which the parts do not make sense without the whole (Lakoff 1987: 489f.; Lakoff & Johnson 1999: 32). Robert Musil's use of gestalts, however, is primarily part of aesthetical and philosophical reflection and can best be understood in the broader framework of his interest in the interplay of rational and non-rational cognition. As both a philosopher and a literary writer, Musil extended his notion of cognition beyond that of purely rational thinking to also include non-rational thinking (Musil 1978f). He found this duality exemplified in the idea of the gestalt. Gestalts are comprised of stable, structurally analysable parts and are therefore not entirely irrational; neither, however, are they entirely rational, as they constitute an emergent whole which cannot be identical, but only similar to other gestalts (Musil 1978d: 1218).

Musil's view of the connection between rational and non-rational thinking, on the one hand, and figurative language on the other becomes clearer in his essay "Geist und Erfahrung" ("Mind and Experience" [1921], Musil 1978c). In this essay, he attacks the reasoning of anti-rationalists for their use of unfounded analogies, their reliance on intuition and their disparagement of the rational. However, Musil does not simply adopt a rationalist position. Even if he praises the precision of rationalist language he also cherishes the cognitive effect of analogies which cannot be fully understood (rationally), but which need to be re-experienced:

> Genauigkeit, Richtigkeit töten; was sich definieren läßt, Begriff ist, ist tot, Versteinerung, Skelett. [...] In Geistesgebieten aber, wo der Satz gilt: Erkennen ist Wiedererinnern [...], macht man diese Erfahrung bei jedem Schritt. Das Wort soll dort nichts Fixiertes bezeichnen. Es ist das lebendige Wort, voll Bedeutung und intellektueller Beziehung im Augenblick, von Wille und Gefühl umflossen; eine Stunde später ist es nichtssagend, obwohl es alles sagt, was ein Begriff sagen kann. Ein solches Denken mag man wohl lebend nennen. (Musil 1978c: 1051)

> Precision, correctness kill; that which can be defined, [or what] is conceptualized, is dead, fossil, skeleton. [...] In the realms of the intellectual, however, where the sentence is valid: to cognize is to re-remember, [...] one has this experience with every step. There, the word should not signify anything fixed. It is the living word, full of meaning and intellectually grounded in the moment, bathed in will and feeling; an hour later it may be meaningless, although it says everything that a concept may say. Such a thought can indeed be called alive. (my translation)[1]

This intricate relationship between rational analytical truth and the non-rational is also at the centre of philosophical and poetical reflections in Musil's novel *Der Mann ohne Eigenschaften* (1930–32; *The Man without Qualities*, Musil 1978a). Whilst pondering the nature of analogy or parable ("Gleichnis"), the protagonist Ulrich recognizes that they contain both a truth and an untruth. If the analogy is perceived through the senses, it becomes dream and art; if it is rationally analysed in terms of correspondences and differences, it produces truth, but it destroys feeling (Musil

1978a: 581–82). Consequently, it can be said that Musil adopts a position somewhere between rationalism and anti-rationalism, or irrationalism. His approach combines the unrestrained creative potential of the non-rational with the scientific precision of the rational. Literature, therefore, plays an important role as a means of conveying knowledge that extends beyond propositional rational thinking.

In his memorial speech for the poet Rainer Maria Rilke, Musil emphasized that metaphors and similes may reinvigorate somewhat worn-out domains of experience ("etwas erschöpfter Gefühls- und Vorstellungsbereich", cf. Musil 1978e: 1237). The following analysis based on Musil's novella "Die Portugiesin" ("The Lady from Portugal") will show how Musil arranged metaphors and similes to reinvigorate the relevant domains of experience.

2   METAPHOR IN MUSIL'S NOVELLA "DIE PORTUGIESIN"

Musil's historical novella "Die Portugiesin" ("The Lady from Portugal", Musil 1999), first published in 1923, and republished in the collection *Drei Frauen* (*three women*), is set in the Middle Ages and narrates the adventures of the robber Baron von Ketten. In the story, von Ketten is not only engaged in a long-lasting feud with the Bishop of Trent, but he also has to overcome a serious illness and faces a marital crisis with his mysterious Portuguese wife.

One of the crucial turning points of the novella arrives when von Ketten falls ill after winning the war. The passage describing von Ketten's experience of the fever contains many figurative expressions. In order to identify these metaphorical expressions and similes we first need to clarify what is *actually* going on in the novella. The cause of the fever (the sting of a fly) is—despite possible symbolic interpretations (cf. Bernauer 1992)—beyond doubt an actual event in the text world of the story. However, the boundary between actual and imagined events becomes less clear as von Ketten's fever worsens, and seems to affect his sense of self:

> Er hatte nie gewußt, daß Sterben so friedlich sei; er war mit einem Teil seines Wesens vorangestorben und hatte sich aufgelöst wie ein Zug Wanderer: Während die Knochen noch im Bett lagen, und das Bett da war, seine Frau sich über ihn beugte [. . .], war alles, was er liebte, schon weit voran. Der Herr von Ketten und dessen mondnächtige Zauberin waren aus ihm herausgetreten und hatten sich sacht entfernt: er sah sie noch, er wußte, mit einigen großen Sprüngen würde er sie danach einholen, nur jetzt wußte er nicht, war er schon bei ihnen oder noch hier. (Musil 1978b: 262)

> He had never known that dying was so peaceful. Part of his being had gone ahead into death, separating and scattering like a cavalcade of travelers. While the bones were still lying in bed, and the bed was

there, his wife bending over him, [. . .] everything he loved had already gone a long way ahead. Herr von Ketten and his moon-lady, his nocturnal enchantress, had issued forth from him [in original: the bed] and softly withdrawn to a distance: he could still see them, he knew that by taking a few great leaps he could still catch up with them, only he no longer knew whether he was already there with them or still here. (Musil 1999: 56)

The unconventional use of spatial deictics ("voransterben"/ 'dying ahead'; "weit voran"/ 'long way ahead') and of the personal deictics ('here'; 'he'; 'them') has been observed in earlier studies (e.g. Bernauer 1992). The deictics develop two different spatial-temporal worlds. On the one hand, there is an actual text world in which von Ketten really is lying in his bed, absent-mindedly watching his wife bend over him; on the other hand, there is an imagined world in which von Ketten experiences his possible departure into death as a dispersion of himself into multiple individuals. This imagined text world is set up by a series of metaphors and similes ("going ahead into death" or "scattering and separating like a cavalcade of travellers"). Together these metaphorical statements provide a portrayal of von Ketten's personality ("Wesen") as being 'dissolved' ("aufgelöst"), i.e. fragmented, into several individuals (in particular, into the figures of von Ketten and his wife), and these seem to have parted company with their corporeal selves. In summary, this passage conceptualizes the human self as a conglomerate of personalities that disperse at the point of death.

The number of mundane metaphors we use to talk and think about life and death (He's gone; He's left us; He's passed on) has for a long time been a subject of critical interest for theorists of conceptual metaphor (Lakoff & Turner 1989: 1). As the theory of conceptual metaphors has demonstrated convincingly, such expressions are not mere stylistic choices, but are connected to the patterns of thought of which they are manifestations. We can therefore see that the description of von Ketten's fever makes use of the rather conventional conceptual metaphor DEATH IS DEPARTURE, which maps the experiential source domain of a 'journey' onto the process of dying.

3   USING CORPORA IN THE LITERARY STUDY OF METAPHORS

The theory of conceptual metaphor has served to raise an awareness of the fact that literary texts often use established conceptual metaphors. At the same time, linguistic studies of conceptual metaphors tend to identify expressions as metaphorical which, in literary studies, are typically regarded as dead metaphors. For instance, container metaphors are often highly conventionalised, and one might question the extent to which the expression "issuing forth from somebody" can in fact be regarded as metaphorical. In recent years, studies examining the relationship between linguistic expression and metaphorical conceptualization have been increasingly influenced by corpus analyses (cf. Deignan 2005; Stefanowitsch & Gries 2006).

A corpus is a large database of digital texts which can be analysed by computer programmes. Corpus studies for German can draw on various corpora on the Internet: *Cosmas 2* from the institut for the German language at Mannheim is probably the largest corpus; however, the corpus of the *Digitale Wörterbuch der deutschen Sprache des 20. Jahrhunderts* (*DWDS*) provides a more balanced selection of twentieth-century texts and genres and therefore is more useful for literary analysis. Such corpora are quite handy as they allow us to ascertain in what contexts metaphorical expressions appear in conventional language use. In particular, looking at the use of an expression in a large balanced corpus provides a more finely grained picture of the possible contexts in which a word has been used. For instance, it is possible to search for metaphorical and non-metaphorical uses of the verb *heraustreten* ('to issue forth'). In the following analyses, non-metaphorical meanings were considered to be more "basic" by virtue of their being more concrete, their being related to bodily action, or that they are more precise (cf. Pragglejaz 2007: 3). The corpus query showed that most instances of 'heraustreten' were metaphorical in the sense of either 'ending a condition' or of 'becoming salient'. This observation is confirmed by an analysis of the form "aus . . . heraus", which is also frequently used metaphorically.[2] Among the first fifty entries of the *DWDS* there were, in fact, very few instances in which something was literally 'torn out' or 'issued forth' and which were clearly non-metaphorical.

Nonetheless, to draw the conclusion that such expressions should not be considered as literary metaphors would seem too simple. Conventional conceptual metaphors may become more poetical or more deviant if they are combined creatively with other conceptual metaphors. Lakoff and Turner (1989: 70) speak about 'composite metaphors'. In the particular instance of the passage quoted above, the conceptual metaphor DEATH IS DEPARTURE is combined with the idea that the individual self is a container of multiple personalities (which refers to two fundamental conceptual metaphors: personification and container metaphor). This composition provides a fresh conceptualization of death as a dispersion of the self into various selves which depart at the point of death. Consequently, von Ketten's fever experience seems to rely upon the slightly paradoxical metaphorical assertion that von Ketten and his wife may have issued forth from von Ketten himself. The paradox of this metaphorical conceptualization consists in the suggestion that the containing container may issue forth from its own container.

This particular use of a container metaphor seems to conform to a recurring pattern in Musil's novella. In a number of different contexts, von Ketten's self seems to become permeable. For instance in battles, von Ketten would forget himself and "everything followed a single course—a wild slashing and blood-letting" (Musil 1999: 49; "da ging alles diesen Weg gewaltiger, Wunden schlagender Gebärden aus ihm heraus", Musil

1978b: 257). An English translation can only partially reflect the density of localising expressions. Nevertheless, it is important to mention the analogy thus established between von Ketten's berserk fighting and his fever; both seem to imply a certain ecstatic state to which he becomes subject. Moreover, von Ketten's self does not merely issue forth; at the same time, he experiences a return of power. At the end of the novella, von Ketten is able to rediscover his former strength by climbing the cliff below his castle. At this moment, as he is struggling against death, he feels strength and health "flowing back into his limbs as though returning into his body from some place outside him" (Musil 1999: 66; "aber, seltsam zu fühlen begannen bei diesem Kampf mit dem Tod Kraft und Gesundheit in die Glieder zu fließen, als kehrten sie von außen wieder in den Körper zurück", Musil 1978b: 269).

One can therefore recognize that von Ketten's personality is described by way of a series of container metaphors, which, however, also serve to undermine the idea of a personality as a well-defined entity with a clear differentiation between an inside and an outside. Thus, the container metaphors, though used in a conventional sense, acquire a more interesting profile as a result of their slightly paradoxical use throughout this novella.

4   HYPERLITERALIST METAPHORS IN LITERATURE

The above findings suggest that in addition to searching for underlying conceptual metaphors it is also necessary—at least in literary studies—to investigate contextual and stylistic differences between linguistic realizations of conceptual metaphors. This kind of analysis of stylistic differences implies more interest in the particular complexities of metaphorical meaning, even if such complexities are not necessarily taken into account by the theory of conceptual metaphor. Lakoff emphasizes that (most) metaphors are understood in terms of pre-existing mental mappings from source to target domains (Lakoff 1993). Thus, the process of understanding metaphorical expressions is usually seen as an activation of elements from the correspondent conceptual source domain which are then mapped onto a target domain according to certain rules; for instance, an expression such as "The sun set on his life" could be read as an actualisation of the conceptual metaphor A LIFETIME IS A DAY (e.g. Lakoff & Turner 1989: 69). Metaphorical meaning in this approach is therefore only defined in terms of broader mappings, and this has sometimes triggered criticism. McGlone (2001), for instance, considers Lakoff's theory to be "hyperliteral" because it would suggest that "our knowledge of abstract concepts is quite literally subsumed by our knowledge of concrete concepts": "A conceptual system designed this way, however, seems incapable of differentiating the literal from the metaphorical" (McGlone 2001: 105). McGlone's criticism would have some foundation if the theory of conceptual metaphor had not also introduced some principles which delimit the extent of conceptual mappings (principle of invariance) and their direction (principle of unidirectionality).

"Invariance" means that "the conceptual material that is mapped from the source preserves its basic structure in the mapping" (Kövecses 2002: 103). Invariance indicates that metaphorical meaning is developed under certain restrictions which are imposed by the target domain. The principle of invariance ascribes precisely defined roles to source and target domains in such a way that knowledge in the source domain is blocked out if it is not coherent with the target domain. For instance, if we talk about love or life in terms of a journey, we still have to acknowledge that we cannot walk backwards in time. The second principle of "unidirectionality" states that conceptual mappings are typically directed from a more concrete source domain to a more abstract target domain (cf. Kövecses 2002: 6). Thus, the principle of unidirectionality posits that we tend to use more accessible or more concrete domains of experience (e.g. journeys) to understand more complex and abstract domains (e.g. life). These principles rule out a hyper-literalist view of metaphors, as has been critically noted by McGlone (2001). Nevertheless, I would like to suggest in this chapter that hyperliteralism is not necessarily inappropriate for literary analysis (cf. Eder 2007: 187) and that Musil's metaphorical style would profit from an analysis based on a moderate form of hyperliteralism.

In order to demonstrate that Musil's metaphorical style can indeed be described in terms of a moderate hyperliteralism, it is useful to discuss the ways in which hyperliteral metaphors deviate from 'regular metaphors'. In terms of the principle of invariance we can assume that the use of expressions typically differs according to whether they are used metaphorically or non-metaphorically. In fact, less common metaphorical expressions are frequently marked by hedges or by specifications of the target domain in the form of compounds, adjectives or genitive constructions. Moreover, the principle of unidirectionality suggests that concepts which are described metaphorically themselves are not typically used as source domains. In contrast, hyperliteralism can be said to exist when metaphors are treated as if there were no conceptual difference between metaphorical and non-metaphorical meaning. For instance, using an expression both metaphorically and non-metaphorically is a potential indication of hyperliteralism. Additional indications of hyperliteralism could also include the violation of at least one of the above mentioned principles of invariance or of uni-directionality. These principles are not set in stone and may be overridden for poetic effect (e.g. Stockwell 2002: 111). A more dynamic interaction between source and target domain has also been proposed by blending theory: a basic tenet of blending theory is that the mapping process is not necessarily constrained by the principle of invariance. This has often been illustrated by the example THIS SURGEON IS A BUTCHER, which implies the existence of an emergent feature of 'incompetence' that is originally absent from the literal meanings of both 'surgeon' and 'butcher' (cf. Grady, Oakley

& Coulson 1999). Consequently, scholars working within the framework of blending theory propose an understanding of metaphorical meaning as a "blending" in which a "target input space" and a "source input space" feed into a common blend in which new features (such as incompetence) may emerge (cf. Coulson). Even if it is difficult to validate theoretical applications of blending empirically (cf. Gibbs 2000), a more dynamic picture of metaphorical meaning is useful in literary analysis (cf. Eder 2007).

One can illustrate this in reference to Robert Musil's view of the (literary) functions of metaphor. In his memorial address for Rainer Maria Rilke, as mentioned above, Musil explicitly noted that as well as comparing a particular November evening to a woollen cloth, a writer can also compare a particular woollen cloth to a November evening. And finally, he poses the question of whether it is possible to do both at the same time:

> Und nun frage ich Sie: Statt zu sagen, der Novemberabend sei wie ein Tuch *oder* das Tuch sei wie ein Novemberabend, könnte man nicht beides in einem sagen? Was ich frage, Rilke hat es immerwährend getan.
>
> Bei ihm sind die Dinge wie in einem Teppich verwoben; wenn man sie betrachtet, sind sie getrennt, aber wenn man auf den Untergrund achtet, sind sie durch ihn verbunden. Dann verändert sich ihr Aussehen, und es entstehen sonderbare Beziehungen zwischen ihnen. (Musil 1978e: 245–6.)

> But now I ask you: instead of saying the November evening is like a cloth *or* that the cloth is like a November evening, could one not say both at the same time? What my question is asking is what Rilke was perpetually doing.
>
> In his poetry, things are woven as in a tapestry. If one observes them, they are separate, but if one regards the background, it connects the things with each other. Then their appearance changes, and strange relationships arise among them. (Musil 1990: 246)

Musil here not only suggests that the principle of unidirectionality (understanding something more abstract—e.g. a November evening, which cannot be touched and has no distinctive boundaries—in terms of something more concrete, e.g. a cloth) may be overridden for poetic purposes. He also seems to speak about fusing different domains of experience in such a way that it is no longer clear what is the source domain and what is the target domain. These remarks cannot necessarily be taken as a counterargument against the existence of the principles of invariance or unidirectionality. In fact, these principles could explain why Musil's way of arranging metaphors may be perceived as interesting or deviant. Whilst Musil's remarks do not suggest that literary texts deviate necessarily from these principles, by overriding them his prose does nonetheless seem to encourage the reader to use one domain of experience (Musil's "Gefühls- und Vorstellungsbereich") to shed light on another to reach a new idiosyncratic understanding. Such use of metaphors presupposes a moderately hyperliteral view of metaphors on the part of Musil: it is moderate, as it acknowledges that metaphors are typically used in a non-deviant way, and it is hyperliteral, as it assumes that the role of target and source domains is not necessarily differentiated within a single text.

It is, therefore, the complex use of metaphors that adds additional poetic potential to very normal metaphorical similes. Such a use of metaphors explains, for instance, why Musil's figurative language in "Die Portugiesin" at first sight appears conventional (Eibl 1978: 139). And it is indeed true that the novella contains many conventional metaphors and similes. For instance, von Ketten's reaction towards a disobedient servant is described in terms of the anger of a small child:

> Der Knecht zögerte, aber er wurde zornig wie ein Kind [. . .].
> (Musil 1978b: 262)

> The man hesitated. But Herr von Ketten raged like a child [. . .].
> (Musil 1999: 57)

At an intuitive level this simile does not strike the reader as either very poetic or deviant; however, a more reliable assessment of the conventionality of this simile can be achieved through a stylistic comparison in a large corpus (cf. Müller 2010). A query in the *DWDS* corpus[3] shows that "wie" and "Kind" co-occur more frequently in literary texts than in other genres of the corpus (non-fiction, newspapers and scientific texts). This initial finding reminds us that evaluations of creativity should typically refer to texts of the same genre. A refined analysis within the collocations yielded by this query focussed on attributive adjectives. This focus allows an investigation of the different features of a source domain that may be highlighted in similes. For instance, many adjectives which co-occur frequently with "Kind/child" (e.g. "unehelich"/'illegitimate') are uncommon in figurative use. Table 11.1 gives an overview of typical adjectives in figurative similes.[4]

Table 11.1   Attributive Adjectives in Similes in the DWDS Corpus

Age	e.g. "klein"/'small'; "neugeboren" /'newborn'; "unmündig"/'minor'[5]	559
Fear, unhappiness, illness	e.g. "geängstigt"/'frightened', "verweint"/'tearstained'; "krank"/'sick'[6]	229
Bad manners	e.g. "eigensinnig", "trotzig"/'obstinate'[7]	221
Happiness	e.g. "spielend"/'playing'[8]	111
Good manners, well behaved	e.g. "gehorsam"/'obedient'[9]	110

Table 11.1 shows that child-similes are frequently used to highlight a person's potential obstinacy and anger. Where the narrator wants to highlight von Ketten's state of weakness and lack of autonomy during his illness, child-similes—as we find them in this novella—would seem to be a conventional choice. However, the conventionality or creativity of an expression should also be considered in the broader context of the novella; and in this respect, we should pay attention to the interplay between similar metaphors and literal uses of figurative expressions. When we do so we can see, first, how the source domain of childhood is also activated in its literal sense, as the Portuguese lady and von Ketten have children themselves. At the same time, the source domain of childhood is also being used to describe the cute behaviour of a little cat. This cat appears at the end of the novella in the way of some kind of 'deus ex machina' to help von Ketten as he is slowly recovering from his illness and struggles to repair his relationship with his wife. One day, von Ketten, his wife and a rival of his from Portugal in love with his wife encounter a cat. The cat stands in front of the gate of the castle, as if it wished to be admitted in the way normally reserved for people (Musil 1978b: 265–66). And this event is then described in terms of an analogy with the reception of a guest and, subsequently, the adoption of a child:

> Sie wurde eingelassen, aber es war gleich, *als ob man einen Gast empfinge*, und schon am nächsten Tag zeigte sich, daß man *vielleicht ein kleines Kind aufgenommen hatte*, aber nicht bloß eine Katze [...]. (Musil 1978b: 266)

> They let it in, and it was like receiving a guest. The very next day it was apparent that what they had opened the gate to was no mere kitten that had come to stay; it was almost as though they had adopted a small child. (Musil 1999: 61–62.)

The mapping in this simile works differently from the mapping in the characterization of von Ketten; here the playful and friendly behaviour of children is highlighted. The altered evaluative role of this simile becomes more apparent when the playful behaviour of the cat is described by what, at a superficial level, appears to be an identical simile ("wie ein Kind"):

> Die Portugiesin beugte sich zärtlich über das Geschöpfchen, das in ihrem Schoß am Rücken lag und mit den winzigen Krallen nach ihren tändelnden Fingern schlug *wie ein Kind* [...]. (Musil 1978b: 266)

> The lady from Portugal bent tenderly over the little creature lying on its back in her lap, in its childlike way beating its tiny paws at her playful fingers. (Musil 1999: 62)

Although the simile ("wie ein Kind") is a conventional one, Musil arranges and re-uses it in such a way that it initiates a complex interaction between the source and the target domains. It does so by instantiating various elements of the source domain of childlike behaviour and by applying the structure of the simile on different entities (a kitten and von Ketten). This use in different contexts thus highlights different aspects of the source domain (e.g. obstinacy, weakness and playfulness).

So far, the mixing of metaphorical and non-metaphorical language has been demonstrated only by looking at one particular source domain. Further analysis shows, however, that this particular use of metaphor and simile is not an exception in this novella. It constitutes a systematic stylistic choice also employed with other metaphors that, in its aim to create an interplay of various domains of experience, is apt to undermine the principles of invariance and unidirectionality. For instance, while von Ketten is away waging war on the Bishop of Trent, we learn that the Portuguese woman perceives her own children as alien and as young wolves ("Ihre Söhne, [. . .], waren das ihre Kinder? Junge Wölfe [. . .] waren es" [Musil 1978b: 260]). In the immediate co-text, a real wolf-cub enters the story. The Portuguese woman also looks after this wolf, because its appearance and the strength of its gaze remind her of her absent husband, von Ketten (260). It is striking that (again) a member of a source domain which has been used to characterize von Ketten is introduced in the story as a non-figurative entity, and appears as some kind of 'representative' of von Ketten at the castle while he is away (Zeller 2001/2002: 201). This is why von Ketten's order to kill the wolf, which could be interpreted as a symbolic destruction of his former self (Sera 1980: 153), has attracted the particular attention of literary critics. To complicate things further, it should be noted that a particular feature of the wolf, his gaze, is also mentioned in other contexts. At the beginning of the novella, each member of the von Ketten family is said to have a 'straight gaze' (Musil 1978b: 253). When von Ketten himself finally meets the wolf at the castle, its impenetrable gaze is foregrounded as von Ketten tries to look into its 'polished eyes' ("Er blickte ihm in die geschliffenen Augen", 262). A few pages after this passage the epithet 'polished eyes' occurs again in reference to his wife's eyes when he experiences problems in communicating with his wife:

Wenn er seiner Frau in die Augen sah, waren sie wie frisch geschliffen, sein eigenes Bild lag obenauf, und sie ließen seinen Blick nicht ein. (Musil 1978b: 265)

When he gazed into his wife's eyes, they were like new-cut glass, and although what the surface showed him was his own reflection, he could not penetrate further. (Musil 1999: 61)

We have seen that animals (e.g. the wolf) were used to describe features of human beings (e.g. von Ketten) and that the behaviour of animals (e.g. the kitten) was described as analogous to that of human beings (e.g. a small child). This mutual mapping of domains of experience of the human and the animal contradicts the principle of unidirectionality. The ultimate effect is that elements of this novella combine to form a tightly-knit web of mutual correspondences, both metaphorical and symbolical. As a consequence, the fixed roles of source domains and target domains (as predicted by the principle of invariance) become blurred. In fact, the wolf, the cat, von Ketten and his wife become part of a system of metaphorical and symbolical correspondences and oppositions: strong and wild vs. weak; concrete and distinct vs. soft; daylight vs. night and moon; north vs. south; mountain vs. sea. The outcome of von Ketten's illness suggests that he himself is searching for some kind of harmonious balance between these dichotomies, and it is in this context that some critics see connections with Musil's deliberations about the opposition between the state of scientific rationality and the so-called 'other state' of the irrational (cf. e.g. Eibl 1978: 148).

As we have seen, Musil's choice of metaphorical expressions is in most cases not particularly innovative. However, he has arranged metaphors and similes in such a way that they create a dense interplay of source and target domains leading to an interplay of experiential domains. Such interplay (or interaction) is in contrast to the automatised understanding of metaphors in conceptual metaphor theory, which tends to follow the principles of unidirectionality and invariance.

5   OVERRIDING OF COGNITIVE PRINCIPLES AS A POETIC PRINCIPLE?

Musil's technique of overriding cognitive principles suggests that such a mixing of experiential domains is a particular literary (or—at least—"creative") technique of using metaphors; it is rare in less creative discourses. Corpus evidence can also be used to provide further corroboration of this assumption. For instance, the assumption that overriding the principles of unidirectionality or invariance by bringing together different domains of experience is a literary feature, begs the question whether we can show that such mixing is unlikely to occur in less creative journalistic or scientific discourses.

To investigate this issue, the use of the word *Kind*/'child' was analysed in the 500 first entries of the *DWDS* data basis's newspaper section. The question posed was designed to ascertain the extent to which this noun appears both as a literal and as a figurative expression within a single text. First results showed that the newspaper collection did not contain many clearly metaphorical instances of "Kind"/'child' (only 17). Of these instances, there were four texts that contained both a figurative and a non-figurative use of the same word; however, three of these instances were not typical examples of newspaper texts. One example was clearly a non-creative selection of short news items independent from each other (*Berliner Tagblatt*, 18/2/1902), one example showed clear signs of fictionality

(*Vossische Zeitung*, 6/3/1903) and another example was a poem (*Berliner Tagblatt*, 2/2/1906). Ultimately, only one instance—a news story about a prince who had shown symptoms of mental illness in his childhood and who actually seemed to behave like a child—could be considered as an example of a double use of a figurative and non-figurative word in the same newspaper article. By contrast, the *DWDS* collection of *fiction* contained many instances of double use.[10] These preliminary results suggest, first of all, that newspaper articles tend to keep ambiguities to a minimum. And secondly, it seems that the use of metaphors in a 'hyperliteral' way is more of a poetic device.

Of course, it can be assumed that not every reader will either want, or find it necessary, to read the metaphors in this novella as a full and unconstrained exploration of the analogies between experiential domains, as has been suggested by Musil's analysis of Rilke's poetry. However, the text structure of Musil's novella "Die Portugiesin" ("The Lady from Portugal") does encourage such readings. Such interplay might contribute to metaphors being foregrounded, and encourage readers to combine different domains of experience in a way that enables them to gain more understanding of their own experiences (cf. Müller 2009). Thus texts in which metaphors are used in a way that undermines the principle of unidirectionality or invariance carry within them the propensity to enrich a reader's experiential knowledge. From this we can see the importance of the hyperliteral use of metaphors: not only do they demonstrate the benefits of overriding cognitive principles for poetic purposes, they also draw attention to the way subtle analogies create a web of interconnectivity in which everything is linked with everything else, and in doing so provide a deep insight into our own use of language.

NOTES

1. A different translation can be found in Musil (1990: 142).
2. Das Digitale Wörterbuch der deutschen Sprache des 20. Jahrhunderts 2004ff. Query: ["aus #5 heraus*"].
3. Das Digitale Wörterbuch der deutschen Sprache des 20. Jahrhunderts 2004ff. Query: ["wie #3 Kind"].
4. In German "wie" ('like') is not restricted to similes; therefore, the results were checked for clearly figurative similes resulting in a total of 592 entries that have been evaluated.
5. E.g. "[...] ihm war übel wie einem kleinen Kind, wenn es geweckt wird"—*DWDS*, Be 1922 (F. Kafka: *Das Schloß*).
6. E.g. "Wie ein geängstigtes Kind streckte sie [...]"—*DWDS*, Be 1943 (L. Weismantel: *Die höllische Trinität*) .
7. E.g. "Also verharrte er stille, nicht wie ein trotziges Kind"—*DWDS*, Be 1926 (H. Grimm: *Volk ohne Raum*).
8. E.g. "[...] Welle auf Welle rollt an den Sand, schäumt und verebbt, jagt sich und tollt wie ein spielendes Kind"—*DWDS* Ge 1915 (P. Witkop (ed.): *Kriegsbriefe gefallener Studenten*).

9. E.g. "Wieder schmurgelt die Großmutter wie ein gehorsames Kind ein Streichholz an: [. . .]"—*DWDS*, Be 1983 (E. Strittmatter: *Der Laden*).
10. However, fiction samples in the *DWDS* are also larger in size, which certainly increases the statistical chance of a double use with metaphoric and non-metaphoric meaning.

WORKS CITED

Bernauer, Hermann (1992) "Weshalb wird Ketten von einer Fliege gestochen? Zur Deixis in Musils Portugiesin". *Deutsche Vierteljahrsschrift für Literaturwissenschaft und Geistesgeschichte* 66.4: 733–47.
Das Digitale Wörterbuch der deutschen Sprache des 20. Jahrhunderts (2004ff.). Berlin-Brandenburgische Akademie der Wissenschaften. http://www.dwds.de (2005–2008).
Deignan, Alice (2005) *Metaphor and Corpus Linguistics*. Amsterdam: John Benjamins.
Eder, Thomas (2007) "Zur kognitiven Theorie der Metapher in der Literaturwissenschaft: Eine kritische Bestandsaufnahme". *Zur Metapher: Die Metapher in Philosophie, Wissenschaft und Literatur*. Eds. Franz Josef Czernin and Thomas Eder. München: Fink. 167–95.
Ehrenfels, Christian von (1960) "Über 'Gestaltqualitäten'" [1890]. *Gestalthaftes Sehen: Ergebnisse und Aufgaben der Morphologie. Zum hundertjährigen Geburtstag von Christian von Ehrenfels*. Ed. Ferdinand Weinhandl. Darmstadt: Wissenschaftliche Buchgesellschaft. 11–43.
Eibl, Karl (1978) *Robert Musil: Drei Frauen. Text, Materialien, Kommentar*. München: Hanser.
Gibbs, Raymond W. (2000) "Making Good Psychology out of Blending Theory". *Cognitive Linguistics* 11.3–4: 347–58.
Grady, Joseph E., Todd Oakley and Seana Coulson (1999) "Blending and Metaphor". *Metaphor in Cognitive Linguistics: Selected Papers from the Fifth International Cognitive Linguistics Conference*. Eds. Raymond W. Gibbs and Gerard J. Steen. Amsterdam: John Benjamins. 101–24.
Kövecses, Zoltan (2002) *Metaphor: A Practical Introduction*. Oxford: Oxford University Press.
Lakoff, George (1977) "Linguistic Gestalts". *Chicago Linguistic Society* 13: 236–87.
———. (1987) *Women, Fire and Dangerous Things: What Categories Reveal about the Mind*. Chicago: University of Chicago Press.
———. (1993) "The Contemporary Theory of Metaphor". *Metaphor and Thought*. Ed. Andrew Ortony. Cambridge: Cambridge University Press. 202–51.
Lakoff, George, and Mark Johnson (1999) *Philosophy in the Flesh: The Embodied Mind and Its Challenge to Western Thought*. New York: Basic Books.
Lakoff, George, and Mark Turner (1989) *More than Cool Reason: A Field Guide to Poetic Metaphor*. Chicago: University of Chicago Press.
McGlone, Matthew S. (2001) "Concepts as Metaphors". *Understanding Figurative Language*. Ed. Sam Glucksberg. Oxford: Oxford University Press. 90–107.
Müller, Ralph (2009) "Interaction of Metaphor". *Studies in the Literary Imagination*. Eds. Anja Müller-Wood and Katja Mellmann. 61–77.
———. (2010) "Critical Analysis of Creative Metaphors in Political Speeches". *Metaphor and the Real World: Proceedings of the 6th Conference on Researching and Applying Metaphor*. Eds. Lynne Cameron and Alice Deignan. Amsterdam: John Benjamins. 321–32.

Musil, Robert (1978a) *Der Mann ohne Eigenschaften*. Ed. Adolf Frisé. Reinbek: Rowohlt.

———. (1978b) "Die Portugiesin". *Gesammelte Werke: Prosa und Stücke*, Vol. 6. Ed. Adolf Frisé. Reinbek: Rowohlt. 252–70.

———. (1978c) "Geist und Erfahrung: Anmerkungen für Leser, welche dem Untergang des Abendlandes entronnen sind [März 1921]". *Gesammelte Werke: Essays und Reden*, Vol. 8. Ed. Adolf Frisé. Reinbek: Rowohlt. 1042–59.

———. (1978d) "Literat und Literatur: Randbemerkungen dazu [September 1931]". *Gesammelte Werke: Prosa und Stücke, Kleine Prosa, Aphorismen, Autobiographisches, Essays und Reden, Kritik*, Vol. 8. Ed. Adolf Frisé. Reinbek: Rowohlt. 1203–25.

———. (1978e) "Rede zur Rilke-Feier in Berlin am 16. Januar 1927". *Gesammelte Werke: Essays und Reden* Vol. 8. Ed. Adolf Frisé. Reinbek: Rowohlt. 1229–42.

———. (1978f) "Skizze der Erkenntis des Dichters" [1918]. *Gesammelte Werke: Essays und Reden*, Vol. 8. Ed. Adolf Frisé. Reinbek: Rowohlt. 1025–30.

———. (1990) *Precision and Soul: Essays and Addresses*. Transl. Burton Pike and David S. Luft. Chicago: University of Chicago Press.

———. (1999) "The Lady from Portugal". *Five Women*. Transl. Eithne Wilkins and Ernst Kaiser. Boston: David R. Godine.

Pragglejaz Group (2007) "MIP: A Method for Identifying Metaphorically Used Words in Discourse". *Metaphor and Symbol* 22.1: 1–39.

Sera, Manfred (1980) "Werde der du bist! [gnothi seauton!] Die Darstellung der Selbsterfahrung in Robert Musils Novelle 'Die Portugiesin'". *Musil-Forum* 6: 145–56.

Stefanowitsch, Anatol, and Stefan T. Gries (2006) Eds. *Corpus-Based Approaches to Metaphor and Metonymy*. Berlin: de Gruyter.

Stockwell, Peter (2002) *Cognitive Poetics: An Introduction*. London: Routledge.

Zeller, Rosmarie (2001/2002) "Grenztilgung und Identitätskrise: Zu Musils 'Törleß' und 'Drei Frauen'". *Musil-Forum* 27: 189–209.

12 Storyworld Metaphors in Swift's Satire

Michael Sinding

I would like to bring together cognitive narratology and conceptual metaphor theory (CMT) by examining how metaphors enter into the spatial structure of the storyworld of Swift's *A Tale of a Tub*.[1] David Herman defines *storyworlds* as "mental models of who did what to and with whom, when, where, why, and in what fashion in the world to which recipients relocate [...] as they work to comprehend a narrative" (2002: 5). Thus spatial modeling is essential to narrative understanding: stories prompt readers to "*spatialize* storyworlds into evolving configurations of participants, objects, and places"[2] (2002: 263).[3] The technique of spatializing metaphors in storyworlds (sometimes called "realization" or literalization) goes back to Aristophanes (Whitman 1981), and continues in postmodernists like Pynchon. Essentially, the author takes a conceptual connection implicit in linguistic metaphor and uses it to structure an imagined scene or story. J. Paul Hunter notes the centrality of the technique in *Gulliver's Travels*:

> Swift is especially fond of literalizing metaphors and turning them into narrative events; he has, for example, courtiers walk tightropes, dance before the king, etc.; he has Gulliver urinate on the royal palace and land in excrement when he tries too ambitious a leap; and the government of Laputa oppresses its subjects by hovering over them or physically crushing their rebellion. The stable society at the end of *Gulliver* seems to me to have a similar status. (2003: 239 n26)

My list of authors suggests that the technique is often satirical. It is also similar to allegory, but distinct from it, as I will discuss below. CMT claims that "image schemas" structure human perception and are also central to the structure of concepts (both literal and metaphorical). I will argue that, as they also structure narrative spatialization, they therefore guide the projection of metaphors in the spatial structure of imagined storyworlds.

1 IMAGE SCHEMAS, METAPHOR COHERENCE, LITERARY STRUCTURE

CMT sees metaphorical expressions as deriving from systematic mappings between concepts, typically from the well-understood to the abstract or subjective. Concepts are structured by schemas, skeletal arrangements of elements and relations modeling some aspect of the world. LIFE AS JOURNEY maps components like travellers, destinations, routes and impediments, to persons, purposes, means and difficulties (Lakoff & Turner 1989: 3–4).

Central to metaphor are image schemas: simple, skeletal spatial relations concepts with a small number of parts and relations. They are involved in human experience, as "recurring, dynamic pattern[s] of our perceptual interactions and motor programs" (Johnson 1987: xiv), which "structure indefinitely many perceptions, images, and events" (29). Thus, "[w]hen we understand a scene, we naturally structure it in terms of such elementary image-schemas" (Lakoff & Turner 1989: 97). A CONTAINER, for example, is a "bounded space with an interior and an exterior", which we may map "onto other images" such as a house, or a country on a map. But we also use image schemas metaphorically, to structure non-imagistic "abstract target domains [. . .] such as wakefulness, alertness, and living": we may go "in" or "out" of houses and countries, and also pass out, tune out or snuff out a candle (97). Thus image schemas can link the image to the abstraction, or help map one image to another. Other image schemas include PATH, CONTACT and human orientations like UP/DOWN and CENTER/PERIPHERY. Image schemas are dynamic as well as static, combine naturally, involve forces (Cienki 1997) and are shaped by culture and context (Hampe & Grady 2005).[4]

For Lakoff and Johnson, common schematic structure, which is often image schematic, allows metaphors to cohere (1980: ch. 9, 15–17). Literary studies have used CMT and image schemas to show structure and coherence in literature where it is not evident on the linguistic or imagistic surface. Lakoff and Turner (1989) show various kinds of coherence across metaphors within individual poems. Metaphors for the same target may cohere if their source domains are special cases of a more general one (LIFE AS JOURNEY in the form of sea voyage, road trip, uphill struggle, etc.). They may also cohere by sharing more complex structure. For example, LIFETIME AS DAY and YEAR; and LIFE AS FLAME, FIRE, and PRECIOUS POSSESSION, share the "commonplace theory" that life is a cycle (moving from non-existence to living to death) (86). More complexly, LIFE AS YEAR, DAY and FIRE are all instances of the more general composite metaphor of "life as a waxing and waning cycle of heat and light" (88).

However, the distinction between description and described, discourse and storyworld, is not very significant in these analyses of poems: the structure they find in the text is in a poetic vision, a conceptualization structured by metaphor. The same has generally been true of the impressive analyses of image-schematic structure in narrative. Turner (1996) demonstrates how image schemas inform the event structures that narratives recount, particularly the "small spatial stories" of changes in states of objects. But his focus is on the principles of mappings and blends across narratives, rather than on the global structures of literary narratives, or their storyworlds. Don

Freeman (1999) however, shows how a dynamic amalgam of CONTAINER, LINKS and PATH image schemas offers a unified basis for *Antony and Cleopatra*'s figurative language, imagery, plot, stage (and offstage) business and character. He describes a

> three-stage progression in its central metaphors: from those in which the robust and solid outline of Rome, political authority, and all that they contain melt into the liquid of [. . .] passions; to those in which the liquid of those passions evaporates into ever changing cloud shapes; and finally to the death vision of Cleopatra's "marble-constant" body-container sublimating directly into her nobler elements of "fire and air". (446)

The overall metaphor structure proposed here is akin to what Margaret Freeman (1995) calls a "conceptual universe"—a pattern structured by image schemas inferred from metaphors in speakers' discourse; a conceptual universe is not the storyworld but a way of seeing it. For instance, Kimmel's (2005) analysis shows how the plot structure of Conrad's *Heart of Darkness* embodies themes in large-scale image-schematic metaphors, which emerge from the gradual, complex build-up of particular metaphors for major story elements (the overall event structure; multiple sources for targets like the wilderness; multiple targets for sources like darkness). The story of Marlow's journey into the wilderness collapses a series of metaphors "into a single scenario-like gestalt" in order to "narrate multiple facets" of an initiation into the darker aspects of the self; we witness a breaking of the boundaries of "race, nation, class, community, family, church, and gender" (Kimmel 2005: 220–22). However, since the particular metaphors are used by a speaker or the narrator to describe a largely realistic storyworld, that world's spatial structure does not seem to be metaphoric in detail. Kimmel focuses on global metaphoric schematic images on a "mental sketchpad" rather than on the metaphoric structure of this world, as it might manifest itself in particular scenes.

2 STORYWORLD METAPHORS

What I am primarily interested in is the phenomenon of metaphor actually driving the structure of a storyworld as distinct from whatever linguistic metaphors are used by speakers or narrators. To further illustrate these distinctions, consider possible variant uses of metaphors of the air or wind as spirit. In *Antony and Cleopatra*, Cleopatra describes herself as sublimating herself at death ("I am fire, and air; my other elements / I give to baser life" (V, ii, 288–89; qtd. in Freeman 1999: 447), but we do not imagine that her body in the storyworld actually does so: the source domain is in the discourse alone, though it describes Cleopatra's state of mind, or aspirations. Realistic fiction may also use wind symbolism in the storyworld. In the

"Aeolus" episode of Joyce's *Ulysses*, the wind really does move around the newspaper offices, echoing the clichéd, "over-blown" spirit of the language of newspapers that Joyce parodies, but it is not identical to that meaning, and there is no detailed correspondence between them. The source domain is in the storyworld, but its reference to the target is limited by the condition that it remain consistent with that world's realism. In Swift's *A Tale of a Tub*, however, as we will see, both source and target are fully embodied and identical in the storyworld: the priests of the "Æolist" cult acquire and dispense spirit in the form of wind. Metaphor shapes storyworld, rather than being accommodated to it. Thus this technique reverses the usual understanding and evaluation of conventional metaphors. Instead of concrete sources structuring an abstract or subjective target, Swift collapses metaphor and referent to give us a storyworld wherein certain manifestations of the source literally *are* manifestations of the target.[5]

We may further define this phenomenon by distinguishing it from allegory. I suggest the use of storyworld metaphors is but one technique, though a central one, among several which allegory employs to connect story with meanings. We can illustrate several non-metaphorical forms of allegorical meaning with examples from Swift's *A Tale of a Tub*. The *Tale*'s story of how three brothers struggle over their father's will refers metaphorically to how three major Christian denominations struggle over the interpretation of the Bible. One form of non-metaphorical allegorical meaning is implicit reference to real-world entities, as when Swift makes veiled allusions to religious, political and literary figures. In the *Tale*, two of the brothers are named Martin and Jack, and these names allude to Martin Luther and John Calvin, and (by metonymy) to the denominations they founded, Protestantism and Calvinism. Other names with which the boys salute Jack refer to more specific radical individualist sects that the speaker associates with Calvinism: "Dutch Jack" refers to "Jack of Leyden, who gave rise to the Anabaptists", "French Hugh" refers to the Huguenots and so on (68n). A second form of non-metaphorical allegorical meaning is the explicit naming of target concepts. Swift does this relatively rarely. In the *Tale*, the ladies with whom the brothers fall in love are "the Duchess d'Argent, Madame de Grands Titres, and the Countess d'Orgueil" (35), but Swift leaves it to later editors to translate the French into English targets: "*i.e. covetousness, ambition,* and *pride*" (35n). John Bunyan, on the other hand, uses this form of meaning more often, as when in *The Pilgrim's Progress* he names his characters Christian, Faithful, etc. A third form of non-metaphorical allegorical meaning is the use of mythological or historical elements with non-metaphorical conventional meanings. In the *Tale*, brother Peter refers to St. Peter the apostle, conventionally regarded as the founder of the Catholic church. Another example is Swift's creation of the armies of Ancient and Modern authors in *The Battle of the Books*, such that Homer, Plato, Aristotle et al. do battle with Descartes, Hobbes, Dryden and others. Other allegorists often bring in classical and Christian gods, heroes, saints, villains, etc. Storyworld metaphors, on the other hand, are related to, but contrast with, the above forms of allegorical meaning.

Let us consider some principles of storyworld metaphors, using the example of Swift's flying island of Laputa from *Gulliver's Travels*, mentioned above as a metaphor for "oppression". The island is an element of setting, but its metaphorical meaning depends crucially on the fact that it is controlled by the rulers of the country, and that it can descend on the subjects to harm them. Hence setting is related to properties of objects (flying), spatial relations (above and below), events (ascending and descending movements), and to characters and relations among characters (rulers and subjects). However, any scenario that embodies this kind of relationship of pressure from an upper entity upon a lower one could spatialize this metaphor of oppression. Thus it seems that source concepts may be represented in any structure, property and relation in the storyworld and its scenes, specific or general: settings, characters, actions, objects and properties and relations of these elements. Target concepts have a corresponding flexibility of activation and specification. But despite this flexibility as to how sources and targets can be spatialized in the storyworld, that embodiment is not unconstrained. To make storyworld metaphors intelligible, authors may motivate them by basing them on conventional metaphors, however unconventional the spatialization may be. To grasp the metaphorical meaning of the flying island, we need to see how its ability to descend on subjects below and physically crush them embodies the metaphorical etymology of words like *oppress*, and the metaphorical use of words like *crush* (signifying a powerful agent destroying or subjugating another person or group).

Thus storyworld metaphors are often based on image-schematic structure (but they need not be: compare Swift's metaphor of Christian doctrine as the father's will). That is, the source domains used in the storyworld's spatial structure are given clear image-schematic structure, so that they can offer clear inferences about the target domain. Often, the fiction exploits an existing fit between the storyworld element and the metaphor source, but exaggerates it—as when the bodies of the Æolist preachers are seen as "vessels" of spirit, and are moreover inflatable and deflatable like balloons.

Storyworld metaphors can be related to one another in several ways, according to the logic of each of the structures that must be involved: narrative structure, source structure, target structure and image-schematic structure.

3 SWIFT'S *A TALE OF A TUB*

Let us now delineate how storyworld metaphors work in Swift's *A Tale of a Tub*, and how they are related to one another. In the *Tale*, the allegory of the struggles of Christian theology satirises abuses in the fields of religion and learning (Swift 2008: 2), so personifications and their actions are central. The narrator, conventionally identified as "the Grub Street Hack" (Paulson 1960: 28), parodies the literary abuses of writers-for-hire.

We find two metaphor systems for Swift's two main targets, "*fanaticism and superstition*" (Swift 2008: 2), embodied in Jack and Peter respectively. In the metaphor of the brothers' coats as different types of Christianity, the Peter system elaborates the conventional mapping of the appearance/reality distinction as surface/depth. Peter leads the brothers to fall in with a tailor/ clothing sect, whose doctrines conflict with the strictures of the Will. The sect believes that the universe is a "large *suit of clothes*, which *invests* every-thing" (36), that Man is a "*micro-coat*" (36), and suits of clothes are "ratio-nal creatures, or men" (37). Clothes perform all offices of life, define virtues (beauty, wit, etc.) and constitute social institutions and functions, including the most powerful (37). Swift implies not only that people pride themselves on "superficial" qualities, but also that appearances get mistakenly equated with internal mental qualities. Further, one can argue that uniform alone defines social authority: there is no "underlying" basis of status differences. The Jack system, on the other hand, elaborates the conventional mapping of the spirit in the body as force in a container in the metaphors of wind and vapours. Jack's followers in the Æolist sect also see the human body as a microcosm, but for them, "the original cause of all things" (72) and the "*anima mundi*" is "the *spirit*, or *breath*, or *wind* of the world" (73).

Overall, the order and relations of metaphors in the tale highlight the thematic and image-schematic connections between the systems represented by Peter and Jack more than they do the narrative connections between them. Peter and Jack are alternatives (contrasting and complementing one another) rather than being part and whole, or having a relationship of logical consequence. Swift champions a basic containing surface (Martin's original simple belief) by contrasting it, first with spurious added layers of surface (Peter's Catholic superstition), then with spurious interior depths (Jack's Calvinist fanaticism).

Narrative-based relations: Narrative structure creates relations of whole and part, and of sequence and causality. Scenes and events are parts of a larger whole; and they are linked in a temporally ordered causal sequence. The *Tale* has fairly minimal general storyworld structure holding the main metaphors together. In action and setting, the *Tale* recounts a struggle over an inheritance, with ruptures ending in the brothers' isolation in separate lodgings. But the narrative allegorically follows the (perceived) structure of church history. This historical target's event structure is the basis of the narrative's settings, its order and its causality. Thus, at first the brothers all "live together in one house like brethren and friends" as the father com-mands (34); then Martin and Jack split from Peter (59); then Jack splits from Martin (68). This parallels the schisms of Protestantism from Catholi-cism, then Calvinism from more moderate Protestantism like Lutheranism. The focus in the narrative, however, is on the smaller stories of the broth-ers' various madnesses.

Thus the main forms of narrative causation that link Peter's and Jack's stories and their metaphor systems derive from the personification metaphors that turn the sects into Peter, Martin and Jack, and the history of those sects into individual lives. Personification makes the structures and norms of folk psychology available for use in narrative and metaphor. Hence feelings of brotherhood and of sibling rivalry inform the two main schisms. Martin and Jack decide to leave Peter after he tries to foist his mad notions on them (57–59). When they copy the Will while he is abroad, and begin to regain their rights, he angrily kicks them out of doors (59). Consequently, Martin and Jack enact their rejection of Peter's "additions" by stripping the ornament from their coats. But while Martin soon demurs, not wanting to cause damage (65–66), Jack is driven by resentment (66), and in a zealous rage tears "the *main body* of his *coat*", urging Martin also to appear "as unlike the rogue Peter as it is possible" (67). Jack becomes envious of Martin's coat, argues with him, runs mad, splits from him and moves away (68).

Within each story, narrative structures (particularly those beholden to folk psychology) provide further ways to relate the main metaphors to other story events and to other metaphors. In the Peter story, the brothers' simple coats bar them from fashionable society, which is ruled by the tailor-deity. Peter reinterprets the Will to allow fashionable accessories, so that the brothers can court the ladies personifying "*covetousness, ambition,* and *pride*" (35n). In Jack's story, "zeal" is presented as a physical substance that drives Jack's mad actions and inspires the thought and action of his followers in the wind-worshipping Æolist sect (77).

Target-based relations: The sequential logic of the storyworld metaphors also comes in part from the understanding of the target. The specific metaphors in the *Tale*'s two systems connect their targets, though not very coherently. The coats are religion, the wind is spirit. The obvious relation would be that the spirit inspires, fills and gives shape to religion. Swift does not seem to see it this way, presenting no positive role for the spirit. The coats are perhaps linked with the spirit in that the father has "provided" them to the brothers as a legacy (we are not told if he made them) (34). There is more target-based coherence in the broader allegory. Peter's superstition and Jack's fanaticism are both irrational delusions, one idolizing institutions and forms to the exclusion of experience, the other idolizing subjective experience to the exclusion of forms and institutions. They are complementary major errors that define the sects and church history.

Source-based relations: Storyworld metaphors may be connected by virtue of real-world connections between source domains. For example, coats are both instrumental, providing warmth and protection, and ornamental. This allows Swift to present the corruption of essential religion by social wealth and power: frills are added to the basic coverings as these become affected by the changing tastes that entail inclusion in, or exclusion from, fashionable society. We noted above that metaphor coherence often depends on image-schematic coherence across sources. Recent studies have also considered how image schemas function in "gestalt groupings [...] which co-occur in our experience and in metaphorical extensions, especially in spatial and force-dynamic combinations" (Cienki 1997: 4). Coherence in image-schematic experience can translate into metaphor coherence. We will consider below how the Jack metaphors incorporate experiential correlations among substance, force, container and (vertical) displacement. We experience these correlations in gas and fluid pressure in our own bodies, and in other objects. The relations between the two main metaphor systems, on the other hand, are mainly those of contrast/complementation, not coherence: coats are outer surfaces, wind is an inner force and focusing on one means neglecting the other. However, the two metaphor systems do cohere in a passage which I discuss below, where sense objects, particularly bodies, are seen as containers with outer surfaces which are preferable to their interiors.

Image-schema-based relations: Within each system, image-schematic structure holds the metaphors together. Peter's story focuses on surface/depth relations, and touches on containment (exterior/interior) and center/periphery issues. Jack's story relates container, force and up/down (the vertical scale) image schemas.

Peter's story introduces the metaphor of religion as clothing when the dying father leaves his sons coats that are supposed to last them their whole lives and grow with them. His Will prescribes their "wearing and management" (Swift 2008: 34)—mainly "not to add to, or diminish [...] one thread", though they are "very plain" (38). Image-schematically, clothing is a (containing) surface; Swift highlights the coats' durability, organic quality, fit and coherence.

As mentioned above, the doctrines of the tailor/clothing sect favour surface appearances over underlying or inner substance, and even mistake the former for the latter. In a second move, adding new doctrines translates into adding fashionable ornamentation to the brothers' coats. Peter wore "whatever trimmings came up in fashion; never pulling off any, as they went out of the mode" such that "upon the time of their falling out there was hardly a thread of the original coat to be seen" (65). The trimmings, "*lace* and *ribbons*, and *fringe*, and *embroidery*, and *points*" (65) stress that these extra surfaces conceal the coat's basis, and are also peripheral to that (spiritual) center.

Three key sections concerning Jack develop metaphors with different specific sources (wind, vapours, sexual arousal) in image-schematically coherent ways. As we have seen, the main Æolist metaphor figures the spirit as wind. Swift concentrates on the relation between the inflation and expulsion of wind in reference to clerical discourse, but also links wind-force with upwards motion, and with the overturning of the vertical order. The etymological metaphor becomes a pun: "*spiritus, animus, afflatus, or anima*" are "several appellations for *wind*", the "*forma informans of* man" (73). Inspiration proceeds from the wind-gods (74). Humans have an inborn "portion or grain of *wind*" that may be "refined as well as enlarged, by certain methods in education" (73):

> [...] when *blown* up to its perfection, [wind] ought not to be covetously hoarded up, stifled, or hid under a bushel, but freely communicated to mankind. Upon these reasons [...] the wise Æolists affirm the gift of BELCHING to be the noblest act of a rational creature. (73)

Priests cultivate this art by getting more air into their bodies, or "their *vessels*", so as when "replete" to "disembogue [...] a plentiful share of their acquirements into their disciples' chaps" (74). They stand with "*mouths gaping wide against a storm*"; they stand in a circle and inflate each other, "with every man a pair of bellows applied to his neighbour's breech"; and they pursue learning, as it "*puffeth men up*", and words and learning are "*nothing but wind*" (74). The image-schematic structure is very clear. The body is a container, and the spirit is a gaseous substance within, which can enter, exert force and be expelled. The wind can fill and even deform the container, and greater inflation means greater expulsion. The satire is also clear: such inspiration is not divine but worldly, artificially drummed up by emotion and fancy; and audiences likewise absorb and encourage the spread of the same hot air.

Swift develops this inspiration–inflation–expulsion system significantly by connecting it with the force dynamics of "flight" and with the confusion or overturning of high and low: "the mind of man, when he gives the spur and bridle to his thoughts, [...] sallies out into both extremes of high and low, of good and evil", but when this "flight of fancy" takes him "out of his own reach and sight", he plunges "into the lowest bottom of things" (76). The logic of this image-schematic compound is evident, though it is emphasized only later: as forceful rising easily gets disoriented, turning downwards, so a strong imagination easily confuses the desirable with the undesirable.

The section of the *Tale* entitled "Discourse concerning the Mechanical Operation of the Spirit" (126–41) parallels the Jack story as it also concerns the "*fanatic* strain, or tincture of *enthusiasm*" (128) in religion. (It was originally appended to the *Tale*, though it seems to have been planned as part of the book [xvi–xvii].) The "Discourse" investigates artificial methods of "enthusiasm"—taken as "a *lifting up of the soul, or its faculties, above matter*" (or "ejaculating", "transporting" or "launching out" the soul) (129). In its physiological metaphors, the generating of spirit is rendered as inflation, while its communication corresponds to expulsion. The "Discourse" focuses on the displacements of pressurized spirit between the lower and upper regions, especially as a result of sexual causes. The initial analogy refers to the "Longheads'" custom of "squeezing, and bracing up the heads of infants, by which means Nature, shut out at one passage, was forced to seek another, and finding room above, shot upwards" (130). The discussion of the "Art of Canting", or the best control of one's voice in preaching, is significant for us. Eloquence is not about words, but about music, and even inarticulate sounds produce "forcible effects": a preacher "shall *blow his nose so powerfully* as to pierce the hearts of his people, who are disposed to receive the *excrements* of his brain with the same reverence as the *issue* of it. [. . .] For, the *spirit* being the same in all, it is of no import through what vehicle it is conveyed" (136). As with the Æolists, the preacher expels an inner substance that his audience takes in. The role of these forcible effects in inverting upper and lower levels is clarified by the origin of *"snuffling"* or *"conveying the sound through the nose"*, when a Puritan "felt the outward man put into odd commotions, and strangely pricked forward by the inward" (136). Among those inspired in this manner there is "a perpetual game at *leap-frog*" where "sometimes the *flesh* is uppermost, and sometimes the *spirit*" (136). Thus "the *saint* felt his *vessel* full *extended* in every part (a very natural effect of strong *inspiration*)" and, prevented from "evacuating upwards by repetition, prayer, or lecture, he was forced to open an inferior vent" (137). The "great seed or principle of the *spirit*" (138) is sex. Physiologically, this is portrayed as follows:

> [T]he spinal marrow being nothing else but a continuation of the brain, must needs create a very free communication between the superior faculties and those below: and thus the *thorn in the flesh* serves for a *spur* to the *spirit*. [. . .] [I]n the height and *orgasmus* of their spiritual exercise, it has been frequent with them * * * * *; immediately after which they found the *spirit* to relax and flag of a sudden with the nerves, and they were forced to hasten to a conclusion. (140–41)

Spiritual and sexual energy follow the same pattern of "build-up and release" (Johnson 1987: 119), a more specific form of the force-in-container event structure. Much incidental imagery fits this structure, e.g. bagpipes (Swift 2008: 136–37).

The "Digression concerning the Original, the Use, and Improvement of Madness in a Commonwealth" (77–87) develops the aforementioned link between wind and force and high and low. It purports to defend Jack as one "whose intellectuals were overturned" (77) by arguing that such *"madness or frenzy"* (78) is "the parent of all those mighty revolutions" of reason (82) that attend great actions (new empires, philosophies and religions). It focuses on the nature of madness as "transposition of the brain by force of certain *vapours* issuing up from the lower faculties" (82). Inflation and ascent cohere strongly with one another, and also with the overturning or transposing of hierarchies. The Hack then mock-praises delusion as happiness by linking the "madness" image schema complex with the knowledge metaphors of surface/depth and exterior/interior. The latter complex is central not only to the Peter story, but for satire metaphors generally. The metaphors are again physiological, but focus on the appearance of aspects of the body, opposing their exposure. In the Hack's view of understanding, imagination is better than reality (83). With the senses, objects "not conveyed in the vehicle of *delusion*", via false mediums, "varnish, and tinsel", are "fade and insipid" (83)—reminding us of Peter's adornments. Twisting traditional satire metaphors, Swift mock-rejects the sect's aims of "exposing weak sides" and of "*unmasking*" what is concealed (83). The surface/depth schema then becomes quite explicit:

> In the proportion that credulity is a more peaceful possession of the mind than curiosity; so far preferable is that wisdom which converses about the surface, to that pretended philosophy which enters into the depth of things, and then comes gravely back with the informations and discoveries that in the inside they are good for nothing. (83)

Precisely here, the surface vs. depth polarity connects with that of exterior vs. interior. The senses touch surfaces, "the outward of bodies"; reason by contrast, operates beneath, "cutting, and opening, and mangling, and piercing" (83). To avoid future "anatomy" the narrator defends reason's view that in "corporeal beings [. . .] the *outside* hath been infinitely preferable to the *in*" (84), offering famously caustic proofs: "Last week I saw a woman *flayed*, and you will hardly believe how much it altered her person for the worse" (84). The stripped "carcass of a *beau*" reveals amazing "unsuspected faults" and as inner organs are cut open, "the defects increase upon us in number and bulk" (84). Reason is ambiguous here: reprehensibly exposing, yet aiming to avoid further anatomizing. Hence "he that can [. . .] content his ideas with the *films* and *images* that fly off upon his senses from the *superficies* of things; such a man, truly wise, creams off Nature, leaving the sour and the dregs for philosophy and reason to lap up" (84). Despite mock-renouncing satire, the satirist gives his blade a final twist: this "sublime and refined point of felicity" is "*the possession of being well deceived*; the serene peaceful state, of being a fool among knaves" (84). We return to a dark satirical view: humanity is divided between knaves using surface impressions to hide vice, and fools failing (or refusing) to penetrate them; but now the surface-preferring anatomist seems as much a knave as his victim/patient.

Based on this analysis we can venture a few conclusions about patterns of structure in storyworld metaphors, and Swift's use of them. Ryan (2003) extends Schneider's claim regarding the centrality of character for narrative, suggesting that the "cognitive mapping" of story space revolves around character motives, relations, and actions. The present chapter extends Ryan's analysis, suggesting that the spatial organisation of storyworld metaphors likewise centres on character. Specifically, Swift's main causal interest is in bodies, and their props. Place is also significant for establishing relationships among these elements. Peter's metaphors focus on props: the will, the coats and their adornments. Jack's metaphors, by contrast, focus on human bodies: wind, vapours, bodily channels; props are sometimes important (bellows, barrels, bladders, hats, etc.); setting is occasionally involved, but never central.

Storyworld metaphors seem to be interrelated according to certain principles. In our examples, metaphors get coordinated both spatially and temporally. They express synchronic aspects of the target concept's structure via the source images, and delineate the diachronic (causal-temporal) aspects of the target's structure via the narrative unfolding of those images in characters' actions. Specifically, the structure and logic of the target concept guides the selection, specification and arrangement of sources. The target concept induces selection of sources with a certain image-schematic structure, and also guides the way in which these sources are specified and arranged in a certain narrative structure and logic of order and connection. Swift presents the central religious errors as connected by giving them complementary metaphoric sources and image-schematic structures: Peter's pursuit of empty external layers of luxury and power vs. Jack's outwardly austere cultivation of inner force. Swift presents these errors in a narrative so as to reflect the causal-temporal order of their historical referents. Peter's "external" error leads to a justified reaction; but where Martin returns to an original moderate norm, Jack goes too far, swinging to an "internal" excess the opposite of Peter's.

Metaphor very often relies on image-schematic structure, both in everyday language and in literary narrative. But literary narrative tends also to elaborate specific-level structure, the familiar experiential level of people and things and places and events—the narrative level, one might say—and this carries over to storyworld metaphors. I may in passing call someone a wind-bag, knowing you will get my point by grasping the image-schematic structure implied by that combination of words. But Swift describes such persons in detail. Image-schematic structure and specific-level structure seem to have different conceptual functions. The image-schematic level often guides emotional and moral response by attributing causality. This is clearest with force metaphors. Swift's metaphors assign non-cognitive causes to the "enthusiastic" thought and behaviour of Jack's followers, i.e. mechanical force (wind, vapours, etc.), not Christian wisdom or feeling or grace. This alone compels a scornful judgment from the reader. The specific level, on the other hand, modifies emotional and moral evaluation from typical associations of particular causal sources. The wind-bag followers become ludicrous by association of the physiology of gas with that of sexual desire (frustrated, indulged or sublimated), a comparison accentuated by Swift's colourful specifications. Further, because of this specific-level richness, the same narrative element can embody multiple metaphors. Mechanical inflation of a preacher indicates that his "inspiration" is artificial and hence deceptive; but it also implies that his ego is inflated, and that his belief and preaching are empty because they are insubstantial, and that they are foul because they unleash bodily gas.

4   METAPHOR AND NARRATIVE IN SATIRE

Swift's use of storyworld metaphors, and the particular metaphoric structures he uses, may not be unique to him, but instead characteristic of his
genre. I suggest that there is a "commonplace theory" of satire as a kind of
action, and that the metaphors typically used to describe that action appear
in the situations and roles and actions of narrative satire.

First, spatialization of metaphor—turning conceptual metaphors into
storyworld structures—may have a particular affinity with satire. Randolph points out that satirical analogy commonly equates the physical with
the moral (1941: 135). Palmeri too argues that "[t]he plot and the rhetoric
of narrative satire cohere in accomplishing the same movement of lowering
or leveling. [. . .] The reduction of spiritual to physical in satiric narrative
corresponds to the rhetorical reduction of metaphors to literal meanings"
(1990: 10–13). However, not only metaphors, but also rhetorical figures
can be spatialized: iconic relations between abstract forms and meanings
in language can shape storyworlds. Kernan characterizes satire in terms of
figures of "disorder" that expand from forms of style to forms of participants, objects, places, and events:[6]

> The world of satire is built up from [certain] rhetorical figures and the
> moral failings they dramatize. But in considering satiric rhetoric, [. . .]
> it will be more useful to translate these terms to the "scenic" terms
> which they suggest. [. . .] This primitive drive toward disorder is at
> first expressed by the various faults of style Pope includes in this class,
> but it presses on to realize itself in such scenic elements as the wearing
> of fantastic clothing, crowd and mob scenes, labyrinths and other dis-
> ordered buildings, huge, jumbled cities, and at last in primal chaos and
> uncreation. (1965: 34–35)

Curtius's classic study similarly shows literary history projecting the *mun-
dus inversus* or World Turned Upside-Down *topos* to elements of gradually
increasing scale (1963: 94–98). The rhetorical device of "stringing together
impossibilities" to articulate a "complaint on the times" (95) becomes a
principle for patterning rhetorical sequences, then general descriptions,
then whole imagined worlds (96). Comic versions of the motif appear in
the work of satirists like Aristophanes, Lucian and Rabelais (96).

Second, there is a commonplace model of satire as an action. Satire
is conventionally seen as humorously exposing folly or vice by making
them appear ridiculous.[7] In this action's sequence of elements, the satirist
observes follies or vices (in a person, institution, practice, etc.), has an emotional response to them (mild or harsh amusement/disgust/anger/despair)
and then releases this emotion by attacking the targets with ridicule. Recognizing the truth of the satiric vision, the audience responds with laughter,
and the target reacts with shame, which, it is hoped, motivates reform.

Third, this action model of satire is often understood via metaphor, so that we get metaphorical models of what satire is and how it works. Robert Elliott in surveying the metaphors used to describe satire notes their aggression:

> [I]t is a tantalizing fact that dozens of the terms we conventionally apply to satire have direct association with the magical power [of destruction]. [. . .] ["Harsh"] satire, we say, may be cutting, blistering, biting, killing, stinging, stabbing, scorching, searing, burning, withering, flaying, annihilating; satires are sharp, barbed, poisonous, malignant, deadly, vitriolic, and so on. (1960: 281)

Likewise, Mary Claire Randolph in her classic essay on Renaissance satiric theory explores why such words "preserve the primitive notion of destroying or harming the human body" (1941: 142). Randolph, however, explains the coherence of this vocabulary by proposing an underlying metaphorical "medical concept" of satire as curing moral ills. The satirist who analyses a subject to find, expose and correct a folly or vice (pride, vanity, affectation, hypocrisy) is a doctor cutting into a patient's body to discover and remove some disease-causing entity. Something strange is going on here. There seem to be *two* contrasting metaphors: satire as destruction, and satire as doctoring. The existence of the doctoring metaphor shows that satire-as-destruction is too broadly conceived to represent the entire concept. Yet Randolph's way of incorporating violence as an element of doctoring seems to leave out many kinds of attack (biting, killing, etc.), and is therefore too narrow to represent the entire concept.

This conundrum can be solved by recourse to conceptual metaphor theory (CMT). By modeling the main metaphors for satire's action schema in terms of image schemas, CMT is able to reflect the similarities of the two metaphors in a general action pattern, and show the coherence of their differences as variant specifications of that pattern. The action model for satire assumes things can seem better than they really are. In the image-schematic metaphorical model for satire, perception knows realities (underlying/inner substances) by appearances (outer surfaces). Things can be overestimated (enlarged beyond natural size) by unwarranted pride/vanity (often, gas or air: "inflated", "puffed up"). Appearance can become separated from reality. The satirist recognizes affectation/hypocrisy (the disparity between surface and substance). The satirist's action (destructive attack/doctoring) releases negative emotional energy ("venting"), reveals (exposes, "punctures") and removes ("deflates", "cuts down") the false appearance, and hence the disparity. Satirist and audience triumph by restoring true perception ("reducing" the object to its original size) and shaming the target (making "small", "exposed").

Fourth, consider how satire's action sequence might translate into narrative. If perception is essential to satire, then so are perspective and conceptualization. Rhetoric and irony are key means of controlling perspective and conceptualization in discourse. Hence, critics recognizing the importance of perception in satire often emphasize rhetoric and irony in their analyses. Such critics are often uncertain about the importance of "plot" for satire (e.g. Griffin 1994). Frye's influential analysis, however, integrates irony and rhetoric into a basic plot situation. Satire is "militant irony" requiring "wit or humor founded on fantasy or a sense of the grotesque or absurd" and "an object of attack" (Frye 1971: 223–24).[8] Narrative satire adapts the plot situation (central to comedy) of a contest between the two character types of *alazon* (impostor) and *eiron* (self-deprecator) (163–75, 224–32). *Eiron* narrators or characters attack *alazons* rhetorically by offering subversive perspectives on them: "The multitudes of comic scenes in which one character complacently soliloquizes while another makes sarcastic asides to the audience show the contest of *eiron* and *alazon* in its purest form" (172). Bakhtin also emphasizes character relations: it is basic to the novel's satirical dimension that "lower" character types expose higher ones (1981: 158–67). Cognitive research reviving character as a centre of narrative interest (Schneider 2001; Culpeper 2002) dovetails with this sense that character parameters and types are central to narrative structure and genre.[9] Hence we may expect that in this contest, metaphors of satirist and target will enter into narratives by some association with the roles and characters of *alazon* (the satiric butt) and *eiron* (the ironizer).

Thus, finally, consider how the elements of the image-schematic metaphorical model for satire should translate into the storyworlds of satiric narratives. In that model, satire's action penetrates and removes inflated exteriors, exposing the disparity between surface and substance, reducing objects to proper size, venting the satirist's emotion and deflating that of the target. If this model is related to satire's contest of *alazon* and *eiron* character-perspectives, then storyworld metaphors in narrative satire should link *alazons* with inflation and false surfaces, and *eirons* with penetrating, exposing and reducing those *alazon* structures. Let us return to Swift to explore this possibility.

Swift's narrative sees Peter, Jack and Swift's scribbling Hack as *alazons*. Swift, or his implied author, is the only consistent *eiron*, but other characters variously take on the role. All brothers are *alazons* at first, their gaudy coats spatializing the satire's false surfaces. Later Martin and Jack become *eirons* to Peter, and this is spatialized in their stripping of their coats. Soon after, Martin turns *eiron* to Jack by refusing Jack's exaggerated outrage. That outrage is due to Jack's becoming "brimful" of a substance called "zeal" (Swift 2008: 66), a condition that spatializes the *alazon* metaphor of inflation: Jack's zeal causes him to strip his coat excessively, and to run mad and split from Martin.

The main image-schematic metaphors of satire are used in ways central to the structure of the narrative, although they are of course not the only metaphors used, and other authors than Swift may use them differently. Swift moreover plays with his metaphors and questions them explicitly. While his "Apology" uses the traditional metaphors, of the exposure of follies as a cure of disease (2), his introduction, by contrast, employs new metaphors, or new twists on old ones, ironically to deny that his text is satirical. He satirizes satire: much satire is dull, but it may still be effective for that very reason: "[I]t is with *wits* as with *razors*, which are never so apt to *cut* those they are employed on as when they have *lost their edge*. Besides, those whose teeth are too rotten to bite, are best of all others, qualified to revenge that defect with their breath" (22–23). Moreover, satire is too easily deflected by readers: "'Tis but a *ball* bandied to and fro, and every man carries a *racket* about him to strike it from himself among the rest of the company" (24). It remains to be seen how the above image-schematic models for the action of satire might be found in other satirical storyworlds, especially those less given to fantasy, and whether metaphors used to describe other genres are also prominently found in the storyworlds of those genres.

CMT and cognitive narratology have been brought together only rarely, despite favourable conditions for their meeting. After all, they share key notions of structure (schemas, models, mapping); metaphor is central to literary narrative; and questions of metaphor's relation to contexts of experience, discourse and culture are vital in metaphor theory.[10] It is axiomatic in cognitive literary studies that readers draw on knowledge in the form of schemas to construe all aspects of texts. To grasp Swift's *Tale*, we need schemas for (*inter alia*) concepts of family roles and relations, inheritance and wills, clothing, air and breathing, church history, theology, psychology and politics. We also need schemas for literary concepts like scenes, characters, text worlds, plots, genres, styles, rhetorical figures and more. But the schemas for these various structures are typically examined in isolation from one another. We must remember that basic construal asks readers to monitor all text parameters simultaneously, and to combine different kinds of schemas. Metaphor is central in narrative. We cannot grasp its unfolding by an exclusive focusing on either metaphor or narrative by themselves. In their simultaneous monitoring of multiple aspects of text structure, image-schematic processes, as I have tried to argue, may help to interconnect structures of metaphor, narrative and genre. They thus provide a link between metaphor and narrative.

ACKNOWLEDGMENTS

I thank the Alexander von Humboldt Foundation for supporting this research through a postdoctoral fellowship. I also thank Monika Fludernik for assistance above and beyond the call of an editor, in matters both large and small.

NOTES

1. Cognitive narratology uses cognitive theory to extend and recast traditional narrative concepts, and to develop new ones. For an overview, see Herman (2003).
2. Unless otherwise indicated, all italics in quotations are original emphases.

3. *Story Logic* devotes chapter 7 to "Spatialization". Ryan (2003) explores some principles of cognitive mapping of narrative space.
4. For further directions in CMT and image schema research, see Gibbs and Steen (1999), Hampe (2005). In this chapter, I have generally not followed the convention of putting image schema names in small capitals. The chapter deals with the complex relations among various aspects of concepts in thought and discourse (e.g. concrete concept, abstract concept, image schema, metaphor, event, word, story). The use of small capitals assumes and implies an inappropriately sharp distinction between the recognized image schemas and other conceptual elements, which often have image schematic aspects. For example, I touch on possible new image schemas (e.g. substance, as a contrast to surface), image schematic processes (e.g. inflation/deflation), complex or combined image schemas (e.g. stripping an object's surface reduces its size and exposes its interior), lexical items (e.g. "puffed up", "vent") and concrete images and events (e.g. coat, stripping). I have tried to make the identity of conceptual elements sufficiently clear in context.
5. Because storyworlds are emergent relative to language, linguistic analyses of metaphor effective at levels of sentence and discourse may be unable to account fully for storyworld metaphor. Words referring to storyworld-metaphor elements are both literal (they refer literally to the storyworld) and metaphorical (they refer metaphorically to the target meaning). The question is then raised of how we recognize metaphor of this kind, if it need not be explicit in the discourse. But I set this aside for now.
6. Kernan also suggests that rhetorical structures map not only to scene structures, but also to manners of action (crowded, chaotic, disordered).
7. Recent studies of satire include Palmeri (1990), Griffin (1994), Connery and Combe (1995) and Simpson (2003). Griffin stresses the differences between this conventional idea and the complexities of satirical texts.
8. Frye's essay "shaped much criticism thereafter"; its "pithy definition" is "[m]ore widely referenced perhaps than any other single formula" (Simpson 2003: 52), though Simpson regrets that it has been little unpacked and probed (53).
9. See also studies of "mind-reading" in narrative. However, this revival may over-emphasize the modern novel, with its sense of character as rich consciousness.
10. As recent surveys observe, there has been little interaction between cognitive studies of metaphor and of narrative (Sternberg 2003: 321 n16; Pettersson 2005: 310–16). Yet the schema is the most important concept in both CMT and cognitive narratology. Schemas can be construed both statically and dynamically, so there is no sharp line between the concepts that structure metaphoric mappings, and the events that structure stories. CMT has often placed metaphors within background event structures (e.g. for ANGER; LOVE; LIFE; DEATH). Lakoff and Turner (1989) discuss EVENTS ARE ACTIONS as metaphor. Steen (2003) links love metaphors to stages of a scenario defining the genre of love stories.

WORKS CITED

Bakhtin, Mikhail (1981) *The Dialogic Imagination: Four Essays.* Transl. Caryl Emerson and Michael Holquist. Austin: University of Texas Press.

Cienki, Alan (1997) "Some Properties and Groupings of Image Schemas". *Lexical and Syntactic Constructions and the Construction of Meaning.* Eds. Marjolijn Verspoor, Kee Dong Lee and Eve Sweetser. Amsterdam Studies in the Theory and History of Linguistic Science, Series IV: Current Issues in Linguistic Theory, 150. Amsterdam: John Benjamins. 3–15.

Connery, Brian A., and Kirk Combe (1995) *Theorizing Satire: Essays in Literary Criticism.* New York: St. Martin's Press.

Culpeper, Jonathan (2002) "A Cognitive Stylistic Approach to Characterization". *Cognitive Stylistics: Language and Cognition in Text Analysis.* Eds. Elena Semino and Jonathan Culpeper. Amsterdam: John Benjamins. 251–77.

Curtius, Ernst Robert (1963) *European Literature and the Latin Middle Ages.* Transl. Willard R. Trask. Bollingen Library, 36. New York: Harper & Row.

Elliott, Robert C. (1960) *The Power of Satire: Magic, Ritual, Art.* Princeton: Princeton University Press.

Freeman, Donald (1999) "'The rack dislimns': Schema and Metaphorical Pattern in *Antony and Cleopatra*". *Poetics Today* 20: 443–60.

Freeman, Margaret (1995) "Metaphor Making Meaning: Dickinson's Conceptual Universe". *Journal of Pragmatics* 24: 643–66.

Frye, Northrop (1971) *Anatomy of Criticism: Four Essays.* Princeton: Princeton University Press.

Gibbs, Raymond, Jr., and Gerard Steen (1999) Eds. *Metaphor in Cognitive Linguistics. Selected Papers from the Fifth International Cognitive Linguistics Conference, Amsterdam, July 1997.* Amsterdam Studies in the Theory and History of Linguistic Science, Series IV: Current Issues in Linguistic Theory, 175. Amsterdam: John Benjamins.

Griffin, Dustin H. (1994) *Satire: A Critical Reintroduction.* Lexington: University Press of Kentucky.

Hampe, Beate, and Joseph Grady (2005) Eds. *From Perception to Meaning: Image Schemas in Cognitive Linguistics.* Cognitive Linguistics Research, 29. Berlin: de Gruyter.

Herman, David (2002) *Story Logic: Problems and Possibilities of Narrative.* Frontiers of Narrative. Lincoln: University of Nebraska Press.

———. (2003) Ed. *Narrative Theory and the Cognitive Sciences.* CSLI Lecture Notes, 158. Stanford: CSLI.

Hunter, J. Paul (2003) "*Gulliver's Travels* and the Later Writings". *The Cambridge Companion to Jonathan Swift.* Ed. Christopher Fox. Cambridge: Cambridge University Press. 216–40.

Johnson, Mark (1987) *The Body in the Mind: The Bodily Basis of Meaning, Imagination, and Reason.* Chicago: University of Chicago Press.

Kernan, Alvin (1965) *The Plot of Satire.* New Haven: Yale University Press.

Kimmel, Michael (2005) "From Metaphor to the 'Mental Sketchpad': Literary Macrostructure and Compound Image Schemas in *Heart of Darkness*". *Metaphor and Symbol* 20: 199–238.

Lakoff, George, and Mark Johnson (1980) *Metaphors We Live By.* Chicago: University of Chicago Press.

Lakoff, George, and Mark Turner (1989) *More than Cool Reason: A Field Guide to Poetic Metaphor.* Chicago: University of Chicago Press.

Palmeri, Frank (1990) *Satire in Narrative: Petronius, Swift, Gibbon, Melville, and Pynchon.* Austin: University of Texas Press.

Paulson, Ronald (1960) *Theme and Structure in Swift's 'Tale of a Tub'.* New Haven: Yale University Press.

Pettersson, Bo (2005) "Afterword: Cognitive Literary Studies: Where to Go from Here". *Cognition and Literary Interpretation in Practice.* Eds. Harri Veivo, Bo Pettersson and Merja Polvinen. Helsinki: Helsinki University Press. 307–22.

Randolph, Mary Claire (1941) "The Medical Concept in English Renaissance Satiric Theory: Its Possible Relationships and Implications". *Studies in Philology* 38: 125–57.

Ryan, Marie-Laure (2003) "Cognitive Maps and the Construction of Narrative Space". *Narrative Theory and the Cognitive Sciences.* CSLI Lecture Notes, 158. Ed. David Herman. Stanford: CSLI. 214–42.

Schneider, Ralf (2001) "Toward a Cognitive Theory of Literary Character: The Dynamics of Mental-Model Construction". *Style* 35: 607–40.

Simpson, Paul (2003) *On the Discourse of Satire: Towards a Stylistic Model of Satirical Humour.* Linguistic Approaches to Literature, 2. Amsterdam: John Benjamins.

Steen, Gerard (2003) "'Love stories': Cognitive Scenarios in Love Poetry". *Cognitive Poetics in Practice.* Eds. Joanna Gavins and Gerard Steen. London: Routledge. 67–82.

Sternberg, Meir (2003) "Universals of Narrative and Their Cognitivist Fortunes (I)". *Poetics Today* 24: 297–395.

Swift, Jonathan (2008) *A Tale of a Tub and Other Works.* Ed. with introd. and notes by Angus Ross and David Woolley. Oxford World's Classics. Oxford: Oxford University Press.

Turner, Mark (1996) *The Literary Mind: The Origins of Thought and Language.* New York: Oxford University Press.

Whitman, Cedric (1981) "Aristophanes: Discourse of Fantasy". *Comedy: Meaning and Form.* Ed. Robert W. Corrigan. Second Edition. New York: Harper & Row. 231–43.

13 Conventional Metaphor and the Latent Ideology of Racism

Andrew Goatly

1 INTRODUCTION: DEGREES OF IDEOLOGICAL LATENCY, CONVENTIONAL METAPHOR, AND METALUDE

This chapter depends upon two linked assumptions. Firstly, that language is not a neutral medium—it does not simply reflect a pre-existing reality but constructs systems of ideas and ideologies. Since ideology is a notoriously slippery term, I had better, at the outset, introduce my understanding of it.

I provisionally adopt Van Dijk's definition and description in *Ideology*. He characterizes ideology as *"the basis of the social representations shared by members of a group*. This means that ideologies allow people, as group members, to organise the multitude of social beliefs about what is the case, good or bad, right or wrong, *for them* and to act accordingly" (Van Dijk 1998: 8; original emphasis). One major determinant of these social representations is "the material and symbolic interests of the group [. . .]. Power over other groups (or resistance against the domination by other groups) may have a central role and hence function as a major condition and purpose for the development of ideologies" (ibid.). This emphasis on power is central to my understanding of ideology, and one might adopt Thompson's briefer definition: "meaning in the service of power" (1990: 7).

Some approaches to ideological analysis, such as Foucault's, minimize the cognitive element (O'Halloran 2003). But ideology inhabits our minds as well as discourse: "It arises out of cognitive mechanisms as well as out of technology and social practices" (Balkin 1998: 272). Van Dijk's definition emphasizes both its social and cognitive aspects, and their realization in or construction by discourse.

Ideologies can, in principle, be detected in discourse in several ways, among them those listed in Table 13.1. Moving down the table from the blatant to the latent, these ideological aspects of discourse become more difficult to detect. This brings us to the second assumption of this chapter: type (7), conventional metaphors, are powerful ways of creating or reproducing ideologies, and often remain undetected.

Table 13.1 Traces of Ideology in Discourse

	Grammar/Propositions		Lexis	Blatant
1	Explicitly stated propositions	5	Original metaphors	↓
2	Presupposition	6	Disputed terms	↓
3	Inference—implicated assumptions	7	Conventional metaphors	↓
4	Semantic-syntactic patterns	8	'Literal' lexis	Latent

Consider briefly, how ideology might operate in discourse in these eight ways, (1) to (4) to do with grammar/propositions, and (5) to (8) to do with lexis, with the help of examples:

(1) *Xs are lazy beggars.* This is an explicitly-stated proposition showing contempt for the social group X.

(2) *The need to increase competitiveness demands the dismantling of the German welfare system.* This presupposes 'X needs to increase competitiveness', an existential presupposition smuggled into the text through nominalisation. As a presupposition it is not easily refuted, since presupposition remains constant under negation: *It is not the case that the need to increase competitiveness demands the dismantling of the German welfare system* counters the idea that the need demands the dismantling of the welfare system, without denying the existence of the need.

(3) *A Scotsman takes some money out of the bank for a holiday. When it's had its holiday he puts it back again.* Here one implicated premise (Sperber & Wilson 1995) necessary to understand the joke is that Scotsmen are mean with their money, giving the implicated conclusion 'The Scotsman puts the money back in the bank without spending it because he is mean'. Because this implicated premise is provided by the receivers of the joke, in a sense they feel responsible for evoking it, as it appears nowhere in the text, and might, therefore, be less obvious (Fairclough 2001).

(4) At a much more latent level of the grammar, Standard Average European languages divide events into Things (Nouns) and Processes (Verb). Unless we speak a radically different language—e.g. the Algonquin language Blackfoot, which depicts events as interactions of processes, and in which nouns are rare—we may be oblivious of the ideological dimensions of our grammars, among them the reinforcement of the ecologically unhelpful canonical event model (Goatly 2007: ch. 7). Compare, for example, the English sentence *That boy brought a chair* with the Blackfoot equivalent (Leroy & Ryan 2004: 38):

iih	pommaat	oom	wa	ann	wa	saahk	oma	a'pii	wa	amo	yi	a's	opii	a'tsis	yi
by way of	transfer	move	ing	that familiar	ing	young	yet	state of	ing	this near	ing	be- come	sit	facil- itate	ing

Figure 13.1   English vs. Blackfoot.

The absence of nouns in this construction of events precludes the possibility of seeing Humans (Actors) as acting on Nature (Affected) unidirectionally, to dominate a passive nature.

Turning from grammar and propositions let's consider lexis in categories 5 to 8:

(5) *Consumerism is a kind of cancer.* This original metaphor, where the conventional lexeme *growth* is substituted with *cancer*, draws attention to itself by its unconventionality.

(6) *The handicapped.* If a term like this is contested, because disabled people resist being regarded as less likely to be successful than other members of society, we become aware of the negative implications of the phrase. (If it is not contested or disputed, then it may revert to a higher level of latency, such as [8]).

(7) *I don't buy that*, meaning 'I don't accept that opinion'. This is now a conventional metaphorical expression, quite unremarkable, until we realize it belongs to a metaphor theme KNOWLEDGE/INFORMATION IS COMMODITY, the prevalence of which has changed educational institutions over the past thirty years.

(8) *Brother.* This literal lexical item might never reveal its ideology at all, unless one happens to be bilingual and one's other language has no equivalent word. In Thai, for example, siblings are obligatorily classified, not by sex, as in European languages, but in terms of seniority, with all the consequences for ideology that this entails in a hierarchical society.

Lexical metaphor occurs at two levels in examples (5) and (7) above. Literary metaphor is more associated with level 5, but this chapter concentrates on the relatively conventional metaphors of level 7, which I consider more powerful in their effects precisely because of their potential for latent effects on cognition. My focus in this chapter coincides with that of conceptual metaphor theory, the most influential theory of metaphor developed over the last thirty years.

This theory was first popularised by Lakoff and Johnson's *Metaphors We Live By* (1980). Its first insight is that metaphor is everywhere (Paprotté & Dirven 1985), and, though associated with literature, is not confined to it. We cannot escape from metaphor, even if we wanted to. Although philosophers, like Thomas Hobbes and John Locke, regarded it as confused thinking, ironically enough, the terms in which they inveigh against it are themselves loaded with metaphors.

> But yet, if we would speak of things as they are, we must **allow** that [. . .] all the artificial and figurative application of words eloquence hath **invented**, are for nothing else but to insinuate wrong ideas, **move** the passions, and thereby **mislead** the judgment, and so indeed are a perfect **cheat**. (*An Essay Concerning Human Understanding*, bk. 3, ch. 10, par. 34; Locke 1959: 105, my emphasis)[1]

Metaphor is indispensable when discoursing on abstract topics. Indeed, the strong claim of conceptual metaphor theory is that abstract thought is impossible without metaphor. Lakoff demonstrated that even mathematical operations and concepts such as Boolean logic or set theory depend on the metaphor of containers or bounded spaces, with members inside the container and non-members outside it (Lakoff 1987: ch. 20).

An important insight of conceptual metaphor theory is that these concrete sources for abstract targets form patterns, called Conceptual Metaphors or Metaphor Themes. I adopt the latter term, because it includes patterns where the topic and the metaphorical term are both concrete entities, for example the comparison of human bodies with buildings. Metaphor themes are conventionally referred to by the capitalized formula X IS Y, or, terminologically, TARGET IS SOURCE.

According to Lakoff's experientialist hypothesis (Lakoff 1987), the motivation for these metaphorical patterns is infant experience. For example the notion of proximity is acquired from being picked up and separated from our carers with whom we form a relationship, so that RELATIONSHIP IS PROXIMITY. We experience the power of gravity—so POWER IS HIGH. As we develop we learn to handle objects with increasing dexterity, initially using a palm grasp, and progressing until we can pick up small objects between thumb and index finger; this provides both the source for UNDERSTANDING IS HOLDING/GRASPING and the motivation for CONTROL IS HANDLE.

The experientialist hypothesis, therefore, claims that metaphor is based on metonymy. That is, infant experience associates contiguous metonymically-related concepts, such as relationship and proximity, which are later elaborated into patterns of metaphors. Such intertwining between perceived metonymies and metaphors appears in racist discourse, which, for example, metaphorically constructs immigrants as contaminating the purity of the indigenous race, but reinforces this with persistent metonymical claims linking actual food contamination with immigrants; for instance, the claims on the startlingly racist *Bob's Truth* blog that 'Filthy Mexicans Contaminate Our Food'.[2]

One of the complications in identifying metaphor themes is that the same experience may cue different abstractions. Not only are proximity and cohesion source terms figuring relationships, but also sources for different kinds of lack of freedom. We use the word *bonds*, for example, as a metaphor for emotional attachment and also as a metaphor for restrictions to our freedom. Such uses of identical sources for different targets are called *multivalency*. Multivalency is a powerful way of creating cognitive associations between the two targets, in a kind of flawed logic, as we shall observe later.

Another problem for systematic research into metaphor themes is that some of the literature, such as *More than Cool Reason* (Lakoff & Turner 1989) with its index of conceptual metaphors, the database Master List of Metaphors at the University of Berkeley (http://cogsci.berkeley.edu/lakoff/) and Barcelona (2000), fail to specify clear criteria for identifying important conceptual metaphor themes.[3] The research undertaken at Lingnan University over the last few years attempted to establish in a more principled way the important metaphor themes for English, and to compare these with Chinese metaphors. The criteria used were: (1) To count as a significant conceptual metaphor, the theme should be realised by at least six lexical items, taken from a dictionary of contemporary English. (2) There should be at least 200 tokens of this joint set of lexical items with the relevant metaphorical meaning in the Cobuild WordsOnline database (http://www.collinswordbanks.co.uk/).[4] The website 'Metalude' (*Metaphor At Lingnan University Department of English*) is the result of these endeavours.[5] I used intuition, existing lexicographical evidence from the conceptual metaphor literature and dictionaries of metaphors, manual searches of dictionaries of contemporary English such as Cobuild, and the computer concordance database of the *Cambridge International Dictionary of English/CIDE+*, supplemented by *The Encarta Dictionary*, data from *Collins Cobuild English Guides, 7: Metaphor* (Deignan 1995), *A Thesaurus of Traditional English Metaphors* (Wilkinson 2002) and the BBC World Service radio. Examples (printed in parentheses and italicised in the data below) were mostly taken from the dictionaries, which use authentic corpora, though they were slightly modified to avoid copyright problems. For present purposes some have been replaced with web-trawled examples relating the discussed lexis more obviously to the topic of racism and immigration.

Once the important patterns of metaphor themes have been established in Metalude, it is possible to investigate them and hypothesize their ideological effects. I have made a first attempt at this in *Washing the Brain: Metaphor and Hidden Ideology* (Goatly 2007), which might be thought of as a broader version of Lakoff's *Moral Politics* (1996). The remainder of this chapter re-presents, reorders, clarifies and streamlines material from *Washing the Brain* adding more real and extensive examples. The hypothesis of this chapter is that many entrenched metaphor themes facilitate racist thinking through a false metaphoric logic, a thinking that may reinforce racist behaviour.

2   COLOUR CODING AND THE CONSTRUCTION OF RACE

The first point is that racial classification is a cultural rather than a scientific construct. It is often erroneously believed that, because of interbreeding and adaptation to different climates, people living close to each other geographically are similar not only in skin colour and facial features, but also genetically:

> Skin pigment was a sunscreen for the tropics, eyelid folds were goggles for the tundra. The parts of the body that face the elements are also the parts that face the eyes of other people, which fools them into thinking that racial differences run deeper than they really do. (Pinker 2003: 143)

The converse of this belief is that people geographically separated are genetically different. But, according to Jonathan Marks's *What It Means to Be 98% Chimpanzee* (2002),

> [t]he overwhelming bulk of detectable genetic variation in the human species is between the individuals within the same population. About 85% in fact. Another 9% of the detectable variation is between populations assigned to the same "race"; while interracial differences constitute only about 6% of the genetic variation in the human species. (82)

Nevertheless, colour is a convenient imperialist device for constructing the idea of different races. For example, Linnaeus "naturally" uses the colours red, white, yellow and black as labels for American, European, Asian and African respectively (Marks 2002: 57). And colour, although it appears to be applied as an OBJECT AS FEATURE metonymy, is often metaphorical: many so-called "blacks" have brown skin; "whites" are pinkish-grey; "red Indians" and "yellow races" the same basic skin colour, more like light brown than red or yellow.

Colour coding is the main linguistic resource for preserving the illusion of race. **Colour** itself metonymically means 'racial identity' (*he felt he had been passed over for promotion because of his colour*). In racist discourse, Caucasians are **white, whitey, lily-white, pinkies** or **palefaces**, non-Caucasians are **non-whites** or **coloured**, Afro- Caribbeans are **blacks, darkies, spades**, native Americans become **Red Indians** or **redskins**, while Chinese and other East Asians may be called **yellow**.

Caucasians have a vested interest in accepting the label **white** because of the metaphor themes GOOD IS CLEAN/WHITE as in: **white knight** 'person or organisation that rescues a company from financial difficulties', fair 'morally correct or just', **whiter than white** 'having a reputation for high moral standards', **lily-white** 'faultless in character', and even **white lie** 'harmless untruth', and **whitewash** 'cover up mistakes or bad behaviour' (cf. Randerson 2002).

The converse is the metaphor theme EVIL IS DARK/BLACK, as in **black** meaning 'bad, cruel or wicked' (*This is a blacker crime than most I've investigated*), **black and white** 'with clear distinctions between what is morally wrong and right', **black mark** 'fault or mistake that has been noted'; it can mean 'illegal', as in **black market, black economy**; or is associated with loss of reputation: **black sheep** 'bad person in a family who brings it into disrepute', and **blacken** 'destroy the good reputation of'. This prejudicial association of *black* with evil is still widespread. Peter Neufeld's programme of DNA testing to save those who have been wrongfully convicted found that

> [i]n the US most rapes of white women are committed by white men, and of black women by black men. Only about 10% of sexual assaults are cross-racial. Yet approximately 60% of all our wrongful convictions were black men wrongfully convicted of sexually assaulting, or sexually assaulting and killing, white women. (Nowak 2003: 49)

Likewise, a majority of U.S. drug-users, welfare recipients and criminals are white (Balkin 1998: 216).

The metaphor of black versus white gains much of its power from a set of interlocking oppositions or homologies:

white : black
law-abiding : criminal
morality : immorality
higher intelligence : lower intelligence
knowledge : ignorance
industry : laziness (ibid.)

EVIL IS DARK/BLACK and GOOD IS CLEAN/WHITE also link with the metaphor theme GOODNESS IS PURITY, where **pure** means 'unmixed'. A white surface can be spoilt by black marks which are of a different colour: **pure** 'morally good' (*he has pure intentions towards you*) and unalloyed, 'not spoilt by being mixed with anything negative' (*I experienced unalloyed feelings of pleasure*). Conversely, we have: **impure/impurity** 'immoral/-ity, sinful/-ness' (*I begged God to take away my impurities*), **pollute/pollution** and **contaminate** 'have a harmful effect on morals' (*The pollution of young minds by the internet continues uncontrolled*). We should remind ourselves here of the racist or eugenicist metaphors: **ethnic cleansing** 'attempt by one racial group to purge a country of another racial group' and **purify** 'remove weak people from' in sentences like *Hitler wanted to purify the German* *population*. These metaphors often have moral or religious meanings. The desire for racial and other kinds of purity may originate in the moral sphere of divinity amongst primitive societies (Pinker 2003: 273).

Keeping the races pure has been the driving force behind racial segregation, and the banning of intimate contact and mixed marriages. Until the 1950s nineteen U.S. states forbade black-white marriages, and some banned white marriages with Indians, Mongolians, Japanese, Chinese and Malays (Marks 2002: 68). The alternative view is to positively celebrate hybridity:

> By hybridity I mean a kind of mutual entanglement of self and other, a two-way exchange that results in a fusion of belief and lifestyle so that the divide between two creatures, or two cultures, is spanned. [. . .] Hybridity is also the opposite of purity. Children know that if they mix the colour blue with the colour yellow, they will get something new—the colour green. Mixing two cultures as different as yellow and blue can result in something new, and also beautiful, as green is beautiful. [. . .] But a language of hybridity does not yet exist. We are searching for it so that we will not remain speechless in a world of isms: fundamentalism, essentialism, nationalism. (Chan 2003: A13)

This passage demonstrates two points—the naturalness of using colour metaphors when talking about culture, ethnicity or race; and the author's sense that we lack a language for the concept of hybridity. I have shown that, by contrast, the conventional metaphors for purity are highly developed.

3 COMPLEX INTERACTIONS OF METAPHOR THEMES IN ANTI-IMMIGRANT IDEOLOGY

There is a racist myth and agenda that the ideal nation is made up of people who are homogenously alike—by race, by culture, by language and by shared values, and this is supported by a number of metaphor themes.[6]

3.1 CATEGORY IS A DIVIDED AREA and Its Cognitive Effects

Firstly we have CATEGORY IS DIVIDED AREA: **divide** means 'to distinguish as belonging to separate categories' (*How can we divide the middle class from the working class?*), **place** 'categorize in a particular class or group' (*The law places road rage in the same category as wife-beating*), **separate** 'to consider independently as belonging to different categories' (*You can't separate technology from morality*), **pigeon-hole** 'categorize' (*He can't be pigeon-holed as a jazz musician*).

The results of dividing are the categories or sub-categories which are divided spaces: **segment, sector** 'subcategory' (*A segment of the population of the U.S. lives in dire poverty*), **compartment** 'category' (*He keeps* *his studies and his religious beliefs in separate compartments*), **demarcation** 'separate categorization' (*In some English departments there is little demarcation between Literature and Film*).

A boundary is a line which separates spaces and therefore categories: **boundary, dividing line** 'distinction between two types of thing' (*The boundary between medicine and superstition is sometimes unclear*). Some regard the relevant conceptual metaphor as CATEGORY IS A CONTAINER. However the more general CATEGORY IS DIVIDED AREA is preferable, because a closed container has too definite a division between outside and inside. Unclear dividing lines between categories are **blurred, smudged** 'not clearly differentiated or categorized' (*The line between advertising and press reporting is becoming badly smudged/blurred*), a **grey area** 'situation difficult to categorise where the rules are uncertain' (*Surrogate motherhood is a legal grey area*). On the **borderline** means 'in or between subjects' (*Medicine is on the borderline of zoology and psychology*).

The racist myth depends upon the opposite of smudged boundaries. Moreover, the divided area, defined by the boundaries of a nation-state, or other geographical area, becomes a category, so that everything within the bounded area has to be the same or similar. The shared feature selected as the basis for this categorization is, more often than not, colour. For instance, self-governing homelands for Africans ("blacks") were part of the apartheid project.[7]

3.2   RELATIONSHIP IS PROXIMITY AND
RELATIONSHIP IS SIMILARITY

This desire for racial homogeneity within social groups is further boosted by the interaction of two metaphor themes with the same source, proximity. These are RELATIONSHIP IS PROXIMITY and SIMILARITY IS PROXIMITY.

RELATIONSHIP IS PROXIMITY is realized by the following lexis: **close** means 'intimate' and **close circle** 'an intimate group'; relatives with whom you have the most strong or intimate relationship are **next** of kin. Affection towards friends or family is **togetherness**, and if two people are **together** or **go together** they are 'intimately related romantically or sexually'.

Having physical contact or attachment is a metaphor, as well as an index or symbol, of acquaintance, affection and love: **be attached to** 'love, have affection for'; **connections** or **contacts** 'business relationships'. Often the source schema is one of tying with rope or string: **bind** 'make people feel they belong together' (*The English language binds the UK and the U.S. together and encourages political alliances*); **bond, bonding** 'close relationship'; **ties** 'friendly feelings or relationships'; **tie the knot, get spliced, get hitched,** 'get married' (*When are you going to tie the knot?*); **knit** 'unite people closely'; **close-knit** 'united'.

The second metaphor theme featuring proximity as source, SIMILARITY IS PROXIMITY, is cognitively fundamental, equating as it does two of the basic psychological gestalts of perception: if asked to group the following shapes, one is in a dilemma as the proximity gestalt and the similarity gestalt are in conflict:

Figure 13.2 Proximity vs. similarity.

SIMILARITY IS PROXIMITY uses these two gestalts in a target-source relationship. Proximity is used for similarity in general: **near to** 'very similar to' (*The sensation was near to nausea*); **close** 'very similar' (*Clare has a close resemblance to her elder sister*). Such lexemes are also used for 'approximation': **around, about, close to** (*There are around/about/close to six million people infected*); **near** (*The pound ended last year near its annual low*); or slightly more distantly: **in the region/neighbourhood/vicinity of** (*The number of tigers left in India is in the region/neighbourhood/vicinity of 2000*).

Conversely, DIFFERENCE IS DISTANCE: **remote from, far** (**different**) **from** 'very dissimilar' (*Botany might seem remote from engineering*); **a long way from** 'very different from what is desired or expected' (*He's a long way from being a popular prime minister*); **nowhere near** 'very different in amount from' (*They are nowhere near the sales target*). Difference can also be conveyed by separation: compare uses of **separate** 'different' (*Abortion and contraception are two separate issues*) and of **poles apart** 'completely different' (*In terms of musicianship Pavarotti and Domingo are poles apart*).

By association through the multivalency of PROXIMITY, therefore, RELATIONSHIP becomes SIMILARITY and according to this logic the most successful relationships will be with people similar to us. This reinforces the notion that those within a bounded space should be similar, the reversal of which gives us DIVIDED AREA IS CATEGORY: 'birds of a feather flock together.'

In an online article 'Getting Past the Bears: Racist Abuse in Middle School and the Formation of People of Color Consciousness' the author, Atlasien, who is half-Japanese, recounts the racism she suffered in middle-school. Some pertinent quotes are

Did they ever tell the black girls to go back to Africa?

Back then, I didn't know. And I had no idea how to ask. [. . .]

The black girls stuck close together. I had no interaction with them, with one exception.

[. . .]

I always looked at the black girls and wondered: what did I have in common with them? I took this question very, very seriously. If I found something in common with them, maybe I wouldn't have to feel so horribly alone.

[...]

I liked living in America. I was American because my mom and my grandparents were American and I was born in America and I lived in America.

Then, starting about second grade, I noticed that other kids started calling me names and singing funny songs at me. The other kids started telling me I didn't belong. I looked weird and I talked funny. I wasn't a real American. I should go back to China.[8]

Here the criterion for the similarity underlying the categorization and therefore for relationships is colour: 'The black girls stuck close together'. The lack of shared colour prompts the writer to wonder what she has in common with them. Moreover, the white children tell her she is not American, does not belong and should go back to China, though she has never been there, not being Chinese but half-Japanese.

Again colour as coding for race is often the criterion for the categorization of people, and for the decision on who belongs in a geographical space. The largest proportion of immigrants to the UK in the 1980s were Irish, who, being white, were not perceived as an ethnic "problem" (though perhaps a political one). The common use of the term 'visible minorities' indicates the priority given to appearance (colour, facial features) in categorizations of race and ethnicity in immigration discourse.

It is instructive to invoke, at this point, Bourdieu's exploration of class and classification:

The transition from the state of being a practical group to the state of being an instituted group (class, nation etc.), presupposes the construction of the principle of classification capable of producing the set of distinctive properties which characterize the set of members in this group, and capable also of annulling the set of non-pertinent properties which part or all of its members possess in other contexts (e.g. properties of [...] age or sex), and which might serve as the basis for other constructions. The struggle lies therefore at the very root of the construction of class (social, ethnic, sexual, etc.): every group is the site of a struggle to impose a legitimate principle of group construction, and every distribution of properties, whether it concerns sex or age, education or wealth, may serve as a basis for specifically political divisions or struggles. [...] Indeed, any attempt to institute a new division must reckon with the resistance of those who, occupying a dominant position in the space thus divided, have an interest in perpetuating a doxic relation to the social world which leads to the acceptance of established divisions as natural or to their symbolic denial through the affirmation of a higher unity (national, familial, etc.). (Bourdieu 1991: 130)

Defenders of existing classifications of society—for example by race/colour, in which they are the most powerful group—use the language of nature/evolution to justify this classification. The dominance of the most powerful group is the result of an evolutionary competitive struggle, in which that group was destined to prevail. And what could be more natural than the process of evolution except perhaps the colour of one's skin? As a consequence, the idea that those enclosed in the same space and near to each other should be similar in race/colour supports the ghetto mentality and the drive to ethnic cleansing.

3.3   Specific Divided Spaces:
SOCIAL ORGANISATION IS A BUILDING

Regarding society as a divided area or container is rather abstract, and, in practical lexicographical terms, the two most important specific kinds of container sources for the target 'society' are buildings and bodies. Let's consider the evidence for the first of these.

A whole building often stands for a society or social organisation: **house** 'financial, publishing or design company' (*He soon became head of the publishing house*); **pyramid** 'organisation with few people on the top level' (*The management pyramid is very steep*), or **citadel** 'powerful organisation that defends a particular belief or way of life' (*The Monday Club was the citadel of racism in the 1970s*).

The parts or materials of buildings will normally be the parts or materials of a society: **cornerstone** 'something on which society depends' (*Christian heritage is the* cornerstone *of our most cherished civic principles*); **pillar of** 'person who works to maintain or improve a group' (*For years he was a pillar of the music society*) or **fabric** 'basic structure of a society or organisation' (*Immigrants are seen . . . as racial* threats *to the social and cultural* fabric *of American society*).

Creating or improving a society will be metaphorised as building or repairing it: **build** 'create or improve a society or organisation' (*He wanted to build a more equal society*); **rebuild/reconstruct** 'restore, change so that it works more effectively' (*We reconstructed the education system from the bottom up*); **shore up** 'help to function better' (*The government lent billions of dollars in the hope of shoring up the banking system*). Conversely, destroying society will be like destroying or threatening the stability of a building: **shake/rock** ([to] the foundations) 'threaten to destroy the whole (organisation)' (*The scandal shook the party to its foundations*). Analogously, the disintegration of a society is figured as the disintegration of a building: **crumble** 'become gradually weaker' (*Society is crumbling largely due to unemployment*); **collapse** 'failure or end of existence' (*California is near total collapse under the weight of immigration*).

More important in terms of immigration is the way this metaphor is elaborated in terms of being in, or moving in or out of a building. For being or moving in we have: **internal** 'happening or existing inside a country or organisation' (*The New Zealand Department of Internal Affairs encompasses heritage, identity services, community development, etc.*); **enter/ entry** 'join/-ing' (*He entered the country a year ago*); **open-door** 'allowing people or goods to come freely into a place or country' (*Australia's open-door policy on immigrants was abandoned in the late '90s*); **get in through the back door** 'join an organisation or society by unconventional or unfair means' (*Most Mexicans claiming refugee status in Canada are queue jumpers trying to "immigrate to Canada through the back door"*). Conversely, for being, keeping or moving out we have: **external** 'from another organisation or country' (*The U.S. couldn't finance its external deficit by borrowing from private creditors*); **exclude, bar** 'prevent from joining' (*The Australian policy was to exclude families with disabled children*), **expel, sling out, throw out** 'force to leave an organisation or country' (*Italy: Minister says government must expel immigrants who fail to integrate*).

These building metaphors for social groups are probably much influenced by our childhood experiences, as Lakoff's experiential theory predicts. After all, the prototypical building is our house or apartment. Those inside this secure home are typically family, sharing blood relations, and can be opposed to outside, alien and threatening beings. The state or house has control within a clear-cut boundary or wall, its territory or home, with no overlapping of homes or territories. The boundary or walls set up an inclusive/exclusive distinction—you are either in or out, and cannot belong to more than one home or family. The home provides stability and permanence 'by means of exclusion rather than by any other means that are available to human societies' (Chilton 1996: 64). In modern racist societies this metaphor theme expresses itself as the exclusion of immigrants. Keeping racial or national categories separate also meshes with GOOD IS PURE/UNMIXED.

3.4   "Threats" to the Body Politic:
DISEASE IS INVASION → INVASION IS DISEASE

We saw in sections 3.1 and 3.2 that, since categories are divided areas or containers, we can constitute a nation-state with its boundaries in terms of a classification: and according to racist thinking the similarities forming the basis of the classification and the basis for relationships could be visual, primarily colour-related. In section 3.3 we saw that one specific kind of experientially-primary container is the house or childhood home, the space for experiencing family relationships, from which 'outsiders' (prototypically not genetically related) are excluded. When this building becomes the metaphorical source for society, then we identify the excluded outsiders with foreigners.

However, an even more fundamentally experiential container is the human body. Through the basic bodily processes of feeding and excretion as infants we experience the difference between inside and outside and the transitions between them. This section shows how racist thinking might exploit the metaphor themes SOCIAL ORGANISATION IS A BODY, especially as it can be related to DISEASE IS INVASION.

A social organisation is often metaphorised as a body. In fact this metaphor, famously expressed in *Coriolanus* (I, i, 94–156), can be traced back at least as far as Plato, the Roman orator Cicero and St Paul (I Corinthians, ch. 12, vv. 12–21). Current English includes the following lexis: **body** 'organisation or institution' (*We need a new body to regulate genetic modification*); **body politic** 'all citizens of a state' (*Democracy involves the whole body politic in decisions*). A social organisation may also be personified as a person or relation: **parent** 'organisation which created and controls another' (*The zoo's parent body is the Zoological Society of Beijing*); **sister** 'organisation that has close connections with another organisation' (*The International Monetary Fund has a sister organisation, the World Bank*); **neighbour** 'country next to another' (*Uganda is a neighbour of Rwanda*).

Parts of society/organisation are metaphorically body parts: **head** 'leader of an organisation or state' (*The meeting brought together seven heads of state*); **arm** 'part of an organisation responsible for a particular place or activity' (*The British Council acted as the arm of the aid organisation*); **backbone** 'most necessary and effective members' (*Women are the backbone of the church*).

If an organisation or society is in a bad state it suffers from disease: **ills, pestilence, malady** 'serious problems or difficulties' (*Thanks to Mayor Lou Barletta, the pestilence of illegal immigration has not stayed in the proverbial shadows*); **disease** 'bad attitude, habit or situation' (*The real disease affecting the country is poor levels of education*); **epidemic** 'repeated antisocial activity or behaviour' (*What shall we do to tackle the illegal immigration epidemic in the U.S.?*); **cancer/canker** 'evil activity or force which destroys' (*Corruption is still a canker in the Ghanaian society*).

Since the late nineteenth century the dominant metaphor for disease has been invasion, replacing the medieval (and Chinese) metaphor of disease as imbalance. This constructs disease of any kind (whether caused by bacteria/viruses or not) as an **attack** by **invaders** 'viruses or bacteria', or **foreign bodies** from outside. The bacteria **invade**, i.e. 'enter the body', and may **strike down**, i.e. 'cause illness or death' to the victims, if they **succumb** 'become ill'. However, the body may **defend** itself, **fight, combat**, i.e. 'struggle to survive' the disease, for instance through resistance 'immune response'. Medicine as a war of defence can attempt to **conquer** or **vanquish** 'eliminate' a disease once and for all (though the military may keep stocks for biological warfare).

In racist anti-immigrant thinking the workings of DISEASE IS INVASION is complicated by its reversal into INVASION IS DISEASE, exploiting the cognitive association between target and source. This is possible because immigrants are often regarded as invading soldiers (Mehan 1997), 'foot-soldiers in these criminal organisations' (Santa Ana 1999: 205). A more current example is the following: "Silvio Berlusconi branded illegal immigrants an 'army of evil' yesterday in his first day in office after winning Italy's general election."[9]

David Huntwork, in the online magazine *Renew America*, uses the immigrants as invaders metaphor while attempting to retaliate against alleged Mexican claims to American territory:

> This is 'their land,' stolen from Mexico, and the concepts of borders and national citizenship are inherently racist. The implication seems to be that we should all somehow transport ourselves back to pre-1492 borders. It is a far more racist argument than any I've heard from those seeking to stem the illegal immigrant invasion.[10]

So by a loose metaphorical logic of multivalent sources equating common targets, IMMIGRANTS ARE INVADERS in conjunction with DISEASE IS INVASION reinforces the conclusion that IMMIGRANTS ARE DISEASE, a view prevalent in anti-Semitic discourse during the reign of National Socialism (cf. Pinker 2003: 154). That these associations are still current can be seen in the numerous articles in the press.[11]

When Michelle Malkin used the headline 'Immigration still plagues U.S.' for her anti-immigrant article, a reader turned her discourse against her:

> The hypocrisy of Michelle Malkin is mind blowing. The same immigration that "plagues" America is the same immigration that allowed her family to come here from the Philippines in the first place. Is she calling her family a plague? Referring to immigrants as "invaders" or as a "plague" are mere code words used to characterize people as sub-human and inferior—just as it has been done during every major civil and human rights atrocities [sic].[12]

According to Susan Sontag, in medieval Europe associating foreignness and disease was conceived of as a metonymy of cause and effect and less as a metaphor: "Massacres of Jews in unprecedented numbers took place everywhere in plague-stricken Europe of 1347–8; they stopped as soon as the plague receded" (Sontag 1991: 72). Even nowadays there are similar reactions to disease: "Authoritarian political ideologies have a vested interest in promoting fear, a sense of the imminence of takeover by aliens—and real diseases are useful material. Epidemic diseases usually elicit a call to ban the entry of foreigners, immigrants. And xenophobic propaganda has always depicted immigrants as bearers of disease" (147).[13]

Reinforcing this pattern of association between foreignness and disease is the tendency to label diseases, in English, with the names of foreign countries—Hong Kong flu, Japanese encephalitis, German measles, Dutch elm disease and so on. When syphilis first spread at the end of the fifteenth century, "it was 'the French pox' to the English, the *morbus Germanicus* to the Parisians, 'the Naples sickness' to the Florentines, 'the Chinese disease' to the Japanese" (Sontag 1991: 133).

Indeed, it has been tragically true in the history of North and South America that the white man's invasion spread new diseases. For instance, by 1805 smallpox and malaria had killed ninety percent of the Indian population of the lower Columbia River basin (Josephson 2002: 42). So the metaphor of invading foreigners as disease might in some cases reflect a real metonymic relationship of cause and effect. My major point is that *it is the selection of this particular metonymy*, IMMIGRATION AS DISEASE, *and its metaphorical elaboration* which are ideological. One could equally well select more positive metonymies as one's basis for metaphors; the colourfulness of West African clothes on the streets of London, the stimulation to one's palate of the spicy foods brought by immigrants. After all, according to Voltaire in *Candide* (1759), not only syphilis, but also chocolate came from the New World. A second point is that, although the history of the Columbia River basin vouches for the factual metonymy of invasion and disease, this is actually a reversal, if not a deconstruction, of the more familiar metaphoric pattern where it is non-whites who are perceived as the disease-ridden invaders of white lands.

In passages like the following we can even see etymological vestiges of the metaphorical association of disease, invasion and immigration: "The report—which recommended a 3-year moratorium on immigration nationwide and linked illegal immigration to a **host** of society's **ills**—has been branded by Latino and Asian leaders as insensitive and one-sided".[14] Here the word *ills*, meaning 'disease', is alliteratively linked to illegal immigration, and the lexeme *host*, meaning 'army'[15] is likewise indirectly linked to immigration by representing disease as an invading army.

3.5 The Ideological Threat to the Body Politic: IDEA IS DISEASE

Besides keeping out other races, the nationalist/racist myth also seeks to preserve intact and pure the nation's values, uninfluenced by foreign morally-suspect ideas. This, therefore, necessitates the containment of thoughts as well as people. The health of the body politic is also threatened by ideas, since IDEA IS DISEASE.

Ideas and emotions can be a **bug** 'enthusiasm' that is **contagious, catching** or **infectious** 'easily communicated to many people' (*China can no longer protect itself from the contagious foreign ideas on the internet*).

The effects of these ideas and the accompanying emotions can often cause harm: **poison** 'introduce a harmful idea into the mind' (*Young minds all over the world are being poisoned by consumerism*); or be harmful: **noxious** 'harmful and unpleasant' (*These noxious attitudes towards Moslems are a danger to peace*).

According to this metaphorical thinking, external ideological disease must be prevented from penetrating our own body politic: "If communism is viewed as [. . .] disease it follows metaphorically that its spread needs to be contained" (Chilton 1996: 153). Sometimes a metonymic relation holds between military invasion and the spread of ideology, as suggested in the following extract from Dean Acheson's reminiscences on his briefing of Congress about the Truman Doctrine:

> No time was left for appraisal. In the last eighteen months, I said, Soviet pressure on the Straits, on Iran and on northern Greece had brought the Balkans to the point of where a highly possible Soviet breakthrough might open three continents to Soviet penetration. Like apples in a rotten barrel **infected** by one rotten one, the **corruption** of Greece would **infect** Iran and all to the east. It would also **carry infection** through Asia Minor and Egypt, and to Europe through Italy and France, already threatened by the strongest domestic communist parties in Western Europe. (Acheson 1987: 219; my bolding)

Now that the U.S. has a new enemy, not communism but Muslim fundamentalism, such metaphors are predictable applied to radical "jihadists" by the Hudson Institute: "A Virulent Ideology in Mutation: Zaqarwi Upstages Maqdisi".[16] Note the extension of the underlying 'virus' metaphor by the lexeme *mutation*, indicating the author is aware of the metaphor (perhaps pushing it closer to level 5 in Table 13.1). A recent Google search immediately furnished eight examples of the phrase *infectious ideology* too.

4   SUMMARY AND CONCLUSION: THE PLACE OF LEXICOLOGICAL METAPHOR STUDY IN CRITICAL METAPHOR ANALYSIS

I have argued that the racist anti-immigration exploitation of metaphor themes, as discussed in the chapter, operates as follows, given the already metaphorical construction of the concept of race by colour coding. There are certain fundamental cognitive metaphors like CATEGORY IS A DIVIDED AREA/CONTAINER, SIMILARITY IS PROXIMITY, RELATIONSHIP IS PROXIMITY, SOCIETY IS BODY and DISEASE IS INVASION which, while not directly related to racist lexis, nevertheless provide a cognitive template and are recruited to interactively reinforce metaphors of exclusion and inclusion, particularly the exclusion of foreigners/disease.

We can now sum up the kind of metaphorical 'logic' or argument by analogy and association which the interaction of these themes leads to. Since SIMILARITY IS PROXIMITY and RELATIONSHIP IS PROXIMITY, relationships are preferable between similars, maybe those similar in colour; this is a case of multivalency, one source with different targets, equating targets. Logically this may lead to category confusion, by which the ambiguity of the source conflates the targets. Or, metonymically, the ambiguity affects behaviour, with similarity causing/creating relationships.

Since RACE IS COLOUR those similar in colour belong to the same category. And since, metaphorically, CATEGORY IS A DIVIDED AREA, so a divided space or container (e.g. a society, SOCIETY IS BUILDING or BODY) might become a category, with those inside it the same according to the colour criteria for the category. This move depends upon the reversal of target and source (CATEGORY IS DIVIDED AREA → DIVIDED AREA IS CATEGORY). Providing we assume that neat categories are desirable, people are categorized according to certain criteria, and the most salient criterion for classification is colour, the constitution of monochromatic categories follows logically. But whether these categories are constituted as geographical and political areas depends upon the association of containers with categories.

This possibility of instantiating the source (DIVIDED AREA) as a literal target, a nation-state with its boundaries, is reinforced by another case of multivalency (equated targets): CATEGORY IS DIVIDED AREA/CONTAINER and SOCIETY IS CONTAINER (BUILDING or BODY) → SOCIETY IS CATEGORY. Moreover, since the metaphor SOCIETY IS A BUILDING obtains, there is already a strong cognitive association between society and a kind of divided area. This is reinforced by our childhood experiences of the family home, a container for those genetically related.

In addition, we looked at the SOCIAL ORGANISATION IS A BODY and DISEASE IS INVASION metaphors, which suggest that if IMMIGRATION IS INVASION immigrants are a disease that needs to be kept out. This is a further case of multivalent sources (INVASION) leading to the metaphorical equation of the two targets. Moreover, if an IDEA IS A DISEASE, ideas (brought by immigrants or not) threaten the state of health of the body politic, especially when foreign ideology is represented by an army. This 'logic' depends upon two compatible source schemas DISEASE and BODY interrelating or expanding to include each other, in ways which mirror our experience of bodies and diseases. If the validity of these metaphor themes is assumed, then the two schemas logically interact.

There is, however, an irrationality in the so-called metaphorical 'logic' of purity and the defence of the body politic against invasion: many bacteria are, in fact, benign. Isolating ourselves from other organisms and regarding them as invaders to be killed is counterproductive in treating or preventing many diseases or the spread of infections. After all, we live in symbiosis with bacteria, especially in our stomachs and intestines; ninety percent of the dried weight of our faeces comprise the bodies of gut microbes, and we all carry with us twenty times as many living bacteria as we do human cells. We have co-evolved with them in some kind of equilibrium (Ryan 2002: 231). Our bodies, too, consist of a variety of organs with different functions working together and interdependently. As the world faces economic and ecological crises, we need to be positive about biodiversity and the diversity of culture and ideas and avoid tribalism and scapegoating. Yet these developments are stalled, most basically, by our discourse whose dominant metaphors reinforce non-cooperation, exclusiveness and homogeneity.

I have tried to develop and analyse possible cognitive networks and interplays between metaphor themes which underlie racist and anti-immigration thinking. The precise order in which these metaphor themes interact is not really crucial; what is crucial is the existence of this network of mutually-reinforcing themes which encourage racist concepts.

Finally, let's place this kind of cognitive critical analysis in relation to other traditions of cognitive and discoursal metaphor research. What is the relationship of my project here and in *Washing the Brain* (Goatly 2007) to the work of Lakoff, particularly his *Moral Politics* (1996)? Lakoff claims that political thinking in the U.S. is dominated by the metaphor SOCIETY IS A FAMILY. Right-wing political thinking invokes metaphors centred on the Strict Father Family, whereas left-wing or liberal thinking relies on less well-developed metaphors centred on the Nurturant Parent Family. He suggests that many reasonable U.S. citizens think in right-wing or conservative ways, simply because their cognition is dominated by Strict Father Family metaphors. He laments liberals' lack of alternative well-developed conceptual metaphors (metaphor theme), as this stacks the odds against them in political argument, which is fundamentally metaphorical.

Of particular interest is Lakoff's argument that the Strict Father model "metaphorically" equates morality with boundaries, homogeneity and purity. The need for boundaries links back to our exploration of the theme CATEGORY IS A DIVIDED AREA, a theme which interacted dangerously, as we have seen, with ideas of SIMILARITY IS PROXIMITY, RELATIONSHIP IS PROXIMITY/COHESION, GOODNESS IS PURITY. Lakoff claims this morality breeds a divisive culture of exclusion and blame, appealing to the worst human instincts, stereotyping, demonizing and punishing the Other simply for being different, and leading to racism, militarism and the horrors of Bosnia, Rwanda, Somalia and the Ku Klux Klan (1996: 383).

However, in regard to racism, it is difficult to consistently apply Lakoff's binary distinction between Nurture and Strict Parenting. Lakoff claims that the emphasis given to Moral Strength, Moral Authority and Moral Order in the Strict Father family metaphor puts it out of touch with the priority given to human flourishing and empathy of the Nurturant Parent metaphor (1996: 382). However, right-wing theories do not give up the nurturing parent value but apply it to the nurturing of the race/nation rather than individuals. As part of the nation immigrants need nurturing, too, because they are guests, if not members, of the family (186–88).

Lakoff's *Moral Politics* aside, where does this article stand in relation to other critical linguistic work on metaphor? There are three main ways of approaching metaphor theory and its relationship to language.[17] (A) To look at individual texts and analyse the use of metaphors within them, e.g. Cameron (2003), Koller (2004), Musolff (2004), Charteris-Black (2005). (B) To generalise about metaphor use by applying concordancing techniques to a corpus of texts, e.g. Deignan (2005). (C) To use as data the intuitions of native speakers about the metaphors they use in the generative grammar tradition in which Lakoff was nurtured. In practice researchers often combine these approaches. The approach I have taken here is at a higher level of generality than (B) (though with some examples from real texts as in [A]) but without moving into the intuitive tradition of (C). My data is mainly the conventional metaphorical lexis found in contemporary dictionaries of English, themselves based on concordance data (B), and which provided evidence for the lexis instantiating the metaphor themes specified in Metalude.

As already pointed out, however, conceptual metaphor themes implicated in racist and anti-immigrant thought are not always directly related to the lexis instantiated in the concordance data of approach (B) or in the discourse analysed in approach (A). Rather, they provide a resource for reinforcing or a platform for creating these more explicitly racist metaphors; so to characterize my approach as neatly related to (B) and (A) would be too simple.

Nevertheless, to strengthen the suggestions in this chapter, more analysis of instantiations of these metaphors in discourse (according to approach A) should be attempted, as oftentimes the particular uses in co-text and context play out subtle or not so subtle variations on the dictionary meaning. Moreover, the hypothesis presented in this chapter needs to be tested, not only against a larger corpus of discoursal behaviour, but by sociological and ethnographic studies to show whether use of these metaphor themes' lexis in fact correlates with racist behaviour.

NOTES

1. In the following all metaphorical lexemes in example passages will be printed in bold.
2. Retrieved from http://bobstruth.blogspot.com/2007/10/filthy-mexicans-contaminate-our-food. html (May 2, 2009).
3. The result is that the formula X IS Y has become quite ambiguous in the literature. Some writers simply use this formula for any metaphor, while others, as did Lakoff and Johnson (1980) originally, use it to represent a pattern or theme. Still others attempt to justify this typography on the basis of cognitive categories, without any hard or lexical evidence.
4. The research was funded by the Research Grants Council of the Hong Kong SAR, project reference LC3001/99H.
5. http://www.ln.edu.hk/lle/cwd03/lnproject_chi/home.html.
6. See the following extracts from the British National Party webpage on immigration policy:

Given current demographic trends, we, the indigenous British people, will become an ethnic minority in our own country well within sixty years—and most likely sooner. All the signs are there: [. . .]—Fourteen percent of all primary school children do not have English as a mother tongue;—At least 316 primary schools in England have a large majority of children whose first language is not English; [. . .] All these facts point inexorably to the overwhelming and extinguishing of Britain and British identity under a tsunami of immigration. [. . .] We want Britain to remain—or return to—the way it has traditionally been. We accept that Britain always will have ethnic minorities and have no problem with this as long as they remain minorities and do not change nor seek to change the fundamental culture and identity of the indigenous peoples of the British Isles [. . .] . Can anyone imagine Saudi Arabia allowing the mass immigration of Christians, so that in a few decades it would no longer be an Islamic country? Each nation has the right to maintain its own identity. The right of India to remain Indian, the right of China to remain Chinese, the right of Pakistan to remain Pakistani and the right of Saudi Arabia to remain Saudi does not mean that any of these nations "hate" anybody else. All it means is that they wish to preserve their identity and national existence. This is all the British National Party seeks for Britain—the right to be British. (Retrieved from http://www.bnp.org. uk/policies/immigration, August 16, 2010)

7. Compare http://www.worldstatesmen.org/South_African_homelands.html (April 29, 2009).

8. Retrieved from http://www.racialicious.com/2008/12/16/getting-past-the-bears-racist-abuse-in-middle-school-and-the-formation-of-people-of-color-consciousness/ (April 29, 2009).

9. Retrieved from www.telegraph.co.uk/ news/ worldnews/1895799/Silvio-Berlusconi-says-illegal-migrants-are-army-of-evil.html (May 1, 2009).

10. Retrieved from http://www.renewamerica.us/columns/huntwork/060618 (May 1, 2009).

11. See, for instance, the article from *Magharebia* entitled 'Illegal Immigration Plagues Algeria', retrieved from http://www.magharebia.com/cocoon/awi/ xhtml1/en_GB/features/awi/features/2005/08/24/feature-02 (May 2. 2009) or the article 'Italy: Illegal and Mass Immigration Plague the Country', retrieved from http://torchlight.typepad.com/torchlight/2009/04/italy-illegal-and-mass-immigration-plague-the-country.html (May 2, 2009).

12. Posted by "Casiopeia" on January 8, 2009, at 11:22 a.m. Retrieved from http://www.gosanangelo.com/news/2009/jan/08/michelle-malkin-immigration-still-plagues-us/#comments (May 2, 2009).

13. Compare "Conservatives Scapegoating Mexican-Immigrants over Swine Flu Pandemic", retrieved from http://sensico.wordpress.com/2009/04/28/conservatives-scapegoating-mexican-immigrants-over-swine-flu-pandemic/ (May 1, 2009).

14. *Los Angeles Times*, June 29, 1993, p. B1; quoted in Santa Ana (1999: 205); my bolding.

15. Interestingly *host* is both ambiguous in English, 'army' and 'welcomer of guests', and even more so in the Latin from which it derives, *hospes*: 'visitor', 'stranger' or 'innkeeper', 'host'. See also J. Hillis Miller's "The Critic as Host" (1979: 217–53).

16. Retrieved from http://www.futureofmuslimworld.com/research/detail/ a-virulent-ideology-in-mutation-zarqawi-upstages-maqdis (May 2, 2009).

17. For a far more comprehensive overview of the field see Steen (2007).

WORKS CITED

Acheson, Dean (1987) *Present at the Creation: My Years in the State Department*. New York: Norton.

Balkin, Jack M. (1998) *Cultural Software*. New Haven and London: Yale University Press.

Barcelona, Antonio (2000) Ed. *Metaphor and Metonymy at the Crossroads*. New York and Berlin: de Gruyter.

Bourdieu, Pierre (1991) *Language and Symbolic Power*. Ed. John B. Thompson, Transl. Gino Raymond and Matthew Adamson. Cambridge: Polity Press.

Cameron, Lynne (2003) *Metaphor in Educational Discourse*. London: Continuum.

Chan, Kwok-bun (2003) "The Importance of Sympathy". *South China Morning Post* December 20, 2003: A13.

Charteris-Black, Jonathan (2005) *Politicians and Rhetoric: The Persuasive Power of Metaphor*. Basingstoke: Palgrave-Macmillan.

Chilton, Paul A. (1996) *Security Metaphors: Cold War Discourse from Containment to Common House*. New York: Peter Lang.

Deignan, Alice (1995) *Collins Cobuild English Guides 7: Metaphor*. London: HarperCollins.

———. (2005) *Metaphor and Corpus Linguistics*. Amsterdam: John Benjamins.

Fairclough, Norman (2001) *Language and Power*. Second Edition. Harlow: Longman.

Goatly, Andrew (2007) *Washing the Brain: Metaphor and Hidden Ideology*. Amsterdam: John Benjamins.

Josephson, Paul R. (2002) *Industrialized Nature: Brute-Force Technology and the Transformation of the Natural World*. London: Shearwater Books.

Koller, Veronica (2004) *Metaphor and Gender in Business Media Discourse: A Clinical Cognitive Study*. Basingstoke: Macmillan.

Lakoff, George (1987) *Women, Fire and Dangerous Things*. Chicago: University of Chicago Press.

———. (1996) *Moral Politics: What Conservatives Know That Liberals Don't*. Chicago and London: University of Chicago Press.

Lakoff, George, and Mark Johnson (1980) *Metaphors We Live By*. Chicago: University of Chicago Press.

Lakoff, George, and Mark Turner (1989) *More than Cool Reason: A Field Guide to Poetic Metaphor*. Chicago: University of Chicago Press.

Leroy Little Bear and Ryan Heavy Head (2004) "A Conceptual Anatomy of the Blackfoot Word". *Revision: A Journal of Consciousness and Transformation* 26.3: 3138.

Locke, John (1959) *An Essay Concerning Human Understanding* [1690]. Ed. Alexander Campbell Fraser. New York: Dover.

Marks, Jonathan (2002) *What It Means to Be 98% Chimpanzee*. Berkeley: University of California Press.

Mehan, Hugh (1997) "The Discourse of the Illegal Immigration Debate". *Discourse and Society* 8.2: 249–70.

Miller, J. Hillis (1979) "The Critic as Host". *Deconstruction and Criticism*. Eds. Harold Bloom et al. New York: Seabury. 217–53.

Musolff, Andreas (2004) *Metaphor and Political Discourse*. Basingstoke: Palgrave-Macmillan.

Nowak, Rachel (2003) "Rough Justice". *New Scientist* June 7, 2003: 49–50.

O'Halloran, Kieran (2003) *Critical Discourse Analysis and Language Cognition*. Edinburgh: Edinburgh University Press.

Paprotté, Wolf, and René Dirven (1985) Eds. *The Ubiquity of Metaphor*. Amsterdam: John Benjamins.

Pinker, Steven (2003) *The Blank Slate*. Harmondsworth: Allen Lane, Penguin.

Randerson, James (2002) "Cleanliness Is Next to Godliness". *New Scientist* June 1, 2002: 8.

Ryan, Frank (2002) *Darwin's Blind Spot: Evolution beyond Natural Selection*. New York: Houghton Mifflin.

Santa Ana, Otto (1999) "Like an Animal I Was Treated; Anti-immigrant Metaphor in US Public Discourse". *Discourse and Society* 10.2: 191–224.

Sontag, Susan (1991) *Illness as Metaphor and AIDS and Its Metaphors*. Harmondsworth: Penguin.

Sperber, Dan, and Deirdre Wilson (1995) *Relevance: Communication and Cognition*. Oxford: Blackwell.

Steen, Gerard (2007) *Finding Metaphor in Grammar and Usage*. Amsterdam: John Benjamins.

Thompson, John B. *(1990)* Ideology *and Modem Culture*. Cambridge: Polity Press.

van Dijk, Teun A. (1998) *Ideology: A Multidisciplinary Approach*. London: Sage.

Voltaire, Francois (1991) *Candide: ou l'optimisme* [1759]. Paris: Hachette Education.

Wilkinson, Peter R. (2002) *A Thesaurus of Traditional English Metaphors*. London: Routledge.

14 The JOURNEY Metaphor and the Source-Path-Goal Schema in Agnès Varda's Autobiographical GLEANING Documentaries

Charles Forceville

1 INTRODUCTION

Les glaneurs et la glaneuse (*The Gleaners and I*, dir. Agnès Varda, 2000) was a remarkable success, in both the director's native country France and abroad. The many enthusiastic reactions Varda received in response to the documentary inspired her to make a sequel, *Les glaneurs et la glaneuse . . . deux ans après* (*The Gleaners and I: Two Years Later*, 2002). The films are unusual in their apparently episodic structure and in the high degree of interpretative freedom spectators seem to enjoy. In fact, however, Varda's two non-fictional "road movies" (see Cohan & Hark 1997) are profoundly structured by two interrelated conceptual metaphors. The first one is A LIFE IS A JOURNEY (Lakoff 1993: 223; Johnson 1993: 167), which—since it is the goal-pursuing aspect of life that is at stake here—I will reformulate as A QUEST IS A JOURNEY. The second metaphor that helps impose coherence on Varda's complex films is A STORY IS A JOURNEY. In order to capture the interrelations between the two metaphors, it is necessary to examine the schema that underlies their central elements, quest, story and journey: the "Source-Path-Goal" schema.

This chapter sets out to demonstrate that the central metaphors A QUEST IS A JOURNEY and A STORY IS A JOURNEY, both rooted in the "Source-Path-Goal" (henceforth SPG) schema, strongly steer viewers' interpretations of Varda's films. The goal of this exercise is threefold. In the first place, since the SPG schema is often used metaphorically (Katz & Taylor 2008; Ritchie 2008), demonstrating its pertinence to films will shed light on the Cognitive Metaphor Theory (CMT) axiom that metaphor primarily governs thought, and only derivatively governs language (Lakoff & Johnson 1980, 1999; see also Johnson 2007). In this respect, the current chapter ties in with my larger project of confronting CMT claims by considering them in the light of multimodal rather than verbal-only manifestations of metaphor (e.g. Forceville 2005a, 2006a, 2006b, 2008a, 2008b; Forceville & Jeulink, forthcoming; see also Forceville & Urios-Aparisi 2009). In the second place, the intention is to show that the

SPG schema is a useful instrument for analysing films that, in one way or another, are "road movies", and to help theorize their generic features. Finally, although no exhaustive interpretation of the documentaries can be claimed, it is hoped that the analyses provide non-trivial insights into Varda's extraordinary films.

2   THE SOURCE-PATH-GOAL SCHEMA

The SPG schema is one of the most important structures in human thinking (Johnson 1987; Lakoff 1993). It manifests itself most literally in movement: a human being runs, crawls, jumps, rides, flies, sails or moves by any other means from one place ("source") via a trajectory ("path") to another place ("goal"). The prototypical movement is walking, an ability that depends on the human body possessing two legs permitting—typically forward—motion as well as on certain motor skills. I will retain the commonly used term JOURNEY for this literal level of the SPG schema, but I will alternate it with the term RELOCATION, which does not evoke JOURNEY's cultural, goal-related connotations.

Since human beings usually move from A to B with a purpose, arriving at B tends to be equivalent with having achieved something, ranging from getting to the fridge in order to fetch a beer to reaching the destination of a long pilgrimage. Consequently, it is probably no coincidence that we systematically use the language of journeys to describe and conceptualize the never-ending quests we undertake in our lives—that even sum up our lives. Indeed, one of Lakoff and Johnson's (1980, 1999) most radical claims is that human beings systematically understand abstract things in terms of concrete things, the latter deserving that status by virtue of being visible, audible, graspable, smellable, touchable, tasteable—in short, by being "embodied". If Lakoff and Johnson are right, metaphorically structuring the abstract in terms of the concrete is indispensable to come to grips with abstract phenomena. This being said, it has increasingly become accepted in CMT that this concrete, embodied knowledge is heavily complemented by cultural knowledge (e.g. Emanatian 1995; Yu 1998; Gibbs & Steen 1999; Kövecses 2005; Caballero 2006; Forceville, Hekkert & Tan 2006). Let me call this second, purpose-oriented manifestation of the SPG schema the QUEST level.

A third domain in which the SPG schema manifests itself is storytelling. A prototypical story has parts that follow one another in a certain order: usually the beginning is followed by a middle and closed off by an ending. A story may be *straightforward* or it may *meander*, a narrator sometimes *digresses*, or, particularly in film, events sometimes occur in *fast forward*, alternatively lose tempo in *slow motion*, or start *in medias res*. Prototypical narrating, then, is metaphorically following a path from a beginning, via various developments, to a conclusion. Let me call this third manifestation of the SPG schema the STORY level.

There is a fourth concept that is deeply structured by the SPG schema: TIME. The rationale of the TIME IS A MOVING OBJECT metaphor, and its complement TIME IS STATIONARY AND WE MOVE THROUGH IT, discussed in Lakoff and Johnson (1980: ch. 9) and Lakoff (1993), seems evident. Briefly, Western calculations of time depend on planetary movements in the first place, and when human beings move through space, this takes time. This manifestation of the SPG schema constitutes the TIME level.

In the road-movie genre these levels are "naturally" conflated: a hero or heroine departs from somewhere to somewhere else (JOURNEY), which takes TIME; wants to achieve something (QUEST); and the film tells the tale of the journey-cum-quest (STORY) (see Campbell 2008/1949 for an erudite characterization of the typical hero's enterprise). This apparent "naturalness" resides in the fact that all of these concepts are elaborations of the highly embodied SPG schema (Johnson 1993: ch. 7). It is not surprising, then, that humans conceive of abstract phenomena such as time, questing and narrating in terms of the SPG schema. More specifically, it gives rise to the conceptual metaphors TIME IS MOVEMENT, A QUEST IS A JOURNEY and A STORY IS A JOURNEY. Given that the isomorphism between relocating from one place to another, the passing of time, going on a quest and telling a story are all rooted in the SPG schema, the levels often enable the kind of synthesizing conflation that Fauconnier and Turner call "blending" (e.g. Turner 1996: ch. 5; Fauconnier 1997; Fauconnier & Turner 2002). In the terminology of blending theory, the SPG schema constitutes the so-called "generic space" where all the shared elements are found (such as beginning, trajectory and end); JOURNEY, QUEST, STORY and TIME form the "input spaces", allowing for many correspondences; and in particular instances in a road movie or travel documentary (or in a novel, a musical or any other narrative pertaining to a journey), the "blended space" merges elements from two, three or even all four of these input spaces. Concrete examples of such blends will be discussed with reference to Varda's two documentaries later in this chapter. But first it is important to insist that although the blends appear natural and self-evident they are nonetheless *blends*—that is, they combine elements from *different* input spaces; while showing structural similarities, the input spaces are not identical.

It is clear that the literal level of the SPG schema, "movement", does not necessarily involve intention or agency. A marble that falls off a table and rolls on the floor, for instance, exemplifies the SPG schema in beginning its movement at a certain point, following a certain trajectory due to certain physical forces and coming to a standstill at a certain point—but it exemplifies no agency. By contrast, a person's movement is typically a willed, physical relocation from A to B. Since this willed physical relocation usually has a purpose, the level of RELOCATION/JOURNEY already encroaches upon the level of the QUEST. But if we define a quest as a search-for-something with a certain magnitude or grandeur, it makes sense to distinguish between these two levels. The ten steps to the fridge, a trip to the supermarket and walking the dog all serve some purpose, but they do not, under normal circumstances, qualify as quests—although they may contribute to one. Quests pertain to grander purposes, such as competing for a prize, training to become the best, studying for a degree, marrying the prince, winning the lottery, overcoming a trauma or finding a lost one. Quests involve spending energy, money and hope; success or failure have substantial consequences in terms of material well-being, self-esteem, prestige, health and happiness. There is a difference, therefore, between mere purposive relocations and quests.

Prototypical stories, finally, are always about protagonists' quests, not about their relocations per se. But while stories and quests often coincide, they are not identical, since not every quest makes it into a story. I postulate as a criterion for something to qualify as a story that it is by definition *shared*. If somebody has embarked upon a quest, but fails to share the pursuit of whatever it is she pursues with anybody else, this quest does not make it to the story level. As such, this still excludes few situations: we usually tell stories about our quests to beloveds, friends, family and colleagues. Stories about quests that are the subject of this chapter, however, differ from such homely ones in at least one important respect: they are created to be shared with a mass audience. This means that, far more so than private stories, they need to have a certain *form* (which in narratology is equivalent to "syuzhet" or "plot"—see e.g. Bordwell 1985: 50), or even *format*. The fact that these public stories are to be absorbed by strangers (rather than spouses, parents, friends or other intimates), under conditions that are to a considerable extent determined by technology and institutions (printed on paper; preserved on celluloid, tape or electronically; distributed by publishers, financed by studios, scheduled in theatres, etc.) imposes constraints on them. Such conditions include, for instance, that audiences may have to pay for access to the story, have limited time to take it in and must visit a certain place to gain access. Thus public stories, far more so than private ones, need to give value for money in terms of intrinsic interest or entertainment. This alone means that there is a difference between quests and the publicly accessible stories based on them, and warrants distinguishing between the QUEST and STORY levels.

In short, the interest of road movies and travel documentaries (and the numerous computer games that involve motion through space) depends on the fact that they constitute a blend of the levels of (1) RELOCATION/ JOURNEY, (2) QUEST, (3) STORY and (4) TIME, and that all these levels are structured by the SPG schema. Since there are structured resemblances between them, artistically pleasurable ambiguities arise because relations between the levels are triggered via the metaphors A QUEST IS A JOURNEY, A STORY IS A JOURNEY, and even A QUEST IS A STORY. However, the SPG schema not only allows for the proliferation of meanings in road movies, it also helps constrain them. The goal-directed nature of quests, for instance, entails that relocations are always first and foremost evaluated in terms of how they contribute, or fail to contribute, to the success of the quest. Similarly, the story-format elicits ideas concerning future developments: we *expect* that physical relocations will be delayed by all kinds of obstacles and interesting digressions, and we *expect*, paradoxically, that we will sometimes be surprised by what will happen. Finally, we usually know at what stage of the story we are (half-way through the 350-page book, toward the end of the 90-minute film, in the fifth instalment of a 24-part TV series), which means that certain things are (un)likely to happen given how much of the story is left.

Table 14.1 lists some of the correspondences that exist between the three instantiations of the SPG schema. (The TIME level does not allow for this kind of structuring, and is taken to be ever-present in the RELOCATION level; it is therefore not specified here.) It is important to note that the dimension/role designated in each cell matters more than the label chosen to mark it; and that not all cells are necessarily filled.

Table 14.1   The SPG Schema: Correspondences between JOURNEY/RELOCATION, QUEST and STORY

JOURNEY/RELOCATION	QUEST	STORY
Traveller	Person	Character
Progressing	Approaching goal	Developing
Fellow-travellers	Family/friends	Helpers
Dangerous people	Adversaries	Antagonists
Meeting people	Meeting people	Introducing characters
Change in destination	Changes in purpose	Turning point
Pleasant incident	Achievement, happy event	Advancement of plot
Obstacle, delay	Misfortune	Setback in plot
Means of transport	?	?
?	?	Medium

3   BRIEF SUMMARIES OF *LES GLANEURS ET LA GLANEUSE* (2000) AND *DEUX ANS APRÈS* (2002)

Les glaneurs et la glaneuse (henceforth *The Gleaners*) begins with Jean-François Millet's famous and endlessly reproduced painting of female gleaners. Varda is intrigued by people's gleaning—what in *Deux ans après* (henceforth *Two Years Later*) she calls the modest gesture of bending to collect ("le geste modeste de se baisser pour ramasser"). The main theme of the two films is portraying a wide variety of people who are gleaners. Initially, the protagonists are literal gleaners—of potatoes, grapes, tomatoes, figs and other edibles—but gradually, more of them are portrayed as gleaners in the extended sense of collectors of anything left behind by others that they find useful for their own purposes. Scenes include meetings with experts who comment on the legal aspects of gleaning, with *patrons* ('landowners') who communicate their views on gleaning, with gleaners both in the country and in the city, with a famous cook who picks his own herbs, with a vintner who is also a psychoanalyst and with various artists whose art consists of *bricolages* of "found objects". In one of the many voice-over texts that accompany the images, Varda emphasizes that she herself is the "glaneuse" of the film's title: she not only collects heart-shaped potatoes and takes *res relictae* from garbage to her home, but she is also, and above all, a gleaner of images. She makes this clear visually at the beginning of *The Gleaners* when she has somebody film her standing in front of a painting of a *glaneuse* by Jules Breton, first holding a sheaf of corn in the same (but mirroring) posture as the girl in the painting, and then exchanging the corn for her camera.

Two Years Later is a sequel to *The Gleaners*, which Varda decided to make after the overwhelmingly positive response to the earlier film. This success transpired not only from the many prizes it won, but also from the numerous letters and presents she received from viewers. In *Two Years Later*, Varda visits new gleaners, revisits gleaners from the earlier film and deepens and broadens the gleaning theme of people actively, often happily, searching for food and objects that others have left behind. The motif of the heart-shaped potato has become a symbol for *The Gleaners*, and a kind of personal logo for Varda (on the cover and disk of my "Total Film" DVD the heart-shaped potatoes are prominently displayed, and on its menu the "bullets" have the form of red hearts).

Varda's two documentaries are autobiographical in the sense that the director mostly handles the camera, regularly films herself and provides a forcefully present first-person voice-over text in the film. These factors also ensure that viewers are constantly reminded they are watching a film, which makes the documentaries emphatically self-reflexive. Varda herself often calls attention to this in her voice-over, perhaps most pointedly when, during one of various occasions when she films her hand, she says: "That is my project: filming one hand with the other" ("C'est ça mon projet: filmer une main d'autre main"). Given Varda's reputation as *Nouvelle Vague* director of an impressive *oeuvre* of fiction films, it seems moreover reason-able to approach her films as *artistic* documentaries. This means that Varda presumably has a more than average interest in forging aesthetically pleas-ing thematic links in her film—and is probably good at this.

4   SOURCE-PATH-GOAL IN *LES GLANEURS ET LA GLANEUSE* AND *DEUX ANS APRÈS*

I will first examine how each of the JOURNEY, QUEST and STORY levels manifests itself in Varda's documentaries, and how and where they lead to aesthetically pleasing blends (some of the analyses are indebted to Meuzelaar 2001).

JOURNEY/RELOCATION *level*. Varda is continually "on the road" in both films. Her physical relocations are explicitly shown and verbally cued. The film features many shots taken from her car of other cars driving along the motorway, as well as of the scenery passing by. Whereas in *The Gleaners* Varda's use of transport is mainly the car, in *Two Years Later* this is alter-nated with a trip by train and a plane flight, and in one shot she films her own feet, walking. In addition, she shows her protagonists as they move. On a verbal level she often mentions, or shows signs of, names of places where she is heading.

QUEST *level*. Varda's primary quest is to collect material for her film. This includes visits to museums with gleaner-paintings, filming and inter-viewing gleaning protagonists, each with their own ambitious or everyday quest, and her own gleaning—for instance of heart-shaped potatoes and, in the city, *res relictae*.

TIME *level*. Cinema is a time-based art, so film by definition exempli-fies the unfolding of time. But while many films try to make the audience forget the passage of time, Varda constantly reminds the viewer of this, specifically of her own ageing. In *The Gleaners* she films her thinning hair (repeated in *Two Years Later*) but, more importantly, she keeps shooting with one hand her other, wrinkled, hand holding an object or performing an activity (something, incidentally, that has become possible only since the introduction of small, lightweight digital cameras). At one moment Varda refers explicitly to the fact that her hands tell her that she will not have so much longer to live ("mes mains qui me disent que c'est bientôt la fin"). The passing of time is also made visible by the fact that the heart-shaped potatoes, too, become old and wrinkled—but still sprout new outgrowths. There are several references to death, the end of ageing. Varda films a dead sheep once; a woman called Delphine tells Varda in *Two Years Later* that seeing *The Gleaners* was a "renaissance" after the death of a dear friend; and in the second film we learn that one of the protagonists of *The Glean-ers*, Charly Plusquellec, has died. All the other persons she meets again have, naturally, aged as well, and in the conversations with most of the people

Varda recorded for both films there is a reference to the two-year gap, and to what happened in the meantime. Moreover, a number of Varda's inter-locutors tell her that what they do (gleaning herbs, growing wine, collect-ing garbage) is something their (grand)parents did before them, evoking a sense of a tradition of quests pursued by one generation after another. The scenes in which the various *bricolage* artists talk about what they find on the streets also help build up the importance of time: the objects they gather are emphatically things with a past, which are now given a new life.

STORY *level*. Finally, the report of all the questing relocations has turned into the cinematic stories of *The Gleaners* and *Two Years Later*. That these are *plotted* stories is first of all made clear by conventional filmic segments such as opening and closing credits, which frame the events in the film as a more or less coherent whole. *The Gleaners* comes full circle by beginning and ending with a painting pertaining to gleaning, while *Two Years Later* begins and ends with an image showing a heart-shaped potato. In addi-tion, viewers are constantly made to realize that they are watching a quest-turned-into-a-story via the profound self-reflexivity of the films. Varda's voice-over often refers to the film-making process itself, the topic crops up repeatedly in exchanges with protagonists in *Two Years Later* familiar from *The Gleaners*, and several times she films herself in mirrors, or has somebody else film her filming her protagonists. In *Two Years Later* there are intertitles introducing new sequences. The first intertitle is "P.M. (Pre Filmum)"—a three-minute prologue-in-fast-motion with a summary of the earlier film. Moreover, if one views the film on DVD, there is the familiar chapter division—another reminder of a story's segmentation and progress. A story-feature of a different nature is the recurrence of certain motifs; these motifs—of which "hands", "heart" and "chance" are particularly noticeable—significantly help forge coherence.

Blending levels. It is because of the isomorphic structure of the SPG schema in the concepts JOURNEY/RELOCATION, QUEST, TIME and STORY that elements in all four of them can reverberate among each other, leading to aesthetically pleasing polyvalent interpretations. On the most obvious level, Varda's RELOCATING blends with her QUEST: gleaning footage about people gleaning. Every time we see Varda on the move, we are aware of the purpo-sive nature of her movements. Forward movement on the relocation level thus blends with progress on the quest level. Interestingly, however, what counts as "progress" is highly dependent on something that is crucial in gleaning: luck, or chance. Paradoxically, then, in order to achieve her goal, Varda must let herself be guided—or at least give the impression that she is guided—by chance. In many cases, the coincidence seems genuine: when Varda stops at a bric-a-brac shop with the sign "Trouvailles" ("findings"), she not only spots a sheaf of corn there, she also finds yet another gleaning painting—which, she assures us, is really what happened. Similarly, the gust of wind that, at the Hédouin museum, shakes Jules Breton's painting of gleaners in a storm-foreboding landscape, appears to be a piece of good fortune—although

Varda may have helped chance by asking for the painting to be carried out-side in what, she was bound to have noticed, was windy weather. In other cases, the coincidence is at least to some extent imposed; partly it is the result of the serendipity that is the reward for a filmmaker who, on the basis of her key concept, is open to any of its manifestations—surely the essence of glean-ing itself. Since the spectators are invited to share Varda's quest, they come to understand everything they see and hear in the films in terms of glean-ing. Thus when Varda stumbles upon a herd of sheep that blocks the road, this is literally a "blockade" on the RELOCATION level, hindering progress. But since the very purpose of Varda's quest is to be diverted by chance, this blockade is in itself an example of a pleasurable diversion, as she emphasizes in her voice-over text: "I have always liked to be stopped by animals, or to stop in order to watch them" ("d'ailleurs, j'ai bien aimé être arrêtée par des bêtes, ou m'arrêter pour les regarder").

The three-level structure of RELOCATION, QUEST and STORY is often mir-rored in the scenes in which Varda films her gleaners: the gleaners recount something about what they actually glean (potatoes, grapes, rubbish, old copper . . .), but they also tell their stories about what motivates them to glean. And often the literal movements the gleaners make (walking and bending to pick up potatoes on the fields or vegetables on the ground after the closing down of the market, reaching up to wrench fruits from trees, bending over to find treasures in trash bins, driving from one pile of *res relictae* to another) are shown as well. Significantly, the man she meets in the trailer camp at the beginning of *The Gleaners* (we later learn his name is Claude), struggling to survive, tells us he used to be a truck driver but lost his license and his car—and then ended up being divorced. The man's dif-ficulties in life thus started when he could no longer make literal progress, having lost the right to drive. Varda reinforces this connection between Claude's inability to move and the failure to achieve his goals by twice inserting a shot of an upturned car.

The quests that people undertake are often intimately linked to their views of life. The quests for food, of course, are mostly a matter of basic survival, and the stories about them do not much exceed information about the gleanable things available, their quality and good places for gleaning. But Varda also portrays a man who says that he has enough money, explain-ing that he gleans food only to keep his talent for gleaning honed. And the cook of a Michelin-starred restaurant tells us that he always picks his own herbs, since these are far fresher than anything he could buy in shops. In such instances gleaning has become part of people's identities, as projected in the stories they tell about themselves; it involves a rejection of consumer culture, or of readymade machine-processed food. This becomes even more transparent when what is gleaned is not food, but debris in various forms that is transformed into art, as Varda records in several cases. Here, the quests merge strongly with the autobiographic stories people tell about themselves. Many characteristics of gleaning—such as that other people

Figure 14.1   The SPG levels of relocation, time, questing and story-telling all captured in a single frame from *Les glaneurs et la glaneuse* (Agnès Varda, France 2000).

have found the things gleaned useless, or difficult to collect; the blurry legal status of gleaning; the unexpected value or worth of the gleaned object— are transferred to the stories the characters tell about their gleaning, if not by these persons themselves then by Varda. The multiplying meanings of the film reside not only in the interrelationships between relocating, quest- ing and story-telling, but also in the fact that the mini-stories are themselves the things gleaned by Varda for her film. Varda's gleaning of her characters' stories results in a story—the finished film—which in turn helps galvanize her own identity as an artist-filmmaker.

There is one shot which captures the levels of relocating, questing, time and narrating perhaps better than any other still from the film: one shot in a series where Varda makes a frame with her fingers and films passing trucks through them, and then closes her hand—an old childhood game (Figure 14.1). The truck exemplifies the movement of relocating; Varda's (ageing) hand suggests the passing of time; the hand is the instrument *par excel- lence* for the quest of gleaning; and the hole Varda makes with the thumb and index finger of her hand mirrors the camera's viewfinder, and therefore metonymically conveys the story level as well as its autobiographical nature. Varda draws attention to the correspondences in her voice-over text: "And always those trucks: I would like to catch them. To preserve what passes? No, to play". ("Et toujours ces camions. Je voudrais les attraper. Pour rete- nir ce qui passe? Non, pour jouer".) Even the nested structure of the film is reflected in this particular shot: just as Varda gleans footage of gleaning

people, so she here films a vehicle transporting vehicles—means of relocation *par excellence*. Stretching the analogy further, one can see something
protective in both the gesture and the mode of transportation.

One of the strongest motifs in the films, particularly in *The Gleaners*, is
that of the metonymically used "hand". In cognitive metaphor theory terminology, a distinction is made between a metonym's source concept, that
is, the metonym proper as it linguistically appears in the "text", and the
target concept, to which it refers (Ruiz de Mendoza & Díez Velasco 2002).
Usually, a metonym unambiguously refers to a specific target concept, as
in examples such as "the sax was ill" for "the saxophone player was ill",
"I read Donne" for "I read poems by Donne", etc. (see Lakoff & Johnson
1980: ch. 8). However, a metonym may support a degree of ambiguity. In
the phrase "Paris decrees short skirts this spring" it is not completely clear
what precisely "Paris" refers to: Is it the collective fashion industry located
there? The most famous designer houses? Fashion journalists? A mixture of
these? In this case the ambiguity may be convenient, since the metonym's
user is not required to specify the referent (Brdar-Szábo & Brdar 2007; Chen
2007). But in the documentaries under discussion here, the ambiguity of the
hand metonym is made artistically productive: Varda's emphatic use has the
effect of cueing different SPG levels simultaneously, as we saw in the discussion of Figure 14.1. For a viewer knowing that the English word for French
"aiguille" (in reference to clocks) is "hand", the hand-time theme is further
reinforced in the scene where on a nighthawking trip Varda finds a clock
without hands, and gives it pride of place at home. (The "time-arrested"
motif is reinforced by the fact that she films herself quietly passing behind
the clock, as if emphasizing all artists' eternal but doomed hope to stop time
by their art.) In short, the hand is a metonym for the gleaners' quests, for
Varda's story-telling and for time passing—foreboding death (for more
discussion of the hand-metonym in film, see Forceville 2009).

5   MODALITY AND MEDIUM IN
MULTIMODAL METAPHOR: A DETOUR

Before concluding, it may be useful—and in the spirit of Varda's project—to
indulge in a very brief detour and sketch some implications of studying
metaphors and blends in the realm of pictorial and multimodal as opposed
to that of written texts. The discipline of multimodal metaphors and blends
is young, and most of the scholarly work is yet to be done (for more discussion, references and applications, see Forceville 2006b, 2008a; Forceville &
Urios-Aparisi 2009). Here a few pointers and speculations will have to do.

*Films have more opportunities at their disposal to create metaphors and
blends than written texts.* Film can, on a conservative categorization of
modalities, at the very least draw on visuals, written language, spoken language, music and non-verbal sound—with gesture being another strong candidate for the status of modality (see Cienki & Müller 2008; Müller 2008;

Müller & Cienki 2009; Mittelberg & Waugh 2009). In practice, this means that a target in a metaphor (or "input space 1" in a blend) can be cued in one modality, and a metaphorical source ("input space 2") in another one—in a variety of permutations. Since modalities are closely tied to media (in the sense of both material carriers for and institutional providers of discourse), multimodal metaphors will have to be studied with reference to the type of discursive situation in which they occur, including an evaluation of genre.

Whereas the sequential nature of the elements in a verbal metaphor or blend requires unfolding, the elements in a visual metaphor/blend can be cued simultaneously. As Figure 14.1 demonstrates, a single film still can trigger the construal of no less than four input spaces at the same time, although the identification of these input spaces would be impossible outside of the narrative context of the film as a whole.

Since non-verbal modalities do not have a "grammar" in the way language has (pace *Kress & Van Leeuwen 2006; see Forceville 1999), the construal of metaphors that do not draw on the verbal modality tends to be more open to interpretation and controversy.* Briefly, in language many metaphors are already given in an "A is B" format; by contrast, non-verbal modalities have to suggest the "is" in manners that are not subject to the rigor of linguistic grammar. This being said, on the one hand it is important to distinguish between what is possible/impossible in a given modality or combination of modalities and, on the other, between what is possible/impossible in a given genre. Thus, it seems more difficult to deny the necessity to construe metaphors in advertising such as discussed in Forceville (1996, 2008b) than in art (Whittock 1990; Forceville 2005b). Similarly, while in metaphors/blends the features that are to be mapped from source to target/from the input spaces to the blend can be explicitly cued in the verbal mode, they must by definition be inferred in the case of non-verbal modes.

Non-verbal modalities in films trigger emotions quicker, and perhaps more subtly, in audiences than the verbal modality, and this characteristic is inherited by multimodal metaphors. Since not only facts and conceptual structures adhering to a domain or input space may be mapped onto a target or blend, but also the evaluations and emotions evoked by them, the use of non-verbal modalities may be very effective (or manipulative) in the communication of narratively or rhetorically significant metaphors. Inasmuch as "lower" modalities such as sound, taste and smell are less consciously registered than "higher" modalities such as language and visuals (see Cacciari [2008] for discussion of the various modes), this has consequences for their expected effects in multimodal metaphors.

6   CONCLUDING REMARKS

In this chapter I have attempted to demonstrate that the polyvalence of Varda's films is both enhanced and constrained by the interrelations governed by the

SPG schema. The episodic nature of the two films, which alternate between Varda's visits to gleaners and meditations on gleaning when at home, gives the impression of a series of playful coincidences that, however, in fact is prevented from disintegrating into formlessness by the intertwining of the constantly recurring themes of journey, quest, time and story-telling.

This finding corresponds to the conclusion I drew in an examination of three other autobiographical journey documentaries: Ross McElwee's *Sherman's March*, Johan van der Keuken's *De Grote Vakantie/The Long Holiday*, and Frank Cole's *Life without Death* (Forceville 2006a). However, there is one important dimension in which Varda's two films appear to differ from these three films, and that is the role of chance. At first sight, Varda's openness to coincidence seems to be incompatible with the purposiveness that characterizes a quest. There is, after all, a potential tension between, on the one hand, the demands of story-telling and, on the other, the anarchy and unpredictability of coincidence. The norm for classic story-telling is a form of completeness or closure (Bordwell 1985: 157–62) that must somehow have been projected or foreseen from the beginning, while coincidence by definition defies such anticipation. In the case of Varda's films, one response is that, of course, chance is by its very nature part of the quest of gleaning: gleaners need luck to achieve their goals. But that being said, gleaners' searches are not random, for they know more or less what they look for, and in what locations and circumstances they will increase the likelihood of being successful. As we all know, the goddess Fortuna favours those who are receptive to her gifts. Indeed, the idea that certain things have been waiting to be gleaned by somebody surfaces several times, for instance in the view of the artist "VR" (in *The Gleaners*) that the garbage he finds has awaited him to give it a second life ("c'est l'objet qui m'appelle, parce qu'il a sa place ici").

The same holds for Varda, the gleaner of images that are to be transformed into more or less coherent story plots. She is open to coincidence, but the concept of gleaning helps determine what counts as a happy coincidence. Moreover, Varda not only reinforces these coincidences in her voice-overs. Out of the innumerable ways in which she could forge a connection between two phenomena, she chooses one that fits the multifaceted gleaning theme. Examples abound: when filming one of the heart-shaped potatoes in *The Gleaners*, she proposes that potato-gleaning could well be conducted by charitable organisations supplying meals for the needy (in French: "restos du *coeur*", the latter being the French word for "heart"); an old Lu biscuit ad, in the beginning of *Two Years Later*, reminds her of the many letters she has read (in French: "lu") by enthusiastic viewers of *The Gleaners*; a train in which she is seated slows down, "as if by coincidence", when passing a waste-processing firm at Ivry; she reports that the men eliciting bright-looking copper wire spools from old TVs remind her that she began her film after seeing a solar eclipse on TV, continued while a TV program showed the transition to the year 2000, and completed the film by May 1 (Labour Day)—a date also mentioned at the end of *Two Years Later* as the day of an anti-Le Pen protest march in Paris. Clearly, Varda often *creates* these links. As in the documentaries by McElwee, Van der Keuken and Cole, language plays a crucial role in making explicit, sometimes imposing, the connections between levels ensuring that Varda's quest acquires the contours of a plot-like form—indispensable for sharing a story.

Nonetheless, one important difference between Varda's films and those by McElwee, Van der Keuken and Cole deserves to be mentioned; a difference that can be located on the "meeting people/introducing characters" dimension (see Table 14.1) and seems to be related to the "chance" theme. While the three male directors are strongly focussed on their own "quests"—more or less: searching for a marriageable woman (McElwee); coming to terms with a terminal illness or perhaps finding a therapy against it (Van der Keuken); and "transcending death" [sic] (Cole) (Forceville 2006a)—Varda never tires of analogizing between her protagonists' gleanings and her own, thereby emphasizing the connections that exist between her and other people. The new red bag that Varda mentions she has acquired echoes Alain F's red bag—his blue one having been stolen; she films a heart-shaped potato in the album of Delphine and Philippe de Trentemoult; and after "Monsieur Bouton", the button collector, emphasizes that finding a button means you have a link with whoever lost it, Varda chooses a button from his collection to replace the one she lost when on her way to visit him (all in *Two Years Later*). Indeed, the fact that in *Two Years Later* Varda revisits many of those she filmed for *The Gleaners* suggests her interest in their quests is genuine, going beyond a need to glean material for the sequel film. More so than in the quests of McElwee, Van der Keuken and Cole, the open and rich nature of gleaning itself enables and encourages Varda to interact with her protagonists on a virtually equal footing and in a way that simultaneously strengthens the structure of the film. It is perhaps not too far-fetched here to invoke the Surrealist tradition in which French culture is so strongly rooted. The Surrealists after all were great believers in the beneficial influence of chance, and in the release of control in art, as transpires from the role they attributed to the *objet trouvé* ("found object"). Moreover, they were strong advocates of collaborative art, as in their verbal and pictorial *cadavres exquis*.[1] Both elements, finally, contribute to the notion of playfulness (see Bigsby 1972). All of these elements surface in Varda's film. Even the subconscious, celebrated by the Surrealists, makes its appearance in the guise of vintner-cum-psychoanalyst Jean Laplanche, who says that psychoanalysis is a kind of gleaning: the therapist and his client jointly search for what has been "left behind" in the client's mind.

This interest in "connectedness"—due to her Frenchness (?), to her gender (?) or both (?)—stands out in Varda's films, and bestows extra interactions in the blended space where journey, quest, time and story merge. The result is a story that combines a strong internal coherence with numerous ties with the protagonists it portrays, and by extension with the viewers, who can empathize with both Varda's and the protagonists' identity-enhancing quests. One of the *bricoleurs* she visits, Louis Pons, succinctly sums up his art as seeing a pile of opportunities in what other people see as a pile of rubbish. With her two films, Varda pays tribute to how her gleaning protagonists impose form and order on their lives, and celebrates art as the gleaning activity *par excellence.*

NOTES

1. This expression, literally 'exquisite corpses', is a technical term in Surrealist art. It refers to a game in which one person draws a head on a piece of paper, then folds it, after which the next person draws a torso, then folds it, after which the third person draws the legs (sometimes there are four stages).

WORKS CITED

Bigsby, C. W. E. (1972) *Dada and Surrealism.* London: Methuen.

Bordwell, David (1985) *Narration in the Fiction Film.* London: Methuen.

Brdar-Szabó, Rita, and Mario Brdar (2007) "Metonymic Zooming in and out within a Functional Domain in the Process of Meaning Construction". Paper presented at the International Cognitive Linguistics Conference, Jagiellonian University Krákow, Poland, July 15–20.

Caballero, Rosario (2006) *Re-Viewing Space: Figurative Language in Architects' Assessment of Built Space.* Berlin and New York: de Gruyter.

Cacciari, Christina (2008) "Crossing the Senses in Metaphorical Language". *The Cambridge Handbook of Metaphor and Thought.* Ed. Raymond W. Gibbs, Jr. Cambridge: Cambridge University Press. 425–43.

Campbell, Joseph (2008) *The Hero with a Thousand Faces* [1949]. Third Edition. Novato, CA: New World Library.

Chen, Xianglan (2007) "Metonymy and Pragmatic Inference". Paper presented at the International Cognitive Linguistics Conference, Jagiellonian University Krákow, Poland, July 15–20.

Cienki, Alan, and Cornelia Müller (2008) "Metaphor, Gesture, and Thought". *The Cambridge Handbook of Metaphor and Thought.* Ed. Raymond W. Gibbs, Jr. Cambridge: Cambridge University Press. 483–501.

Cohan, Steven, and Ina Rae Hark (1997) *The Road Movie Book.* London and New York: Routledge.

Emanatian, Michelle (1995) "Metaphor and the Expression of Emotion: The Value of Cross-Cultural Perspectives". *Metaphor and Symbolic Activity* 10: 163–82.

Fauconnier, Gilles (1997) *Mappings in Thought and Language.* Cambridge: Cambridge University Press.

Fauconnier, Gilles, and Mark Turner (2002) *The Way We Think: Conceptual Blending and the Mind's Hidden Complexities.* New York: Basic Books.

Forceville, Charles (1996) *Pictorial Metaphor in Advertising.* London and New York: Routledge.

———. (1999) "Educating the Eye? Kress & Van Leeuwen's *Reading Images: The Grammar of Visual Design* (1996)". *Language and Literature* 8: 163–78.

———. (2005a) "Visual Representations of the Idealized Cognitive Model of Anger in the Asterix Album *La Zizanie*". *Journal of Pragmatics* 37: 69–88.

296   Charles Forceville

———. (2005b) "Cognitive Linguistics and Multimodal Metaphor". *Bildwissenschaft: Zwischen Reflektion und Anwendung*. Ed. Klaus Sachs-Hombach. Cologne: Von Halem. 264–84.

———. (2006a) "The Source-Path-Goal Schema in the Autobiographical Journey Documentary: McElwee, Van der Keuken, Cole". *New Review of Film and Television Studies* 4: 241–61.

———. (2006b) "Non-verbal and Multimodal Metaphor in a Cognitivist Framework: Agendas for Research". *Cognitive Linguistics: Current Applications and Future Perspectives*. Eds. Gitte Kristiansen et al. Berlin and New York: de Gruyter. 379–402.

———. (2008a) "Metaphor in Pictures and Multimodal Representations". *The Cambridge Handbook of Metaphor and Thought*. Ed. Raymond W. Gibbs, Jr. Cambridge: Cambridge University Press. 462–82.

———. (2008b) "Pictorial and Multimodal Metaphor in Commercials". *Go Figure! New Directions in Advertising Rhetoric*. Eds. Edward F. McQuarrie and Barbara J. Phillips. Armonk, NY: M.E. Sharpe. 272–310.

———. (2009) "Metonymy in Visual and Audiovisual Discourse". *The World Told and the World Shown: Issues in Multisemiotics*. Eds. Eija Ventola and Jésus Moya Guijarro. Basingstoke and New York: Palgrave Macmillan. 56–74.

Forceville, Charles, Paul Hekkert and Ed Tan (2006) "The Adaptive Value of Metaphors". *Heuristiken der Literaturwissenschaft: Einladung zu disziplinexternen Perspektiven auf Literatur*. Eds. Uta Klein et al. Paderborn: Mentis. 85–109.

Forceville, Charles, and Marloes Jeulink (forthcoming) "The Flesh and Blood of Embodied Understanding: The Source-Path-Goal Schema in Animation Film". *Pragmatics & Cognition*.

Forceville, Charles, and Eduardo Urios-Aparisi (2009) Eds. *Multimodal Metaphor*. Berlin and New York: de Gruyter.

Gibbs, Raymond W., Jr., and Gerard J. Steen (1999) Eds. *Metaphor in Cognitive Linguistics*. Amsterdam and Philadelphia: John Benjamins.

Les glaneurs et la glaneuse. Dir. Agnès Varda. Ciné Tamaris, 2000.

Les glaneurs et la glaneuse . . . Deux ans après. Dir. Agnès Varda. C.N.D.P., 2002.

Johnson, Mark (1987) *The Body in the Mind: The Bodily Basis of Meaning, Imagination and Reason*. Chicago: University of Chicago Press.

———. (1993) *Moral Imagination: Implications of Cognitive Science for Ethics*. Chicago: University of Chicago Press.

———. (2007) *The Meaning of the Body: Aesthetics of Human Understanding*. Chicago: University of Chicago Press.

Katz, Albert N., and Tamsen E. Taylor (2008) "The Journeys of Life: Examining a Conceptual Metaphor with Semantic and Episodic Memory Recall". *Metaphor and Symbol* 23: 148–73.

Kövecses, Zoltán (2005) *Metaphor in Culture: Universality and Variation*. Cambridge: Cambridge University Press.

Kress, Gunther, and Theo van Leeuwen (2006) *Reading Images: The Grammar of Visual Design* [1996]. Revised Edition. London and New York: Routledge.

Lakoff, George (1993) "The Contemporary Theory of Metaphor". *Metaphor and Thought*. Second Edition. Ed. Andrew Ortony. Cambridge: Cambridge University Press. 202–51.

Lakoff, George, and Mark Johnson (1980) *Metaphors We Live By*. Chicago: University of Chicago Press.

———. (1999) *Philosophy in the Flesh: The Embodied Mind and Its Challenge to Western Thought*. New York: Basic Books.

Meuzelaar, Andrea (2001) "Oneindig leven op doodlopende wegen: een onderzoek naar reisstructuur en conceptuele metafoor in twee hedendaagse documentaires".

["Endless lives on dead-end streets: an examination of travel structures and conceptual metaphors in two contemporary documentaries".] Unpublished ms., Dept. of Media Studies, Universiteit van Amsterdam.

Mittelberg, Irene, and Linda R. Waugh (2009) "Metonymy First, Metaphor Second: A Cognitive-Semiotic Approach to Figures of Thought in Co-speech Gesture". *Multimodal Metaphor.* Eds. Charles Forceville and Eduardo Urios-Aparisi. Berlin and New York: de Gruyter. 329–56.

Müller, Cornelia (2008) *Metaphors Dead and Alive, Sleeping and Waking: A Dynamic View.* Chicago: University of Chicago Press.

Müller, Cornelia, and Alan Cienki (2009) "Words, Gestures and Beyond: Forms of Multimodal Metaphor in the Use of Spoken Language". *Multimodal Metaphor.* Eds. Charles Forceville and Eduardo Urios-Aparisi. Berlin and New York: de Gruyter. 297–328.

Ritchie, David L. (2008) "X is a Journey: Embodied Simulation in Metaphor Interpretation". *Metaphor and Symbol* 23: 174–99.

Ruiz de Mendoza, Francisco José, and Olga I. Díez Velasco (2002) "Patterns of Conceptual Interaction". *Metaphor and Metonymy in Comparison and Contrast.* Eds. René Dirven and Ralph Pörings. Berlin and New York: de Gruyter. 490–532.

Turner, Mark (1996) *The Literary Mind.* New York and Oxford: Oxford University Press.

Yu, Ning (1998) *The Contemporary Theory of Metaphor: A Perspective from Chinese.* Amsterdam and Philadelphia: John Benjamins.

Whittock, Trevor (1990) *Metaphor and Film.* Cambridge: Cambridge University Press.

Contributors

Benjamin Biebuyck is Professor of German Literature at Ghent University (Belgium). He studied Germanistik, Anglistik and Literary Theory in Ghent and Basel (Switzerland), and obtained his PhD from Ghent University (in 1996) with a dissertation on metaphor theory and figurativeness in Nietzsche's *Zarathustra*. He has been carrying out and supervising research projects on nineteenth- and twentieth-century German literature, on literary rhetoric and on philosophical writing (particularly on Nietzsche). He authored *Die poietische Metapher: Ein Beitrag zur Theorie der Figürlichkeit* (1998), co-authored a monograph on literature and ethics (*Negen muzen, tien geboden,* 2005) and co-edited *Faith and Fiction: Interdisciplinary Studies on the Interplay between Metaphor and Religion* (1998). Recent publications include articles in *Philologus, Nietzsche-Studien, Einführung in die Erzähltextanalyse* and *Style.*

Beatrix Busse is Professor of English Linguistics at the University of Heidelberg (Germany). She studied English and History at Osnabrück (Germany) and Keele (UK) and was a visiting researcher in Birmingham, Stratford and Lancaster (UK). In 2007, she was a British Academy Visiting Fellow in the UK. Among others, her scholarly interests include the history of English, (historical) pragmatics, Shakespeare studies and Early Modern English, stylistics, narratology, cognitive linguistics, corpus linguistics as well as e-learning. Her doctoral dissertation is an investigation of Vocative Constructions in the Language of Shakespeare and was published with Benjamins in 2006. Her 'Habilitationsschrift' is on speech, writing and thought presentation in nineteenth-century English narrative fiction.

Elżbieta Chrzanowska-Kluczewska is Professor of Linguistics and Head of the Institute of English Philology at the Jagiellonian University of Kraków, Poland. Her main areas of interest include theoretical and literary semantics, stylistics and the philosophy of language, on which she has published extensively in various periodicals and collective volumes. Her research has centred, among others, around the issue of possible worlds, especially in what concerns their application in discourse analysis and poetics. In turn, her monograph *Language-Games: Pro and Against* (2004) is devoted to theoretical and philosophical aspects of linguistic games. At present she is working on another monograph focussed on metatropes as large figures of human thought and language. She has delivered guest lectures at various universities in Poland, Germany, Armenia, Taiwan, Ukraine and Georgia. An active board member of IALS (International Association of Literary Semantics), she is serving currently on the editorial board of *Journal of Literary Semantics*. She is also a member of PASE (Polish branch of ESSE), PTJ (Polish Linguistic Society) and PALA. As a collaborator of the National Museum in Kraków she has translated into English over thirty books on fine arts in Poland.

Hans Georg Coenen studied Romance Languages, Ancient History and Philosophy in Münster and Paris. After completing his teacher training and his PhD in 1961, he taught at the Department of Romance Studies in Münster. From 1971 to his retirement he held the position of a Studien-professor. Professor Coenen's major fields of interest are poetics, rhetoric and the French literature of the classical period. Recent publications include: *Französische Verslehre* (1998), *Die Gattung Fabel* (2000), *Analogie und Metapher* (2002), *Ein Kapitel Poetik* (2005), *Rhetorisches Argumentieren im Licht antiker und moderner Theorien* (2006) and *Die vierte Kränkung: Das Maximenwerk La Rochefoucaulds* (2008).

John Douthwaite is Professor of English Linguistics at the University of Genoa. He was formerly Professor of English Linguistics at the University of Cagliari, where he also directed the University Language Centre. He is an Executive Board member of the Associazione Italiana di Anglistica, a co-editor of the AIA journal *Textus* and member of the Board of Editors of Englishes. He has published widely in national and international journals, edited volumes and published essays/chapters on both the theory of stylistics as well as close textual readings, and on postcolonialism, gender, ethnicity, identity, crime fiction, language variety, humour, psycholinguistics and language pedagogy, as well as in comparative literature. Among his publications are *Metaphors of Power: Aspects of the Linguistic Approach to Text Analysis* (1990), *Teaching English as a Foreign Language* (1991), *Towards a Linguistic Theory of Foregrounding* (2000) and *Migrating the Texts: Hybridity as a Postcolonial Literary Construct* (with Alessandro Monti; 2003).

Monika Fludernik is Professor of English at the University of Freiburg in Germany. Her publications include *The Fictions of Language and the Languages of Fiction* (1993), *Towards a 'Natural' Narratology* (1996) and *An Introduction to Narratology* (2009). She has edited several special issues of journals (on second-person fiction, *Style* 1994; on metaphor, *Poetics*

Today 1999; on voice, *New Literary History* 2001; and on German narratology, *Style* 2004). She also (co-)edited many collections of essays, among others, *Hybridity and Postcolonialism* (1998), *Diaspora and Multiculturalism* (2003) and *In the Grip of the Law* (2004). Homepage: http://www.portal.uni-freiburg.de/angl/Englisches_Seminar/Lehrstuehle/LS_Fludernik/index

Charles Forceville lectures in the University of Amsterdam's Media Studies department, where he coordinates the Research Master. After *Pictorial Metaphor in Advertising* (Routledge 1996), he has broadened his scholarly work, which is embedded in a Relevance Theory framework, to multimodal metaphor in moving and multi-panel images in various media and genres. Considering the structure and rhetoric of multimodal discourse his core business, he tries to be a cognition scholar in the humanities. Forceville is on the editorial board of *Metaphor and Symbol*, and member of the advisory boards of *Journal of Pragmatics*, the *Public Journal of Semiotics* and the *Applied Cognitive Linguistics* series of Mouton de Gruyter. With Eduardo Urios-Aparisi he edited *Multimodal Metaphor* (de Gruyter 2009). Forceville teaches courses on documentary film, metaphor and animation film, while narratology never lost its appeal for him since studying English language and literature at the Vrije Universiteit Amsterdam. He rides a bicycle.

Margaret H. Freeman is Emeritus Professor of English at Los Angeles Valley College. She was a founder and first president of the Emily Dickinson International Society (1988–92), and is co-director of the Myrifield Institute for Cognition and the Arts (MICA) in Heath, Massachusetts. She has published articles on cognitive poetics in several journals and anthologies which mark the expansion of her research from studies in cognitive linguistics to include semiotics, cognitive science and aesthetics (http://www.emilydickinson.org/edis/scholars/freeman.htm). She is currently engaged in developing her theory of aesthetic iconicity in the arts, with especial reference to poetry. Email: freemamh@lavc.edu.

Andrew Goatly: After studying with Randolph Quirk for his PhD at University College London, Andrew Goatly taught in colleges and universities in the UK, Thailand and Singapore. He is at present Professor in the Department of English at Lingnan University, Hong Kong. He has published the following books: *The Language of Metaphors* (1997/2nd Edition 2011), *Critical Reading and Writing* (2000), *Washing the Brain: Metaphor and Hidden Ideology* (2007), *Explorations in Stylistics* (2008) and *Meaning and Humour* (2011). He is also the chief investigator of a cross-linguistic study of metaphors in the lexicons of English and Chinese, which led to the interactive website Metalude.

You can access this website on the net at http://www.ln.edu.hk/lle/cwd03/lnproject_chi/introduction.html (User ID: <user>; password <edumet6>).

Ina Habermann is Professor of English at the University of Basel. Until spring 2007, she was Lecturer in English and Cultural Studies at the University of Erlangen. Her fields are early modern literature, early twentieth-century literature, cultural history and theory as well as gender and film studies. She is the author of *Staging Slander and Gender in Early Modern England* (2003) and *Myth, Memory and the Middlebrow: Priestley, du Maurier and the Symbolic Form of Englishness* (2010).

Michael Kimmel is a cognitive linguist based at Vienna University, Austria, where he earned his PhD in 2002. In the past he has worked on metaphor in varied fields including political discourse and metaphor clusters. His current work in the field of literary cognition centres on sensorimotor processes in reading as well as narrative macrostructure, thematics and mega-metaphor. Another major area of interest relates to socio-cultural embodiment, and particularly the role of image schemas as shapers of cultural thought, habitus and embodied interaction skills. In the past few years Dr. Kimmel has been engaged in a phenomenological study of bodily skills in tango argentino, with a focus on multimodal aids used by teachers. Across all these applied fields he takes interest in the development of software-assisted qualitative coding tools. Homepage: http://www.michaelkimmel.at.

Gunther Martens is Research Professor at the German Department of Ghent University (Belgium). He holds an MA in German, English and Literary Theory from the Universities of Ghent, Eichstätt and Antwerp. He obtained his PhD from Ghent University in 2003. Until 2010, he was a Professor of Literary Theory and German Literature at the Universities of Brussels and Antwerp. He has published on German and Austrian literature, on narrative theory and on literary polemics. He is on the editorial board of *Musil Forum Online,* and on the advisory boards of *Cahier voor literatuurwetenschap* and *Authorship.* One of his current projects is on the encyclopaedic German novel (1650–2010). His recent publications include: *Tradition and Renewal in the Twentieth-Century First-Person Novel: The Case of Narrative (Un)Reliability* (co-edited with Elke D'hoker, 2009); "Narrative and Stylistic Agency: The Case of Overt Narration", in *Point of View, Perspective, Focalization: Modeling Mediation in Narrative,* eds. Peter Hühn, Wolf Schmid and Jörg Schönert (de Gruyter 2009), pp. 99–118; "De(ar)ranged Minds, Mindless Acts, and Polemical Portrayal in Kleist and Canetti", in *Style* 43.3 (2009), pp. 388–406. Homepage: http://users.ugent.be/~gnmarten/

Ralph Müller is Associate Professor at the German Department of the University of Fribourg, Switzerland. He is author of a monograph entitled *Theorie der Pointe*, and he has published various articles on humour and metaphor. During a three-year scholarship funded by the Swiss Research Foundation he wrote his habilitation-dissertation on the stylistic analysis of political metaphors, and he was, subsequently, awarded the 'venia legendi' in German literature in 2009.

Bo Pettersson is Professor of the Literature of the United States and Head of the English Department of Modern Languages, University of Helsinki. He holds an MA from the University of California, Berkeley, and a PhD from Åbo Akademi University in Finland. He has published widely on Anglo-American literature, literary theory and aesthetics and is author of *The World According to Kurt Vonnegut: Moral Paradox and Narrative Form* (1994) and co-editor of *Cognition and Literary Interpretation in Practice* (with Harri Veivo and Merja Polvinen, 2005) and *Narrative and Identity: Theoretical Approaches and Critical Analyses* (with Birgit Neumann and Ansgar Nünning, 2008). He also serves on several editorial boards, including *Journal of Literary Semantics* and *Nordic Journal of English Studies*. In 2006 he was awarded the Oskar Öflund Prize for his academic achievements.

Michael Sinding is an independent scholar based in Innsbruck, Austria. He studies cognitive approaches to cultural and literary forms, including genre, narrative and metaphor. He focuses particularly on analyzing genres as "idealized cognitive models", and genre mixture as conceptual blending. He has held postdoctoral fellowships from the Social Sciences and Humanities Research Council of Canada, and from the Alexander von Humboldt Foundation. He has published articles and reviews in *The Wallace Stevens Journal*, *New Literary History*, *Genre*, *Semiotica*, *Style*, *SubStance*, *Cognitive Linguistics*, *The Journal of Literary Theory* and *Postmodern Culture*, and a chapter in *Northrop Frye: New Directions from Old*. He has work forthcoming in *Poetics Today* and in edited collections.

Tamar Yacobi is Senior Lecturer in the Literature Department, Tel Aviv University. She has written on narratology, particularly the narrator's (un)reliability, on ekphrasis and on poetics (the modernist Hebrew poet Dan Pagis, Henry James, Isak Dinesen) in *Poetics Today*, *Style*, *Narrative*, as well as published chapters in books. Her recent publications include: "Authorial Rhetoric, Narratorial (Un)Reliability, Divergent Readings: Tolstoy's *Kreutzer Sonana*", in *A Companion to Narrative Theory*, eds. James Phelan and Peter J. Rabinowitz (Blackwell: 2005), pp. 108–23; and "Fiction and Silence as Testimony: The Rhetoric of Holocaust in Dan Pagis", in *Poetics Today* 26 (2005), pp. 209–55.

Author Index

Subject Index